EMERGENCE OF MAHARAJA RANJIT SINGH

Encyclopaedic History of Indian Freedom Movement Series

EMERGENCE OF MAHARAJA RANJIT SINGH

Edited by

OM PRAKASH

ANMOL PUBLICATIONS PVT. LTD.
NEW DELHI - 110 002 (INDIA)

ANMOL PUBLICATIONS PVT. LTD.
4374/4B, Ansari Road, Daryaganj
New Delhi - 110 002
Ph.: 23261597, 23278000
Visit us at: www.anmolpublications.com

Emergence of Maharaja Ranjit Singh

First Edition, 2004

ISBN 81-261-1511-4

PRINTED IN INDIA

Published by J.L. Kumar for Anmol Publications Pvt. Ltd., New Delhi - 110 002 and Printed at Mehra Offset Press, Delhi.

Contents

Preface

'Golden bird' as India was known in yore days, rich in natural resources and well-developed cottage industries it was considered an affluent country. Indian spices, fabrics and other handicrafts were in great demand the world over. In the lure of having these goods and riches, many European powers made adventurous voyages to locate India.

The story of European expansions in Asia forms one of the great epics of modern times. India was the cornerstone of European imperialism in Asia. It was the lure of the lucrative 'Indian trade' which incited European adventurers to seek a new route to India, thus inaugurating a new era of contact between these two distant lands. Among the European empires in Asia, the British empire was the most enduring and prosperous one. And India was the finest jewel of the British dominion. It is worthwhile to remember that European exploration and adventure in the east were encouraged by the great demand in Europe for the products from Malabar like spices and calicoe cloth. Symbolically, the European age in Indian and indeed Asian history began with the landing of Vasco-de-Gama at Calicut on the 27th of May 1498. During this period, there was a continuous struggle between European traders and their native rivals and among the Europeans themselves. By the end of the eighteenth century this struggle for supremacy had been resolved in favour of the English.

The European traders were originally in the position of supplicants before the native rulers in India. For example, when William Hawkins arrived at the court of Jehangir with a letter from King James I asking for trade facilities, he had brought with him, a gift of 25,000 Gold pieces. As Lane Poole observes,

"There was nothing to suggest the most distant dream that in two centuries and a half the slight introduction Hawkins was then effecting between England and India would culminate in the sovereignty of a British Queen over the whole empire."

But unlike their European rivals like the Portuguese and the Dutch, the English made their bid for power in India only when the powerful Mughal empire had begun to decline. In any case the Portuguese and the Dutch had only small coastal settlements in India even at the height of their power and influence in this country.

By the end of the seventh Century, the Portuguese had been displaced by their Dutch rivals in Malabar and in the islands, of the East Indies. As for the Dutch, they were compelled by force of circumstances to regard the factories "which they established on the main land merely as marketing points for the products of an Empire which had its capital at Batavia in the East Indies."

Moreover, the Dutch power in India was largely jeopardised on European battle fields.

The wars with England and France drained the resources of this nation. Thus, it was left to the French to provide real opposition to the English in India.

The same pattern can be detected in the story of European activity in Malabar. Here the intensity of their rivalry was greater because of three main reasons. Malabar with its many fine harbours and backwaters was more accessible from the sea, increasing the scope for European interference.

Thus, European powers who came to India with the intention of trade snatched the political power and sovereignty from the local states, principalities and feudal lords. And established complete control over India. After over hundred years colonial rule, the feeling of national integration and freedom from the clutches of foreign power developed among the Indians. Thus, began the saga of freedom movement.

This encyclopaedic study is phased into two most significant and historic diversions having deep bearing on varied kinds of events which moulded the destiny of millions of people of Indian sub-continent. These events having complete political overtones, became a glaring phenomenon with the downfall of the Mughal Empire almost with the commencement of the 18th century. The ambitious piercing eyes of four European powers — the British, the French, the Portuguese and the Dutch—did cast upon several gainful economic successes in India.

Of these powers, the East India Company's government, with well organised force, bureaucracy and diplomats achieved phenomenal successes against their adversaries. The first phase,—therefore has been marked from Plassey to the Mutiny of 1857 (The First War of Independence) when the Company's role came to an end.

The second phase, naturally, came very much in the hands of the British Government functioning under the Whitehall and ended with the dawn of Swaraj on 15 August 1947.

This multi-volumes study would take up several themes, viz. political, socio-economic, religious, constitutional, educational, press, revolutionaries, local pioneers, legislation, revenues and judicial policy, on-going process of reaction — violent and non-violent, moderates and extremists, local and all India movements, reaction of the British Raj, efforts for conciliation, significant Acts passed by the Central Legislature, the impact of two global wars, 1914-1919 and 1939-1945; Congress, Muslim League, Hindu Mahasabha and the British Policy, a significant change in Britain soon after 1945, the Labour Government of Clement Attlee and Partition of India in August 1947.

In the first lot eleven volumes have appeared while in the present second lot ten volumes are being brought out namely the Marathas and their administration; Lord William Bentinck and Metcalf era of reforms; Raja Rammohun Roy: the reformer; Mutiny and its aftermath; History of Anglo-Sikh wars;

Emergence of Maharaja Ranjit Singh; Lord Hastings and his administrative measures; Ranjit Singh administration and British policy; British policy of intervention and expansion; and Lord Wellesley and policy of expansion.

This prestigious project is arranged, managed and looked after by a team of most dedicated and long experienced scholars of modern Indian history.

In gathering the authentic information, we have taken liberty to draw the material from the learned works of many great scholars in the field. We are deeply beholden to all those whose works are partially cited or substantially made use of in the project. I am indebted to Mr. J.L. Kumar, Managing Director, Anmol Publications Pvt. Ltd., New Delhi for his constant inspiration and moral support and finally to bring out this work. Last but not the least I am thankful to all those who have assisted me one way or other while preparing the manuscript.

—**Om Prakash**

1

Ascendancy of Ranjit Singh

The Sikhs had mastered the upper plains from Karnal and Hansi to the banks of the Jhelum. The necessity of union was no longer paramount, and rude untaught men are ever prone to give the rein to their passions, and to prefer their own interests to the welfare of the community. Some dwelt on real or fancied injuries, and thought the time had come for ample vengeance; others were moved by local associations to grasp at neighbouring towns and districts; and the truer Sikh alone at once resolved to extend his faith, and to add to the general domain of the Khalsa, by complete conquest or by the imposition of tribute. When thus about to arise, after their short repose, refreshed and variously inclined, they were again awed into unanimity by the final descent of Ahmad Shah. That monarch, whose activity and power declined with increase of years and the progress of disease, made yet another attempt to recover the Punjab, the most fertile of his provinces. He crossed the Indus in 1767, but he avoided Lahore and advanced no farther than the Sutlej. He endeavoured to conciliate when he could no longer overcome, and he bestowed the title of Maharaja, and the office of military commander in Sirhind, upon the warlike Amar Singh, who had succeeded his grandfather as chief of Patiala, or of the Malwa Sikhs. He likewise saw a promising ally in the Rajput chief of Katotch, and he made him his deputy in the Jullundur Doab and adjoining hills. His measures were interrupted by the defection of his own troops; twelve thousand men marched back towards Kabul, and the Shah found it prudent to follow them. He was harassed in his retreat, and he had scarcely crossed the Indus before Sher Shah's mountain stronghold of Rohtas was blockaded by the Sukerchukias, under the grandfather of Ranjit Singh, aided by a detachment of the neighbouring Bhangi confederacy. The place fell in 1768, and the Bhangis almost immediately afterwards occupied the country as far as Rawalpindi and the vale of Khanpur, the Gakhars showing but little of that ancient hardihood which distinguished them in their contests with invading Mughals.[1]

The Bhangis, under Hari Singh, next marched towards Multan, but they were met by the Muhammadan Daudputras, who had migrated from Sind on learning Nadir Shah's intention of transplanting them to Ghazni, and had established the principality now known as Bhawalpur.[2] The chief, Mobarik Khan, after a parley with Hari Singh, arranged that the neutral town of Pakpattan, held by a Musalman saint of eminence, should be the common boundary. Hari Singh then swept towards Dera Ghazi Khan and the Indus, and while thus employed, his feudatory of Gujarat, who had recently taken Rawalpindi, made an attempt to penetrate into Kashmir by the ordinary road, but was repulsed with loss. On the Jumna, and in the great Doab, the old Najib-ud-daula was so hard pressed by Rai Singh Bhangi, who emulated him as a paternal governor in his neighbouring town and district of Jagadhri, and by Baghel Singh Krora Singhia, that he proposed to the Marathas a joint expedition against these new lords. His death, in 1770, put an end to the plan, for his succeeding son had other views, and encouraged the Sikhs as useful allies upon an emergency.[3]

Hari Singh Bhangi died, and he was succeeded by Jhanda Singh, who carried the power of the Misal to its height. He rendered Jammu tributary, and the place was then of considerable importance, for the repeated Afghan invasions, and the continued insurrections of the Sikhs, had driven the transit trade of the plans to the circuitous but safe route of the hills; and the character of the Rajput chief, Ranjit Deo, was such as gave confidence to traders, and induced them to flock to his capital for protection. The Pathans of Kasur were next rendered tributary, and Jhanda Singh then deputed his lieutenant, Mujja Singh, against Multan; but that leader was repulsed and slain by the united forces of the joint Afghan governors and of the Bhawalpur chief. Next year, or in 1772, these joint managers quarrelled, and as one of them asked the assistance of Jhanda Singh, that unscrupulous leader was enabled to posses himself of the citadel. On his return to the northward, he found that a rival claimant of the Jammu chiefship had obtained the aid of Charat Singh Sukerchukia, and of Jai Singh, the rising leader of the Kanhaya Misal. Charat Singh was killed by the bursting of his own matchlock, and Jai Singh was then so base as to procure the assassination of Jhanda Singh. Being satisfied with the removal of this powerful chief, the Kanhaya left the Jammu claimant to prosecute his cause alone, and entered into a league with the old Jassa Singh Ahluwalia, for the expulsion of the other Jassa Singh the Carpenter, who had rendered Ahmad Shah's nominal deputy, Ghamand Chand of Katotch, and other Rajputs of the hills, his tributaries. The Ramgarhia Jassa Singh was at last beaten, and he retired to the wastes of Hariana to live by plunder. At this time, or about 1774, died the Muhammadan governor of Kanga. He had contrived to maintain himself in independence, or in reserved subjection to Delhi or Kabul, although the rising chief of Katoch had long desired to possess so famous a stronghold. Jai Singh Kanhaya was prevailed on to assist him, and the place fell; but the Sikh chose to keep it to himself, and the possession of the imperial fort aided him in his usurpation of Jessa Singh's authority over the surrounding Rajas and Thakurs.[4]

In the south of the Punjab the Bhangi Sikhs continued predominant; they seem to have possessed the strong fort of Mankera as well as Multan, and to have levied exactions from

Kalabagh downwards. They made an attempt to carry Shujabad, a place built by the Afghans on losing Multan, but seem to have failed. Taimur Shah, who succeeded his father in 1773, was at last induced or enabled to cross the Indus, but his views were directed towards Sind, Bhawalpur, and the Lower Punjab, and he seems to have had no thought of a reconquest of Lahore. In the course of 1777-8, two detachments of the Kabul army unsuccessfully endeavoured to dislodge the Sikhs from Multan, but in the season of 1778-9 the Shah chiefs, and his lieutenant surrendered the citadel after a show of resistance. Taimur Shah reigned until 1793, but he was fully occupied with Sindian, Kashmiri and Uzbeg rebellions; the Sikhs were even unmolested in their possession of Rawalpindi, and their predatory horse traversed the plains of Chach up to the walls of Attock.[5]

In the direction of Hariana and Delhi, the young Amar Singh Phulkia began systematically to extend and consolidate his authority. He acquired Sirsa and Fatehabad, his territories marched with those of Bikaner and Bhawalpur, and his feudatories of Jind and Kaithal possessed the open country around Hansi and Rohtak. He was recalled to his capital of Patiala by a final effort of the Delhi court to re-establish its authority in the province of Sirhind. An army, headed by the minister of the day, and by Farkhunda Bukht, one of the imperial family, marched in the season 1779-80. Karnal was recovered; some payments were promised; and the eminent Krora-Singhia leader, Baghel Singh, tendered his submission. Dehsu Singh, of Kaithal, was seized and heavily muleted, and the army approached Patiala. Amar Singh promised fealty and tribute, and Baghel Singh ascend sincere in his mediation; but suddenly it was learnt that a large body of Sikhs had marched from Lahore, and the Mughal troops retired with precipitation to Panipat, not without a suspicion that the cupidity of the minister had been gratified with Sikh gold, and had induced him to betray his master's interests. Amar Singh died in 1781, leaving a minor son of imbecile mind. Two years afterwards a famine desolated Hariana; the people perished or sought other homes; Sirsa was deserted, and a large tract of country passed at the time from under regular sway and could not afterwards be recovered by the Sikhs.[6]

In the Doab of the Ganges and Jumna, the Sikhs rather subsidized Zabita Khan, the son of Najib-ud-daula, than became his deferential allies. That chief had designs, perhaps, upon the titular ministry of the empire, and having obtained a partial success over the imperial troops, he proceeded, in 1776, towards Delhi, with the intention of laying siege to the city. But when the time for action arrived he mistrusted his power; the emperor, on his part, did not care to provoke him too far; a compromise was effected, and he was confirmed in his possession of Saharanpur. On this occasion Zabita Khan was accompanied by a body of Sikhs, and he was so desirous of conciliating them, that he is credibly said to have adopted their dress, to have received the Pahul, or initiatory rite, and to have taken the new name of Dharam Singh.[7]

Jassa Singh Ramgarhia, when compelled to fly to the Punjab by the Kanhaya and Ahluwalia confederacies, was aided by Amar Singh Phulkia in establishing himself in the country near Hissar, whence he proceeded to levy exactions up to the walls of Delhi. In 1781 a body of Phulkia and other Sikhs marched down the Doab, but they were successfully attached under the walls of Meerut by the imperial commander Mirza Shafi Beg, and Gajpat Singh of Jind was taken prisoner. Nevertheless, in 1783, Baghel Singh and other commanders were strong enough to propose crossing the Ganges, but they were deterred by the watchfulness of the Oudh troops in the opposite back. The destructive famine already alluded to seems to have compelled Jassa Singh to move into the Doab, and, in 1785, Rohilkhand was entered by the confederates and plundered as far as Chandosi, which is within forty miles of Bareilly. At this period Zabita Khan was almost confined to the walls of his fort of Ghausgarh, and the hill raja of Garhwal, whose ancestor had received Dara as a refugee in defiance of Aurangzeb, had been rendered tributary, equally with all his brother Rajputs, in the lower hills westward to the Chenab. The Sikhs were predominant from the frontiers of Oudh to the Indus, and the traveller Forster amusingly describes the alarm caused to a little chief and his people by the appearance of two Sikh horsemen under the walls of their fort, and the assiduous services and respectful attention which the like number of troopers met with from the local authorities of Garhwal, and from the assembled wayfarers at a place of public reception.[8]

In the Punjab itself Jai Singh Kanhaya continued to retain a paramount influence. He had taken Mahan Singh, the son of Charat Singh Sukerchukia, under his protection, and he aided the young chief in capturing Russulnaggar on the Chenab, from a Muhammadan family. Mahan Singh's reputation continued to increase, and, about 1784-5, he so far threw off his dependence upon Jai Singh as to interfere in the affairs of Jammu on his own account. His interference is understood to have ended in the plunder of the place; but the wealth he had obtained and the independence he had shown both roused the anger of Jai Singh, who rudely repelled Mahan Singh's apologies and offers of atonement, and the spirit of the young chief being fired, he went away resolved to appeal to arms. He sent to Jassa Singh Ramgarhia, and that leader was glad of an opportunity of recovering his lost possessions. He joined Mahan Singh, and easily procured the aid of Sansar Chand, the grandson of Ghamand Chand of Katoch. The Kanhayas were attacked and defeated; Gurbakhsh Singh, the eldest son of Jai Singh, was killed, and the spirit of the old man was effectually humbled by this double sorrow. Jassa Singh was restored to his territories, and Sansar Chand obtained the fort of Kangra, which his father and grandfather had been so desirous of possessing. Mahan Singh now became the most influential chief in the Punjab, and he gladly assented to the proposition of Sudda Kour, the widow of Jai Singh's son, that the alliance of the two families should be lamented by the union of her infant daughter with Ranjit Singh, the only son of Mahan Singh, and who was born to him about 1780. Mahan Singh next proceeded to attack Gujarat, the old Bhangi chief of which, Gujar Singh, his father's confederate, died in 1791; but he was himself taken ill during the siege, and expired in the beginning of the following year at the early age of twenty-seven.[9]

Shah Zaman succeeded to the throne of Kabul in the year 1793, and his mind seems always to have been filled with idle hopes of an Indian empire. In the end of 1795 he moved to Hassan Abdul, and sent forward a party which is said to have recovered the fort of Rohtas; but the exposed state of his western dominions induced him to return to Kabul. The rumours of another Durrani invasion do not seem to have been unheeded by the princes of Upper India, then pressed by the Marathas and the English. Ghulam Muhammad, the defeated usurper of Rohilkhand, crossed the Punjab in 1795-6, with the view of inducing Shah Zaman to prosecute his designs, and he was followed by agents on the part of Asaf-ud-daula of Oudh, partly to counteract, perhaps, the presumed machinations of his enemy, but mainly to urge upon his majesty that all Muhammadans would gladly hail him as a deliverer. The Shah reached Lahore, in the beginning, of 1797, with thirty thousand men, and he endeavoured to conciliate the Sikhs and to render his visionary supremacy an agreeable burden. Several chiefs joined him, but the proceedings of his brother Mahmud recalled him before he had time to make any progress in settling the country, even had the Sikhs been disposed to submit without a struggle; but the Sikhs were perhaps less dismayed than the beaten Marathas and the ill-informed English. The latter lamented, with the Wazir of Oudh, the danger to which his dominions were exposed; they prudently cantoned a force at Anupshahr in the Doab, and their apprehensions led them to depute a mission to Teheran, with the view of instigating the Shah of Persia to invade the Afghan territories. Shah Zaman renewed his invasion in 1798; a body of five thousand men, sent far in advance, was attacked and dispersed on the Jhelum, but he entered Lahore without opposition, and renewed his measures of mixed conciliation and threat. He found an able leader, but doubtful partisan, in Nizam-ud-din Khan, a Pathan of Kasur, who had acquired a high local reputation, and he was employed to coerce such of the Sikhs, including the youthful Ranjit Singh, as pertinaciously kept aloof. They distrusted the Shah's honour; but Nizam-ud-din distrusted the permanence of his power, and the prudently forbore to proceed to extremities against neighbours to whom he might soon be left a prey. Some resultless akirmishing took place, but the designs of Mahmud, who had obtained the support of Persia, again withdrew the ill-fated king to the west, and he quitted Lahore in the beginning of 1799. During this second invasion the character of Ranjit Singh seems to have impressed itself, not only on other Sikh leaders, but on the Durrani Shah. He coveted Lahore, which was associated in the minds of men with the possession of power, and, as the king was unable to cross his heavy artillery over the flooded Jhelum, he made it known to the aspiring chief that their transmission would be an acceptable service. As many pieces of cannon as could be readily extricated were sent after the Shah, and Ranjit Singh procured what he wanted, a royal investitute of the capital of the Punjab. Thenceforward the history of the Sikhs gradually centres in their great maharaja; but the revival of the Maratha power in Upper India, and the appearance of the English on the scene, require that the narrative of his achievements should be somewhat interrupted.[10]

The abilities of Madhagi Sindhia restored the power of the Marathas in Northern India, and the discipline of his regular brigades seemed to place his administration on a firm and lasting basis. He mastered Agra in 1785, and was made deputy vicegerent of the empire by the titular emperor, Shah Alam. He entered at the same time into an engagement with the confederate Sikh chiefs, to the effect that of all their joint conquests on either side of the Jumna, he should have two-thirds and the 'Khalsa' the remainder.[11] This alliance was considered to clearly by point at the kingdom of Oudh, which the English were bound to defend, and perhaps to affect the authority of Delhi, which they wished to see strong; but the schemes of the Maratha were for a time interrupted by the Rohilla Ghulam Kadir. This chief succeeded his father, Zabita Khan, in 1785, and had contrived, by an adventurous step, to become the master of the emperor's person a little more than a year afterwards. He was led on from one excess to another, till at last, in 1788, he put out the eyes of his unfortunate sovereign, plundered the palace in search of imaginary treasures, and declared an unheeded youth to be the successor of Akbar and Aurangzeb. These proceedings facilitated Sindhia's views, nor was his supremacy unwelcome in Delhi after the atrocities of Ghulam Kadir and the savage Afghans. His regular administration soon curbed the predatory Sikhs, and instead of being received as allies they found that they would merely be tolerated as dependent or as servants. Raj Singh, the patriarchal chief of Jagadhri, was retained for the time as farmer of considerable districts in the Doab, and during ten years, three expeditions of exaction were.directed against Patiala and other states in the province of Sirhind. Parialsa was managed with some degree of prudence by Nanu Mal, the Hindu Diwan of the deceased Amar Singh; but the seems to have trusted for military support to Baghel Singh, the leader of the Krora Singhias, who contrived to maintain a large body of horse, partly as a judicious maintain, and partly by helping Patiala in levying contributions on weaker brethren, in a aid of the Mughal and Maratha demands, which could neither be readily met nor prudently resisted.[12]

General Perron succeeded his countryman, De Boigne, in the command of Daulat Rao Sindhia's largest regular force, in the year 1797, and he was soon after appointed the Moharaja's deputy in Northern India. His ambition surpassed his powers; but his plans were nevertheless systematic, and might have temporarily extended his own, or the Maratha, authority to Lahore, had not Sindhia's influence been endangered by Holkar, and had not Perron's own purposes been crossed by the hostility and success of the adventurer George Thomas.[13] This Englishman was bred to the sea, but an eccentricity of character, or a restless love of change, caused him to desert from a vessel of war at Madras in 1781-2, and to take military service with the petty chiefs of that presidency. He wandered to the north of India, and in 1787 he was employed by the well-known Begum Samru,[14] and soon rose high in favour with that lady. In six years he became dissatisfied, and entered the service of Appa Khande Rao, one of Sindhia's principal officers, and under whom De Boigne had formed his first regiments. While in the Maratha employ, Thomas defeated a party of Sikhs at Karnal, and he performed various other services; but seeing the distracted state of the country, he formed the not impracticable scheme of establishing a separate authority of his own. He repaired the crumbling walls of the once important Hansi, he assembled soldiers about him, cast guns, and deliberately proceeded to acquire territory. Perron was apprehensive of his power—the more so, perhaps as Thomas was encouraged by Lakwa Dada and other Marathas, who entertained a great jealousy of the French commandant.[15]

In 1799 Thomas invested the town of Jind, belonging to Bhag Singh, of the Phulkia confederacy. The old chief, Baghel Singh Krora Singhia, and the Amazonian sister of the imbecile Raja of Patiala, relieved the place, but they were repulsed when they attacked Thomas on his retreat to Hansi. In 1800 Thomas took Fatehabad, which had been deserted during the famine of 1783, and subsequently occupied by the predatory Bhattis of Hariana, then rising into local repute, not-withstanding the efforts of the Patiala chief, who, however, affected to consider them as his subjects, and gave them some aid against Thomas. Patiala was the next object of Thomas's ambition, and he was encouraged by the temporary secession of the sister of the chief; but the aged Tara Singh, of the Dallehwala confederacy, interfered, and Thomas has to act with caution. He obtained, nevertheless, a partial success over Tara Singh, he received the submission of the Pathans of Maler Kotla, and he was welcomed as a deliverer by the converted Muhammadans of Raikot, who had held Ludhiana for some time, and all of whom were equally jealous of the Sikhs. At this time Sahib Singh, a Bedi of the race of Nanak, pretended to religious inspiration, and, having collected a large force, he invested Ludhiana, took the town of Maler Kotla, and called on the English adventurer to obey him as the true representative of the Sikh prophet. But Sahib Singh could not long impose even on his countrymen, and he had to retire across the Sutlej. Thomas's situation was not greatly improved by the absence of the Bedi, for the combination against him was general, and he had to retire across the Sutlej. Thomas's situation was not greatly improved by the absence of the Bedi, for the combination against him was general, and he retired from the neighbourhood of Ludhiana towards his stronghold of Hansi. He again took the field, and attacked Safidon, an old town belonging to the chief of Jind. He was repulsed, but the place not appearing tenable, it was evacuated, and he obtained possession of it. At this time he is said to have had ten battalions and sixty guns, and to have possessed a territory yielding about 450,000 rupees, two-thirds of which he held by right of seizure and one-third as a Maratha feudatory; but he had rejected all Perron's overtures with suspicion, and Perron was resolved to crush him. Thomas was thus forced to come to terms with the Sikhs, and he wished it to appear that he had engaged them on his side against Perron; but they were really desirous of getting rid of one who plainly designed their ruin, or at least their subjection and the alacrity of Patiala in the Maratha service induced a promise, on the part of the French commander, of the restitution of the conquests of Amar Singh in Hariana. After twice beating back Perron's troops at points sixty miles distant, Thomas was compelled to surrender in the beginning of 1802, and he retired into the British provinces, where he died in the course of the same year.[16]

Perron had thus far succeeded. His lieutenant, by name Bourquin, made a progress through the Cis-Sutlej states to levy contributions, and commander himself dreamt of a dominion reaching to the Afghan hills, and of becoming as independent of Sindhia as that chief was of the Peshwa.[17] He formed an engagement with Ranjit Singh for a joint expedition to the Indus, and for a partition of the country south of Lahore,[18] but Holkar had given a rude shock to Sindhia's power, and Perron had long evaded a compliance with the Maharaja's urgent calls for troops to aid him where support was most essential. Sindhia became involved with the English, and the interested hesitation of Perron was punished by his supersession. He was not able, or he did try, to recover his authority by vigorous military operations; he knew he had committed himself, and he effected his escape from the suspicious Marathas to the safety and repose of the British territories, which were then about to be extended by the victories of Delhi and Laswari, of Assaye and Argaon.[19]

In the beginning of the eighteenth century the agents of the infant company of English merchants were vexatiously detained at the imperial court by the insurrection of the Sikhs under Banda, and the discreet 'factors', who were petitioning for some trading privileges, perhaps witnessed the heroic death of the national *Singhs,* the soldiers of the 'Khalsa', without comprehending the spirit evoked by the genius of Gobind, and without dreaming of the broad fabric of empire about to be reared on their patient labours.[20] Forty years afterwards, the merchant Omichand played a conspicuous part in the revolution which was crowned by the battle of Plassey; but the sectarian Sikh, the worldly votary of Nanak, who used religion as a garb of outward decorum, was outwitted by the audacious falsehood of Clive; he quailed before the stern scorn of the English conqueror, and he perished the victim of his own base avarice.[21] In 1784 the progress of the genuine Sikhs attracted the notice of Hastings, and he seems to have thought that the presence of a British agent at the court of Delhi might help to deter them from molesting the Wazir of Oudh.[22] But the Sikhs had learnt to dread others as well as to be a cause of fear, and shortly afterwards they asked the British Resident to enter into a defensive alliance against the Marathas, and to accept the services of thirty thousand horsemen, who had posted themselves near Delhi to watch the motions of Sindhia.[23] The English had then a slight knowledge of a new and distant people, and an estimate, two generations old, may provoke a smile from the protectors of Lahore, 'The Sikhs', says Col. Francklin, 'are in their persons tall.... their aspect is ferocious, and their eyes piereing; ... they resemble the Arabs of the Euphrates, but they speak the language of the Afghans; ... their collected army amounts to 250,000 men, a terrific force, yet from want of union not much to be dreaded.'[24] The judicious and observing Forster put some confidence in similar statements of their vast array, but he estimated more surely than any other early writer the real character of the Sikhs, and the remark of 1783, that an able chief would probably attain to absolute power on the ruins of rude commonwealth, and become the terror of his neighours, has been amply borne out by the carrer of Ranjit Singh.[25]

The battle of Delhi[26] was fought on the 11th September, 1803, and five thousand Sikhs swelled an army which the speedy capture of Aligarh had taken by surprise.[27] The Marathas were overthrown, and the Sikhas dispersed; but the latter soon afterwards tendered their allegiance to the British commander. Among the more important chiefs whose alliance or whose occasional services were accepted were Bhai Lal Singh of Kaithal, who had witnessed the success of Lord Lake Bhag Singh, the patriarchal chief of Jind, and, after a time, Bhanga Singh, the savage master of Thanesar.[28] The victory of Laswari was won within two months, and the Maratha power seemed to be annihilated in Northern India. The old blind emperor Shah Alam was again flattered with the semblance of kingly power, his pride was soothed by the demeanour of the conqueror, and as the Mughal name was still imposing, the feelings of the free but loyal soldier were doubtless gratified by the bestowal of a title which declared an English nobleman to 'the sword of the state' of the great Tamerlane.[29]

The enterprising Jaswant Rao Holkar had by this time determined on the invasion of Upper India, and the retreat of Col. Monson[30] buoyed him up with hopes of victory and dominion. Delhi was invested, and the Doab was filled with troops; but the successful defence of the capital by Sir David Ochterlony, and the reverse of Dig, drove the great marauder back into Rajputana. During these operations a British detachment, under Col. Burn, was hard pressed at Shamli near Saharanpur, and the opportune assistance of Lal Singh of Kaithal and Bhag Singh of Jind contributed to its ultimate relief.[31] The same Sikh chiefs deserved and received the thanks of Lord Lake for attacking and killing one Ika Rao, a Maratha commander who had taken up a position between Delhi and Panipat; but others were disposed to adhere to their sometime allies, and Sher Singh of Buriya fell in action with Col. Burn, and the conduct of Gurdit Singh of Ladwa induced the British general to deprive him of his villages in the Doab, and of the town of Karnal.[32]

In 1805 Holkar and Amir Khan again moved northward and proclaimed that they would be joined by the Sikhs, and even by the Afghans; but the rapid movements of Lord Lake converted their advance into a retreat or a flight. They delayed some time at Patiala, and they did not fail to make a pecuniary profit out of the differences then existing between the imbecile Raja and his wife;[33] but when the English army reached the neighbourhood of Karnal, Holkar continued his retreat towards the north, levying contributions where he could, but without being joined by any of the Sikh chiefs of the Cis-Sutlej states. In the Punjab itself he is represented to have induced some to adopt his cause, but Ranjit Singh long kept aloof, and when at last he met Holkar at Amritsar, the astute young chief wanted aid in reducing the Pathans of Kasur before he would give the Marathas any assistance against the English. Amir Khan would wish it to be believed, that he was unwilling to be a party to an attack upon good Muhammadans, and it is certain that the perplexed Jaswant Rao talked of hurrying on to Peshawar; but Lord Lake was in force on the banks of the Beas, the political demands of the British commander were moderate, and, on the 24th December, 1805, an arrangement was come to, which allowed Holkar to return quietly to Central India.[34]

Lord Lake was joined on his advance by the two chiefs, Lal Singh and Bhag Singh, whose services have already been mentioned, and at Patiala he was welcomed by the week and inoffensive Shaib Singh, who presented the keys of his citadel, and expatiated on his devotion to the British Government. Bhag Singh was the maternal uncle of Ranjit Singh, and his services were not unimportant in determining that calculating leader to avoid an encounter with disciplined battalions and a trained artillery. Ranjit Singh is believed to have visited the British camp in disguise, that he might himself witness the military array of a leader who had successively vanquished both Sindhia and Holkar,[35] and he was, moreover, too acute to see any permanent advantage in linking his fortunes with those of men reduced to the condition of fugitives. Fateh Singh Ahluwalia, the grand-nephew of Jassa Singh Kalal, and the chosen companion of the future Maharaja, was the medium of intercourse, and an arrangement was soon entered into with 'Sardars' Ranjit Singh and Fateh Singh jointly, which provided that Holkar should be compelled to retire from Amritsar, and that so long as the two chiefs conducted themselves as friends the English Government would never form any plans for the seizure of their territories.[36] Lord Lake entered into a friendly correspondence with Sansar Chand, of Katotch, who was imitating Ranjit Singh by bringing the petty hill chiefs under subjections; but no engagement was entered into, and the

British commander returned to the Provinces by the road of Ambala and Karnal.[37]

The connexion of Lord Lake with many of the Sikh Chiefs of Sirhind had been intimate, and the services of some had been opportune and valuable. Immediately after the battle of Delhi, Bhag Singh of Jind was upheld in a jagir which he possessed near that city, and in 1804 another estate was conferred jointly on him and his friend Lal Singh of Kaithal. In 1806 these leaders were further rewarded with life grants, yielding about £11,000 a year, and Lord Lake was understood to be willing to give them the districts of Hansi and Hissar on the same terms; but these almost desert tracts were objected to as unprofitable. Other petty chiefs received rewards corresponding with their services, and all were assured that they should continue to enjoy the territorial possessions which they held at the time of the British interference without being liable to the payment of tribute. These declarations or arrangements were made when the policy of Lord Wellesley was suffering under condemnation; the reign of the English was to be limited by the Jumna, a formal treaty with Jaipur was abrogated, the relations of the Indian Government with Bharatpur were left doubtful, and, although nothing was made known to Sikh chiefs of Sirhind, their connexion with the English came virtually to an end, so far as regarded the reciprocal benefits of alliance.[38]

It is now necessary to return to Ranjit Singh, whose authority had gradually become predominant among the Sikh people. His first object was to master Lahore from the incapable chiefs of the Bhangi confederacy who possessed it, and before Shah Zaman had been many months gone, effect was given to his grant by a dexterous mixture of force and artifice. Ranjit Singh made Lahore his capital, and, with the aid of the Kanhayas (or Ghani) confederacy, he easily reduced the whole of the Bhangis to submission although they were aided by Nizam-ud-din Khan of Kasur. In 1801-2 the Pathan had to repent his rashness; his strongholds were difficult to capture, but he found it prudent to become a feudatory, and to send his best men to follow a new master. After this success Ranjit Singh went to bathe in the holy pool of Taran Taran, and, meeting with Fateh Singh Ahluwalia. He conceived a friendship for him, as has been mentioned, and went through a formal exchange of turbans, symbolical of brotherhood. During 1802 the allies took Amritsar from the widow of the last Bhangi leader of note, and, of their joint spoil, it fell to the share of the master of the other capital of the Sikh country. In 1803 Sansar Chand, of Katotch, in prosecution of his schemes of aggrandizement, made two attempts to occupy portions of the fertile Doab of Jullundur, but he was repulsed by Ranjit Singh and his confederate. In 1804 Sansar Chand again quitted his hills, and captured Hoshiarpur and Bajwara; but Ranjit Singh's approach once more came involved with the Gurkhas, a new people in search of an empire which should comprise the whole range of Himalayas.[39]

In little more than a year after Shah Zaman quitted the Punjab, he was deposed and blinded by his brother Mahmud, who was in his turn supplanted by a third brother, Shah Shuja, in the year 1803. These revolutions hastened the fall of the exotic empire of Ahmad Shah, and Ranjit Singh was not slow to try his arms against the weakened Durrani governors of districts and provinces. In 1804-5 he marched to the westward; he received homage and presents from the Muhammadans of Jhang and Sahiwal, and Muzaffar Khan of Multan, successfully deprecated an attack by rich offerings. Ranjit Singh had felt his way and was satisfied; he returned to Lahore, celebrated the festival of the Holi in his capital, and then went to bathe in the Ganges at Hardwar, or to observe personally the aspect of affairs to the eastward of the Punjab. Towards the close of 1805 he made another western inroad, and added weight to the fetters already imposed on the proprietor of Jhang; but the approach of Holkar and Amir Khan recalled, first Fateh Singh, and afterwards himself, to the proper city of the whole Sikh people . The danger seemed imminent, for a famed leader of the dominant Marathas was desirous of bringing down and Afghan host, and the English army, exact in discipline, and representing a power of unknown views and resources, had reached the neighbourhood of Amritsar.[40]

A formal council was held by the Sikhs, but a portion only of their leaders were present. The singleness of purpose, the confident belief in the aid of God, which had animated mechanics and shepherds to resent persecution, and to triumph over Ahmad Shah, no longer possessed the minds of their descendants, born to comparative power and affluence, and who, like rude and ignorant men broken loose from all law, gave the rein to their grosser passions. Their ambition was personal and their desire was for worldly enjoyment. The genuine spirit of Sikhism had again sought the dwelling of the peasant to reproduce itself in another form; the rude system of mixed independence and confederacy was unsuited to an extended dominion; it had served its ends of immediate agglomeration, and the 'Misals' were in effect dissolved. The mass of the people remained satisfied with their village freedom, to which taxation and inquisition were unknown, but the petty chiefs and their paid followers, to whom their faith was the mere expression of a conventional custom, were anxious for predatory licence, and for additions to their temporal power. Some were willing to join the English, others were ready or link their fortunes with the Marathas, and all had become jealous of Ranjit Singh, who alone was desirous of excluding the stranger invaders, as the great obstacles to his own ambition of founding a military monarchy which should ensure to the people the congenial occupation of conquest. In truth, Ranjit Singh laboured, with more or less of intelligent design, to give unity and coherence to diverse atoms and scattered elements; to mould the increasing Sikh nation into a well-ordered state or commonwealth, as Gobind had developed a sect into a people, and had given application and purpose to the general institutions of Nanak.[41]

Holkar retired, and Ranjit Singh, as has been mentioned, entered into a vague but friendly alliance with the British Government. Towards the close of the same year he was invited to interfere in a quarrel between the chief of Nabha and the Raja of Patiala, and it would be curious to trace whether the English authorities had first refused to mediate in the dispute in consequence of the repeated instructions to avoid all connexion with powers beyond the Jumna. Ranjit Singh crossed the Sutlej, and took Ludhiana from the declining Muhammadan family which had sought the protection of the adventurer George Thomas. The place was bestowed upon his uncle, Bhag Singh of Jind, and as both Jaswant Singh of Nabha, whom he had gone to aid, and Sahib Singh of Patiala, whom he had gone to coerce, were glad to be rid of his destructive arbitration, he retired with the present of a piece of artillery and some treasure, and went towards the hills of Kangra, partly that he might pay his superstitious devotions at the natural flames of Juala Mukhi.[42]

At this time the unscrupulous ambition of Sansar Chand of Katotch had brought him into fatal collision with the Gurkhas. That able chief might have given life to a confederacy against the common enemies of all the old mountain principalities, who were already levying tribute in Garhwal: but Sansar Chand in his desire for supremacy had reduced the chief of Kahlur, or Belaspur, to the desperate expedient of throwing himself on the support of the Nepal commander. Amar Singh Thappa gladly advanced, and, notwithstanding the gallant resistance offered by the young chief of Nalagarh, Sansar Chand's coadjutor in his own aggressions, the Gurkha authority was introduced between the Sutlej and Jumna before the end of 1805, during which year Amar Singh crossed the former river and laid siege to Kangra. At the period of Ranjit Singh's visit to Juala Mukhi, Sansar Chand was willing to obtain his aid; but, as the fort was strong and the sacrifices required considerable, he was induced to trust to his own resources, and no arrangement was then come to for the expulsion of the new enemy.[43]

In 1807 Ranjit Singh first directed his attention to Kasur, which was again rebellious, and the relative independence of which caused him disquietude, although its able chief, Nizam-ud-din, had been dead for some time; nor was he, perhaps, without a feeling that the reduction of a large colony of Pathans, and the annexation of the mythological rival of Lahore, would add to his own merit and importance. The place was invested by Ranjit Singh, and by Jodh Singh Ramgarhia, the son of his father's old ally, Jassa the Carpenter. Want of unity weakened the resistance of the then chief, Kutb-ud-din, and at the end of a month he surrendered at discretion, and received a tract of land on the opposite side of the Sutlej for his maintenance. Ranjit Singh afterwards proceeded towards Multan, and succeeded in capturing the walled town; but the citadel resisted such efforts as he was able to make, and he was perhaps glad that the payment of a sum of money enable him to retire with credit; he was, nevertheless, unwilling to admit his failure, and, in the communications which he then held with the Nawab of Bahawalpur, the ready improver of opportunities endeavoured to impress that chief with the belief that a regard for him alone had caused the Afghan governor to be left in possession of his stronghold.[44]

During the same year, 1807, Ranjit Singh took into his employ a Kshattriya, named Mohkam Chand, an able man, who fully justified the confidence reposed in him. With this new servant in his train he proceeded to interfere in the dissensions between the Raja of Patiala and his intriguing wife, which were as lucrative to the master of Lahore as they had before been to Holkar and Amir Khan. The Rani wished to force from the weak husband a large assignment for the support of her infant son, and she tempted Ranjit Singh, by the offer of a necklace of diamonds and a piece of brass ordinance, to espouse her cause. He crossed the Sutlej, and decreed to the boy a maintenance of 50,000 rupees per annum. He then attacked Naraingarh, between Ambala and the hills, and held by a family of Rajputs, but he only secured it after a repulse and a heavy loss. Tara Singh, the old chief of the Dallehwala confederacy, who was with the Lahore force on this occasion, died before Naraingarh, and Ranjit Singh hastened back to secure his possessions in the Jullundur Doab. The widow of the aged leader equalled, the sister of the Raja of Patiala in spirit, and she is described to have girded up her garments, and to have fought, sword in hand, on the battered walls of the fort of Rahon.[45]

In the beginning of 1808 various places in the Upper Punjab were taken from their independent Sikh proprietors, and brought under the direct management of the new kingdom of Lahore, and Mohkam Chand was at the same time employed in effecting a settlement of the territories which had been seized on the lefty bank of the Sutlej. But Ranjit Singh's systematic aggressions had begun to excite fear in the minds of the Sikhs of Sirhind, and a formal deputation, consisting of the chiefs of Jind and Kaithal, and the Diwan, or minister, of Patiala, proceeded to Delhi, in March 1808, to ask for British protection. The communications of the British. Government with the chiefs of the Cis-Sutlej states had not been altogether broken off, and the Governor-General had at this time assured the Muhammadan Khan of Kunjpura, near Karnal,[46] that he need be under no apprehensions with regard to his hereditary possessions, while the petty Sikh chief of Sikri had performed some services which were deemed worthy of a pension.[47] But the deputies of the collective states could obtain no positive assurances from the British authorities at Delhi, although they were led to hope that, in the hour of need, they would not be deserted. This was scarcely sufficient to save them from loss, and perhaps from ruin; and, as Ranjit Singh had sent messengers to calm their apprehensions, and to urge them to join his camp, they left Delhi for the purpose of making their own terms with the acknowledge Raja of Lahore.[48]

The Governor-General of 1805,[49] who dissolved or deprecated treaties with princes beyond the Jumna, and declared that river to be that limit of British dominion, had no personal knowledge of the hopes and fears with which the invasions of Shah Zaman agitated the minds of men for the period of three or four years; and had the Sikhs of Sirhind sought protection from Lord Cornwallis, they would doubtless have received a decisive answer in the negative. But the reply of encouragement given in the beginning of 1808 was prompted by renewed danger; and the belief that the French, the Turkish, and the Persian emperors meditated the subjugation of India led another new Governor-General to seek alliances, not only beyond the Jumna, but beyond the Indus.[50] The designs or the desires of Napoleon appeared to render a defensive alliance with the Afghans and with the Sikhs imperative; Mr. Elphinstone was deputed to the court of Shah Shuja, and in September 1808 Mr. Metcalfe was sent on a mission to Ranjit Singh for the purpose of bringing about the desired confederation.[51] The chiefs of Patiala, Jind, and Kaithal were also verbally assured that they had become dependent princes of the British Government; for the progress of Ranjit Singh seemed to render the interposition of some friendly states, between his military domination and the peaceful away of the English, a measure of prudence and foresight.[52]

Mr. Metcalfe was received by Ranjit Singh at his newly conquered town of Kasur, but the chief affected to consider himself as the head of the whole Sikh people, and to regard the possession of Lahore as giving him an additional claim to supremacy over Sirhind. He did not, perhaps, see that a French invasion would be ruinous to his interests; he rather feared the colossal power on his borders, and he resented the intention of confining him to the Sutlej.[53] He suddenly broke off negotiations, and made his third inroad to the south of the Sutlej. He seized Faridkot and Ambala, levied exactions in Maler Kotla and Thanesar, and entered into a symbolical brotherhood or alliance with the Raja of Patiala. The British envoy remonstrated against these virtual acts of hostility, and he remained on the banks of the Sutlej until Ranjit Singh recrossed that river.[54]

The proceedigns of the ruler of Lahore determined the Governor-General, if doubtful before, to advance a detachment of troops to the Sutlej, to support Mr. Metcalfe in his negotiations, and to effectually confine Ranjit Singh to the northward of that river.[55] Provision would also be thus made, it was said, for possible war-like operations of a more extensive character, and the British frontier would be covered by a confederacy of friendly chiefs, instead of threatened by a hostile military government. A body of troops was accordingly moved across the Jumna in January 1809, under the command of Sir David Ochterlony. The General advanced, by way of Buriya and Patiala, towards Ludhiana, he was welcomed by all the Sirhind chiefs, save Jodh Singh Kalsia, the nominal head of the Krora Singhia confederacy; but during his march he was not without apprehensions that Ranjit Singh might openly break with his government, and, after an interview with certain agents whom that chief had sent to him with the view of opening a double negotiation, he made a detour and a halt, in order to be near his supplies should hostilities take place.[56]

Ranjit Singh was somewhat discomposed by the near presence of a British force but he continued to evade compliance with the propositions of the envoy, and he complained that Mr. Metcalfe was needlessly reserved about his acquisitions on the south banks of the Sutlej, with regard to which the Government had only declared that the restoration of his last conquests, and the absolute withdrawal of his troops to the northward of the river, must form the indispensable basis of further negotiations.[57] Affairs were in this way when intelligence from Europe induced the Governor-General to believe that Napoleon must abandon his designs upon India, or at least so far suspend them as to render defensive precautions unnecessary.[58] It was therefore made known that the object of the English Government had become limited to the security of the country south of the Sutlej from the encroachments of Ranjit Singh; for that, independent of the possible approach of a European enemy, it was considered advisable on other grounds to afford protection to the southern Sikhs. Ranjit Singh must still, nevertheless, withdraw his troops to the right bank of the Sutlej, his last usurpations must also be restored, but the restitution of his first conquests would not be insisted on; while, to remove all cause of suspicion, the detachment under Sir David Ochterlony could fall back from Ludhiana to Karnal, and take up its permanent position at the latter place.[59] But the British commander represented the advantage of keeping the force where it was; his Government assented to its detention, at least for a time, and Ludhiana thus continued uninterruptedly to form a station for British troops.[60]

In the beginning of February 1809, Sir David Ochterlony had issued a proclamation declaring the Cis-Sutlej states to be under British protection, and that any aggressions of the Chief of Lahore would be resisted with arms.[61] Ranjit Singh then perceived that the British authorities were in earnest, and the fear struck him that the still independent leaders of the Punjab might likewise tender their allegiance and have it accepted. All chance of empire would thus be lost, and he prudently made up his mind without further delay. He withdrew his troops as required, he relinquished his last acquisitions, and at Amritsar, on the 25th April, 1809, the now single Chief of Lahore signed a treaty which left him the master of the tracts he had originally occupied to the south of the Sutlej, but confined his ambition for the future to the north and westward of that river.[62]

The Sikh, and the few included Hindu and Muhammadan chiefs, between the Sutlej and Jumna, having been taken under British protection, it became necessary to define the terms on which they were secured from foreign danger. Sir David Ochterlony observed,[63] that when the chiefs first sought protection, their jealousy of the English would have yielded to their fears of Ranjit Singh, and they would have agreed to any conditions proposed, including a regular tribute. But their first overtures had been rejected, and the mission to Lahore had taught them to regard their defence as a secondary object, and to think that *English* apprehensions of remote foreigners had saved *them* from the arbiter of the Punjab. Protection, indeed, had become no longer a matter of choice; they must have accepted it, or they would have been treated as enemies.[64] Wherefore, continued Sir David, the chiefs expected that the protection would be gratuitous. The Government, on its part, was inclined to the liberal to its new dependants, and finally a proclamation was issued on the 3rd May, 1809, guaranteeing the chiefs of 'Sirhind and Malwa' against the power of Ranjit Singh, leaving them absolute in their own territories exempting them from tribute, but requiring assistance in time of war, and making some minor provisions which need not be recapitulated.[65]

No sooner were the chiefs relieved of their fears of Ranjit Singh, than the more turbulent began to pray upon one another, or upon their weaker neighbours; and, although the Governor-General had not wished them to consider themselves as in absolute subjection to the British power,[66] Mr. Metcalfe pointed out[67] that it was necessary to declare the chiefs to be protected singly against one another, as well as collectively against Ranjit Singh; for, if such a degree of security were not guaranteed, the oppressed would necessarily have recourse to the only other person who could use coercion with effect, viz., to the Raja of Lahore. The justness of these views was admitted, and, on the 22nd August, 1811, a second proclamation was issued, warning the chiefs against attempts at unsurpation, and reassuring them of independence and of protection against Ranjit Singh.[68] Nevertheless, encroachments did not at once cease, and the Jodh Singh Kalsia, who avoided giving in his adhesion to the British Government on the advance of Sir David Ochterlony, requried to have troops sent against him in 1818 to compel the surrender of tracts which he had forcibly seized.[69]

The history of the southern or Malva Sikhs need not be continued, although it presents many points of interest to the general reader, as well as to the student and to those concerned in the administration of India. The British functionaries soon became involved in intricate questions about interference between equal chiefs, and between chiefs and their confederates or dependants; they laboured to reconcile the Hindu laws of inheritance with the varied customs of different races, and with the alleged family usages of peasants suddenly become princes. They had to decide on questions of escheat, and being strongly impressed with the superiority of British municipal rule, and with the undoubted claim of the paramount to some benefit in return for the protection it afforded, they strove to prove that collateral heirs had a limited right only, and that exemption from tribute necessarily implied an enlarged liability to confiscation. They had to define the common boundary of the Sikh states and of British rule, and they were prone to show, after the manner of Ranjit Singh, that the present possession of a principal town gave a right to all the villages which had ever been attached to it as the seat of a local authority, and that all waste lands belonged to the supreme power, although the dependant might have last possessed them in sovereignty and intermediately brought them under the plough. They had to exercise a paramount municipal control, and in the surrender of criminals, and in the demand for compensation for property stolen from British subjects, the original arbitrary nature of the decisions enforced has not yet been entirely replaced by rules of reciprocity. But the government of a large empire will always be open to obloquy, and liable to misconception, from the acts of officious and ill-judging servants, who think that they best serve the complicated interests of their own rulers by lessening the material power of others, and that any lessening the material power of others, and that any advantage they may seem to have gained for the state they obey will surely promote their own objects. Nor, in such matters, are servants alone to blame and the whole system of internal government in India requires to be remodelled and made the subject of a legislation at once wise, considerate, and comprehensive. In the Sikh states ignorance has been the main cause of mistakes and heart-burnings, and in 1818 Sir David Ochterlony frankly owned to the Marquis of Hastings[70] that his proclamation of 1809 had been based on an erroneous idea. He thought that a few great chiefs only existed between the Sutlej and Jumna, and that on them would devolve the maintenance of order; whereas he found that the dissolution of the 'Misals', faulty as was their formation, had almost thrown the Sikhs back upon the individual independence of the times of Ahmad Shah. Both in considering the relation of the chiefs to one another, and their relation collectively to the British Government, too little regard was perhaps had to the peculiar circumstances of the Sikh people. They were in a state of progression among races as barbarous as themselves, when suddenly the colossal power of England arrested them, and required the exercise of political moderation and the practice of a just morality from men ignorant alike of despotic control and of regulated freedom[71]

Sir David Ochterlony even thought it prudent to lay in supplies and to throw up defensive lines at Ludhiana.[72] Ranjit Singh had likewise *his* suspicions, but they were necessarily expressed in ambiguous terms, and were rather to be deduced from his acts and correspondence, and from a consideration of his position, that to be looked from in overt statements or remonstrances. By degrees the apprehensions of the two governments mutually vanished and while Ranjit Singh felt he could freely exercise his ambition beyond the Sutlej, the English were persuaded he would not embroil himself with its restless allies in the south, so long as he had occupation elsewhere. In 1811 presents were exchanged between the Governor-General and the Maharaja,[73] and during the following year Sir David Ochterlony became his guest at the marriage of his son, Kharak Singh,[74] and from that period until within a year of the late war, the rumours of a Sikh, invasion served to amuse the idle and to alarm the credulous, without causing uneasiness to the British viceroy.

On the departure of Mr. Metcalfe, the first care of Ranjit Singh was to strengthen both his frontier post of Phillaur opposite Ludhiana, and Gobindgarh the citadel of Amritsar, which he had begun to build as soon as he got possession of the religious capital of his people.[75] He was invited, almost at the same time, by Sansar Chand of Katotch, to aid in resisting the Gurkhas, who were still pressing their long-continued siege of Kangra, and who had effectually dispelled the Rajput prince's dreams of a supremacy reaching from the Jumna to the Jhelum. The stronghold was offered to the Sikh ruler as the price of his assistance, but Sansar Chand hoped, in the meantime, to gain admittance himself, by showing to the Gurkhas the futility or resisting Ranjit Singh, and by promising to surrender the fort to the Nepal commander, if allowed to withdraw his family. The Maharaja saw through the schemes of Sansar Chand, and he made the son of his ally a prisoner, while he dexterously cajoled the Khatmandu general, Amar Singh Thappa, who proposed a joint warfare against the Rajput mountaineers, and to take, or receive, in the meantime, the fort of Kangra as part of the *Gurkha* share of the general spoil. The Sikhs got possession of the place by suddenly demanding admittance as the expected relief. Sansar Chand was foiled, and Amar Singh retreated across the Sutlej, loudly exclaiming that he had been grossly duped.[76] The active Nepalese commander soon put down some disorders which had arisen in his rear, but the disgrace of his failure before Kangra rankled in his mind, and he made preparations for another expedition against it. He proposed to Sir David Ochterlony a joint march to the Indus, and a separate appropriation of the plains and the hills;[77] and Ranjit Singh ignorant alike of English moderation and of international law, became apprehensive lest the allies of Nepal should be glad of a pretext for coercing one who had so unwillingly acceded to their limitation of his ambition. He made known that he was desirous of meeting Amar Singh Thappa on his own ground; and the reply of the Governor-

General that he might not only himself cross the Sutlej to chastise the invading Gurkhas in the hills, but that, if they descended into the plains of Sirhind, he would receive English, assistance gave him another proof that the river of the treaty was really to be an impassable barrier. He had got the assurance he wanted and he talked no more of carrying his horsemen into mountain recesses.[78] But Amar Singh long brooded over his reverse, and tried in various ways to induce the British authorities to join him in assailing the Punjab. The treaty with Nepal, he would say, made all strangers the mutual friends or enemies of the two governments, and Ranjit Singh had wantonly attacked the Gurkha possessions in Katotch. Besides, he would argue, to advance is the safest policy, and what could have brought the English to the Sutlej but the intention of going beyond it?[79] The Nepal war of 1814 followed, and the English became the neighbours of the Sikhs in the hills as well as in the plains, and the Gurkhas, instead of grasping Kashmir, trembled, for their homes in Khatmandu. Ranjit Singh was no then asked to give his assistance, but Sansar Chand was directly called upon by the English representative to attack the Gurkhas and their allies—a hasty requisition, which produced a remonstrance from the Maharaja, and an admission on the part of Sir David Ochterlony, that his supremacy was not questioned; while the experienced Hindu chief had forborne to commit himself with either state by promising much and doing little.[80]

Ranjit Singh felt secure on the Upper Sutlej, but a new danger assailed him in the beginning of 1810, and again set him to work to dive to the bottom of British counsels. Mr. Elphinstone had scarcely concluded a treaty with Shah Shuja against the Persians and French, before that prince was driven out of his kingdom by the brother whom he had himself supplanted, and who had placed his affairs in the hands of the able minister, Fateh Khan. The Maharaja was at Wazirabad, sequestering that place from the family of a deceased Sikh chief, when he heard of Shah Shuja's progress to the eastward with vague hopes of procuring assistance from one friendly power or another. Ranjit Singh remembered the use he had himself made of Shah Zaman's grant of Lahore, he feared the whole, Punjab might similarly be surrendered to the English in return for a few battalions, and he desired to keep a representative of imperial power within his own grasp.[81] He amused the ex-king with the offer of cooperation in the recovery of Multan and Kashmir, and he said he would himself proceed to meet the Shah to save him further journeying towards Hindustan.[82] They saw one another at Sahiwal, but no determinate arrangement was come to, for some prospects of success dawned upon the Shah, and he felt reason to distrust Ranjit Singh's sincerity.[83] The conferences were broken off; but the Maharaja hastened, while there was yet an appearance of union to demand the surrender of Multan for himself in the name of the king. The great gun called 'Zamzam',[84] or the 'Bhangi Top', was brought from Lahore to batter the walls of the citadel; but all his efforts were in vain, and he retired, foiled, in the month of April, with no more than 180,000 rupees to soothe his mortified vanity. The Governor, Muzaffar Khan, was by this time in correspondence with the British viceroy in Calcutta, and Ranjit Singh feared that a tender of allegiance might not only be made but accepted.[85] He therefore proposed to Sir David Ochterlony that the two "allied powers" should march against Multan and divide the conquest equally.[86] It was surmised that he wanted the siege train of the English, but he may likewise have wished to know whether the Sutlej was to be as good a boundary in the south as in the north. He was told reprovingly that the English committed aggressions upon no one, but otherwise the tenor of the correspondence was such as to lead him to believe that he would not be interfered with in his designs upon Multan.[87]

Shah Shuja proceeded towards Attock after his interview with Ranjit Singh, and having procured some aid from the rebellious brother of the Governor of Kashmir, he crossed the Indus, and in March 1810, made himself master of Peshawar. He retained possession of the place for about six months, when he was complied to retreat southward by the Wazir's brother Muhammad Azim Khan. He made an attempt to gain over the Governor of Multan, but he was refused admittance within its walls, and was barely treated with courtesy, even when he encamped a few miles distant. He again moved northward and, as the enemies of Mahmud were numerous, he succeeded in mastering Peshawar a second time, after two actions, one a reverse and the other a victory. But those who had aided him became suspicious that he was in secret league with Fateh Khan the Wazir, or, like Ranjit Singh, they wished to possess his person; and, in the course of 1812, he was seized in Peshawar by Jahan Dad Khan, Government of Attock, and removed, first to that fort, and afterwards to Kashmir, where he remained as a prisoner for more than twelve months.[88]

After the failure before Multan, Ranjit Singh and his minister, Mohkam Chand, were employed in bringing more fully under subjection various Sikh and Muhammadan chiefs in the plains, and also the hill Rajas of Bhimbar, Rajaori, and other places. In the month of February 1811, the Maharaja had reached the salt mines between the Jhelum and Indus, and hearing that Shah Mahmud had crossed the latter river, he moved in force to Rawalpindi, and sent to ascertain his intentions. The Shah had already deputed agents to state that his object was to punish or overawe the Governor of Kashmir, who had sided with his brother, Shah Shuja, then in the neighbourhood of Multan; and the two princes being satisfied, they had a meeting of ceremony before the Maharaja returned to Lahore to renew his confiscation of lands held by the many petty chiefs who had achieved independence or sovereignty while the country was without a general controlling power, but who now fell unresistingly before the systematic activity of the young Maharaja.[89]

In the year 1811, the blind Shah Zaman crossed the Punjab, and was visited by Ranjit Singh. He took up his residence in Lahore for a time and deputed his son Eunus to Ludhiana, where he was received with attention by Sir David Ochterlony; but as the prince perceived that he was not a welcome guest, his father quitted Ranjit Singh's city and became a wanderer for a time in Central Asia.[90] In the following year the families of the two ex-kings took up their abode at Lahore, and as the Maharaja was preparing to bring the hill chiefs south of Kashmir under his power, with a view to the reduction of the valley itself, and as he always endeavoured to make success more complete or more easy by appearing to labour in the cause of others, he professed to the wife of Shah Shuja that he would release her husband and replace Kashmir under the Shah's sway; but he hoped the gratitude of the distressed lady would make the great diamond, Koh-i-nur, the reward of his chivalrous labour when they should be crowned with success. His principal object was doubtless the possession of the Shah's person, and when, after his preliminary successes against the hill chiefs, including the capture of Jammu by his newly married son, Kharak Singh, he heard, towards the end of 1812, that Fateh Khan the Kabul Wazir had crossed the Indus with the design of marching against Kashmir, he sought an interview with him, and said he would assist in bringing to punishment both the rebel, who detained the king's brother, and likewise the Governor of Multan, who had refused obedience to Mahmud. Fateh Khan had been equally desirous of an interview, for the felt that he could not take Kashmir if opposed by Ranjit Singh, and he readily promised anything to facilitate his immediate object, The Maharaja and the Wazir each hoped to use the other as a tool, yet the success of neither was complete. Kashmir was occupied in February 1813. But Fateh Khan outstripped the Sikhs under Mohkam Chand, and he maintained that as he alone had achieved the conquest, the Maharaja could not share in the spoils. The only advantage which accrued to Ranjit Singh was the possession of Shah Shuja's person, for the illfated king was allowed by Fateh Khan to go whither he pleased, and he preferred joining the Sikh army which he accompanied to Lahore, to becoming virtually a prisoner in Kabul.[91] But the Maharaja's expedients did not entirely fail him, and as the rebel Governor or Attock was alarmed by the success of Shah Mahmud's party in Kashmir, he was easily persuaded to yield the fort to Ranjit Singh. This unlooked for stroke incensed Fateh Khan, who accused the Maharaja of barefaced treachery, and endeavoured further to intimidate him by pretending to make overtures to Shah Shuja; but the Maharaja felt confident of his strength, and a battle was fought on the 13th July, 1813, near Attock, in which the Kabul Wazir, and his brother Dost Muhammad Khan, were defeated by Mohkam Chand and the Sikhs.[92]

Ranjit Singh was equally desirous of detaining Shah Shuja in Lahore, and of securing the great diamond which had adorned the throne of the Mughals. The king evaded a compliance with all demands for a time, and rejected even the actual offer, of moderate sums of money; but at last the Maharaja visited the Shah in person, mutual friendship was declared, an exchange of turbans took place, the diamond was surrendered,[93] and the king received the assignment of a jagir in the Punjab for his maintenance, and a promise of aid in recovering Kabul. Ranjit Singh then moved towards the Indus to watch the proceedings of Fateh Khan, who was gradually consolidating the power of Mahmud, and he required Shah Shuja to join him, perhaps with some design of making an attempt on Kashmir; but Fateh Khan was likewise watchful, the season was advanced, and the Maharaja suddenly returned. Shah Shuja followed slowly, and on the way he was plundered of many valuables, by ordinary robbers, as the Sikhs said but by the Sikhs themselves, as the Shah believed. The inferior agents of Ranjit Singh may not have been very scrupulous, but the Shah may not have been very scrupulous, but the Shah had traitors in his own household, and the high officer who had been sent to conduct Mr. Elphinstone to Peshawar, embezzled much of the Shan's property when misfortune overtook him. This Mir Abdul Hassan had originally informed the Sikh chief of the safety of the Koh-i-nur and other valuables, he plotted when in Lahore to make it appear the king was in league with the Governor of Kashmir, and he finally threw difficulties in the way of the escape of his master's family from the Sikh capital. The flight of the Begums to Ludhiana was at last effected in December 1814; for Shah Shuja perceived the design of the Maharaja to detain him a prisoner and to make use of his name for purposes of his own. A few months afterwards the Shah himself escaped to the hills; he was joined by some Sikhs discontented with Ranjit Singh, and he was aided by the chief of Kishtwar in an attack upon Kashmir. He penetrated into the valley, but he had to retreat, and, after residing for some time longer with his simple, but zealous, mountain host, he marched through Kulu, crossed the Sutlej, and joined his family at Ludhiana in September 1816.[94] His presence on the frontier was regarded as embarrassing by the British Government, which desired that he should be urged to retire to Karnal or Saharanpur, and Sir David Ochterlony was further discretionally authorized to tell Ranjit Singh that the ex-king of Kabul was not a welcome guest within the limits of Hindustan. Nevertheless the annual sum of 18,000 rupees, which had been assigned for the support of his family, was raised to 50,000 on his arrival, and personally he was treated with becoming respect and consideration.[95]

Shah Shuja thus slipped from the hands of the Maharaja, and no use could be made of his name in further attempts upon Kashmir; but Ranjit Singh continued as anxious as ever to obtain possession of the valley, although the Governor had, in the meantime, put himself in communication with the English.[96] The chiefs south of the Pir Panjal range having been brought under subjection, military operations were commenced towards the middle of the year 1814. Sickness detained the experienced Mohkam Chand at the capital, but he warned the Maharaja of the difficulties which would beset him as soon as the rains set in and he almost urged the postponement of the expedition. But the necessary arrangements had been completed, and the approach was made in two columns. The more advanced division surmounted the lofty barrier, a detachment of the Afghan force was repulsed, and the town of Supain was attacked; but the assault failed, and the Sikhs retired to the mountain passes. Muhammad Azim Khan, the Governor, then fell on the main body of Ranjit Singh, which had been long in view on the skirts of the valley, and compelled the Maharaja to retreat with precipitation. The rainy season had fairly set in the army became disorganized, a brave chief, Mith Singh Behrania, was slain, and Ranjit Singh reached his capital almost alone about the middle of August. The advanced detachment was spared by Muhammad Azim Khan, out of regard, he said, for Mohkam Chand, the grandfather of its commander; and as doubtless the aspiring brother of the Wazir Fateh Khan had views of his own amid the struggles then going on for power, he may have thought it prudent to improve every opportunity to the advantage of his own reputation.[97]

The efforts made during the expedition to Kashmir had been great, and the Maharaja took some time to reorganize his means. Towards the middle of 1815 he sent detachments of troops to levy exactions around Multan, but he himself remained at Adinanagar, busy with internal arrangements, and perhaps intent upon the war then in progress between the British and the Nepalese, which for a period of six months, was scarcely worthy of the English name. The end of the same year was employed in again reducing the Muhammadan tribes south-east of Kashmir, who had thrown off their allegiance during the retreat of the Sikhs. In the beginning of 1816 the refractory hill Raja of Nurpur sought poverty and an asylum in the British dominions, rather than resign his territories and accept a maintenance. The Muhammadan chief-ship of Jhang was next finally confiscated, and Leiah, a dependency of Dera Ismail Khan was laid under contribution. Uch on the Chenab, the seat of families of Saiyids, was temporarily occupied by Fateh Singh

Ahluwalia, and the possessions of Jodh Singh Ramgarhia, lately deceased, the son of Jassa the Carpenter (the confederate of the Maharaja's father), were seized and annexed to the territories of the Lahore government. Sansar Chand was honoured and alarmed by a visit from his old ally, and the year 1816 terminated with the Maharaja's triumphant return to Amritsart.[98]

The northern plains and lower hills of the Punjab had been fairly reduced to obedience and order, and Ranjit Singh's territories were bounded on the south and west by the real or nominal dependencies of Kabul, but the Maharaja's meditated attacks upon them were postponed for a year by impaired health. His first object was Multan, and early in 1818 an army marched to attack it, under the nominal command of his son, Kharak Singh, the titular reducer of Jammu. To ask what were the Maharaja's reasons for attacking Multan would be futile; he thought the Sikhs had as good a right as the Afghans to take what they could, and the actual possessor of Multan had rather asserted his own independence than faithfully served the heirs of Ahmad Shah. A large sum of money was demanded and refused. In the course of February, the city was in possession of he Sikhs, but the fort held out until the beginning of June, and chance had then some share in its capture. An Akali, named Sadhu Singh, went forth to do battle for the 'Khalsa', and the very suddenness of the onset of his small band led to success. The Sikhs, seeing the impression thus strangely made, arose together carried the outwork, and found an easy entry through the breaches of a four months' batter. Muzaffar Khan, the governor and two of his sons, were slain in the assault, and two others were made prisoners. A considerable booty fell to the share of the soldiery but when the army reached Lahore, the Maharaja directed that the plunder should be restored. He may have felt some pride that his commands were not altogether unheeded, but he complained that they were not so productive as he had expected.[99]

During the same year, 1818, Fateh Khan, the Kabul Wazir was put to death by Kamran, the son of Mahmud, the nominal ruler. He had gone to Herat to repel an attack of the Persians, and he was accompanied by his brother, Dost Muhammad, who again had among his followers a Sikh chief, Jai Singh Atariwala, who had left the Punjab in displeasure. Fateh Khan was successful, and applause was freely bestowed upon his measures; but he wished to place Herat, then held by a member of Ahmad Shah's family, within his own grasp, and Dost Muhammad and his Sikh ally were employed to eject and despoil the prince-governor. Dost Muhammad effected his purpose somewhat rudely, the person of a royal lady was touched in the eagerness of the riflers to secure her jewels, and Kamran made this affront offered to a sister a pretext for getting rid of the man who from the stay had become the tyrant of his family. Fateh Khan was first blinded and then murdered; and the crime saved Herat, indeed, to Ahmad Shah's heirs, but deprived them for a time, and now perhaps for ever, of the rest of his possessions. Muhammad Azim Khan hastened from Kashmir, which he left in charge of Jabbar Khan, another of the many brothers. He at first thought of reinstating Shah Shuja, but he at last proclaimed Shah Ayub as king, and in a few months he was master of Peshawar and Ghazni, of Kabul and Kandahar. This change of rulers favoured, if it did not justify, the views of Ranjit Singh, and towards the end of 1818 he crossed the Indus and entered Peshawar, which was evacuated on his approach. But it did not suit his purposes, at the time to endeavour to retain the district; he garrisoned Khairabad, which lies on the right bank of the river, so as to command the passage for the future, and then retired, placing Jahan Dad Khan, his old ally of Attock, in possession of Peshawar itself, to hold it as he could by his own means. The Barakzai governor, Yar Muhammad Khan, returned as soon as Ranjit Singh had gone, and the powerless Jahan Dad made no attempt to defend his gift.[100]

Ranjit Singh's thoughts were now directed towards the annexation of Kashmir, the garrison of which had been reduced by the withdrawal of some good troops by Muhammad Azim Khan; but the proceedings of Desa Singh Majithia and Sansar Chand for a moment changed his designs upon others into fears for himself. These chiefs were employed on an expedition in the hills to collect the tribute due to the Maharaja; and the Raja of Kahlur, who held territories on both sides of the Sutlej, who held territories on both sides on the Sutlej, ventured to resist the demands made. Sansar Chand rejoiced in this opportunity of revenge upon the fried of the Gurkhas; the river was crossed, but the British authorities were prompt, and a detachment of troops stood ready to oppose force to force. Ranjit Singh directed the immediate recall of his men, and he desired Sirdar Desa Singh to go in person, and offer his apologies to the English agent.[101] This alarm being over, the Maharaja proceeded with his preparations against Kashmir, the troops occupying which had, in the meantime been reinforced by a detachment from Kabul. The Brahman, Diwan Chand, who had exercised the real command at Multan, was placed in advance; the Prince Kharak Singh headed a supporting column and Ranjit Singh himself headed a supporting column, and Ranjit Singh himself remained behind with a reserve and for the purpose of expediting the transit of the various munitions of war. The choice of the Sikh cavalry marched on foot over the mountains along with the infantry soldiers, and they dragged with them a few light guns; the passes were scaled on the 5th July 1819, but Jabbar Khan was found ready to receive them. The Afghans repulsed the invaders, and mastered two guns; but they did not improve their success, and the railed Sikhs again attacked them, and won an almost bloodless victory.[102]

A few months after Kashmir had been added to the Lahore dominions, Ranjit Singh moved in person to the south of the Punjab, and Dera Ghazi Khan on the Indus, another dependency of Kabul, was seized by the victorious Sikhs.

The Nawab of Bahawalpur, who held lands under Ranjit Singh in the fork of the Indus and Chenab, had two years before made a successful attack on the Durrani chief of the place, and it was now transferred to him in form, although his Cis-Sutlej possessions had virtually but not formally, been taken under British protection in the year 1815, and he had thus become, in a measure, independent of the Maharaja's power.[103] During the year 1820 partial attempts were made to reduce the turbulent Muhammadan tribes to the south-west of Kashmir, and in 1821, Ranjit Singh proceeded to complete his conquests on the Central Indus by the reduction of Dera Ismail Khan. The strong fort of Mankera, situated between the two western most rivers of the Punjab was held out for a time by Hafiz Ahmad Khan the father of the titular governor, who scarcely owned a nominal subjection to Kabul; but the promise of honourable terms induced him to surrender before the end of the year, and the country on the right bank of the Indus, including Dera Ismail Khan, was left to him as a feudatory of Lahore.[104]

Muhammad Azim had succeeded to the power of his brother Fateh Khan, and, being desirous of keeping Ranjit Singh to the left bank of the Indus, he moved to Peshawar in the year 1822, accompanied by Jai Singh, the fugitive Sikh chief, with the intention of attacking Khairabad opposite Attock. Other matters caused him hastily to retrace his steps, but his proceedings had brought the Maharaja to the westward, who sent to Yar Muhammad Khan, the Governor of Peshawar, and demanded tribute. This leader, who apprehended the designs of his brother, Muhammad Azim Khan, almost as much as he dreaded Ranjit Singh, made an offering of some valuable horses.[105] The Maharaja was satisfied and withdrew perhaps the more readily as some differences had arisen with the British authorities regarding the right to a place named Whadni to the south of the Sutlej, which had been transferred by Ranjit Singh to his intriguing and ambitious mother-in-law, Sada Kaur, in the year 1808. The lady was regarded by the English agents as being the independent representative of the interests of the Kanhaya (or Ghani) confederacy of Sikhs on *their* side of the river, and therefore as having a right to their protection. But Ranjit Singh had quarrelled with and imprisoned his mother-in-law, and had taken possession of the fort of Whadni. It was resolved to eject him by force, and a detachment of troops marched from Ludhiana and restored the authority of the captive widow. Ranjit Singh prudently made no attempt to resist the British agent, but he was not without opprehensions that his occupation of the place would be construed into a breach of the treaty, and he busied himself with defensive preparations. A friendly letter from the superior authorities at Delhi relieved him of his fears, and allowed him to prosecute his designs against Peshawar without further interruption.[106]

Muhammad Azim Khan disapproved of the presentation of horses to Ranjit Singh by Yar Muhammad Khan, and he repaired to Peshawar in January 1823. Yar Muhammad fled into the Usufzai hills rather than meet his brother, and the province seemed lost to one branch of the numerous family; but the chief of the Sikhs was at hand, resolved to assert his equality of right or his superiority of power. The Indus was forded on the 13th March, the guns being carried across on elephants. The territory of the Khattaks bordering the river was occupied, and at Akora the Maharaja received and pardoned the fugitive Jai Singh Atariwala. A religious war had been preached, and twenty thousand men, of the Khattak and Usufzai tribes, had been assembled by their priests and devotees to fight for their faith against the unbelieving invaders. This body of men was posted on and around heights near Noshahra, but on the left bank of the Kabul river, while Muhammad Azim Khan, distrustful of his influence over the independent militia, and of the fidelity of his brothers, occupied a position higher up on the right bank the Wazir in check and crossed the river to attack the armed peasantry. The Sikh 'Akalis' at once rushed upon the

Muhammadan 'Ghazis', but Phula Singh, the wild leader of the fanatics of Amritsar, was slain, and his horsemen made no impression on masses of footmen advantageously posted. The Afghans than exultingly advanced, and threw the drilled infantry of the Lahore ruler into confusion. They were checked by the fire of the rallying battalions, and by the play of the artillery drawn up on the opposite bank of the river, and at length Ranjit Singh's personal exertions with his cavalry converted the check into a victory. The brave and believing mountaineers reassembled after their rout, and next day they were willing to renew the fight under their 'Pirzada', Muhammad Akbar; but the Kabul Wazir had fled with precipitation, and they were without countenance or support. Peshawar was sacked, and the country plundered up to the Khaibar Pass; but the hostile spirit of the population rendered the province of difficult retention, and the prudent Maharaja gladly accepted Yar Muhammad's tender of submission. Muhammad Azim Khan died shortly afterwards, and with him expired all show of unanimity among the bands of brothers who possessed the three capitals of Peshawar, Kabul, and Kandahar; while Shah Mahmud and his son Kamran exercised a precarious authority in Herat, and Shah Ayub, who had been proclaimed titular monarch of Afghanistan, remained a cipher in his chief city.[107]

Towards the end of the year 1823, Ranjit Singh marched to the south-west corner of his territories, to reduce refractory Muhammadan Jagirdars, and to create an impression of his power on the frontiers of Sind—to tribute from the Amirs of which country he had already advanced some claims.[108] He likewise pretended to regard Shikarpur as a usurpation of the Talpur dynasty; but his plans were not yet matured, and he returned to his capital to learn of the death of Sansar Chand. He gave his consent to the succession of the son of a chief whose power once surpassed his own, and the Prince Kharak Singh exchanged turbans, in token of brotherhood, with the heir of tributary Kaṭotch.[109]

Ranjit Singh had now brought under his sway the three Muhammadan provinces of Kashmir, Multan and Peshawar: he was supreme in the hills and plains of the Punjab proper; the mass of his dominion had been acquired; and although his designs on Ladakh and Sind were obvious, a pause in the narrative of his actions may conveniently take place, for the purpose of relating other matters necessary to a right understanding of his character, and which intimately bear on the general history of the country.

Shah Shuja reached Ludhiana, as has been mentioned, in the year 1816, and secured for himself an honoured repose: but his thoughts were intent on Kabul and Kandahar; he disliked the British notion that he had tamely sought an asylum, and he wished to be regarded as a prince in distress, seeking for aid to enable him to recover his crown. He had hopes held out to him by the Amirs of Sind when hard pressed, perhaps, by Fateh Khan, and he conceived that an invasion of Afghanistan might be successfully prosecuted from the southward. He made offers of advantage to the English, but he was told that they had no concern with the affairs of strangers, and desired to live in peace with all their neighbours. He was thus casting about for means when Fateh Khan was murdered, and the tenders of allegiance which he received from Muhammad Azim Khan at once induced him to quit Ludhiana. He left that place in October 1818: with the aid of the Nawab of Bahawalpur, he mastered Dera Ghazi Khan; he sent his son Timur to occupy Shikarpur, and he proceeded in person towards Peshawar, to become, as he believed, the king of the Durranis. But Muhammad Azim Khan had, in the meantime, seen fit to proclaim himself the Wazir of Ayub, and Shah Shuja, hard pressed, sought safetly among some friendly clans in the Khaibar hills. He was driven thence at the end of two months, and had scarcely entered Shikarpur when Muhammad Azim Khan's approach compelled him to retire. He went first to Khairpur, and afterwards to Hyderabad, and, having procured some money from the Sindians, he returned and recovered Shikarpur, where he resided for a year. But Muhammad Azim Khan again approached, the Hyderabad chiefs pretended that the Shah was plotting to bring in the English, and their money was this time paid for his expulsion. The ex-king, finding his position untenable, retired through Rajputana to Delhi and eventually took up his residence a second time at Ludhiana in June 1821. His brother, the blind Shah Zaman, after visiting Persia, and perhaps Arabia, arrived at the same place about the same time and nearly by the same road. Shah Shuja's stipend had all along been drawn by his family, represented by the able and faithful Wafa Begum, and an allowance, first of 18,000 and afterwards of 24,000 rupees a year, was assigned for the support of Shah Zaman, when he also became a petitioner to the English Government.[110]

In the year 1820, Appa Sahib, the deposed Raja of the Maratha kingdom of Nagpur, escaped from the custody of the British' authorities and repaired to Amritsar. He would seem to have had the command of large sums of money, and he endeavoured to engage Ranjit Singh in his cause; but the Maharaja had been told the fugitive was the violent enemy of his English allies, and he ordered him to quit his territories. The chief took up his abode for a time in Sansar Chand's principality of Katotch, and while there he would appear to have entered into some idle schemes with Prince Haidar, a son of Shah Zaman, for the subjugation of India south and east of the Sutlej. The Durrani was to be monarch of the whole, from Delhi to Cape Comorin; but the Maratha was to be Wazir of the empire, and to hold the Deccan as a dependent sovereign. The Punjab was not included; but it did not transpire that either Ranjit Singh or Sansar Chand, or the two ex-kings of Kabul, were privy to the design, and as soon as the circumstance became known, Sansar Chand compelled his guest to proceed elsewhere. Appa Sahib repaired, in 1822, to Mandi, which lies between Kangra and the Sutlej; but he wandered to Amritsar about 1828, and only finally quitted the country during the following year; to find as asylum with the Raja of Jodhpur. The state had become an English dependency, and the ex-Raja's surrender was required; but the strong objections of the Rajput induced the Government to be satisfied with a promise of his safe custody, and he died almost forgotten in the year 1840.[111]

As has been mentioned, the Raja Bir Singh, of Nurpur, in the hills, and been dispossessed of his chiefship in the year 1816. He sought refuge to the south of the Sutlej, and immediately made proposals to Shah Shuja, who had just reached Ludhiana to enter into a combination against Ranjit Singh. The Maharaja had not altogether despised similar tenders of allegiance from various discontented chiefs, when the Shah was his prisoner-guest in Lahore; he remembered the treaty between the Shah and the English, and he knew his readily dethroned kings might be made use of by the ambitious. He wished to ascertain the views of the English authorities, but he veiled his suspicions of *them* in terms of apprehension of the Nurpur Raja. His troops, he said, were absent in the neighbourhood of Multan, and Bir Singh might cross the Sutlej and raise disturbances. The reception of emissaries by Shah Shuja was then discountenanced, and the residence of the exiled Raja at Ludhiana was discouraged; but Ranjit Singh was told that his right to attempt the recovery of his chiefship was admitted, although he would not be allowed to organize the means of doing so within the British limits. The Maharaja seemed satisfied that Lahore would be safe while he was absent in the south or west, and he said no more.[112]

In the year 1819 the able and adventurous traveller, Moorcroft, left the plains of India in the hope of reaching Yarkand and Bukhara. In the hills of the Punjab he experienced difficulties, and he was induced to repair to Lahore to wait upon Ranjit Singh. He was honourably received and any lurking suspicions of his own designs, or of the views of his Government were soon dispelled. The Maharaja conversed with frankness of the events of his life; he showed the traveller his bands of horsemen and battalions of infantry, and encouraged him to visit any part of the capital without hesitation, and at his own leisure. Mr Moorcroft's medical skill and general knowledge, his candid manner and personal activity, produced an impression favourable to himself and advantageous to his countrymen; but his proposition that British merchandise should be admitted into the Punjab at a fixed scale of duties was received with evasion. The Maharaja's revenues might be affected, it was said, and his principal officers, whose advice was necessary, were absent on distant expeditions. Every facility was afforded to Mr. Moorcroft in prosecuting his journey and it was arranged that if he could not reach Yarkand from Tibet, he might proceed through Kashmir to Kabul and Bukhara, the route which it was eventually found necessary to pursue. Mr Moorcroft reached Ladakh in safety, and in 1821 he became possessed of a letter from the Russian minister, Price Nesselrode, recommending a merchant to the good offices of Ranjit Singh and assuring him that the traders of the Punjab would be well received in the Russian dominions—for the emperor was himself a benign ruler, he earnestly desired the prosperity of other countries, and he was especially the well-wisher of that reigned over by the King of the Sikhs. The person recommended had died on his way southward from Russia; and it appeared that, six years previously, he had been the bearer of similar communications for the Maharaja of Lahore, and the Raja of Ladakh.[113]

Ranjit Singh now possessed a broad dominion, and an instructed intellect might have rejoiced in the opportunity accorded for wise legislation, and for consolidating aggregated provinced into one harmonious empire. But such a task neither suited the Maharaja's genius nor that of the Sikh nation; nor is it perhaps, agreeable to the constitution of any political society, that its limits shall be fixed, or that the pervaditing spirit of a people shall rest, until its expansive force is destroyed and becomes obnoxious to change and decay. Ranjit Singh grasped the more obvious characteristics of the impulse given by Nanak and Gobind; he dexterously turned them to the purposes of his own material ambition and he appeared to be an absolute monarch in the midst of willing and obedient subjects. But he knew that he merely directed into a particular channel a power which he could neither destroy nor control, and that, to prevent the Sikhs turning upon himself, or contending with one another, he must regularly engage them in conquest and remote warfare. The first political system of the emancipated Sikhs had crumbled to pieces, partly through its own defects, partly owing to its contact with a well-ordered and civilized government, and partly in consequence of the ascendancy of one superior mind. The 'Misals' had vanished or were only represented by Ahluwalia and Patiala (or Phulkia), the one depending on the personal friendship of Ranjit Singh for its chief, and the other upheld in separate portions by the expediency of the English. But Ranjit Singh never thought his own or the Sikh sway was to be confined to the Punjab and his only wish was to lead armies as far as faith in the Khalsa and confidence in his skill would take brave and believing men. He troubled himself not at all with the theory or the practical niceties of administration, and he would rather have added a province to his rule than have received the assurances of his English neighbours that he legislated with discrimination in commercial affairs and with a just regard for the amelioration of his ignorant and fanatical subjects of various persuasions. He took from the land as much as it could readily yield, and he took from merchants as much as they could profitably give; he put down open marauding; the Sikh peasantry enjoyed a light assessment; no local officer dared to oppress a member of the Khalsa; and if elsewhere the farmers of revenue were resisted in their tyrannical proceedings, they were more likely to be changed than to be supported by battalions. He did not ordinarily punish men who took redress into their own hands, for which, indeed his subordinates were prepared, and which they guarded against as they could. The whole wealth and the whole energies of the people were devoted to war, and to the preparation of military means and equipment. The system is that common to all feudal government, and it gives much scope to individual ambition, and tends to produce independence of character. It suited the mass of the Sikh population; they had ample employment they loved contention and they were pleased that city after city admitted the supremacy of the Khalsa and enabled them to enrich their families. But Ranjit Singh never arrogated to himself the title or the powers of despot or tyrant. He was assiduous in hid devotions; he honoured men of reputed sanctity, and enabled them to practise an enlarged charity; he attributed every success to the favour of God and he styled himself and people collectively the 'Khalsa', or commonwealth of Gobind. Whether in walking barefooted to make his obeisance to a collateral representative of his prophets, or in rewarding a soldier distinguished by that symbol of his faith, a long and ample beard, or in restraining the excesses of the fanatical Akalis, or in beating an army and acquiring a province, his own name and his own motives were kept carefully concealed, and everything was done for the sake of the Guru, for the advantage of the Khalsa, and in the name of the Lord.[114]

In the year 1822 the French Generals, Ventura and Allard, reached Lahore by way of Persia and Afghanistan, and after some little hesitation, they were employed and treated with distinction.[115] It has been usual to attribute the superiority of the Sikh army to the labours of these two officers, and of their subsequent coadjutors, the Generals Court and Avitabile; but in truth, the Sikh owes his excellence as a soldier to his own hardihood of character to that spirit of adaptation which distinguished every new people, and to that feeling of a common interest and destiny implanted in him by his great teachers. The Rajputs and Pathans are valiant and high-minded warriors: but their pride and their courage are personal only, and concern them as men of ancient family and noble lineage; they will do nothing unworthy or their birth, but they are indifferent to the political advancement of their race. The efforts of the Marathas, in emancipating themselves from a foreign yoke, were neither guided nor strengthened by any distinct hope or desire. They became free, but knew not how to remain independent, and they allowed a crafty Brahman.[116] to turn their aimless aspirations to his own profit, and to found a dynasty of 'Peshwas' on the achievements of unlettered Sudras. Ambitious soldiers took a further advantage of the spirit called up by Sivaji, but as it was not sustained by any pervading religious principle of action a few generations saw the race yield to the expiring efforts of Muhammadanism, and the Marathas owe their present position, as rulers to the intervention of European strangers. The genuine Maratha can scarcely be said to exist, and the two hundred thousands spearmen of the last century are once more shepherds and tillers of the ground. Similar remarks apply to the Gurkhas, that other Indian people which had risen to greatness in latter times by its own innate power, unmingled with religious hope. They became masters, but no peculiar institution formed the landmark of their thoughts, and the vitality of the original impulse seems fast waning before the superstition of an ignorant priesthood and the turbulence of a feudal nobility. The difference between these races and the fifth tribe on Indian warriors will be at once apparent. The Sikh looks before him only, the ductility of his youthful intellect readily receives the most useful impression, or takes the most advantageous form, and religious faith is ever present to sustain him under any adversity, and to assure him of an ultimate triumph.

The Rajput and Pathan will fight as Pirthi Raj and Jenghiz Khan waged war; they will ride on horses in tumultuous array, and they will wield a sword and spear with individual dexterity: but neither of these cavaliers will design to stand in regular ranks and to handle the musket of the infantry soldier, although the Muhammadan has always been a brave and skilful server of heavy cannon. The Maratha is equally averse to the European system of warfare, and the less stiffened Gurkha has only had the power or the opportunity of forming battalions of footmen, unsupported by an active cavalry and a trained artillery. The early force of the Sikhs was composed of horsemen, but they seem intuitively to have adopted the new and formidable matchlock of recent times, instead of their ancestral bows, and the spear common to every nation. Mr. Forster noticed this peculiarity in 1783, and the advantage it gave in desultory warfare.[117] In 1805, Sir John Malcolm did not think the Sikh was better mounted than the Maratha;[118] but, in 1810, Sir David Ochterlony considered that, in the confidence of untried strength, his great native courage would glow him more formidable than a follower of Sindhia or Holkar, and readily lead him to face battery of well-served guns.[119] The peculiar arm of the contending nations of the last century passed into a proverb, and the phrase, the Maratha spear, the Afghan sword, the Sikh matchlock, and the English cannon, is still of common repetition; nor does it gratify the pride of the present masters of India to hear their success attributed rather to the number and excellence of their artillery, that to that dauntless courage and firm array which have enabled the humble footmen to win most of those distant victories which add glory to the English name. Nevertheless it has always been the object of rival powers to obtain a numerous artillery; the battalions of De Boigne would never separate themselves from their cannon, and the presence of that formidable arm is yet, perhaps, essential to the full confidence of the British Sepoy.[120]

Ranjit Singh said that in 1805, he went to see the order of Lord Lake's army,[121] and it is known that in 1809 he admired and praised the discipline of Mr. Metcalfe's small escort, who repulsed the sudden onset of a body of charged Akalis.[122] He began, after that period, to give his attention to the formation of regular infantry, and in 1812 Sir David Ochterlony saw two regiments of Sikhs, besides several of Hindustanis, drilled by then who had resigned or deserted the British service.[123] The next year the Maharaja talked of raising twenty-five battalions,[124] and his confidence in discipline was increased by the resistance which the Gurkhas offered to the British arms. He enlisted people of that nation, but his attention was chiefly given to the instruction of his own countrymen, and in 1820 Mr. Moorcroft noticed with approbation the appearance of the Sikh foot-soldier.[125] Ranjit Singh had not got his people to resign their customary weapons and order of battle without some trouble. He encouraged them by good pay, by personal attention to their drill and equipment, and by himself wearing the strange dress, and going through the formal exercise.[126] The old chiefs disliked the innovation, and Desa Singh Majithia, the father of the present mechanic and disciplinarian Lahna Singh, assured the companions of Mr. Moorcroft that Multan and Peshawar and Kashmir had all been won by the free Khalsa cavalier.[127] By degrees the infantry service came to be preferred, and before Ranjit Singh died, he saw it regarded as the proper warlike array of his people. Nor did they give their heart to the musket alone, but were perhaps more readily brought to serve guns than to stand in even ranks as footmen.

Such was the state of change of the Sikh army, and such were the views of Ranjit Singh when Generals Allard and Ventura obtained service in the Punjab. They were fortunate in having an excellent material to work with and like skilful officers, they made a good use of their means and opportunities. They gave a moderate degree of precision and completeness to a system already introduced; but their labours are more conspicuous in French words of command, in treble ranks, and in squares salient with guns, than in the ardent courage, the alert obedience, and the long endurance of fatigue, which distinguished the Sikh horsemen sixty years ago, and which pre-eminently characterize the Sikh footman of the present day among the other soldiers of India.[128] Neither did Generals Ventura and Allard, Court and Avitabile, ever assume to themselves the merit of having created the Sikh army and perhaps their ability and independence of character added more to the general belief in European superiority, than all their instructions to the real efficiency of the Sikhs as soldiers.

When a boy, Ranjit Singh was betrothed, as has been related, to Mehtab Kaur, the daughter of Gurbakhsh Singh, the young heir of the Kanhaya (or Ghani) chiefship, who fell in battle with his father Mahan Singh. Sada Kaur, the mother of the girl, possessed a high spirit and was ambitious of power, and, on the death of the Kanhaya leader. Jai Singh, about 1793, her influence in the affairs of the confede-body of brave and banded men which furnishes the most obvious examples of degradation.[129] The husband man of the Punjab, as of other provinces in Upper India, is confined to his cakes of millet or wheat and to a draught of water from the well; the soldier fares not much better, and neither indulge in strong liquors, except upon occasions of rejoicing. The indolent man of wealth or station, or the more idle religious fanatic, may seek excitement, or a refuge from the vacancy of his mind, in drugs and drink; but expensiveness of diet is rather a Muhammadan than an Indian characteristic, and the Europeans carry their petitions and the pleasures of the table to an excess unknown to the Turk and Persian and which greatly scandalize the frugal Hindu.[130]

Yet Ranjit Singh not only yielded more than was becoming to the promptings of his appetites, but, like all deposts and solitary authorities, he laid himself open to the charge of extravagant partiality and favouritism. He had placed himself in some degree in opposition to the whole Sikh people; the free followers of Gobind could not be the observant slaves of an equal member of the Khalsa, and he sought for strangers whose applause would be more ready if less sincere, and in whom he could repose some confidence as the creatures of his favour. The first who thus rose to distinction was Khushal Singh, a Brahman from near Saharanpur who enlisted in one of the first raised regiments, and next became a runner or footman on the Maharaja's establishment. He attracted Ranjit Singh's notice, and was made Jamadar of the Devni, or master of the entry, about the year 1811. His brother seemed likely to supplant him, but refusal to become a Sikh favoured Khushal Singh's continuance in power, until both yieldid to the Jammu Rajputs in the year 1820. Gulab Singh, the eldest of three sons, claimed that his grandfather was the brother of the well-known Ranjit Deo; but the family was perhaps illegitimate, and had become impoverished, and Gulab Singh took service as a horseman in a band commanded by Jamadar Khushal Singh. He sent for his second brother, Dhian Singh and then, again like the reigning favourite, they both became running footmen under Ranjit Singh's eye. Their joint assiduity, and the graceful bearing of the younger man, again attracted the Maharaja's notice and Dhian Singh speedily took the place of the Brahman chamberlain, without however, consigning him to neglect, for he retained his estates and his position as a noble. Gulab Singh obtained a petty command and signalized himself by the seizure of the turbulent Muhammadan Chief of Rajauri. Jammu was then conferred in jagir or fire upon the family, and the youngest brother, Suchet Singh, as well as the two elder, were one by one raised to the rank of Raja, and rapidly obtained an engrossing and prejudicial influence in the counsels of the Maharaja, excepting perhaps in connexion with his English relations, the importance of which required and obtained the exercise of his own unbiassed opinion. The smooth and crafty Gulab Singh ordinarily remained in the hills, using Sikh means to extend his own authority over his brother Rajputs, and eventually into Ladakh; the less able, but more polished. Dhian Singh, remained continually in attendance upon the Maharaja, ever on the watch, in order that he might anticipate his wishes; white the elegant Suchet Singh fluttered as a gay courtier and gallant soldier, without grasping at power or creating enemies. The nominal fakir or devotee, the Muhammadan Aziz-ud-din, never held the place of an ordinary favourite, but he attached himself at an early period to Ranjit Singh's person, and was honoured and trusted as one equally prudent and faithful; and during the ascendancy both of Khushal Singh and Dhian Singh he was always consulted, and invariably made the medium of communication with the British authorities. The above were the most conspicuous persons in the Lahore court; but the mind of Ranjit Singh was never prostrate before that of others, and he conferred the government of Multan on the discreet Sawan Mal, and rewarded the military racy became paramount. She encouraged her young son-in-law to set aside the authority of his own widow mother, and at the age of seventeen the future Maharaj is not only said to have taken upon himself the management of his affairs, but to have had his mother put to death as an adultress. The support of Sada Kaur was of great use to Ranjit Singh in the beginning of his career, and the cooperation of the Kanhaya Misal mainly enabled him to master Lahore and Amritsar. Her hope seems to have been that, as the grandmother of the chosen heir of Ranjit Singh, and as a chieftainess in her own right, she would be able to exercise a commanding influence in the affairs of the Sikhs; but her daughter was childless, and Ranjit Singh himself was equally able and wary. In 1807 it was understood that Mehtab Kaur was pregnant and it is believed that she was really delivered of a daughter; but, on Ranjit Singh's return from an expedition, he was presented with two boys as his offspring. The Maharaja doubted: and perhaps he always gave credence to the report that Sher Singh was the son of a carpenter, and Tara Singh the child of a weaver, yet they continued to be brought up under the care of their reputed grandmother as if their parentage had been admitted. But Sada Kaur perceived that she could obtain no power in the names of the children, and the disappointed woman addressed the English authorities in 1810 and denounced her son-in-law as having usurped her rights, and as resolved on war with his new allies. Her communications received some attention, but she was unable to organize an insurrection, and she became in a manner reconciled to her position. In 1820 Sher Singh was virtually adopted by the Maharaja, with the apparent object of finally setting aside the power of his mother-in-law. She was required to assign half of the lands of the Kanhaya chiefship for the maintenance of the youth: but she refused, and she was in consequence seized and imprisoned, and her whole possessions confiscated. The little estate of Whadni, to the south of the Sutlej, was however restored to her through British intervention, as has already been mentioned.[131]

Ranjit Singh was also betrothed, when a boy, to the daughter of Khazan Singh a chief of the Nakkais confederacy and by her he had a son in the year 1802, who was named Kharak Singh, and brought up as his heir. The youth was married, in the year 1812, to the daughter of a Kanhaya leader, and the nuptials were celebrated amid many rejoicings. In 1816 the Maharaja placed the mother under some degree of restraint owing to her mismanagement of the estates assigned, for the maintenance of the prince and he endeavoured to rouse the spirit of his on to exertion and enterprise; but he was of a weak and indolent character, and the attempt was vain. In the year 1821 a son was born to Kharak Singh, and the child, Nau Nihal Singh soon came to be regarded as the heir of the Punjab.[132]

REFERENCES

1. Forster, *Travels,* i. 323; Elphinstone, *Kabul,* ii. 297; Murray, *Ranjit Singh,* p. 27; Moorcroft, *Travels,* i. 127; and manuscript accounts consulted by the author.
2. When Nadir Shah proceeded to establish his authority in Sindh, he found the ancestor of the Bhawalpur family a man of reputation in his native district of Shikarpur. The Shah made him the deputy of the upper their of the province; but, becoming suspicious of the whole clan, he resovled on removing it to Ghazni. The tribe then migrated up the Sutlej, and seized lands by force. The Daudputras are so-called from Daud (David), the first of the family who acquired a name. They fabulously trace their origin to the Caliph Abbas; but they may be regarded as Sindian Baluchis, or as Baluchis changed by a long residence in Sind. In establishing themselves on the Sutlej, they reduced the remains of the ancient Langahs and Johiyas to further insignificance; but they introduced the Sindhian system of canals

of irrigation, and both banks of the river below Pakpattan bear witness to their original industry and love of agriculture.

3. The memoirs of the Bhawalpur family, and manuscript Sikh histories. Cf. also Forster, *Travels, i.* 148.
4. The memoirs of the Bhawalpur chief and manuscript Sikh accounts. Cf. Murray, *Ranjit Singh*, p. 38, &c.; and Forster, *Travels*, i. 283, 286, 336.

   Ranjit Deo, of Jammu, died in A.D. 1770.

   Charat Singh was killed accidentally, and Jhanda Singh was assassinated, in 1774.

   Hari Singh Bhangi appears to have been killed in battle with Amar Singh of Patiala, about 1770.
5. Memoirs of the Bhawalpur chief, and other manuscript histories. Cf. Browne, *India Tracts*, ii. 28, and Forster, *Travels*, i. 324; Elphinstone (*Kabul*, ii. 303) makes 1781, and not 1779, the date of the recovery of Multan from the Sikhs.
6. Manuscript histories, and Mr. Ross Bell's report of 1836, on the Bhattiana boundary. Cf. Francklin, *Shah Alam*, pp. 86, 90, and Shah Nawaz Khan's Epitome of Indian History, called *Mirrit-i-Aftab Numa.*
7. Cf. Forster *Travels*, i. 325; *Browne*, India Tracts, ii. 29; and Francklin, *Shah Alam*, p. 72.
8. Forster, *Travels*, i. 228, 229, 262, 326 and note. Ct. also Francklin, *Shah Alam*, pp. 93, 94, and the Persian epitome *Mirrit-i-Aftab Numa.*
9. Manuscript histories and chronicles. Cf. Forster, *Travels*, i. 288; Murray, *Ranjit Singh*, pp. 42, 48; and Moorcroft, *Travels*, i. 127. The date of 1785-6, for the reduction of the Kanhayas and the restoration of Jassa Singh, &c., is preferred to 1782, which is given by Murray, partly because the expedition to Rohilkhand took place in 1785, as related by Forster (*Travels*, i. 326 note), and Jassa Singh is generally admitted to have been engaged in it, being then in banishment.
10. Elphinstone (*Kabul*, ii. 308) states that Shah Zaman was exhorted to undertake his expedition of 1795 by a refugee prince of Delhi, and encouraged in it by Tipu Sultan. The journey of Ghulam Muhammad, the defeated Rohilla chief, and the mission of the Wazir of Oudh, are given on the authority of the Bhawalpur family annals, and from the same source may be added an interchange of deputations on the part of Shah Zaman and

Sindhia, the envoys, as in the other instance, having passed through Bhawalpur town. A suspicion of the complicity of Asaf-ud-daula, of Lucknow, does not seem to have occurred to the English historians, who rather dilate on the exertions made by their government to protect their pledged ally from the northern invaders. Nevertheless, the statements of the Bhawalpur chronicles on the subject seem in every way credible.

11. Browne, *India Tracts,* ii. 29.

12. Manuscript accounts. Cf. Francklin, *Shah Alam,* pp. 179-85.

13. [For an excellent sketch of the life of this adventurer see the article 'A Free lance from Tipperary' in *Strangers within the Gates,* by G. Festing. Edinburgh, and London, 1914.—Ed.]

14. [This remarkable woman, whose origin is wrapped in mystery, was said to have been a dancing-girl in Delhi. She subsequently married 'Somru', a European adventurer, who had entered the service of the Emperor and had received the Jagir of Sardhana, a few miles from Delhi. 'Somru'—whose real name was Reinhard—was a man of the foulest antecedents, and among his other exploits he had been principally concerned in the murder of the English prisoners at Patna in 1763. Upon her husband's death the Begum succeeded to his estate and to the leadership of the disreputable band of cut-throats who formed his army. After the battle of Assaye he submitted to the English, embraced Christiantiy about 1781, and was publicly embraced by Lord Lake, to the great horror of the spectators. She ended her days in great sanctity, and was buried in the Roman Catholic Cathedral at Sardhana which she herself had built. She also Sleeman, *Rambles and Recollections,* ed. V.A. Smith, chap. 75, Oxford University Press, 1915 Ed.]

15. Francklin, *Life of George Thomas,* pp. 1, 79, 107, &c., and Major Smith, *Account of Regular Corps in the Service of Indian Princes,* p. 118, &c.

16. See generally Francklin, *Life of George Thomas,* and Major Smith, *Account of Regular Corps in Indian States,* p. 21, &c. The Sikh accounts attribute many exploits to the sister of the Raja of Patiala, and among them an expedition into the hill territory of Nahan, the state from which Patiala wrested the vale of Pinjaur, with its hanging gardens, not, however, without the aid of Bourquin, the deputy of Perron.

17. Malcolm (*Sketch,* p. 106) considers that Perron could easily have reduced the Sikhs, and mastered the Punjab.

18. This alliance is given on the authority of a representation made to the Resident at Delhi agreeably to his letter to Sir David Ochterlony of July 5, 1814.

19. Cf. Major Smith, *Account of Regular Corps in Indian States,* p. 31, &c.

20. See Orme, *History,* ii, 22, &c., and Mill, Wilson's edition, iii. 34, &c. The mission was two years at Delhi during 1715, 1716, 1717, and the genuine patriotism of Mr. Hamilton, the surgeon of the deputation, mainly contributed to procure the cession of thirty-seven villages near Calcutta, and the exemption from duty of goods protected by English passes. This latter privilege was a turning-point in the history of the English in India, for it gave an impulse to trade, which vastly increased the importance of British subjects, if it added little to the profits of the associated merchants. [It may be added that a dispute about the issue of those passes brought about an open rupture between the East India Company and Mir Kasim, Nawab of Bengal, in 1763. The later was utterly defeated at the Battle of Bunar in 1764 and as one of the terms of peace in the following year—the year of Clive's return to India—the Diwani (fiscal administration) of Bengal, Bihar and Orissa was granted by the Emperor Shah Alam to the Company, in return for a yearly payment of 26 lakhs, while the Nawab, the sucessor of Mir Kasim, was deprived of all power and pensioned.—Ed.]

    In the *Granth* of Guru Gobind there are at least four allusions to Europeans, the last referring specially to an Englishman. First, in the *Akal Stut,* Europeans are enumerated among the tribes inhabiting India; second and third, in the *Kalki* chapters of the 24 *Autars,* apparently in praise of the systematic modes of Europeans; and Fourth, in the Persian *Hikayats,* where both a European and an Englishman appear as champions for the hand of a royal damsel, to be vanquished, of course, by the hero of the tale.

21. That Omichand was a Sikh is given on the authority of Forster, *Travels,* i. 337. That he died of a broken heart is doubted by Professor Wilson. (Mill, *India,* iii. 192 note, ed 1840.)

22. Browne, *India Tracts,* ii. 20, 30: and Franklin, *Shah Alam,* pp. 115-116.

23. Auber, *Rise and Progress of the British Power in India,* ii. 26, 27. The chief who made the overtures was Dulcha Singh of Rudaur on the Jumna, who afterwards entered Sindhia's service. Cf. Francklin, *Shah Alam,* p. 75, 77, 78 note.

24. *Francklin, Shah Alam,* p. 75, 77, 78.
25. Forster's *Travels,* ii. 340. See also p. 324, where he says the Sikhs had raised in the Punjab a solid structure of religion. The remark of the historian Robertson may also be quoted as apposite, and with the greater reason as prominence has lately been given to it in the House of Commons on the occasion of thanking the army for its services during the Sikh campaign of 1848-9. He says that the enterprising commercial spirit of the English, and the martial ardour of the Sikhs, who possess the energy natural to men in the earlier states of society, can hardly fail to lead sooner or later to open hostility. (*Disquisition Concerning Ancient India,* note iv. sect. 1. written in 1789-90.)
26. For an interesting discussion as the exact site of this battle, the result of which was the occupation of Delhi by the English and the placing of the Emperor Shah Alam under their protection, the reader is referred to an article by Sir Edward Maclagan, in the *Journal of the Punjab Historical Society,* vol. iii—Ed.]
27. Major Smith, *Account of Regular Corps in Indian States,* p. 34.
28. Manuscript memoranda of personal inquiries.
29. Mill, *History of British India,* Wilson's ed., vi. 510.
30. [He had made a rash advance into Holkar's territory in July 1804, to unite with another English force under Col. Murray. Lack of supplies caused him to retreat, and he only reached Agra at the end of August, after losing the major part of his army. However, he took his revenge at Dig. as that victory was mainly his work.—Ed.]
31. Manuscript memoranda. Both this aid in 1804, and the opposition of the Sikhs at Delhi, in 1803, seem to have escaped the notice of English observers, or to have been thought undeserving of record by English historians. (Mill, *History,* vi. 503, 592 ed. 1840.)
32. Manuscript memoranda of written documents and of personal inquiries.
33. Amir Khan, in his Memoirs (p. 276), says characteristically, that Holkar remarked to him, on observing the silly differences between the Raja and the Rani, 'God has assuredly sent us these two pigeons to pluck; do you espouse the cause of the one, while I take up with the other.'
34. Cf. Amir Khan, *Memoirs,* pp. 276, 285; and Murray *Ranjit Singh,* p. 57, &c.

35. See Moorcroft, *Travels*, i. 102.
36. See the treaty itself, Appendix XXIII.
37. The public records show that a newswriter was maintained for sometime in Katotch, and the correspondence about Sansar Chand leaves the impression that Ranjit Singh could never wholly forged the Raja's original superiority, nor the English divest themselves of a feeling that he was independent of Lahore.
38. The original graints to Jind, Kaithal, and others, and also similar papers of assurance, are carefully preserved by the several families; and the various English documents show that Bhag Singh, of Jind, was always regarded with much kindliness by Lord Lake, Sir John Malcolm, and Sir David Ochterlony.
39. Cf. Murray, *Ranjit Singh*, pp. 51, 55.

    Capt. Murray, the political agent at Ambala, and Capt. Wade, the political agent at Ludhiana, each wrote a narrative of the life of Ranjit Singh, and that of the former was printed in 1834, with a few corrections and additions, and additions, and some notes, by Mr. Thoby Prinsep, secretary to the Indian Government. The author has not seen Capt. Wade's report or narrative, but he believes that it, even in a greater degree than Capt. Murray's, was founded on personal recollections and on oral report, rather than on contemporary English documents, which reflected the opinions of the times, and which existed in sufficient abundance after 1803 especially. The two narratives in question were, indeed, mainly prepared from accounts drawn up by intelligent Indians, at the requisition of the English functionaries, and of these the chronicles of Buta Shah, a Muhammadan, and Sohan Lal, a Hindu, are the best known, and may be had for purchase. The inquiries of Capt. Wade, in especial, were extensive, and to both officers the public is indebted for the preservation of a continuous narrative of Ranjit Singh's actions.

    The latter portion of the present chapter, and also chapters VI and VII, follow very closely the author's narratives of the British connexion with the Sikhs, drawn up for Government, a [*literary*] use which he trusts may be made, without any impropriety, of an unprinted paper of his own writing.
40. See Elphinstone, *Kabul*, ii. 325; and Murray, *Ranjit Singh*, pp. 56-57.
41. Malcolm (*Sketch*, pp. 106-107) remarks on the want of unanimity among the Sikhs at the time of Lord Lake's expedition. Cf. Murray, *Ranjit Singh*, pp. 57-58.

42. See Murray, *Ranjit Singh,* pp. 59-60. The letter of Sir Charles Metcalfe to Government, of June 17, 1809, shows that Ranjit Singh was not strong enough at the time in question, 1806, to interfere, by open force, in the affairs of the Malwa Sikhs, and the letters of Sir David Ochterlony, of February 14, March 7, 1809 and July 30, 1811, show that the English engagements of 1805, with the Patiala and other chiefs, were virtually at an end, so far as regarded the reciprocal benefits of alliance.

43. Cf. Murray, *Ranjit Singh,* p. 60; and Moorcroft, *Travels,* i. 127, &c.

    Sansar Chand attributed his overthrow by the Gurkhas to his dismissal of his old Rajput troops and employment of Afghans, at the instigation of the fugitive Rohilla chief, Ghulam Muhammad, who had sought an asylum with him.

    The Gurkhas crossed the Jumna to aid the chief of Nahan against his subjects, and they crossed the Sutlej to aid one Rajput prince against another—paths always open to new and united races. References in public records show that the latter river was crossed in A.D. 1805.

44. Murray, *Ranjit Singh,* pp. 60-61, and the manuscript memories of the Bahawalpur family.

45. Cf. Murray, *Ranjit Singh,* pp. 61-63. The gun obtained by Ranjit Singh from Patiala on this occasion was named Karri Khan, and was captured by the English during the campaign of 1845-6.

46. In a document dated 18th January, 1808.

47. Mr. Clerk of Ambala to the agent at Delhi, 19th May, 1837.

48. See Murray, *Ranjit Singh,* pp. 64-65.

49. [Lord Cornwallis had been sent out in 1805 with strict orders to pursue a pacific and economizing policy, as the Directors were alarmed at the expense of the wars waged by his predecessor—Lord Wellesley. But Cornwallis died two months after his arrival, and was temporarily succeeded by Sir G. Barlow.—Ed.]

50. Mr. Auber (*Rise and Progress of the British Power in India,* ii. 461), notices the *triple* alliance which threatened Hindustan (Lord Minto had arrived as Governor-General in 1807.—Ed.]

51. [Col. Malcolm was dispatched on a similar mission to Persia at the same time, and concluded a treaty (1809) which did away with the possibility of French interference in that quarter.—Ed.]

52. Government to Sir David Ochterlony, 14th Nov., 1808, Cf. Murray, *Ranjit Singh,* pp. 65-66.

53. Moorcroft ascertained (*Travels*, i. 94) that Ranjit Singh had serious thoughts of appealing to the sword, so unpalatable was English interference. The well-known Fakir Uziz-ud-din was one of the two persons who dissuaded him from war.

54. Murray, *Ranjit Singh*, p. 66.

55. Government to Sir David Ochterlony, 14th Nov. and 29th Dec., 1808.

56. Sir David Ochterlony to Government, 20th Jan., and 4th, 9th, and 14th Feb., 1809, with Government to Sir David Ochterlony, of 13th March, 1809. Government by no means approved of what Sir David Ochterlony had done, and he, feeling aggrieved, virtually tendered his resignation of his command. (Sir David Ochterlony to Government, 19th April, 1809.)

57. Sir David Ochterlony to Government, 14th Feb., 1809, and Government to Sir David Ochterlony, 30th July, 1809 Lieut.-Col. Lawrence (*Adventures in the Punjab*, p. 131, note *g*) makes Sir Charles Metcalfe sufficiently communicative on this occasion with regard to other territories, for he is declared to have told the Maharaja that by a compliance with the then demands of the English, he would ensure their neutrality with respect to encroachments elsewhere.

58. Government to Sir David Ochterlony, 30th Jan., 1809. [Probably the altered relations between Napoleon and Turkey were the main cause of this. The Franco-Turkish alliance of 1807 had come to an end with the deposition of Mustapha IV and accession of Mahmud II—July 1808—and the improved relations of England and Turkey led to the signature by the latter powers of the Treaty of the Dardanelles (January 1809)—Ed.]

59. Government to Sir David Ochterlony, 30th Jan., 6th Feb., and 13th March, 1809.

60. Sir David Ochterlony to Government, 6th May, 1809, and Government to Sir David Ochterlony, 13th June, 1809.

61. See Appendix XXIV.

62. See the treaty itself, Appendix XXV. Cf. Murray, *Ranjit Singh*, pp. 67-68.

63. Sir David Ochterlony to Government, 17th March, 1809.

64. See also Government to Resident at Delhi, 26th Dec., 1808. Baron Hugel (*Travels*, p. 279) likewise attributes the interference of the English, in part at least, to selfishness, but with him the motive was the petty desire of benefiting by escheats, which the

dissipated character of the chiefs was likely to render speedy and numerous! This appetite for morsels of territory, however, really arose at a subsequent date, and did not move the English in 1809.

65. See Appendix XXVI.

66. Government to Sir David Ochterlony, 10th April, 1809.

67. Mr. Metcalfe to Government, 17th June, 1809.

68. See the proclamation, Appendix XXVII.

69. Resident at Delhi to Agent at Ambala, 27th Oct., 1818, mulching the chief in the military expenses incurred, 65,000 rupees. The head of the family, Jodh Singh, had recently returned with Ranjit Singh's army from the capture of Multan, and he was always treated with consideration by the Maharaja; and, bearing in mind the different views taken by dependent Sikhs and governing English, of rights of succession, he had fair grounds of dissatisfaction. He claimed to be the head of the 'Krora Singhia' Misal, and to be the heir of all childless feudatories. The British Government, however, made itself the valid or efficient head of the confederacy.

70. In a private communication, dated 17th May, 1818.

71. In the Sikh States on either side of the Sutlej, the British Government was long fortunate in being represented by such men as Capt. Murray and Mr. Clerk, Sir David Ochterlony, and Lieut-Col. Wade—so different from one another, and yet so useful to one common purpose of good for the English power. These men, by their personal character or influence, added to general reputation of their countrymen, and they gave adaptation and flexibility to the rigid unsympathizing nature of a foreign and civilized supremacy. Sir David Ochterlony will long live in the memory of the people of Northern India as one of the greatest of the conquering English chiefs; and he was among the very last of the British leaders who endeared himself both to the army which followed him and to the princes who bowed before the colossal power of his race.

    Nevertheless, the best of subordinate authorities, immersed in details and occupied with local affairs, are liable to be biassed by views which promise immediate and special advantage. They can seldom be more than upright or dexterous administrators, and they can still more rarely be men whose minds have been enlarged by study and reflexion as well as by actual experience of the world. Thus the ablest but too often resemble merely the practical man of the moment; while the supreme authority, especially when absent from his councillors and intent upon some great undertaking, is of necessity dependent mainly upon the local representatives of the Government, whose notions must inevitably be partial or one-sided, for good, indeed, as well as for evil.

72. Sir D. Ochterlony to Government, 31st Dec., 1809, and 7th Sept., 1810.

73. A carriage was at this time sent to Lahore. See, further, Resident of Delhi to Sir D. Ochterlony, 25th Feb., 1811, and Sir D. Ochterlony to Government, 15th Nov., 1811.

74. Sir D. Ochterlony to Government, 18th July, 1811 and 23rd Jan., 1812.

75. Cf. Murray, *Ranjit Singh*, p. 76.

76. Murray, *Ranjit Singh*, pp. 76-77. The Maharaja told Capt. Wade that the Gurkhas wanted to share Kashmir with him, but that he thought it best to keep them out of the Punjab altogether. (Cap. Wade to Government, 25th May, 1831.).

77. Sir D. Ochterlony to Government, 16th and 30 Dec., 1809.

78. Sir D. Ochterlony to Government, 12th Sept., 1811, and Government to Sir D. Ochterlony, 4th Oct. and 22nd Nov., 1811.

79. Sir D. Ochterlony to Government, 20th December, 1813.

80. Government to Sir D. Ochterlony, Ist and 20th Oct., 1814. Resident at Delhi to Sir D. Ochterlony, 11th Oct., 1814, and Sir David's letter to Ranjit Singh, dated 29th Nov., 1814.

    During the war of 1814 Sir David Ochterlony sometimes almost despaired of success; and, amid his vexations, he once at least recorded his opinion that the Sepoys of the Indian army were unequal to such mountain warfare as was being waged. (Sir D. Ochterlony the Government, 22nd Dec., 1814). The most active and useful ally of the English during the war was Raja Ram Saran of Hindur (or Nalagarh), the descendant of the Hari Chand slain by Guru Gobind and who was himself the ready coadjutor of Sansar Chand in many aggressions upon others, as well as in resistance to the Gurkhas. The venerable chief was till alive in 1846, and he continued to talk with admiration of Sir David Ochterlony and his 'eighteen pounders', and to expatiate upon the aid he himself rendered in dragging them up the steeps of the Himalayas.

81. Sir D. Ochterlony to Government 10th and 30th Dec., 1809.

82. Sir D. Ochterlony to Government, 7th, 10th, 17th, and 30th Dec., 1809, and 30th Jan., 1810.

83. Shah Shuja's 'Autobiography's chap. xxii, published in the *Calcutia Monthly Journal* for 1839. The original was undoubtedly revised, if not really written, by the Shah.

84. [Known to all the world as 'Kim's' gun, it now reposes in its jast resting-place outside the Central Museum in Lahore.—Ed.]

85. Sir D. Ochterlony to Government, 29th March and 23rd May, 1810. In the latter it is stated that 250,000 rupees were paid, and the sum of 180,000 is given on Capt. Murray's authority. (*Life of Ranjit Singh*, p. 81).

86. Sir D. Ochterlony to Government, 23rd July and 13th Aug. 1810.

87. Sir D. Ochterlony to Government, 29th March and 17th Sept., 1810, and Government to Sir D. Ochterlony, 25th Sept., 1840. (Cf. Murray, *Ranjit Singh*, pp. 80-81.).

88. Sir, D. Ochterlony to Government, 10th Jan. and 26th Feb., 1810, and 27th April, 1812. Shah Shuja's 'Autobiography' chaps. xxiii-xxv, in the *Calcutta Monthly Journal* for 1839, and Murray, *Ranjit Singh*, pp. 79, 87, 92.

    Shah Shuja's second appearance before Multan in 1810-11 is given mainly on Capt. Murray's authority, and the attempt is not mentioned in the Shah's memoirs although it is admitted that he went into the Derajat of the Indus, *i.e.* to Dera Ismail Khan &c.

89. Murray, *Ranjit Singh*, p. 83, &c. The principal of the chiefs whose territories were usurped was Budh Singh, of the Singhpuria or Feizulapuria Misal. See also Sir D. Ochterlony to Government, 15th Oct., 1811.

90. Murray, *Ranjit Singh*, p. 87. The visit of the prince was considered very embarrassing with reference to Ranjit Singh: for Shah Shuja might follow, and he was one who claimed British aid under the treaty of 1809. It was regretted that the 'obligations of political necessity should supersede the dictates of compassion', it was argued that the treaty referred to defence against the French, and not against a brother; and the loyal-hearted Sir David Ochterlony was hidden for the reception he gave to the distressed Shahzada. (Government to Sir D. Ochterlony; 19th Jan., 1811, and the correspondence generally of Dec. 1810 and Jan. 1811).

91. Murray, *Ranjit Singh*, pp. 92, 95; Sir D. Ochterlony to Government, 4th March, 1813; and Shah Shuja's 'Autobiography' chap. xxv.

92. Murray, *Ranjit Singh*, pp. 95, 100; Sir D. Ochterlony to Government, 1st July, 1813.

93. Murray, *Ranjit Singh*, p. 96, &c.: Shah Shuja's 'Autobiography', chap. xxv; Sir D. Ochterlony to Government, 16th and 23rd April, 1813, and to the Resident at Delhi, 15th Oct., 1813. The Shah's own account of the methods practised to get possession of the diamond is more favourable than Capt. Murray's to Ranjit Singh. The Shah wanted a jagir of 100,000 rupees, and one of 50,000 was assigned to him; but effect to the assignment was never given, nor perhaps expected.

94. Murray, *Ranjit Singh*, pp. 102, 103; Shah Shuja's 'Autobiography', chaps. xxv-xxvi.

95. Government to Sir D. Ochterlony, 2nd and 20th Aug., 1815, and 14th, 21st, and 28th Sept., 1816. The Wafa Begam had before been told that the Shah's family had no claims to British protection or intervention. (Government to Resident at Delhi, 19th Dec., 1812, and 1st July, 1813).

96. Government to Sir D. Ochterlony, 29th Oct. and 23rd Nov., 1813.

97. Murray, *Ranjit Singh*, pp. 104, 108, and Sir D. Ochterlony to Government, 13th Aug., 1814. Diwan Mohkam Chand died soon after Ranjit Singh's return.

98. Cf. Murray, *Ranjit Singh*. pp. 108, 111.

99. The place fell on the 2nd June, 1818. See Murray, *Ranjit Singh*, p. 114, &c. The Maharaja told Mr. Moorcroft that he got very little of the booty he attempted to recover. (Moorcroft, *Travels, i.* 102.) Muhammad Muzaffar Khan, the governor, had held Multan from the time of the expulsion of the Sikhs of the Bhangi 'Misal', in 1779. In 1807 he went on a pilgrimage to Mecca, and although he returned in two years, he left the nominal control of affairs with his son. Sarafraz Khan. On the last approach of Ranjit Singh, the old man refused, according to the Bahawalpur annals, to send his family to the south of the Sutlej, as on other occasions of siege; but whether he did so in the confidence, or in the despair, of a successful resistance is not clear.

100. *Cf.* Murray, *Ranjit Singh*, pp. 117, 120; Shah Shuja's 'Autobiography', chap. xxvii; and Munshi Mohan Lal, *Life of Dost Muhammad, i.* 99, 104.

Capt. Murray (p. 131) places the defection of Jai Singh of Atari in the year 1822; but cf. also Mr. Masson, *Travels, iii*, 21, 32, in support of the earlier date assigned.

101. Cf. Murray, *Ranjit Singh*, pp. 121-122, and Moorcroft, *Travels*, 110, for the duration of the Maharaja's displeasure with Desa Singh.

102. Cf. Murray, *Ranjit Singh*, pp. 122-4.

103. Government to Superintendent Ambala. 15th Jan., 1815. and Sir D. Ochterlony to Government, 23rd July, 1815. Cf. Murray, *Ranjit Singh*, p. 124. The Bahawalpur Memoirs state that Ranjit Singh came down the Sutlej as far as Pakpattan, with the view of seizing Bahawalpur, but that show of resistance having been made, and some presents offered, the Maharaja moved westward.

104. Cf. Murray, *Ranjit Singh*, pp. 129-130. and Sir A. Burnes' *Kabul*. p. 92.

105. Cf. Murray, *Ranjit Singh*, pp. 134-7.

106. Cf. Murray, *Ranjit Singh*, p. 134, where the proceedings are given very briefly, and scarcely with accuracy. Capt. Murray's and Capt. Ross's letters to the Resident at Delhi, from Feb. to Sept. 1822, give details, and other information is obtainable from the letters of Sir D. Ochterlony to Capt. Ross, dated 7th Nov., 1821, and of the Governor-General's Agent at Delhi to Capt. Murray, of 22nd June, and to Government of the 23rd Aug. 1822; and from those of Government to the Government-General's Agent, 24th April, 13th July, and 18th Oct., 1822. On this occasion the Akali Phula Singh is reported by and Ranjit Singh to have commissioned him to embody a thousand of his brethren. Sir Claude Wade (*Narrative of Personal Services*, p. 10 note) represents Sir Charles Metcalfe to have considered the proceedings of the English with regard to Whadni as unwarranted—for with the domestic concerns of the Maharaja they had no political concern.

107. Cf. Murray, *Ranjit Singh*, p. 137, &c.; Moorcroft, *Travels, ii*. 333, 334; and Masson, *Journeys, iii*. 58-60. Ranjit Singh told Capt. Wade that, of his disciplined troops, his Gurkhas alone stood firm under the assault of the Muhammadans. (Capt. Wade to Resident at Delhi, 3rd April, 1839.)

The fanatic, Phula already referred to in the preceding note, was a man of some notoriety. In 1809 he attacked Sir Charles Metcalfe's camp, and afterwards the party of a British officer employed in surveying the Cis-Sutlej states. In 1814-15 he fortified himself in Abohar (between Ferozepur and Bhatnair), since construed into British possession (Capt. Murray to Agent, Delhi, 15th May, 1823); and in 1820 he told Mr. Moorcroft that he was dissatisfied with Ranjit Singh, that he was ready to join the English and that, indeed, he would carry fire and sword wherever Mr. Moorcroft might desire. (*Travels, i*. 110.)

With regard to Dost Muhammad Khan it is well-known, and Mr. Masson (*Journeys, iii.* 59-60) and Munshi Mohan Lal (*Life of Dost Muhammad, i.* 127-128) both show the extent to which he was an intriguer on this occasion. This circumstance was subsequently lost sight of by the British negotiators and the British public, and Sikh and Afghan leaders were regarded as essentially antagonistic, instead of as ready to coalesce for their selfish ends under any of several probable contingencies.

108. Capt. Murray to the Governor-General's Agent, Delhi, 15th Dec. 1825, and Capt. Wade to the same, 7th Aug. 1823.

109. Murray, *Ranjit Singh,* 141. For an interesting account of Sansar Chand, his family, and his country, see Moorcroft, *Travels, i.* 126-46.

110. Cf. Shah Shuja's 'Autobiography', chaps. xxvii, xxviii, xxix, in the *Calcutta Monthly Journal* for 1839, and the *Bahawalpur Family Annals* (Manuscript). Capt. Murray (*History of Ranjit Singh*, p. 103) merely states that Shah Shuja made an unsuccessful attempt to recover his throne; but the following letters may be referred to in support of all that is included in the paragraph: Government to Resident, Delhi, 10th May and 7th June 1817; Capt. Murray to Resident, Delhi, 22nd Sept. and 10th Oct. 1818, and 1st April 1825; and Capt. Murray to Sir D. Ochterlony, 29th April, 30th June, and 27th Aug. 1821.

111. Cf. Murray, *Ranjit Singh*. p. 126; Moorcroft, *Travels*. i. 109; and the quasi-official authority, the *Bengal and Agra Gazetteer* for 1841-1842 (articles 'Nagpur' and 'Jodhpur'). See also Capt. Murray, letters to Resident at Delhi, 24th Nov. and 22nd Dec. 1821, the 13th Jan. 1822, and 16th June 1824; and likewise Capt. Wade to Resident at Delhi, 15th March 1828.

112. The public correspondence generally of 1816-17 has here been referred to and especially the letter of Government to Resident at Delhi, dated 11th April 1817. In 1826 Bir Singh made another attempt to recover his principality; but he was seized and imprisoned. (Murray, *Ranjit Singh*, p. 145, and Capt. Murray to Resident at Delhi, 25th Feb. 1827). He was subsequently released and was alive, but unheeded, in 1844.

113. Moorcroft, *Travels*, i. 99, 103; and see also pp. 383, 387, with respect to a previous letter to Ranjit Singh.

114. Ranjit Singh, in writing or in talking of his government, always used the term 'Khalsa'. On his seal he wrote, as any Sikh usually writes, his name, with the prefix 'Akal Sahai', that is, for instance, 'God the helper, Ranjit Singh'—an inscription strongly

resembling the 'God with us' of the Commonwealth of England. Professor Wilson (*Journal Royal Asiatic Society*. No. xvii, p. 51) thus seems scarcely justified in saying that Ranjit Singh deposed Nanak and Gobind, and the supreme ruler of the universe, and held himself to be the impersonation of the Khalsa!

With respect to the abstract excellence or moderation, or the practical efficiency or suitableness of the Sikh government, opinions will always differ, as they will about all other governments. It is not simply an unmeaning truism to say that the Sikh government suited the Sikhs well, for such a degree of fitness is one of the ends of all governments of ruling classes, and the adaptation has thus a degree of positive merit. In judging of *individuals*, moreover, the extent and the peculiarities of the civilization of their times should be remembered, and the present condition of the Punjab shows a combination of the characteristics of rising mediaeval Europe and of the decaying Byzantine empire—semi-barbarous in either light, but possesed at once of a native youthful vigour, and of an extraneous knowledge of many of the arts which adorn life in the most advanced stages of society.

The fact, again, that a city like Amritsar is the creation of the Sikhs at once refutes many charges of oppression or misgovernment, and Col. Francklin only repeats the general opinion of the time when he says (*Life of Shah Alam*, p. 77) that the lands under Sikh rule were cultivated with great assiduity. Mr. Masson could hear of no complaints in Multan (*Journeys*, i. 30, 398), and although Moorcroft notices the depressed condition of the Kashmiris (*Travels*, i. 123) he does.

115. Murray, *Ranjit Singh*, p. 131, &c.

116. [The reference is to Nana Farnavis, who became Prime Minister of the Peshwa in 1775 and who died in 1800, having exercised an extraordinary influence over Maratha politics during his years of ascendancy. 'He had consistently been opposed to the political progress of the English as subversive of Maratha power, and he objected to the employment of foreign troops under any conditions; but he was faithful to his political engagements, and his devotion to the maintenance of the honour of his own nation is attested by the respect of all his contemporaries. The faithless materials with which he had to deal at the close of his life threw him into intrigues and combinations for his own preservation which would otherwise have been avoided and left him at liberty to continue the able administration he had conducted for twenty-

five years' (Meadows Taylor). On the occasion of his death the English Resident at Poona wrote: 'With him has departed all the wisdom and moderation of the Maratha Government.' See Grant Duff, *History of the Marathas*, ed. 1826, p. 188.—Ed.]

117. Forster, *Travels*, i. 332.

118. Malcolm, *Sketch of the Sikhs*, pp. 150-151.

119. Sir D. Ochterlony to Government, 1st Dec. 1810.

120. This feeling is well-known to all who have had any experience of Indian troops. A gunner is a prouder man than a musketeer: when battalions are mutinous, they will not allow strangers to approach their guns, and the best-dispositioned regiments will scarcely leave them in the rear to go into action unencumbered, an instance of which happened in Perron's warfare with George Thomas. (Major Smith, *Regular Corps in Indian Employ*, p. 24).

The ranks of the British Army are indeed filled with Rajputs and Pathans so called, and also with Brahmans; but nearly all are from the provinces of the Upper Ganges, the inhabitants of which have become greatly modified in character by complete conquest and mixture with strangers; and, while they retain some of the distinguishing marks of their races, they are, as soldiers, the merest mercenaries, and do not possess the ardent and restless feeling or that spirit of clanship, which characterize the more genuine descendants of Kshattriyas and Afghans. The remarks in the text thus refer especially to the Pathans of Rohilkhand and Hariana and similar scattered colonies, and to the yeomanry and little proprietors of Rajputana. [Much of this is of course incorrect and refers to the pre-Mutiny conditions of the Army. With the exception of a few mountain batteries the artillery is now entirely in the hands of British troops. The Brahman element in the Army has also been greatly reduced. At the present time 63 per cent of the efficient fighting forces of the Indian Army came from the Punjab.—Ed].

121. Moorcroft, *Travels*, i. 102. [The fact of this visit having been made is also borne out by a passage in the Diary of L. Sohan Lal. The latter was Court Vakil to Ranjit Singh.—Ed].

122. Murray. *Ranjit Singh*, p. 68.

123. Sir D. Ochterlony to Government, 27th Feb. 1812.

124. Sir D. Ochterlony to Government, 4th March 1813.

125. Moorcroft, *Travels*, i. 98. There were at that time, as there are still, Gurkhas in the service of Lahore.

126. The author owes this anecdote to Munshi Shahamat Ali, otherwise favourably known to the public by his book on the Sikhs and Afghans.

127. Moorcroft, *Travels*, i. 98. Ranjit Singh usually required his feudatories to provide for constant service, a horseman for every 500 rupees which they held in land, besides being ready with other fighting men on an emergency. This proportion left the Jagirdar one-half only of his estate untaxed, as an efficient horseman cost about 250 rupees annually. The Turks (Ranke, *Ottoman Empire*, ed. 1843, Introd., p. 5) required a horseman for the first 3,000 *aspers*, or 50 dollars, or say 125 rupees, and an additional one for every other 5,000 aspers, or 208 rupees. In England, in the seventeenth century, a horseman was assessed on every five hundred pounds of income. (Macaulay, *History of England*, i. 29)

128. For notices of this endurance of fatigue, see Forster, *Travels*, i. 332-333; Malcolm, Sketch, p. 141; Mr. Masson, *Journeys*, i. 433; and Col. Steinbach, *Punjab*, pp. 63-64.

The general constitution of a Sikh regiment was a commandant and adjutant, with subordinate officers to each company. The men were paid by deputies of the 'Bakshi', or paymaster; but the rolls were checked by 'Mutasaddis', or clerks, who daily noted down whether the men were absent or present. To each regiment at least one 'Granthi', or reader of the scriptures, was attached, who, when not paid by the government, was sure of being supported by the men. The Granth was usually deposited near the 'jhanda', or flag, which belonged to the regiment, and which represented its headquarters. Light tends and beasts of burden were allowed in fixed proportions to each battalion, and the state also provided two cooks, or rather bakers, for each company who baked the men's cakes after they had themselves kneaded them, or who, in some instances, provided unleavened loaves for those of their own or an inferior race. In cantonments the Sikh soldiers lived to some extent in barracks, and not each man in a separate hut, a custom which should be introduced into the British service. [The barrack system has been introduced. The whole organization of the Sikh army under Ranjit Singh is of much interest. Quite recently some research has been initiated and is still in progress upon the Sikh records in the Secretariat at Lahore. The result of this, as far as it concerns the army, will be found in the Appendix, section XXXIX.—Ed].

129. Col. Steinbach (*Punjab*, pp. 76-77) admits general simplicity of diet, but he also makes some revolting practices universal. Capt.

Murray (*Ranjit Singh*, p. 85) and Mr. Masson (*Journeys*, i. 435) are likewise somewhat sweeping in their condemnations, and even Mr. Elphinstone (*History of India*, ii. 565) makes the charge of culpable devotion to sensual pleasures very comprehensive. The morals, or the manners, of a people however, should not be deduced from a few examples of profligacy: but the Indians equally exaggerate with regard to Europeans, and in pictorial or pantomimes pieces, they usually represent Englishmen drinking and swearing in the society of courtesans, and as equally prompt to use their weapons with or without a reason.

130. Forster (*Travels*, i. 333) notices the temperance of the Sikhs, and their forbearance from many enervating sensual pleasures, and he quotes, he thinks, Col. Polier to a similar effect, Malcolm (*Sketch*, p. 141) likewise describes the Sikhs as hardy and simple; but, doubtless as the power of the nation has increased since these times luxuries and vicious pleasures have, in numerous instances, followed wealth and indolence.

131. Cf. Murray, *Ranjit Singh*, pp. 46-51, 63, 127-128, 134-135. See also Sir D. Ochterlony to Government 1st and 10th Dec. 1810, and p. 144 of this volume.

132. Cf. Murray, *Ranjit Singh*, pp. 48, 53, 90-91, 112, 129.

133. Cf. Murray, *Ranjit Singh*, p. 85.

2

The Sukarchakia Misal

Budha Singh

Budha Singh,[1] an affluent Jat farmer of the village of Sukarchak in the Majha tract of the Punjab, was the first historically known ancestor of Maharaja Ranjit Singh. His original name was Desu.[2] He was born in 1670.[3] He possessed 25 acres of land and three ploughts and a well. On this land he had built a couple of houses for his family and cattle. The place was named Sukarchak. *Sukar* means small and narrow and *chak* signifies a petty tract of land. It also assumed the meaning of a village. On account of this Desu began to be called Sukarchakia.[4] According to a tradition, it is also said that Sukarchak was so named as it was founded on Friday (Shukarwar).[5] Sukarchak was situated near Gujranwalas, 70 kms. north of Lahore.

It is said that in his early days Desu sometimes indulged in cattle-lifting. Once Desu carried off some good cattle from the village Narkhona. After a few days he met an old woman in the jungle. She enquired of Desu's whereabouts. She told him that Desu had taken away her buffaloes and a pair of oxen and she was going to get them back. He told her that Desu was a man of fierce nature and he would maltreat her. She said that when he knew her miserable condition he would take pity on her. She could not find Desu in the village but on return to her place she was surprised to find all her cattle tied up there safe and sound.[6] One of his ancestors was initiated into Sikhism by Guru Gobind Singh in 1692.[7] Budha Singh was a daring adventurer and is said to have taken part in the battles of Guru Gobind Singh and Banda Singh Bahadur. The success, which attended his exploits, won him the reputation of being one of the boldest and the most resolute of the Sikhs of the Punjab. He built a fortress-like mansion at his village. He was always held in high esteem by the Sikhs.[8]

He used to rise a piebald mare called after him as Desi which had crossed with its rider the rivers of Jhelum, Ravi and Chenab fifty times. It is said that sometimes Budha Singh covered on his mare's back a distance of over one hundred miles a day. The brave and courageous Budha Singh, who was a giant in strength, is said to have received during his life time some forty sword cuts and nine matchlock wounds, without his physical strength failing him.[9] In the words of Carmichael Smyth, Budha Singh "was distinguished for the most intrepid courage; for his sagacity and shrewdness which bore him successfully through all his schemes, and for his ready wit and good humour. He was also famed for his regard to the rights and property of the poor.[10] He was very kind and sympathetic to the *faqirs,* the poor and the travellers. He died of apoplexy in 1716.[11]

Sardar Naudh Singh

On his death, Budha Singh left behind two sons, named Naudh Singh and Chanda Singh, the latter being the ancestor of the Sandhanwalia Sardars of Raja Sansi. Naudh Singh grew up into a healthy and beautiful youngman. During the time of drought he used to bring his cattle to graze to the Majitha village in the present Amritsar district. Gulab Singh, a baptised Sikh of Majitha, married his daughter Lali to Naudh Singh in 1730, on the condition that he should get himself duly baptised.[12] Gulab Singh was a devoted follower of the *Khalsa Panth*. Under the inspiration of his father-in-law, Naudh Singh joined the *Dal Khalsa* under the command of Kapur Singh Faizullapuria.[13] He left his home and moved about in the inhospitable jungles along with his companions.[14] He came into prominence when, in the accompaniment of Kapur Singh, he relieved Ahmad Shah Durani of his baggage and heavy booty in 1749.

Sultan Khan Chatha, Pathan of Rasulnagar, forcibly converted six Sikhs to Islam. Naudh Singh and Chanda Singh attacked Rasulnagar, plundered Sultan Khan's property and brought back the Sikhs and baptised them again. Shahab-ud-Din of Firozwala captured a few Sikhs of village Karyala and removed the hair of their heads and beards. Naudh Singh and Chanda Singh plundered his village and put Shahab-ud-Din to death.

In 1749, Naudh Singh was wounded by a gun-shot in the head while fighting against the Afghan invaders. The wound did not prove fatal but he was incapaciated and he lingered on for a few years without participating in the Sikh movement in the Punjab and died in 1792.[15]

Sardar Charhat Singh (1732-1770)

Naudh Singh had four sons: Charhat Singh, Dal Singh, Cher Singh and Maghi Singh. At the time of his father's death in 1752, Charhat Singh was 20 years of age. At that time Jassa Singh Ahluwalia and Hari Singh and Jhanda Singh Bhangis were well on their way to carve out their Misals. They had their *dals* at their command and had established *rakhi* in certain areas. The *rakhi* system sowed the seeds of the Sikh political authority in the land. In the early stages, the *rakhi* or protection was sought by the people from the Sikhs and later, in order to bring more territories under the *rakhi* system, the offer of *rakhi* was made to the people of the towns and villages of the Punjab, and was actively pursued by the Sikhs as a regular feature of their activities. The world *rakhi* literally means 'protection' and in practice, it was a tribute received by the Sikhs to provide or guarantee protection against external aggression to the people paying it. The circumstances which led to the creation of this system were correlated with the rise of the Sikh power.[16]

Charhat Singh, to start with, was in the Bhangi *dal* but soon thereafter he began to nurse, in his heart, political ambition (*bu-i-riyast*) and came out of the Bhangi contingent and declared himself as holding an independent status.[17] In a short time he collected about 100 followers, and the number of his men began to grow rapidly, and soon he had, at his command, 400 horse and foot.[18] He placed the tracts of Rohtas, Dhani and salt mines under his *rakhi* (protection) and received the due revenue of protection money from them.[19] Though young in years he started his career as a very active, ambitious and pushing youngman with a good fund of intelligence and capacity to take decisions immediately. He was resourceful and very influential among the Sikhs.

His father-in-law, Amir Singh, and brother-in-law, Gurbakhsh Singh, helped him in the execution and fulfilment of his political designs. Amir Singh, though in the grip of old age, exercised tremendous influence on the people of his native place, Gujranwala. He had been a very brave and a fearless soldier. His guidance facilitated Charhat Singh's rise considerably.[20]

Charhat Singh's essential condition, for recruitment to his contingents, was that the incumbent must be a duly deprised 'Singh.' Those who were not already initiated into Sikhism with the baptism of the double-edged sword receive the *amrit* from his hands before joining his ranks.[21] He made his headquarters at Gujranwala. He placed, the *taaluqas* of Gujranwala, *qila* Didar Singh, *qila* Mian Singh and *qila* Sahib Singh and a number of villages around Akalgarh, under his control. He named his Misal after the name of his native village Sukarchak.

The Muslim governor of Eminabad harassed the Hindu and Sikh population. Charhat Singh, at the head of his young companions, besieged Eminabad. A lot of cash, arms, including rifles and war munition and hundreds of horses, fell into his hands.[22] Flushed with victory, he planned more ambitious enterprises.

For Charhat Singh's action against Eminabad, Khwaja Ubaid Khan, the Governor of Lahore, decided to teach a lesson to the former. Charhat Singh took asylum in his fortress newly constructed at Gujranwala in 1758. It was besieged by the forces of the Lahore Governor in September 1761. Jassa Singh Ahluwalia, Bhangi chiefs Hari Singh, Jhanda Singh, Lehna Singh and Gujjar Singh, Jai Singh and Sobha Singh Kanaihyas came for the relief of Charhat Singh and encamped about 6 kms away from Gujranwala. Charhat Singh's men resorted to night-attacks on the besiegers. Ubaid was compelled to lift the siege and retire to Lahore. Charhat Singh, accompanied by his daring young followers, made an assault on the returning forces of Ubaid. They plundered much of the war material, camels and horses from the fleeing forces of Lahore,[23] and many soldiers of Lahore were murdered or wounded. In 1762, during the *Wada Ghallughara* Charhat Singh played a dominant role in opposing the enemy and raising the morale and spirits of the Sikhs.

Conquests

Charhat Singh strengthened his fortress at Gujranwala. His possession began to assume the shape of a strong Misal, not so easy to reckon with. Right from his early days, he had been imbued with plans of creating a state for himself. He drove away the Muslim ruler of Wazirabad and placed it under his control, appointing his brother-in-law, Bakhshish Singh, as its *thanedar* or administrator.[24] Crossing river Jhelum, Charhat Singh extended his sway over Pind Dadan Khan and its surrounding areas, including Ahmedabad, Khushab, Soen, etc., which were formerly held by Chanda Singh and Ganda Singh.[25] He also constructed a fortress at Pind Dadan Khan.[26] He captured the salt mines of Kheora[27] as well from the Bhangis, that proved a good source of income to him. He also conquered the areas of Dhani and Pothohar. The *zamindars* of Chakwal, Jalalpur and Sayidpur also accepted his overlordship.[28] He conquered Rohtas about which Qazi Nur Muhammad wrote in 1765, "Chartu holds Rohtas in his *jagir* and this has grown into a city by his efforts".[29] He attained victory, in August 1761, over Nur-ud-Din Bamzai, a military commander of Ahmad Shah Durrani, on the left bank of the Chenab at Sialkot.[30] After holding out for eight days, against Charhat Singh, Nur-ud-Din escaped to Jammu in the disguise of a beggar. His troops, that surrendered, were allowed to go in safety. This victory made Charat Singh a front-rank leader among the Sikh Sardars. He also seized some war material including guns and other arms.

There are many incidents on record to show Charhat Singh's uttar fearlessness and dauntless courage. After the *faujdar* of Sirhind was killed by the Sikh Sardars in 1764, Ahmad Shah Abdali appointed one of his brave generals. Jahan Khan, to head an expedition against the Sikhs. When the Afghan general reached Sialkot, Charhat Singh, accompanied by Jhanda Singh and Gujjar Singh Bhangis, inflicted a crushing defeat on him.[31]

In December 1764, when Ahmad Shah invaded India for the seventh time he was joined by Naseer Khan Baluch, chief of Kalat, with 12,000 Baluchi troops. Qazi Nur Muhammad, who had accompanied his protege Naseer Khan, writes that in a battle at Lahore, Naseer Khan was opposed by Charhat Singh Sukarchakia. Naseer Khan's horse was killed by a bullet and he escaped to his camp. On his return journey also he was harassed by Charhat Singh.[32]

Jhelum town stood on the right bank of river Jhelum. In May 1767, Charhat Singh and Gujjar Singh marched upon it. Its Gakhar chief fled away to the fort of Rohtas for shelter. Charhat Singh entrusted Jhelum town to Dada Ram Singh.

A little later, Sarbuland Khan, paternal uncle of Ahmad Shah Durrani, after having been relieved of his charge as Governor of Kashmir, left for Kabul, accompanied by 10 or 12 thousand troopers. When he was encamped near Attock, Charhat Singh and Gujjar Singh Bhangi marched towards Rohtas to attack this Afghan *faujdar* in the early summer of 1764. The two Sardars crossed the Chenab into the Chaj Doab, overpowered the Afghan resistance and pushed forward beyond the Jhelum. Sarbuland Khan came out to confront the Sikhs, but was forced back to seek shelter in his fort. The Sikhs laid siege to Rohtas, but there was no reduction of the fort for four months. The Sikhs under Charhat Singh pretended to raise the siege and move away. Sarbuland Khan pursued the Sikhs and fell into their trap. Charhat Singh suddenly turned back and took the fort unawares. Sarbuland Khan was made a captive but was treated with respect due to his position both as a highly placed Afghan official and as an uncle of Ahmad Shah Durrani. Pleased with the kindness received at the hands of Charhat Singh, Sarbuland Khan offered to serve under him as a governor, if he (Charhat Singh) proclaimed, himself king. Charhat Singh said. "The kingship is already bestowed on us by the Guru, we want to keep you as a prisoner so that the world may know that Charhat Singh had captured the uncle of the Shah." "But there is a still greater name in releasing me," said Sarbuland Khan. "They will say," he continued, "that Charhat Singh captured the uncle of Ahmad Shah and, then, set him at liberty." The Khan then paid two lakh rupees to the Sardar, who allowed him to return to his country.[33]

Consequent upon the victory of the Sikhs, the entire territory between the Jhelum and Indus came into the hands of Charhat Singh and his Bhangi allies.

In a short period of fifteen years, Charhat Singh became the master of Gujranwala, Wazirabad, Ramnagar, Sialkot, Rohtas, Pind Dadan Khan and the areas of Dhani and Pothohar which gave him a good amount of revenue. Charhat Singh had on his administrative staff a number of efficient *kardars* which included Dal Singh Gill, Bhag Singh Virk, Budh Singh, Gaur Singh, Dharam Singh Batasa, Tahal Singh Chhachhi, Nirmal Singh, Himat Singh, Dada Ram Singh and Sahaj Singh.[34]

The Awans, the Janjuas, the Ghebas, the Alpials, the Bhandials, the Jodras and the Sagri Pathans of Makhad also accepted the overlordship of Sardar Charhat Singh.

Ever since Charhat Singh took possession of Pind Dadan Khan and the salt mines of Kheora Bhangis became his deadly enemies. The biggest salt mine was at Kheora, 8 kms from Pind, Dadan Khan, in Jhelum district. The others were at Nurpur in Jhelum district, at Warcha in Shahpur district and at Kalabagh in Mianwali district. The mineral exists in vertical layers. The hills are nearly 400 metres high from the valley of river Jhelum and about 8 kms in breadth. The work in the mines could be conducted for nine or ten months in the year.[35]

Bhangis and Sukarchakias took hostile postures and there were occasional confrontations between the two. In 1827 Bk. corresponding to A.D. 1770, when Jhanda Singh Bhangi and Charhat Singh were facing each other for a clash, Charhat Singh was mortally wounded by the bursting of his own matchlock.[36] At the time of Charhat Singh's death his successor, Mahan Singh, was only ten years of age.[37] Mahan Singh's younger brother Sahaj Singh had died in his early boyhood. During his life time Charhat Singh had contracted some matrimonial alliances which strengthened his position. Dal Singh of Alipur, renamed Akalgarh, was married to the sister of Charhat Singh. Sahib Singh Bhangi was married to the daughter of Charhat Singh. Charhat Singh's son Mahan Singh was married to the daughter of Jai Singh Mann. Some more matrimonial alliances followed Charhat Singh's death.

Charhat Singh left behind a son, a daughter and his widow, Mai Desan. Mahan Singh being too young to handle the state affairs, his step-mother Desan took over the reigns of the administration of the Sukarchakia Misal. In the words of Gordon, "Sikh ladies played an important part in the history of the warlike times...and Mai Desan ruled with vigour and diplomacy."[38] Her brothers, Gurbakhsh Singh and Dal Singh, rendered her great service in this regard. Desan was a worldly-wise, experienced and an intelligent lady. In order to strengthen her position she married her daughter, Raj Kaur, to Sahib Singh, son of Gujjar Singh of Gujarat.[39] Shortly thereafter, she married her son Mahan Singh to the daughter of Gajpat Singh, ruler of Jind, in 1774.[40] These matrimonial relations united the three Misals for the purpose of combined action.

Sardar Mahan Singh (1760-1790)

Mahan Singh was born in 1760.[41] He inherited a state from his father, though small in size, but had all the attributes of an independent principality. Jai Singh Kanaihya, a close friend of Charhat Singh, became foster-father of the young Sukarchakia chief. As soon as he found himself strong enough to strike, Mahan Singh snatched the fort of Rohtas from the hands of Nur-ud-Din Bamzai and occupied Kotli Ahangaran, near Sialkot. The artisans of this place were very adept in manufacturing rifles.[42] Mahan Singh benefitted of this possession by arming his soldiers with new rifles. Then, he proceeded against Pir Muhammad, the ruler of the Chathas, on the eastern bank of river Chenab.[43] Assisted by Jai Singh Kannaihya, Mahan Singh marched at the head of 6,000 troops and besieged Rasulnagar in 1799. Pir Muhammad surrendered himself along with his family. His territory was occupied. Rasulnagar was renamed as Ramnagar.[44] Dal Singh was appointed as the administrator or the governor of the place. The victory added lustre to the Sukarchakia Misal, and many other chiefs who were the dependents of the Bhangis offered to transfer their allegiance to the Sukarchakias.[45]

In the words of Muhammad Latif, "Mahan Singh's fame spread throughout the length and breadth of the country, owing to his having captured Rasulnagar, and the reputation for valour obtained by him was so great that many Sardars who had hitherto been dependent on the Bhangi Misal, now acknowledged the Sukarchakia Sardar as their chief, and transferred their allegiance to him, and deemed it an honour to fight under his banners."[46] The Chathas did not accept the defeat lying down and soon got refractory against Mahan Singh. The army had again to be led against them. This time, Alipur and mancher were also occupied and Alipur was renamed Akalgarh.[47]

Chet Singh, the younger brother of Gujjar Singh Bhangi, had come to help the Chathas. Mahan Singh captured and imprisoned him in the fort of Gujranwala. Sahib Singh's wife, Raj Kaur, who was the sister of Mahan Singh, came from Gujarat to Gujranwala to secure Chet Singh's release. Mahan Singh paid no attention to her imploring and did not liberate the Bhangi Sardar.

On his return from Rasulnagar, Mahan Singh received the happy tidings of the birth of a son who was originally named Budh Singh,[48] but later named Ranjit Singh as he was born in the days of conquest. The birth took place on November 13, 1780,[49] at Gujranwala.

Mahan Singh led his next expeditions against Pindi Bhatian, Sahiwal, Jhang, Isa Khel and Musa Khel. Desa Singh Bhangi failed to protect his territories. He asked his brother-in-law Sahib Singh's help. Sahib Singh could not help because of his own strained relations with his younger brother, Sukha Singh.

In 1783, Punjab passed through a very critical period. For the past three years not a drop of rain had fallen, and one of the severest famines had broken out in northern India. *Adam adam ra me khurd, wa madar bachchan ra firo me burd. Jahan talaf shud.* (Men ate men and the mothers sold their children. Everything was ruined). Mahan Singh distributed grains to every body who approached him.[50]

Ranjit Deo, the ruler of Jammu, died in 1782. His death was followed by a dispute of succession between his sons, Brij Raj and Dalet Singh. Brij Raj emerged victorious. But Brij Raj Deo proved to be a weak and an inefficient ruler. The Kanaihyas and Bhangis, taking advantage of this position, occupied some of the territories of Jammu. Brij Deo made an appeal to Mahan Singh for help. He marched at the head of his army to Jammu but the powerful combination of his enemies compelled Brij Raj Deo to pay tribute of 30,000 rupees to the victorious Haqiqat Singh Kanaihya[51] and thus the Sukarchakia chief could not be of any help to Brij Deo.

About six months later, Mahan Singh again got a chance to go to Jammu, this time not in support of Brij Raj Deo but against him. Brij Deo refused to pay the stipulated tribute to the Kanaihyas who invited Mahan Singh to join them in their invasion of Jammu. Brij Raj Deo, finding himself unequal to the situation, run away into the hills of Vaishno Devi. This took place towards the close of January 1784. Haqiqat Singh Kanaihya and Mahan Singh had made a pact to attack and plunder Jammu jointly, but the Sukarchakia chief did it alone. Mahan Singh came back with a heavy baggage of booty from Jammu.[52] It is said that Mahan Singh's booty was worth a crore of rupees.

In the year 1784, Mahan Singh came to Amritsar,[53] on the occasion of *Diwali*. Most of the chiefs of the Misals, including Jai Singh Kanaihya, had assembled there. Jai Singh was held in high esteem by all other Sardars of the Misals. Mahan Singh visited Jai Singh to pay his regards to him. During the meeting, Jai Singh, who was jealous of the growing power of the Sukarchakias, insulted Mahan Singh by his remarks, "Go away, you Bhagtia (dancing boy); I do not want to hear your sentimental talk." This was too much to be borne in silence by so haughty and impervious a young chief as Mahan Singh was."[54] Jai Singh also demanded a share from the booty which he had brought from Jammu,[55] Mahan Singh felt highly engaged at the rude treatment shown to him by the Kanaihya chief who ordered his men that Mahan Singh should not be allowed to go out of Amritsar. He should be made captive and produced before him. After a minor clash outside Amritsar both sides withdrew and went to their respective places, but Mahan Singh was not in a position to take revenge single-handed. He invited Jassa Singh Ramgarhia from Hansi and Hissar where he was living in a sort of exile as he had been driven out of his possessions by Jai Singh.[56] Sansar Chand Katoch, the ruler of Kangra, who was another enemy of the Kanaihyas, was also called by Mahan Singh to join him. The three chiefs, with their combined forces marched against the Kanaihyas. The battle was fought at Achal Batala, and Jai

Singh's son Gurbaksh Singh, who had advanced with a force of 8,000 to oppose Mahan Singh, was struck by a bullet at the very first charge and was killed.[57] In the course of fighting the Kanaihyas were routed, thus humbling the old Kanaihya chief. After the battle of Achal Batala, Jai Singh retired to Naushehra where another battle was fought against Mahan Singh. Both sides sustained heavy losses, but Jai Singh suffered a defeat. The Ramgarhia and Katoch chiefs got back their territories already captured by the Kanaihyas.[58]

Finding the Sukarchakia Misal in its ascendancy, Sada Kaur, widow of Gurbakhsh Singh Kanaihya, proposed in 1786, the betrothal of her only daughter, Mehtab Kaur, to Ranjit Singh, the young son of Mahan Singh.[59] After Ranjit Singh's recovery from an attack of small pox and high fever at Jammu during Mahan Singh's campaign to that place in 1786, the latter held a magnificence function at Gujranwala. Many Sardars came to offer congratulations. Jai Singh Kanaihya also attended the function. There he made a formal proposal of his grand-daughter's betrothal with Mahan Singh's son, which was accepted. With this matrimonial alliance peace was restored between the two contending Misals. This alliance proved very helpful to Ranjit Singh in his future conquests and consolidation of Punjab under his sway.[60]

As referred to above, Mahan Singh's sister was married to Sahib Singh of Gujarat. After the death of his father, Gujjar Singh in 1788, Sahib Singh became the ruler of Gujarat. Mahan Singh demanded *haq-i-hakmana,* succession money, or tribute from Sahib Singh who refused to give any. The hackneyed maxim that, "kingship knows no kinship" so aptly applied to the situation. To promote the interests of ones state even close blood relationship was disregarded. Sahib Singh was the husband of Mahan Singh's real sister. Hostilities commenced between the two. Sahib Singh took asylum in the fort of Sodhra which was besieged by Mahan Singh.[61] Mahan Singh's sister, Raj Kaur, waited upon her brother and tried to dissuade him from fighting. Mahan Singh did not care to heed to her entreaties. The Sukarchakia chief was having a failing health due to overwork and exhaustion and in the course of the siege of Sodhra when the victory was just in sight he was suddenly taken ill by a violent attack of fever. Handing over the charge of the siege to his ten-year old son Ranjit Singh, Mahan Singh retired to Gujranwala where he expired on the 5th Baisakh, 1847 Bk, corresponding to April 15, 1790,[62] as a result of severe dysentery.[63] Thus, the death removed the ambitious and courageous Sukarchakia chief from the stage of history in early youth at the age of thirty. According to Hari Ram Gupta, "There is not the least doubt about it that if he had lived ten years longer, he would have become the sole monarch of the whole of northern India from the Khyber Pass to the Ganga, and from the Himalayas to the Arabian Sea, and Emperor Shah Alam II would have become his protege."[64]

In the words of Muhammad Latif, "Mahan Singh was brave, enterprising and prudent beyond his years; and the age in which he lived highly favoured him ambitious schemes.....His early feats in arms had acquired for him so great a reputation that many influential independent Sardars joined his banner. His rapid successes gave him an ascendancy over all the Sikh chiefs. His military genius, undaunted courage, stern temper and rigid observance of the rules of delicacy and honour, at times, involved him in serious trouble, but he honourably acquitted himself on all such occasions. At an early age, he shook off the trammels of his mother's guardianship to pave the way for his own greatness."[65]

James Browne, in 1787, estimated the military strength of Mahan Singh at 15,000 horse and 5,000 food in the Rachna Doab and about 5,000 horse and foot in the Chaj and Sind Sagar Doabs.[66] Imam-ud-Din Husaini wrote in 1796 that Mahan Singh commanded about 22,000 horse and foot.[67] "He left to his son and successor a state beset with danger; but he bequeathed to him at the same time the qualities by which dangers are best overcome-courage combined with a natural genius for command and enterprise tempered by prudence and foresights."[68]

After his father's death Ranjit Singh succeeded to the chiefship of his Misal. Only at the age of nineteen he occupied Lahore and put his Misal on the road to glory of a consolidated kingdom of the Punjab. His rule gave to the history of Punjab a remarkable era of independence, pride, magnificence, security and stability.

Maharaja Ranjit Singh (1780-1839)

Ranjit Singh was born on November 13, 1780[69], at Gujranwala. Very little is known about his childhood except that he had a virulent attack of small pox which deprived him of his left eye.

Right from the beginning he had displayed a spirit of bravery and adventure. Even at the young age of six he, along with other boys, did swimming in river Chenab.[70] In his early boyhood he was sent to Bhagu Singh's *dharamsala* at Gujranwala to learn Gurmukhi but he did not assimilate anything at school.[71] Later, he received training in shooting from a Brahman, named Amir Singh, who was matchless in that art.[72] At the time of his father's death he was a young boy of ten years old.[73] It is said that the *pagri* or turban-tying ceremony, in respect of Ranjit Singh, had already been performed in the life time of Mahan Singh. Ranjit Singh was too young to handle the state affairs but the had no difficulty in accession to his father's *gaddi*.

As told earlier Ranjit Singh had been engaged to the daughter of an intelligent and a brave lady, Rani Sada Kaur, widow of Gurbakhsh Singh[74] of Kanaihya Misal. In his early years Ranjit Singh was fortunate in having the help of a shrewd and far sighted woman as Sada Kaur was. Sardar Dal Singh Gill and Gurbaksh Singh of Wazirabad were appointed to look after the army and the administrative affairs were conducted by Diwan Lakhpat Rai, popularly known as Lakhu.[75] Ranjit Singh's mother, Raj Kaur, also supervised the administrative business.'[76]

In 1795,[77] at the age of 15, Ranjit Singh got himself married to Mehtab Kaur, daughter of Sada Kaur.

He had his second marriage with Datar Kaur, sister of Sardar Gian Singh Nakkai, in 1798. She was popularly known as Mai Nakkain. Kharak Singh was born to her on February 22, 1801.

At the time of Ranjit Singh's accession to power, the Punjab was divided into a number of petty principalities and some of the leaders were not on happy terms with one another. The people of the province were generally devoid of a sense of unity. The Sikh confederacies had already been weakened. The Afghans under Zaman Shah were again threatening to establish their overlordship in the Punjab. The English had also started to take interest in this part of the country as their future sphere of influence. Besides, there were some Pathan possessions, adjoining hill states under the Hindu Rajas and several small and petty principalities that dotted the map of the Punjab. "In the 1790s, the Punjab looked like a jig-saw puzzle consisting of fourteen pieces with five arrows piercing it from the sides. Twelve of these fourteen pieces were the Sikh *Misals;* the other two, the Pathan-controlled district of Kasur in the neighbourhood of Lahore, and Hansi in the south-east under the English adventurer, George Thomas. The five arrows were: The Afghans in the north-west; the Rajputs of Kangra in the north; the Gorkhas in the north-east; the British in the east; and the Marathas in the south-east."[78]

The province was a congeries of small disintegrated states and there was no individual power in the province which could pose any formidable danger to the adventures of a strong man. As early as 1783. George Forster had predicted that "we may see some ambitious chief, led on by his enius and success, absorbing the power of his associates, display from the runs of their commonwealth the standard of monarchy."[79]

Anarchy and political upheaval always hold out an opportunity to men of genius. In the words of Lepel Griffin, "There is perhaps no more notable and picturesque figure among the chiefs who rose to power on the ruins of the Mughal Empire than Maharaja Ranjit Singh, the founder of the short-lived Sikh kingdom of Lahore. In the stormy days at the beginning of the century, amid a fierce conflict of races and creeds, he found his opportunity and, seizing it with energy, promptitude and genius welded the turbulent and warlike secretaries, who followed the teachings of Gobind Singh into a homogeneous nation."[80]

Young Ranjit Singh, who was aspiring for the consolidation of the Punjab, had to face an ambitious aggrandiser, Zaman Shah Durrani, who succeeded to the throne of Kabul in 1793, and had plans to seize the Punjab.

Zaman Shah marched to the Punjab in the winter of 1798, and reached Lahore on 27th November.

The Shah dispatched a contingent of Afghans to Amritsar. Ranjit Singh issued out of the town and gave a tough fight to the Afghans and forced them to retire to Lahore.[81] Every night Ranjit Singh visited, with a few *sawars,* the suburbs of the city of Lahore and attacked the forces of the Shah at night with a view to harassing him.[82]

According to Sohan Lal Suri,[83] Ranjit Singh, at this time, thrice rushed upon the Samman Burj of the Lahore fort with a few Sardars, fired a number of shots, killed and wounded a number of Afghans, and on an occasion challenged the Shah himself to a hand to hand fight, "Come out you, O, grandson of Ahmad Shah," shouted Ranjit Singh to him, "and try two or three hands with the grandson of the great Sardar Charhat Singh." But as there was no response from the other side, Ranjit Singh had to retire without a trial of strength with the Durrani.

During the four-week stay of the Shah at Lahore some of the Sardars met him there.

During his visit to the Shah, Ranjit Singh's representative probably negotiated for the *subedari* of Lahore.[84] But at this stage the reversed Sikh Baba Sahib Singh Bedi pleaded with the Sardars to stop negotiating with the Durrani invader. They agreed to abide by his decision and when the Shah's agents came to the Sikh Sardars again, Sahib Singh Bedi told them on behalf of the Sikhs. "We took the country by the sword and will preserve it by the same."[85] Then, the Shah gave up the plan to win over the Sikhs.

According to Ali-ud-Din Mufti, Zaman Shah left for Kabul after a month's stay at Lahore as Mahmud Shah, in collaboration with Baba Khan Qachar, had attacked Kabul. Diplomatically enough, Ranjit Singh did not harass Zaman Shah on his return march rather facilitated his return so that he might not get irritated against him and think of hitting back at him at the earliest opportunity. Since the Shah had to go back hurriedly 12 of his guns sank in river Jhelum that was in spate because of rainy season. It is said that Shah addressed a letter to Ranjit Singh that after the level of the river water went down he might extricate his guns and get them sent to Kabul. Ranjit Singh brought out all the 12 guns from the river. He despatched eight of them to Kabul and retained four with him in his arsenal one of which was of iron and three of brass.[86]

Ranjit Singh's Occupation of Lahore (1799)

Twenty six days after Zaman Shah's exit from Lahore, on 4th January 1799, the Bhangi Sardars re-entered Lahore. The three rulers of Lahore were not functioning in collaboration with one another.

According to Munshi Sohan Lal, the people of Lahore were suffering hardships under the misrule of their chiefs.[87] The respectable people of Lahore, including the Hindus,. Muslims and Sikhs, met secretly and decided to address an invitation to Ranjit Singh, to come to Lahore and arrange its occupation. Ranjit Singh accepted the invitation.[88] The letter of invitation sent to him was signed by Muhammad Ashaq,

Gurbakhsh Singh, Hakim Rai, Mufti Muhammad Mukarram, Muhammad Bakar, Mir Shadi and Mehar Mohkam Din. It was sent through Hakim Rai.[89]

Ranjit Singh started from Rasulnagar and reached Batala and discussed the matter of occupation of Lahore with Rani Sada Kaur.[90] She accompanied him to Lahore. They had at their command an army of about twenty five thousand horsemen and foot soldiers. The people of Lahore had earlier promised Ranjit Singh to open the Lohari Gate at his arrival there. On the day Ranjit Singh reached Lahore, the Lohari Gate could not be opened as it was strongly defended by Chet Singh.

Next morning, that is, on July 6, 1799,[91] Ranjit Singh led his men to Lohari Gate which was opened unto him. The eighteen year old conqueror entered the city triumphanity.

Mohar Singh was captured and produced before Ranjit Singh. Graciously enough, he allowed him to proceed to his *Jagirs,* along with his goods. Chet Singh evacuated the fort next morning, that is, on July 7, 1799 (29th of the month of Har, Samat 1856), and Ranjit Singh occupied the fort the same day.[92]

Confrontation of Bhasin (March 1800)

Ranjit Singh's power was growing day by day. With the occupation of Lahore—the traditional capital of the Punjab. Ranjit Singh's power received a fillip. Other Sardars got jealous of him.

So, they joined hands to restrain Ranjit Singh from his policy of territorial aggrandisement. After the festival of *Holi* Sahib Singh of Gujarat, Gulab Singh Bhangi, Jassa Singh Ramgarhia and Nizam-ud-Din of Kasur assembled their forces at the village of Bhasin, about 9 *kos* on the east of Lahore.[93] Ranjit Singh came from Lahore. Both sides arrayed themselves in the battle-field and no action took place between the contending forces for two months.[94] Each side was apprehensive of the other and did not consider proper to initiate fighting. After the expiry of about eight weeks, Gulab Singh Bhangi, who had invited the other chiefs to fight on his side, drank himself to death.[95]

The death of their leader dispirited the confederate army which dispersed without achieving anything and their plans fizzled out.

Invasion of Jammu (1800)

After he was free from the expedition of Bhasin, Ranjit Singh attacked Jammu. The ruler of Jammu had an audience with Ranjit Singh and offered him a *nazarana* of 20 thousand rupees and an elephant.[96]

Possession of Akalgarh (1801)

Akalgarh had been conferred on Dal Singh by Sardar Mahan Singh. Since Dal Singh had become hostile to Ranjit Singh the former was brought to Lahore by the latter and intended there in 1800.[97] Dal Singh assured Ranjit Singh of his perfect innocence and he was released on the intercession of Sada Kaur and Baba Kesra Singh Sodhi.[98] Dal Singh died shortly after arriving back at Akalgarh. Ranjit Singh visited Akalgarh for condolence. He granted a *jagir* of two villages to Dal Singh's widow for her subsistence,[99] and placed Akalgarh under his control.

Assumed the Title of Sarkar (April 12, 1801)

A grand *durbar* was organised on *Baisakhi* day, Sunday, April 12, 1801, in which many Sardars and notables and prominent citizens were invited to participate. Ranjit Singh assumed the title of *sarkar* or *sarkar-i-wala,* and not that of 'Maharaja' as some writers believe.[100]

Siege of Kasur (1801)

It has already been referred to that the Pathan ruler of Kasur was keen contestant for Lahore but Ranjit Singh had stolen a march over him. Nawab Nizam-ud-Din had come to Bhasin along with the Sikh chiefs. He had also been inciting Sahib Singh of Gujarat against Ranjit Singh. The Maharaja wanted to punish the Nawab for his intrigues against him. According to Amar Nath, the Maharaja sent a big army against him under the command of Sardar Fateh Singh Kalianwala. The Nawab suffered a defeat at the hands of the Lahore army and obtained peace through submission. He became a tributary *subedar* of the Maharaja and paid a huge amount as war indemnity. He also sent his younger brothers, Qutab Din, and Haji Khan and Wasil Khan to Lahore as hostages.[101]

Attack on Kangra (1801)

Some of the territories of Rani Sada Kaur had been usurped by Sansar Chand Katoch of Kangra. In the words of Khushwaqat Rai, "Sansar Chand often uttered these remarks from his tongue: from the hair of the Sikhs I shall prepare the ropes for my horses, and spoke very ill of Guru Nanak and Guru Gobind Singh."[102] He was planning to further penetrate into Sada Kaur's territories. She informed Ranjit Singh of Sansar Chand's designs. Sansar Chand captured the fort of Garhdiwala and gave it to Jodh Singh Ramgarhia and Bhunga to Nawab Fatu Khan, brother of Ghulam Qadar.[103]

The Maharaja led an army of six thousand horsemen into Kangra. Sansar Chand ran away for his life. The territories of Sada Kaur occupied by Sansar Chand were restored to her. Nurpur was also taken from Sansar Chand.[104]

Exchange of Turban with Fateh Singh Ahluwalia (1802)

When the Maharaja went to Tarn Taran for a dip in the holy tank he expressed a desire to have a meeting with Fateh Singh Ahluwalia. Both the rulers met in the presence of the holy *Guru Granth Sahib* and exchanged turbans to profess brotherhood.[105]

Occupation of Chiniot (1802)

Territory of Chiniot was in the hands of Jassa Singh, son of Karam Singh Dullu. His subjects were sick of him.

The Maharaja led an army to Chiniot. Jassa Singh closed the gates of the fort. The siege continued for about two months. At last Jassa Singh evacuated the fort and Ranjit Singh placed it under his own control. The Maharaja gave Jassa Singh a suitable *jagir*.[106]

Occupation of Amritsar (1805)

It was, then, held by Mai Sukhan, widow of Gulab Singh Bhangi, who had died at Bhasin by excessive drinking in 1800. She had the support of the Ramgarhia Sardar.

On the advice of Jodh Singh, the Ramgarhia chief, and the Akali leader Phula Singh, the fort and the city of Amritsar were evacuated by Mai Sukhan on February 24, 1805.[107] The occupation of Amritsar, the religious capital of the Sikhs, brought additional lustre to Ranjit Singh's name.

Jaswant Rao Holkar's Visit (1805)

Jaswant Rao met Ranjit Singh and requested him for help against the British. Ranjit Singh made all arrangements for his comfortable stay at Amritsar. After consultations with some other Sardars, Ranjit Singh advised Jaswant Rao to sue for peace with the English. General Lake was also told that it was in the interest of both to conclude peace. Both agreed and the fighting between them was avoided.[108]

Malwa Campaigns (1806-08)

From 1806 to 1808, Ranjit Singh led three campaigns into the cis-Satluj areas. In 1806, there cropped up a sharp dispute between Patiala and Nabha over the possession of village Daladi, barely 2 kms from the town of Nabha. Ranjit Singh was invited to mediate in the dispute.[109] On his way to Patiala and back he placed a large number of villages and territories under his own control in the cis-Satluj areas.[110]

In 1807, the Maharaja was again invited to settle the dispute between Rani Aus Kaur and Sahib Singh, the ruler of Patiala.[111] During this visit also Ranjit Singh followed the same policy of territorial aggrandisement.

In 1808, again he entered the cis-Satluj areas with a view to subjugating the cis-Satluj region. During all the three incursions he conquered and distributed a large number of villages and territories among his followers including Fateh Singh Ahluwalia, Mai Sada Kaur and Diwan Mohkham Chand.

Ranjit Singh Helped the Ruler of Kangra (1807)

The Gurkhas of Nepal planned the conquest and occupation of the whole of Himachal Pradesh. After conquering Sirmur, Garhwal and Nalagarh the Gorkhas proceeded towards Kangra under the command of Amar Singh Thapa. Raja Sansar Chand of Kangra sent his brother Mian Fateh Chand to meet Maharaja Ranjit Singh and seek help against the Nepalese who were encamped near Kangra. Ranjit Singh expressed his readiness to help Sansar Chand.

Amar Singh Thapa, finding himself no match for the allies, that is Sansar Chand and Ranjit Singh, retired quickly from Kangra.[112]

Occupation of Kasur (1807)

After the death of Nawab Nizam-ud-Din in 1807, his brother, Qutb-ud-Din Khan, succeeded him. He did not like to remain under the overlordship of Ranjit Singh and got refractory. On the other hand, Ranjit Singh did not like an independent Afghan state to function so close to his capital. So he decided to occupy Kasur at the earliest. Lahore forces attacked Kasur on the 10th of February 1807, and the siege of the fort continued for a month and during this time a mine was laid under a wall of the fort which was battered. The captured Nawab was produced before Ranjit Singh who received him graciously and gave him the *jagir* of Mamdot that brought an annual income of one lakh rupees.[113]

Occupation of Jhang (1807)

Jhang was under Ahmad Khan Sial. In 1807, the Maharaja came to know that Ahmad Khan had concluded a secret treaty with Nawab Muzaffar Khan of Multan. This Maharaja sent a heavy force against Jhang and it was annexed to the Lahore kingdom in 1807. Ahmad Khan was provided with a *jagir* for a decent living.[114]

Submission of Bahawalpur and Akhnur (1807-08)

As a result of Maharaja's invasion of Bahawalpur in 1807, Nawab Bahawal Khan submitted to the Maharaja and promised to pay annual tribute regularly.[115] In 1808, Alam Singh, the ruler of Akhnur, accepted the overlordship of the Maharaja.[116]

Annexation of Dallewalia Misal (1807)

Dallewalia Misal was annexed by Ranjit Singh in 1807. It had been under Tara Singh Ghaiba who was supporter of Ranjit Singh. He had accompanied the Maharaja to Patiala a few days earlier. On learning about Tara Singh's death the Maharaja went to Rahon to condole Ghaiba's death to his widow. Ranjit Singh occupied the entire territory of Tara Singh and gave a *jagir* of a few villages to his widow.[117]

Occupation of the Fort of Kangra (1809)

For some time past Amar Singh Thapa had been busy fighting against Sansar Chand of Kangra.[118] According to Diwan Amar Nath, the Gurkha army, thrown against Sansar Chand, was about 50 thousand with two guns.[119] The Kangra chief sent his brother Fateh Chand as his emissary to Ranjit Singh for help against the Gurkhas. Ranjit Singh demanded a heavy price for the help in the form of possession of the fort of Kangra. Sansar Chand agreed to surrender the fort and it passed into the hands of Lahore forces on August 25, 1809.[120]

On September 24, 1809, Ranjit Singh valiantly entered the Kangra fort and held a grand Durbar there in which the rulers of Kangra, Chamba, Nurpur, Kotla, Shahpur, Jasrota, Basohli, Mankot, Jaswan, Guler, Mandi, Suket, Kulu and Datarpur participated. All the hill chiefs offered *nazaranas* to the Maharaja, and on their return they received robes of honour from him. Ranjit Singh appointed Desa Singh Majithia in charge of the fort of Kangra with Pahar Singh Mann, as its deputy *nazim*.[121]

Occupation of Gujarat (1810)

Gujarat was under the control of Sahib Singh Bhangi. He developed strained relations with his son. Gulab Singh,[122] who occupied a couple of forts against the wishes of his father. Ranjit Singh availed of this opportunity and in the course of two or three months he occupied the whole of Gujarat. Sahib Singh excapted to the hilly areas.[123]

Conquest of Khushab and Sahiwal (1810)

The territories of Khushab and Sahiwal were inhabited by the Baloch tribes and they had built, at many places, very strong forts. On the arrival of Lahore forces near Khushab its ruler Jafar Khan Baloch, finding himself no match for the Sikhs, fled from the town of Khushab.[124] After a severe fighting, the Maharaja conquered the fort of Sahiwal on February 10, 1810.[125]

Conquest of Jammu (1810)

Before the Maharaja started for Khushab he had despatched a contingent to Jammu under the command of Hukma Singh Chimni. After a brief resistance the chief administrator, Mian Mota, handed over the state to the Maharaja.[126]

Annexation of Wazirabad (1810)

Jodh Singh, the ruler of Wazirabad, died in November 1809. The Maharaja appointed the former ruler's son. Ganda Singh, as the successor of his father. In June 1810, there were riots between Ganda Singh and his relatives.[127] The Maharaja ordered Faqir Aziz-ud-Din, the administrator of Gujarat, to go and occupy Wazirabad.[128] Ganda Singh was relieved of his charge and was given a reasonable *jagir* for his subsistence.

Annexation of the Territories of Faizullapurias (1811), Nakkais (1811) and Kanaihyas (1821)

The territories of the Faizullapurias were situated on both sides of river Satluj. Budh Singh, the Sardar of this Misal, was not willing to accept Ranjit Singh as his overlord. The Maharaja ordered Mohkam Chand to mobilize forces against Budh Singh. Mohkam Chand, accompanied by Jodh Singh Ramgarhia and Fateh Singh Ahluwalia, besieged Jalandhar. Budh Singh escaped to Ludhiana and sought the protection of the British. The fort of Jalandhar and its surrounding areas were conquered by Mohkam Chand.[129] Budh Singh's possessions near Tarn Taran were also captured by the Maharaja's artillery officer, Ghaus Khan.

REFERENCES

1. Khuswant Rai, *Tawarikh-i-Sikhan* (1811), MS., Ganda Singh collection, Patiala, p. 130; Sohan Lal Suri, *Umdat ut-Towarikh*, Daftar II, Lahore, 1885, p. 2; Ganesh Das, *Char Bagh-i-Punjab* (1855), Amritsar, 1965, p. 134; Gian Singh, *Tawarikh Guru Khalsa*, Part-II, reprint 1970, p. 277; Lapel Griffin, *Ranjit Singh*, Oxford, 1905, p. 153; Muhammad Latif, *History of the Panjab*, (1891), reprint, Delhi, 1964, p. 337. Some modern writers wrongly name him as Budh Singh.
2. Some writers believe that Desu was the nickname given to Budha Singh after his mare called Desai (Muhammad Latif, *op. cit.*, p. 337; Gian Singh, *op. cit.*, p. 227; Prem Singh Hoti, *Maharaja Ranjit Singh*, 3rd ed. Amritsar, 1931, pp. 17-18).
3. Carmichael Smyth, *A History of the Reigning Family of Lahore* (1847), Patiala reprint, 1970, p. 14.
4. Hari Ram Gupta, *History of the Sikhs*, Vol. IV Delhi, 1982, p. 293.
5. Kirpal Singh, 'Maharaja Ranjit's Birth place, Gujranwala, *The Panjab Past and Present'*, Vol. XVI-II, October, 1980, p. 20.
6. Carmichael Smyth, *op. cit.*, p. 5.
7. Gian Singh, *op. cit.*, p. 277, Waheed-ud-Din, *The Real Ranjit Singh*, reprint, Delhi, 1976, p. 56.
8. Carmichael Smyth, *op. cit.*, p. 4.
9. Lepel Griffin, *op. cit.*, p. 153; Muhammad Latif, *op. cit.*, p. 337.

10. Carmichael Smyth, *op. cit.*, p. 5.
11. *Ibid.*
12. Prinsep, *Origin of the Sikh Power in the Punjab and Political Life of Maharaja Ranjit Singh* (1834), Patiala reprint, 1970, p. 18; Ali-ud-Din Mufti, *Ibratnama,* Vol. I (1854), Lahore, 1961, p. 369. Carmichael Smyth, *op. cit.*, p. 6; Muhammad Latif *op. cit.*, p. 388.
13. Carmichael Smyth, *op. cit.*, p. 6.
14. Ganesh Das Badehra, *op. cit.*, p. 135; cf., Prinsep, *op. cit.*, p. 18.
15. Carmichael Smyth, *op. cit.*, p. 6; Muhammad Latif, *op. cit.*, p. 338; Lepel Griffin, *op. cit.*, p. 154; Prem Singh Hoti, *op. cit.*, p. 19.
16. Bhagat Singh, *Sikh Polity in the Eighteenth and Nineteenth Centuries,* Delhi, 1978, pp. 77-78.
17. Ganesh Das Badehra, *op. cit.*, p. 135.
18. Bute Shah, *Tarikh-i-Punjab,* Daftar, V (1848), MS., Ganda Singh collection, Patiala, pp. 2-3; Sohan Lal Suri, *op. cit.*, II. p. 5; cf., M'Gregor, *The History of the Sikhs,* I (1846), Allahabad reprint, 1979, p. 149.
19. Bute Shah, *op. cit.*, p. 3.
20. Muhammad Latif, *op. cit.*, p. 338.
21. Sohan Lal Suri, *op. cit.*, II, p. 5; Bute Shah, *op. cit.*, V. pp. 2-3.
22. Muhammad Latif, *op. cit.*, pp. 338-39; Prem Singh Hoti, *op. cit.*, p. 21.
23. Sohan Lal Suri, *op. cit.*, II. p. 8; Bute Shah, *op. cit.*, V, pp. 3-4; Ali-ud-Din Mufti, *op. cit.*, Vol. I, p. 373; Prinsep, *op. cit.*, pp. 18-19; Baron Hugel, *Travels in Kashmir and Punjab* (1845), Patiala reprint, 1970, pp. 270, 358; Lepel Griffin *op. cit.*, p. 154.
24. Muhammad Latif, *op. cit.*, p. 339.
25. Ali-ud-Din Mufti, *op. cit.*, Vol. I, p. 375.
26. Sohan Lal Suri, *op. cit.*, II, p. 9; Bute Shah, *op. cit.*, V. p. 4; Muhammad Latif, *op. cit.*, p. 339.
27. Sohan Lal, *op. cit.*, p. 10; Bute Shah, *op. cit.*, p. 5; Ahmad Shah Batalia, Appendix to Sohan Lal Suri's *Umdai-ut-Tawarikh,* Daftar I, p. 29.
28. Bute Shah, *op. cit.*, V, p. 4; Sohan Lal Suri, *op. cit.*, II, p. 9.
29. Qazi Nur Muhammad, *Jang Nama* (1765), (ed. Ganda Singh), Amritsar, 1939, p. 60.
30. Bute Shah, *op. cit.*, V, p. 3.

31. Sohan Lal Suri, *op. cit.*, II, p. 11; Bute Shah, *op. cit.*, V, p. 5.
32. Qazi Nur Muhammad, *op. cit.*, pp. 30-31.
33. Sohan Lal Suri, *op. cit.*, II, pp. 11-12; Ganesh Das Badehra, *op. cit.*, p. 131; Rattan Singh Bhangu, *Prachin Panth Prakash* (1841), Amritsar, 1939, p. 390.
34. Hari Ram Gupta, *op. cit.*, IV, pp. 303-04.
35. Prem Singh, *Punjab da Samajak Ithas*, Patiala, 1979, pp. 68-70.
36. Sohan Lal Suri, *op. cit.*, II, p. 13; Bute Shah, *op. cit.*, V, p. 6; Ahmad Shah Batalia, Appendix Sohan Lal Suri's *Umdat-ut-Tawarkh*. p. 29; Prinsep, *op. cit.*, p. 31; M'Gregor, *op. cit.*, I, p. 150; Ganesh Das, *op. cit.*, p. 135; Lepel Griffin, *op. cit.*, 154. Some writers say that Charhat Singh died in 1774, when he was encamped on the bank of Basanti river where he had gone to support the cause of Brij Raj Deo, the eldest son of Ranjit Deo, the ruler of Jammu, against his younger brother Dalel Singh. But none of the contemporary Persian writers corroborate it. Murray seems to be the originator of this information which was followed and copied by the later writers like Kanaihya Lal and Muhammad Latif. But all writers are unanimous about the cause of death.
37. Prinsep, *op. cit.*, p. 31; Baron Hugel, *op. cit.*, p. 359.
38. Gordon, *The Sikhs*, London, 1904, p. 81.
39. Bute Shah, *op. cit.*, V, p. 7; Sohan Lal Suri, *op. cit.*, II, p. 9; Ganesh Das Badehra, *op. cit.*, p. 131; Ali-ud-Din Mufti, *op. cit.*, Vol. I, p. 378; Carmichael Smyth, *op. cit.*, p. 5; M'Gregor, *op. cit.*, I, p. 152.
40. Ali-ud-Din Mufti, *op. cit.*, Vol. I, p. 378; Lepel Griffin, *op. cit.*, p. 155.
41. Ahmad Shah Batalia, *op. cit.*, p. 29; Carmichael Smyth, *op. cit.*, p. 9.
42. Sohan Lal Suri, *op. cit.*, II, p. 15; Bute Shah, *op. cit.*, V, p. 8.
43. Bute Shah, *op. cit.*, V, p. 9.
44. Prinsep, *op. cit.*, pp. 41-42; Ali-ud-Din Mufti, *op. cit.*, I, pp. 382-84; Carmichael Smyth, *op. cit.*, p. 10.
45. *Ibid.*, p. 42.
46. Muhammad Latif, *op. cit.*, p. 341.
47. Sohan Lal Suri, *op. cit.*, II, p. 20; Bute Shah, *op. cit.*, V, pp. 9-10; Ali-ud-Din Mufti, *op. cit.*, I, p. 99.
48. Sohan Lal Suri, *op. cit.*, I, p. 19.

49. *Ibid.*, p. 17.
50. Hari Ram Gupta, *History of the Sikhs,* Vol. IV, Delhi, 1982, p. 309.
51. Lapel Griffin, *op. cit.*, p. 156; Muhammad Latif, *op. cit.*, p. 342; C.H. Payne, *History of the Sikhs,* London, n.d., p. 68.
52. Bute Shah, *op. cit.*, V. p. 10; Sohan Lal Suri, *op. cit.*, II, p. 21; Prinsep, *op. cit.*, p. 34; Lepel Griffin, *op. cit.*, pp. 156-57.
53. Sohan Lal Suri, *op. cit.*, II, p. 21; Prinsep. *op. cit.*, II, p. 34, Muhammad Latif, *op. cit.*, p. 343.
54. Muhammad Latif, *op. cit.*, p. 343; Prinsep *op. cit.*, p. 35; Baron Hugel, *Travels in Cashmere and Punjab,* London, 1845, p. 361.
55. Bute Shah, *op. cit.*, V, p. 10; Ali-ud-Din Mufti, *op. cit.*, I, p. 278; Lepel Griffin, *op. cit.*, p. 157.
56. Sohan Lal Suri, *op. cit.*, II, p. 22; Bute Shah, *op. cit.*, V, p. 12; Prinsep, *op. cit.*, p. 35; Muhammad Latif, *op. cit.*, p. 343.
57. Khushwaqat Rai, *op. cit.*, p. 92; Sohan Lal Suri, *op. cit.*, II, p. 22; Prinsep, *op. cit.*, p. 36; Ali-ud-Din Mufti, *op. cit.*, I, pp. 278-79; Bute Shah, *op., cit.*, V, p. 12; Baron Hugel, *op. cit.*, p. 361.
58. Ahmad Shah Batalia, *op. cit.*, p. 24; Sohan Lal Suri, *op. cit.*, II, pp. 24-26.
59. Sohan Lal Suri, *op. cit.*, II, p. 26; Bute Shah, *op. cit.*, V, pp. 15-16.
60. Prinsep, *op. cit.*, p. 36; Ahmad Shah Batalia, *op. cit.*, p. 25; Gian Singh, *op. cit.*, II, p. 285.
61. Sohan Lal Suri, *op. cit.*, II, p. 27; Bute Shah, *op. cit.*, V, p. 16; Prinsep, *op. cit.*, p. 37.
62. Sohan Lal Suri, *op. cit.*, II, p. 28; Bute Shah, *op. cit.*, V, p. 17; Ganesh Das, *op. cit.*, p. 137; J. Skinner, *Haqaaiq-i-Rajgan,* (MS, GS. collection). (1830). p. 105. A letter written by a Maratha *vakil,* at Delhi, to the Peshwa, at Poona, in May 1790, conveyed the news that, "a great Sikh Sardar, named Mahan Singh, died." (DYMR-II, letter No. 15 dated May 1790, English version in Ganda Singh's private collection. Patiala); Gian Singh, *op. cit.*, II, p. 285. Some writers, depending on later or unreliable sources, fix Mahan Singh's death in 1792, which is incorrect.
63. Ahmad Shah Batalia, *op. cit.*, p. 29.
64. Hari Ram Gupta, *op. cit.*, IV, p. 313.
65. Muhammad Latif, *op. cit.*, p. 344-45; cf., Prinsep, *op. cit.*, pp. 37-38.
66. James Browne, 'History of the Origin and Progress of the Sicks,' *Early European Accounts of the Sikhs,* (edited Ganda Singh), p. 43.

67. Imam-ud-Din Husaini, *Tarikh-i-Husain Shahi,* (MS, 1798), quoted by Hari Ram Gupta, *op. cit.*, p. 313.
68. C.H. Payne, *op. cit.*, pp. 69-70.
69. Some writers wrongly consider November 2, 1780, to be the date of his birth in place of November 13, 1780. The following books give November 13, as the date of Ranjit Singh's birth: Sohan Lal Suri, *op. cit.*, II, pp. 17, 19; Bute Shah, *op. cit.*, V, p. 8; Diwan Amar Nath, *op. cit.*, p. 6; Gian Singh, *op. cit.*, p. 282; *Tarkh-i-Makhzan-i-Punjab* by Mufi Ghulam Sarwar (1867-68); *Tarikh-i-Gujranwala* by Gopal Das (1873); *Tarikh-i-Punjab* by Kanaihya Lal (1877) and *Maharaja Ranjit Singh* by Sita Ram Kohli (1933).
70. Bute Shah, *op. cit.*, V, p. 8.
71. *Ibid.*
72. *Ibid.*, pp. 8-9.
73. As told earlier Mahan Singh died in 1790, when Ranjit Singh was 10 years old and not 11 years as written by Ali-ud-Din Mufti or 12 years as written by Muhammad Latif and prinsep. But Mufti agrees with Amar Nath and Sohan Lal that at the time of assumption of turban of royalty Ranjit Singh was 10 years old.
74. Bute Shah, *op. cit.*, V, pp. 15-16; Muhammad Latif, *op. cit.*, p. 346.
75. Ganesh Das, *op. cit.*, p. 137; Ali-ud-Din Mufti, *op. cit.*, I, p. 390.
76. Ganesh Das, *op. cit.*, p. 137; Muhammad Latif, *op. cit.*, . 346.
77. Sohan Lal Suri, *op. cit.*, Daftar II, pp. 32-33; Bute Shah, *op. cit.*, V, p. 19.
78. Khushwant Singh, *Ranjit Singh,* London, 1962, p. 28.
79. Forster, *A Journey from Bengal to England,* Vol. I, London, 1798, p. 295.
80. Lepel Griffin, *op. cit.*, p. 9.
81. *Imperial Records, Foreign Department,* 24th December, 1798, No. 24.
82. Ganesh Das, *op. cit.*, p. 140; Sohan Lal Suri, *op. cit.*, Daftar II, p. 39. Ranjit Singh gave this information to Captain Wade in 1827 (Wade's letter, 31st May, 1831).
83. Sohan Lal Suri, *op. cit.*, Daftar 11, p. 39; cf., Bute Shah, *op. cit.*, V, p. 22; Ganesh Das, *op. cit.*, p. 140.
84. *Imperial Records, Political Proceedings,* 1799, No. 24; cf., Bute Shah, *op. cit.*, V, pp. 22-23.

85. Khushwant Singh, *op. cit.*, p. 36.
86. Ali-ud-Din Mufti, *op. cit.*, I, p. 397.
87. Sohan Lal Suri, *op. cit.*, Daftar II, p. 40, cf., Bute Shah, *op. cit.*, V, p. 22; Ali-ud-Din Mufti, I. p. 397; Gian Singh, *op. cit.*, p. 290).
88. *Ibid.*, p. 41.
89. *Ibid.*, p. 41; Bute Shah, *op. cit.*, V, p. 23; Ali-ud-Din Mufti, *op. cit.*, I, p. 398; Gian Singh, *op. cit.*, p. 290.
90. Sohan Lal Suri, *op. cit.*, II, p. 41; Bute Shah, *op. cit.*, V, p. 23; Muhammad Latif, *op. cit.*, p. 349.
91. Bute Shah, *op. cit.*, V, p. 24.
92. Sohan Lal Suri, *op. cit.*, II, pp. 42-43.
93. Sohan Lal Suri, *op. cit.*, II, p. 46; Amar Nath, *op. cit.*, p. 11; Khushwaqat Rai, *op. cit.*, 138-39; Ali-ud-Din Mufti, *op. cit.*, I, pp. 402-03.
94. Amar Nath, *op. cit.*, p. 12; Khushwaqat Rai, *op. cit.*, p. 139.
95. Sohan Lal Suri, *op. cit.*, II, p. 46; Khushwaqat Rai, *op. cit.*, p. 140; Ganesh Das, *op. cit.*, p. 142; Muhammad Latif, *op. cit.*, p. 352.
96. Amar Nath, *op. cit.*, p. 12.
97. Amar Nath, *op. cit.*, p. 13; Sohan Lal Suri, *op. cit.*, II, p. 49, Muhammad Latif, *op. cit.*, p. 354.
98. Sohan Lal Suri, *op. cit.*, II, p. 49.
99. *Ibid.*, p. 50; Muhammad Latif, *op. cit.*, p. 354.
100. Amar Nath, *op. cit.*, p. 16; Gian Singh, *op. cit.*, p. 293; Bhagat Singh, *Maharaja Ranjit Singh and His Times*, New Delhi, 1990, pp. 35-36. *op. cit.*,
101. Amar Nath, *op. cit.*, p. 19.
102. Khushwaqat Rai, *op. cit.*, p. 144.
103. *Ibid.*, pp. 143-44.
104. Amar Nath, *op. cit.*, p. 19.
105. Sohan Lal Suri, *op. cit.*, II, p. 51; Amar Nath, *op. cit.*, p. 20; Bute Shah, *op. cit.*, V, p. 27; Muhammad Latif, *op. cit.*, p. 317.
106. Sohan Lal Suri, *op. cit.*, pp. 54-55.
107. *Ibid.*, pp. 56-57. The date of occupation of Amritsar has been given differently by different authors. According to Ali-ud-Din Mufti, (Vol. I, p. 404) and Ganesh Das (p. 146), Ranjit Singh,

conquered Amritsar in 1803, and according to Amar Nath the occupation of Amritsar took place in 1802 (p. 27).

108. Amar Nath, *op. cit.*, p. 36; All-ud-Din Mufti, *op. cit.*, I, pp. 408-09.
109. Sohan Lal Suri, *op. cit.*, II, p. 60; Bute Shah, *op. cit.*, V. 35.
110. Sohan Lal Suri, *op. cit.*, II, pp. 60-61; Bute Shah, *op. cit.*, V, pp. 35-36.
111. *Ibid.*, p. 65-66.
112. *Ibid.*, p. 62; Bute Shah, *op. cit.*, V, pp. 38-39.
113. *Ibid.* p. 64; Amar Nath, *op. cit.*, p. 40, cf., Bute Shah, *op. cit.*, V, p. 40.
114. Sohan Lal Suri, *op. cit.*, II, p. 212.
115. Sohan Lal Suri, *op. cit.*, II, p. 65.
116. *Ibid.*, pp. 68-69.
117. *Ibid.*, II, p. 67, Bute Shah, *op. cit.*, V, p. 42; Muhammad Latif, *op. cit.*, pp. 369-10; Gian Singh, *op. cit.*, p. 253.
118. *Ibid.*, II, p. 86; Ganesh Das, *op. cit.*, p. 151; Bute Shah, *op. cit.*, V, p. 60.
119. Amar Nath, *op. cit.*, p. 52.
120. Sohan Lal Suri, *op. cit.*, II, p. 87.
121. *Ibid*, p. 90; Amar Nath, *op. cit.*, pp. 53-54; Ganesh Das, *op. cit.*, p. 151.
122. Ganesh Das, *op. cit.*, p. 152.
123. Sohan Lal Suri, *op. cit.*, II, pp. 100-01; Ganesh Das, *op. cit.*, p. 134.
124. *Ibid.*, pp. 97-98.
125. *Ibid.*, p. 98.
126. *Ibid.*, p. 92.
127. *Ibid.*, p. 101.
128. *Ibid.*, pp. 101-02.
129. Ahmad Shah Batalia, *op. cit.*, p. 34; Lepel Griffin, *Rajas of the Punjab* (1870), pp. 480-81.

3
The Ahluwalia Misal

Whatever the real origin of this Misal it appear first in history as of the Jat caste to which Sadao Singh, the founder of the villages of Ahlu, Hallu-Sadho, Tor and Chak, belonged.[1]

As the tradition goes, Sadawa,[2] the younger brother of Sadao Singh fell violently in love with a girl of the Kalal (or distiller) caste. The marriage of Sadawa with the Kalal girl was not approved by his relatives. But finding the lover getting dangerously ill the marriage was allowed. The parents of the bride imposed the condition on Sadawa that, in future, all their children would be married among the Kalals to which he agreed. Thus, Ahluwalias or residents of the village of Ahlu came to be called Kalals.[3] Four sons, including Gopal were born to Sadawa. Later, Dewa Singh was born to Gopal. Dewa and Gurbakhsh Singh. Badar Singh was married to the sister of Bagh Singh, a petty *zamindar* of the Lahore district.

Jassa Singh (1718-1783)

For many years, Badar Singh had no child. It is said that Badar Singh sought the blessings of the Guru imploring that if a son was born to him he would be made the disciple of the Guru. As a result of his father's prayers, Jassa Singh was born on Baisakh Sudi 15, Puranmashi, Samvat 1775, May 3, 1718.[4] Badar Singh died in 1722, when Jassa Singh was just five years of age.[5] Badar Singh's widow went to Delhi with her child to place him in the care of Guru Gobind Singh's widow. *Mata* Sundari who was living there. Jassa Singh and his mother remained at Delhi for quite some time.[6] *Mata* Sundari became much attached to both the mother and the son.

When Jassa Singh was seven years of age,[7] his maternal uncle Bagh Singh, who was issueless, requested *Mata* Sundari to spare the young boy to succeed him. *Mata* Sundari blessed and allowed Jassa Singh and his mother to go to Bagh Singh's house.[8]

According to Sohan Lal Suri. Bagh Singh raided and captured many villages and exacted tributes from the *zamindars*.[9]

On their return from Delhi Jassa Singh, his mother and his maternal uncle, Bagh Singh, stayed at Jalandhar where they were visited by Kapur Singh Faizullapuria. He was very much pleased to hear Bagh Singh's sister or Jassa Singh's mother singing *bani* (holy hymns) with melodious voice.[10] He demanded the custody of her son Jassa Singh who was entrusted to his care. Jassa Singh was baptised by Kapur Singh[11] who, later, put him on the duty of distributing grains to his followers for their horses. When he resented that duty he was told that, in future, he would be shouldering a much greater responsibility.[12] Kapur Singh always treated Jassa Singh as his own son.

Jassa Singh once brought a complaint to Nawab Kapur Singh saying that the Sikhs in his camp ridiculed his manner of speech. Having spent his earlier days in Delhi he had acquired the habit of mixing Urdu words with his Punjab. The Sikhs ragged him for this and called him *'ham ko—tum ko'*. Kapur Singh tried to console him with the words: 'Why should you mind what the Khalsa say? They got for me a *nawabship*, and might make you a *padshah*.' The Sikhs at once caught up the words as a prophecy and began to call Jassa Singh a *padshah*.[13]

Soon after, Bagh Singh died. At the time of Bagh Singh's death Jassa Singh was only 13. He inherited the property of his maternal uncle.[14] He grew into a very brave and fearless youngman. His 'political talent, religious zeal and lofty aspirations combined, rendered him one of the most powerful federal chiefs of the Punjab."[15]

The Sikhs considered it a privilege to take baptism of double-edged sword at Jassa Singh's hands. Raja Amar Singh, the successor of Ala Singh of Phulkian family, was once of the many prominent Sikhs to have been administered *pahul* by Jassa Singh.[16]

Like others, Jassa Singh created a *jatha* of his own and with the resources inherited form his maternal uncle, he became one of the leading Sikh Sardars.

Nadir Shah attacked India in 1739, and when, on his return, he was carrying away an enormous amount of money as booty he was attacked by the Sikhs and was dispossessed of most of his plunder. Sardar Jassa Singh Ahluwalia is said to have played an important part in this enterprise. Shortly thereafter, the Ahluwalia chief built the fort of Dallewal on the bank of the Ravi. In 1743, he attacked and carried away a large government treasure that was being taken from Eminabad to Lahore. Jaspat Rai, the brother of Diwan Lakpat Rai, was killed by the Sikhs fighting under the command of Jassa Singh Ahluwalia.

By 1747, the Sikhs had created among them as many as 65 *jathas*, each under its respective leader. There was an imperative need of uniting these *jathas* into a lesser number and placing them under the overall commands of a competent leader. In the words of Hari Ram Gupta, "Luckily for the Sikhs, a very capable leader who commanded high respect from all the Sikhs and possessed remarkable power of organization had appeared among them. This was Jassa Singh Ahluwalia, who had received his training under the famous leader Nawab Kapur Singh. The Nawab was the most venerable Sikh leader. Owing to the constant nelp and guidance of the Nawab and his own sterling virtues Jassa Singh Ahluwalia had come to occupy a very prominent position among the Sikh leaders. The Nawab was growing old and he wanted to give the leadership of the warlike Khalsa to somebody else. He had his eye on the promising Jassa Singh and he was on the look out for an opportunity to do so."[17]

After Ahmad Shah Durrani's return from the province, following his first invasion of India, the Sikhs met at Amritsar on the *Baisakhi* day, March 29, 1748, and on the proposal of Nawab Kapur Singh that the Panth needed solidarity and union, the entire fighting body of the Sikhs was named, the Dal Khalsa jio, and placed under the supreme command of Jassa Singh Ahluwalia.[18] The various groups were leagued together under twelve prominent chiefs.

In 1749, Jassa Singh, whose reputation had, by then, become great because of his bravery and ability was invited by Diwan Kaura Mal, to help him expelling Shah Nawaz Khan, the former governor of Lahore, who was, then in occupation of Multan on the authority of Ahmad Shah Durrani. Mir Mannu, the Governor of Lahore, could not stand a rival in the Punjab. Jassa Singh willingly offered help and cooperated with Kaura Mal in reducing Multan to Mir Mannu's submission. Shah Nawaz was killed in the battle and Jassa Singh received a rich share of booty and honours for him from Muin-ul-Mulk (Mir Mannu).[19]

The Lahore government again began to follow the policy of persecution against the Sikhs. In 1753, a large army under Aziz Khan was sent against the Sikhs and the government force was utterly routed by Jassa Singh. In 1755, the Ahluwalia chief defeated Adeena Beg at Kadar and snatched from him the territory of Fatehbad. He established his headquarters at Fatehbad on the right bank of river Beas, where he set up his military post in the *serai* which was developed into a fort and was called Khalwara. Fatehbad continued to be Jassa Singh's headquarters up to 1780, when it was shifted to Kapurthala. Shortly thereafter, Umed Khan and Aziz Khan were defeated in yet another trial. In 1756,

Sarbuland Khan, one of the Afghan generals whom Ahmad Shah Durrani the ruler of Kabul, had left behind him in charge of Jalandhar was defeated by Jassa Singh and his comrades. In 1758, Adeena Beg invited the help of the Marathas and the Sikhs to occupy Lahore. Prince Timur and his minister Jahan Khan fled to Afghanistan.[20]

In October 1759, Ahmad Shah Durrani appointed Raja Ghamand Chand of Kangra as Governor of Jalandhar Doab and the hill territory lying between the Ravi and the Satluj. Jassa Singh moved against Ghamand Chand and routed him in the battle of Mahilpur near Hoshiarpur and made him pay tribute to the Dal Khalsa. He realised tributes from the hill states of Mandi and Kulu. Nalagarh and Bilaspur were made tributary in March 1763.

He also placed under his control Jalalpur, Goindwal, Istala, Butala, Tarn Taran and Khadur.[21] After crossing river Beas he occupied Sultanpur, Talwandi and some other territories.

According to Ahmad Shah Batalia, Jassa Singh Ahluwalia gave away Nidala, Miani, Begowal, etc., totalling about hundred villages, to the Sikhs of Wazir village and Machunki, Dhilwan, Sidhwan, Haliwal, Brahmwal, Chakoki, Boh, Dogran and the surrounding areas and portions of the *pargana* of Nurmahal were conferred upon his *tumandars* and Misaldars. The *zamindars* of Phagwara, who were very affluent and maintained big contingents accepted his fealty and coceded to pay regular annual revenue to him. The Afghans of Urmar Tanda and Yahiyapur had take and employment under Jassa Singh. Crossing river Satluj he occupied Isru and Kot Isa Khan and their *zamindars* accepted to pay a fixed *nazarana*. Rai of Jagraon also came under his overlordship and accepted to pay revenue to him. In short, in the Bist Jalandhar Doab, Jassa Singh became the most important and powerful Sardar.[22]

After the celebration of *Diwali* Jassa Singh directed, the Dal Khalsa to attack Lahore in November 1761. Khawaja

Ubaid Khan Governor of Lahore, sought protection in the fort. The prominent citizens of Lahore waited upon Jassa Singh and offered to admit the Sikhs into the city provided the people were promised safety and security. After occupying the city the Sikhs attacked the fort. Ubaid Khan was killed in the course of fighting and the fort was captured by the Sikhs.

Jassa Singh, very actively, participated against the Afghans during the *wada ghallughara* in 1762.

After the departure of Ahmad Shah Abdali the Sikhs decided to turn upon Ala Singh who had been taken a prisoner early in the year 1762, by the Afghans, but he had pleased the conqueror so much that he had been created a Raja and honoured with rich presents. But Jassa Singh's influence prevented an open quarrel and he tried to persuade his co-religionists that Ala Singh had no option as to his acceptance of the title, which had not, till then, been known among the Sikhs.[23]

The Sikhs now prepared to attack the Afghan garrisons which Ahmed Shah had left behind him. But before anything else they decided to try their strength against Kasur, a rich Pathan colony, and a very strongly fortified town which had long been the object of desire of the Sikhs. Kasur was invested by the combined forces of Jassa Singh Ahluwalia, Hari Singh, Jhanda Singh and Ganda Singh Bhangi, Jai Singh Kanaihya, Jassa Singh Ramgarhia and many more Sardars. Alif Khan the Pathan leader was beaten back with great loss, two of the Afghan chiefs, Kamul-ud-Din Khan and Hasan Khan were stain and the town was sacked. The fort, holding out for some days more, also fell. Kasur territory was made over to the Bhangi chiefs who held it till 1794,[24] when Nizam-ud-Din Khan occupied it.

Under the general command of Jassa Singh Ahluwalia the Karora Singhia, Bhangi, Shahid Kanaihya and Phulkian chiefs led an expedition against Shirhid. Zain Khan, the Governor of Sirhind, gave them battle but was defeated and killed on January 14, 1764.[25] The town was razed to the ground as the Sikhs nursed a deep-rooted hatred against as the place where Baba Fateh Singh and Baba Zorawar Singh, the younger sons of Guru Gobind Singh, had been bricked alive. The whole of the surrounding territory fell into the hands of the Sikhs.

From Sirhind Jassa Singh proceeded to Naraingarh, 85 kilometers away. Raja Kirat Parkash of Nahan presented to him a horse and a sum of rupees 10,000 as a *nazar* through his Diwan Bulaqi Mal. The Mir of Garhi Kotla and Garib Das of Manimajra (near Chandigarh) also paid him *nazars*. The Raja of Garhwal came from Srinagar to pay homage to him.

In the district of Ambala Singh seized twentyfour village forming the *ilaqa* of Suhoran. Some of these villages were given by him to Bundalia Sikhs who were in his train.[26] The villages retained by the Ahluwalia chief were seized by the chief of Patiala, shortly after his recrossing the Satluj.

Jassa Singh, then, returned to Amritsar where he contributed liberally towards rebuilding the Harmandir Sahib (the Golden Temple) which Ahmed Shah Abdali, before his departure to his country, had defiled with the blood of cows and then blown up with gun-powder.[27] He also built the Ahluwalia bazar.

Najib-ud-Doulah, the Rohilla chief, who had been stationed at Delhi by Ahmad Shah in 1756, had, in due course of time, become a powerful minister there. Jassa Singh had for sometime been a close ally of Suraj Mal, the Jat ruler of Bharatpur. When this chief was killed in a skirmish in 1764, his son Jawahar Singh invited Jassa Singh to join him to take vengeance on Sher Khan Jassa Singh accompanied by Maratha forces, marched against their common enemy Najib Khan who refused to surrender Sher Khan and the allied emerged victorious near Shahjahanabad.[28] Najib Khan took refuge in Delhi which was invested by the Sikhs and the Marathas and it would have fallen had not the besiegers learnt about the invasion of the Punjab by Ahmed Shah

Durrani. The Durrani invader could come up to Sirhind from where he retired to Kabul not without molestation from the Sikhs who captured almost the whole of his baggage at Chenab.

The Sikhs resented Jammu Raja Ranjit Deo's being tributary of Ahmad Shah Durrani. In 1765, on Durrani's return to Kabul the Jammu chief paid him a tribute. A section of the Dal Khalsa under Jassa Singh Ahluwalia, attacked Jammu and realised from Ranjit Deo, by way of fine, a sum of three lakh and seventy five thousand rupees and made him a tributary of the Dal Khalsa.[29]

On the death of Ala Singh in 1765, his grandson Amar Singh succeeded him. Since Amar Singh had been baptised by Jassa Singh the former had great regards for the latter. Amar Singh made a request to Jassa Singh to attend his coronation as chief guest, to confer on him the emblems of royalty which he did. Jassa Singh received the *pargana* of Isru as a *nazar*.[30] This *pargana* remained with the Ahluwalias till the First Anglo-Sikh war when it was reverted to its former owner —the ruler of Patiala.

When Ahmad Shab entered the Punjab for the first time in the winter of 1766, he was constantly by the Sikhs. He is said to have written letters to Jassa Singh Ahluwalia and other Sardars that they should meet him to conclude peace with him. The suggestion was spurned and the Afghan invader returned to Kabul.[31]

In 1766, Jassa Singh marched southward with the chiefs of Patiala and Jind and ravaged Jhajjar, Rewari and Baghpat. He captured Payal, etc., from the Kotla Afghans. During his last invasion in 1766-1767, Ahmad Shah found that it was not possible to reconquer the Punjab most of which had, by this time, come in the hands of the Sikhs. In 1768, Jassa Singh overan the neighbourhood of Delhi and Anupshahr defeating Mirza Sukhan, who was sent against him by the Emperor.

In 1769, Jassa Singh captured Jalandhar and the adjoining territory in collaboration with the Singhpuria chief, Khushal

Singh. Jassa Singh kept Jalandhar with him and the neighbouring villages were given to Khushal Singh. After a few years, out of respect and affection which Jassa Singh had for his patron Newab Kapur Singh, he gave Jalandhar also to Khushal Singh who made it his headquarters.

In 1771, Jassa Singh captured Raikot from the Pathans and Rajputs of Berowal. Next year, that is in 1772, he marched against Kapurthala, held by Rai Ibrahim[32] who had promised to pay annual tribute. It was only after reducing thirteen forts in the neighbourhood of Kapurthala, and investing the town itself, that the Rai paid what was due. But Jassa Singh's authority was not really established and in 1777, his son-in-law, Mohar Singh, was shot at from the fort and killed. It was pretended that this was an accident, and Jassa Singh was compelled to accept the explanation offered. In 1780, Jassa Singh took advantage of the tribute again falling into arrears to seize the town of Kapurthala and he made it his capital.[33] Rai Ibrahim was allowed to leave the place with his moveable property and his family. According to James Skinner, Jassa Singh gave a village in *jagir* to Ibrahim's son and daughter gor their subsistence.[34] Jassa Singh lived at Kapurthala till his death.

In 1775 one day when Jassa Singh Ahluwalia was on his way to Achal, near Batala, to attend a fair, Jassa Singh Ramgarhia's brother, Mali Singh, who was going from Sri Hargobindpur to Batala with his men, wounded him by a bullet. Mali Singh carried him to Batala. The Ahluwalia chief felt so much hurt in his mind and humiliated that during his two days' stay there he did not eat or drink any thing, nor did he talk to anybody. Jassa Singh Ramgarhia felt extremely sorry for the incident and sincerely apologized. On the third day the Ahluwalia chief was sent back to his headquarters Fatehbad in a *palki* (palanquin) with all honours and adequate escort.[35]

In 1776. to avenge an attack made on him by the Ramgarhia Sardars, Jassaa Singh formed a coalition with the Bhangis, Kanaihyas, Sukarchakias and some others, to expel

Jassa Singh Ramgarhia from the Punjab and seize his possessions. The expedition was a complete success. The Ramgarhias were utterly defeated and the Ramgarhia chief was forced to fly to cis-Satluj areas especially towards Hansi and Hisar in the Haryana[36] from where he returned later with the help of Mahan Singh Sukarchakia and Katoch chief of Kangra.

In September 1779, which Abdul Ahad, a minister of Delhi, invaded Patiala, Maharaja Amar Singh of Patiala invited help from Jassa Singh Ahluwalia who responded immediately and came to Patiala with his collaborators Khushal Singh Singhpuria and Tara Singh Ghaiba whose son was married to the princess of Patiala. The minister from Delhi got frightened and retired to the Mughal capital.

In 1782, Jassa Singh Ahluwalia attended the marriage of Raja Sahib Singh with the daughter of Ganda Singh Bhangi. He joined the marriage party when it passed through Kapurthala. He administered *pahul* to Samo Singh at the Gurdwara of Tarn Taran.[37] The marriage was solemnized at Panjwar and, on the return of the marriage party, he gave rich presents to Sahib Singh.

Accompanied by Sardar Baghel Singh and others Jassa Singh Ahluwalia entered Delhi in early March 1783. On March 11, he made for the Red Fort. The Emperor and his courtiers hid themselves in their private apartments. The Sikhs entered the Diwan-i-Am. In a fit of enthusiasm they fulfilled the prophecy of Nawab Kapur Singh who had expressed his hope for *padshahi* for Jassa Singh Ahluwalia. The Sikhs made him sit on the throne and waved peacock feathers, tied in a knot, over his head.[38] Jassa Singh Ramgarhia and some other Sardars resented it. So the Ahluwalia chief immediately declined the honour thrust upon him, and he left the Durbar. Jassa Singh Ahluwalia discarded the distinction of royalty twice, once in 1761, and again in 1783.

Jassa Singh died on October 22, 1783,[39] at the age of 65, due to his having eaten a water melon at Bandala which gave him colic pain of which he could not survive. His body was taken to Amritsar where it was cremated, and a monument to his memory was raised in the *derah* of Baba Atal, near that of Nawab Kapur Singh.

'He was a man of the greatest ability, and much respected by the Sikhs'. In person he was tall with a fair complexion, over-hanging eye-brows, broad fore-head, wide chest, sonrous voice and piercing eyes. He was famous as a marksman, both with the matchlock and the bow. He was a great warrior, a valiant general and a splendid organiser. He had nearly three dozen scars of sword cuts and bullet marks[40] in the front part of his body and none on the back which he never turned to the enemy. Qazi Nur Mohammad who saw him fighting during Ahmad Shah's seventh invasion in 1765, wrote in his *Jangnama*, "In the centre was Jassa Kalal, who fearlessly stood like a mountain."[41]

Although a most successful general in the battlefield, it was rather as the most saintly and orthodox of their leaders that the Sikhs respected him and many powerful and prominent Sardars, including Amar Singh of Patiala, received *pahul* from his hands.[42] The rulers of Patiala and Jind stood before him in all reverence and humility. The Rajas of Jammu, Kangra, Bilaspur and Nalagarh touched his knees. The Nawabs of Malerkotla and Kunjpura paid him homage. This did not turns his head. He always considered himself a humble and decide devotee and disciple of Guru Gobind Singh.

Although the Ahluwalia Misal was not the biggest, yet the influence of Jassa Singh was great and whenever any combination of Misals took place he was made the commander-in-chief though each body of troops fought under its own leader.

Jassa Singh did more than any other chief to consolidate the Sikh Power which after his death got disorganised, until the strong hand of Maharaja Ranjit Singh again forced it into cohesion.

Jassa Singh was an enlightened and liberal-minded man. He practised an utmost religious toleration. He was not an enemy of the Muslims or Islam. A very large number of Muhammadans were employed in his service and they were allowed to follow their own religious observances without any ban or molestation. In his behavious he was never prejudiced against the Muslims rather his attitude towards them was praise-worthy.[43] He was opposed only to the Muhal or Afghan rule based upon deep religious bigotry and bitter fanaticism. He was always liberal and considerate. The Sodhis of Kartarpur, who had been boycotted by the Sikhs who neither ate nor drank anything from their hands, beseeched Jassa Singh to readmit them in the Sikh faith by publically eating and drinking with them. Jassa Singh who was busy in his consolidation work deputed Bhag Singh along with some prominent Sikhs to go to Kartarpur to eat with them. They ate from their plates and readmitted them into Sikhism. He had strictly prohibited the slaughter of cow. He took expeditions against the cow-killers of Kasur and Lahore.

The liberality of the Ahluwalia chief was very great. He wore a new dress and when it was soiled in a day or so he would put it off and give it to his people to wear and thus never put on washed clothes.[44] He, at great expense, constructed a large reservoir at Anandpur and gave large grants to the Sodhis residing there. His hospitality was extended to all who asked for it and hundreds were fed daily in his *langar* or public kitchen.[45]

In normal days Jassa Singh had a very regular daily programme. At day-dreak he would rise, perform his ablutions, and dress himself, repeating the morning prayer and the *Sukhmani*. He, then, took his morning meal and set about the business of the day and at 3-00 p.m., held Durbar or assembly for all who chose to attend, where all matters of general interest were discussed. After the evening meal musicians played and sung hymns called *rahras* and an hour after sunset all retired to rest, having repeated the *ardas* or the evening prayer. And in the words of Lepel Griffin, "he was a Sikh by honest conviction." He never kept a visitor waiting and called him immediately without any consideration of time at his hands.

The city of Amritsar was, in a great measure, rebuilt and beautified by him. A bazar called Katra Ahluwalian was laid out by him.

Some writers believe that the Sikhs after the conquest of Lahore in November 1761, seizing the royal mint, struck the first rupee which bore the inscription:

Sikka zad dar jahan ba fazle Akal,
Mulke Ahmed grift Jassa Kalal.

[Jassa Kalal having seized the country of Ahmad (Shah Durrani) struck coin in the world by the grace of God].

But it does not seem to be correct. It is very improbable that any Sikh ruler, much less a religious zealot like Jassa Singh, should have issued a coin in his own name, and that too a clipped name, *i.e.*, mere 'Jassa' instead of 'Jassa Singh'. In reality the local Muslims and Mullahs felt very perturbed on Jassa Singh's occupation of Lahore and the establishment of his *badshahat* there. With a view to instigating the Durrani invader they struck a few coins and sent the same to Ahmad Shah.[46]

Since Jassa Singh remained the indisputed leader of the Sikh community they had begun to call him *Sultan-ul-qaum* or the *badshah,*[47] but he never arrogated to himself any prerogatives of the *badshah*. He only considered himself as one of the senior members of the Dal Khalsa.

Towards his later years he could not keep the whole Sikh community and their rulers united. They got split up into different groups and Jassa Singh joined one of them. He was friendly to the Kanaihyas and hostile to the Ramgarhias. Despite his open opposition to the Ramgarhias, the Ramgarhia chief had maintained personal regards for the Ahluwalia chief.

Bhag Singh (1783-1801)

Jassa Singh Ahluwalia had no male child. He had two daughters of whom one was married to Mehar Singh and the other to Mohar Singh.[48] Jassa Singh's wife Raj Kaur had impressed upon him to nominate one of their sons-in-law or her brother to succeed him but he did not agree as he did not find the necessary qualities of a ruler in any of them.

Bhag Singh, a close relative of Jassa Singh and Diwan Burha Mal, and been responsibly shouldering most of the burden of the administrative affairs of the state. Bhag Singh believed that the Diwan was not an honest man who sometimes misappropirated the state funds. But since the Diwan was an important man Bhagh Singh could not do any against him during Jassa Singh's time.[49]

After Jassa Singh's death, both of his sons-in-law claimed inheritance to his territory and property. The Sikhs assembled on condolence of Jassa Singh at Kapurthala and desired that the late Sardar's elder son-in-law should succeed him. But Jai Singh Kahaihya, who was friendly to Jassa Singh's cousin Bhag Singh, born in 1747, managed to get the latter appointed as the new ruler of the Ahluwalia Misal.[50] He was in his 38th year at the time of succession to the *gaddi*.[51] Bhag Singh had to face a constant challenge from the sons-in-law of his predecessor. Although Bhag Singh did not have high opinion of Diwan Burha Mal he did not like to take a drastic step of doing away with his services at the very outset of his rule.

Appointing Diwan Burha Mal and Sher Karim Did to look after his administration Bhag Singh came out of Kapurthala and toured the whole of the Doaba. He realised *nazaranas* from the *jagirdars* of Phagwara and Nurmahal.[52] The first quarrel that Bhag Singh found at his hands was one bequeathed to him by the late Ahluwalia chief who had joined Hakikat Singh Kanaihya in attacking Jammu, then ruled by Raja Brij Raj Deo. Bhag Singh renewed his alliance with the Kanaihya chief and his first expedition was, in company with Jai Singh Kanaihya, against Wazir Singh and

Bhagwan Singh chiefs of the Nakka territory between Lahore and Gogaira. In the next year Bhag Singh went to the assistance of Jai Singh, when Mahan Singh Sukarchakia, Jassa Singh Ramgarhia and Raja Sansar Chand of Kangra united to destroy him. His help could not be effective and Jai Singh suffered a defeat near Batala.[53]

In 1784, on the complaint of the people of Salan, Sardar Gurbakhsh Singh was removed from the territory placed under his care. Then, Bhag Singh took Sharkpur from the Nakkais. Accompanied by some other Sardars, he conquered Kasur. It was there that he learnt the news of the birth of his son who was named Fateh Singh in memory of their victory at Kasur.[54]

Shortly after this, he allied himself with Raja Sansar Chand of Kangra and their infant sons Fateh Singh and Anrodh Chand exchanged turbans in the fort of Kangra in token of brotherhood. Bhag Singh and Raja Sansar Chand are also said to have exchanged turbans.[55]

In 1787, Bhag Singh dismissed Diwan Burha Mal whom he had found to be a man of questionable character. He was insolent and disrespectful to the extent of smoking *huqa* at the Durbar.[56] In 1787, the Diwan occupied Begowal and came in open confrontation with the state forces. He was captured and later released. He again revolted in 1789, and occupied Chakoki. Encouraged by Burha Mal's action Diwan Sheikh Karim Allah also revolted and captured Sultanpur. Diwan Burha Mal was made captive from Chakoki and ordered to be beheaded but his life was spared on the intercession of Sayad Chirag Shah of Sultanpur.[57] A contingent was also sent against Sheikh Karim Allah who ran away from Sultanpur. He was overpowered by some robbers and killed near Mianwind village.[58]

Diwan Singh was appointed in Burha Mal's place. He made some changes on administrative grounds.[59] Hamir Singh was made the administrator of Sultanpur.

Bhag Singh then quarrelled with Gulab Singh Bhangi who owned Amritsar and the neighbouring areas and whose people had put to death an Ahluwalia agent at Jhubal. He occupied Jandiala and Tarn Taran but made no effort to retain these acquisitions and returned to Kapurthala satisfied with his success. This took place is 1793.[60]

After some time Bhag Singh crossed river Beas and got the territory of Chamkaur for the Bedis who had been dispossessed of that area by Sardar Hari Singh Dallewalia.[61]

In 1796, Bhag Singh jointed the Kanaihyas, under the leadership of Sada Kaur, in their attack upon Jassa Singh Ramgarhia who had entrenched himself at Miani in the present district of Jalandhar. But there was a sudden rise of the river Beas that compelled the allies to retreat in all haste with the loss of their baggage.[62]

In 1801, Bhag Singh, along with his son Fateh Singh, went to the *Akal Takht* (at Amritsar) and got his son baptised there by Sadhu Singh Akal Bungia.[63] Next year Fateh Singh was married with befitting pomp and show.[64]

In 1801, Bhag Singh sent a force under Hamir Singh against the Ramgrhias, who had been joined by Raja Sansar Chand of Kangra. The Ahluwalias were completely routed, Hamir Singh being severely wounded. Learning about this defeat Bhag Singh collected his remaining forces and marched as far as Phagwara against his opponents. He got a serious and painful trouble in his foot which grew worse day by day. He was taken to Kapurthala where he passed away soon after, on July 10, 1801.[65]

Sardar Bhag Singh was a man of docile and affable disposition which sometimes stood in the way of an efficient administration. Griffin considered him, "a man of very slight calibre". At times he could not exhibit the needed statesmanship and diplomacy which resulted in the alienation of some of his Misaldars and *tumandars* who got independent of the Ahluwalia chief.[66] Certain places as Begowal and Miani went out of his hands and the payments of revenue of some areas, including Jagraon, were withheld by the officials and *zamindars* of these places.[67] Bhag Singh was constantly on war-path against Jassa Singh Ramgarhia. Sometimes he was defeated by the Ramgarhias and at other times he defeated them.[68]

The Ahluwalia Sardar even tried to befriend Sansar Chand Katoch of Kangra but they, mostly arranged themselves on opposite sides in the event of a battle. The important battles of this period were those of Nagoke. Miani, Begowal and Garhdiwala. The assistance rendered to the Ahluwalia chief by the Kanaihyas and Sukarchakias against the Ramgarhias marked the continuing pattern of politics practised in this part of the Punjab.

Bhag Singh was given to constant meditation and he gave alms to Brahmans.[69] He got excavated at Kapurthala a Devi Tank and Devi Dawara was also got repaired. The *pujaris* were provided with subsistence. All the new Sadhus entering Kapurthala were entertained sumptuously by him.[70] He was an extremely kind-hearted man and would not tolerate cruelty even to the animal and insect life. In his early days he was required to look after the needs of the mendicants.[71] This had made him sympathetic to the poor to whom he gave a great deal in charity. He ruled his Misal for nearly eighteen years.

Fateh Singh (1801-1837)

As referred to earlier, according to Lepel Griffin and Giani Gian Singh, Fateh Singh was born in 1784, but according to Khushwaqat Rai[72] and Bute Shah[73] Fateh Singh was twelve years of age at the time of his accession to the *Sardari* of the Misal in 1801. He was the only son of Bhag Singh. One of his first acts was to form an alliance, offensive and defensive, with Ranjit Singh, who was, then, gaining power in the Punjab. The young Ahluwalia and Sukarchakia chiefs exchanged turbans at Fatehbad and swore on *Guru Granth Sahib* to become each other's brothers.[74] They also exchanged some gifts including horses and dresses. In the presence of the holy *Guru Granth Sahib* they accepted to abide by three conditions. One that the enemy of one would be considered as enemy of the other. Two, in the course of their meetings in the territory of Ranjit Singh or that of Fateh Singh, they would not claim any expenses from each other. Three, if they jointly conquered any territory suitable *jagir* from the same would be given to Fateh Singh.[75]

Mehar Singh, son-in-law of Jassa Singh, and some Misaldars including Thakur Singh and Brar Singh, who had consolidated power during the period of Bhag Singh and had become independent of the Ahluwalia chief, were attacked and deprived of their estates and property by Fateh Singh.[76]

Fateh Singh appointed Qadar Bakhsh, a Rajput, and a resident of Talwandi, as his *mukhtar* or administrator and then sent him to Maharaja Ranjit Singh as his envoy.[77]

When Jaswant Rao Holkar came to the Punjab in 1805, he met Ranjit Singh and Fateh Singh Ahluwalia at Amritsar. Holkar was obliged to make a treaty with the English. Ranjit Singh and Fateh Singh made a supplementary treaty with the English by which they caused Holkar to leave Amritsar, pledging themselves to maintain no connection or friendship with him, while on the other hand, the British Government promised to them a peaceful possession of their territories so long as their conduct remained friendly.[78]

Fateh Singh accompanied Ranjit Singh in his expedition to the south of the Satluj in October 1806. In the next year he accompanied the Maharaja to Jhang, when its fort was captured and Sial chief, Ahmad Khan expelled.

During Ranjit Singh's second expedition to cis-Satluj region in 1807, Fateh Singh also accompanied him.[79] The Ahluwalia chief requested Ranjit Singh to recover his territory of Naraingarh from Kanwar Kishan Singh of Nahan who held it. Mohkam Chand besieged the fort of Naraingarh. The Maharaja personally supervised the siege and the fort fell after a hard battle for nearly three weeks. Kanwar Kishan Singh ran into the hills. In the course of operations at the fort of Naraingarh Ranjit Singh lost a prominent commander, Fateh Singh Kalianwala. Tara Singh Ghaiba was also seriously wounded there and he died on his way back to Rahon.[80]

Fateh Singh also accompanied the Maharaja on his campaign against Kasur which was captured after an obstinate resistance. When Metcalfe came to Kasur in September 1808 to meet Ranjit Singh the Ahluwalia chief was deputed to meet him with Diwan Mohkam Chand and ten thousand troops, at a distance of four miles from the Maharaja's camp and escort him to his tents.[81]

Fateh Singh was present in the Kangra expedition of 1809, when Ranjit Singh took possession of the fort of Raja Sansar Chand, which had been long besieged by the Gurkhas under Amar Singh Thapa.

In February 1811, Fateh Singh accompanied the Maharaja to Rawalpindi to meet Shah Mahmud, the brother of Shah Shujah who was on his way to Kashmir. On October 1811, the Ahluwalia chief Marched against Budh Singh of Jalandhar along with Diwan Mohkam Chand and Jodh Singh Ramgarhia. Budh Singh fled across the Satluj and his estates were confiscated to Lahore.

After Jodh Singh's death, the Ramgarhia possessions were occupied by Ranjit Singh. The areas of Tanda and Yahyapur, which were formerly Ramgarhia. Possessions, were given over to Fateh Singh by the Maharaja. The Ahluwalia chief received the *pargana* of Phagwara from Ranjit Singh in return for Sharakpur.[82]

In the majority of Ranjit Singh's campaigns Fateh Singh served him with his contingents. He fought at the battle of Hazro on July 13, 1813,[83] when Fateh Khan, the Kabul minister, was utterly defeated. The Ahluwalia chief held a command in the Bhimbar, Rajauri and Bahawalpur campaigns. In 1818, he participated in the siege of Multan when the whole province fell into the hands of Ranjit Singh.

During the Kashmir campaign of 1819, Fateh Singh remained in charge of Lahore.[84] In 1821, he assisted the Lahore Durber in the reduction of the fort of Mankera. In 1823, when Ranjit Singh went to Khushab he left Lahore in the charge of Fateh Singh.[85]

Besides the above mentioned expeditions Fateh Singh accompanied the Maharaja in the following expeditions also:

Jamke and Kathua (1802), Sujanpur (1803), Kasur (1804 and 1807), Amritsar (1805), Jhang (1807), Sialkot (1807), and across the Satluj (1806-08). He was also present in the expeditions against Pind Dadan Khan (1809-10), Jalandhar (1810-11), Mandi (1811), Kulu (1811), Hazara (1813), Kashmir (1814), and the Yusufzai territories (1824).

The estate of Bhirog which consisted of about one hundred villages was conferred by Jassa Singh Ahluwalia on a dependent, Mirza Singh, whose son Jawahar Singh fought and died under the Ahluwalia standard. When Jawahar Singh's son Mahan Singh was directed in 1810, and 1814, by the British representative to fulfil his engagements as a chief under the protection of the British government, he declared to be the vassal of Fateh Singh Ahluwalia. In 1817, David Ochterlony, because of Mahan Singh's outrageous conduct, called upon Fateh Singh to confiscate his territory, who accordingly took possession of the whole estate. In consideration of Mahan Singh's young age of thirteen Ochterlony pardoned him and asked the Ahluwalia chief to reinstate him, who unwillingly did so. In 1825, Mahan Singh refused to acknowledge the supremacy of the Ahluwalia chief and also paid no attention to the remonstrances of the British agent who recommended the attachment of his *jagir* until he obeyed the orders conveyed to him. Mahan Singh was not prepared to acknowledge the supremacy of Fateh Singh. The British allowed Fateh Singh to enforce his supremacy by any measures he might see fit to employ but they would no give permission to the Lahore troops to cross the Satluj with those of Karpurthala.[86]

The small fort of Kotla was situated in the centre of Fateh Singh's cis-Satluj territories and was owned by a Pathan family, the eldest representative of which was Nihang Khan. The Ahluwalia chief was determined to assert his supremacy and in the summer of 1822, forcibly occupied the fort of Kotla and retained it despite the repeated orders of the British officer at Ambala. Balwant Khan, one of the younger brothers of the Kotla chief, was friendly to Fateh Singh and inimical to his own family members. He encouraged the Ahluwalia chief to continue retaining the possession of the Kotla fort. Ultimately, the British warned Fateh Singh against attempting to exercise any intervention in the affairs of the Kotla chiefship. Nihang Khan was reinstated in his rights and the fort was forfeited to his elder brother.[87]

Qadir Bakhsh, the *Wazir* of Fateh Singh Ahluwallia, had become very powerful. He visited Ranjit Singh very often, as envoy of the Ahluwalia chief. He wrongly conveyed to the Maharaja that Fateh Singh was planning to revolt against the Lahore Durbar. Ranjit Singh sent two battalions of the Lahore army to Doaba Bist Jalandhar. Qadar Bakhsh provoked and frightened Fateh Singh by telling him that Ranjit Singh had sent a force to conquer his territory and make him a captive.[88]

Fateh Singh got terribly alarmed and crossed river Satluj on December 27, 1825, and went to his possession of Jagraon in the cis-Satluj area and sought the British protection there. Ranjit Singh took possession of the territories of Fateh Singh in the trans-Satluj area and appointed Faqir Aziz-ud-Din to look after the same.[89]

The Ahluwalia chief wanted to obtain from the British government some sort of guarantee for the security of his trans-Satluj possessions. What Fateh Singh wanted was not possible for the British government to grant. Under the treaty of 1809, they could not interfere with the Maharaja's proceeding north of the Satluj nor were the whole of his cis-Satluj estates under British protection. These consisted at this time, of 454 villages of which 291 were held by Fateh Singh in sovereignty, and 163 were in possession of *jagirdars*. Naraingarh and Jagraon, consisting respectively of 46 and 66 villages, had been received by grant from the Maharaja in 1807, and over these two estates the supremacy of Lahore was admitted by the British.[90]

The apprehensions of Fateh Singh were totally baseless and Ranjit Singh was as sincere to him as ever. In the words of Lepel Griffin, "The fears of Fateh Singh were exaggerated and that he was one of the few men for whom the Maharaja had any sincere feeling of regard".[91]

Ranjit Singh sincerely wanted Fateh Singh to return. According to Ahmad Shah Batalia. Fateh Singh unable to secure adequate support from the British, decided to approach Ranjit Singh and beg pardon from him for his conduct and entertaining baseless apprehensions regarding the Maharaja's treatment towards him. He sent his *vakil*, Diwan Sher Ali Khan, to the Maharaja with the desired request which the latter accepted with utmost magnanimity.[92]

Ranjit Singh sent Dhian Singh his seven year old grandson Nau Nihal Singh, Desa Singh Majithia, Shiv Dyal and Jawahar Singh Bastini to Jagraon to convince Fateh Singh of his sincerity towards him and bring him to the Maharaja with all the honours due to him. Fateh Singh came back to Kapurthala in 1827, and met Maharaja at Lahore. His territories including Kapurthala and Sultanpur, were restored to him. But Ranjit Singh retained his possession of some of the territory of Fateh Singh despite assurances otherwise.[93] His cis-Satluj possessions of Jagraon. Isru, Naraingarh, etc., remained in his hands.

During the later years of his life Fateh Singh remained at Kapurthala in comparative retirement. He died on October 20, 1837, with malarial fever.[94]

In the words of the contemporary British diplomat. Charles Metcalfe, "The quiet character of Fateh Singh, who was the equal, if not the superior, in rank and power, of Ranjit Singh, has yielded to the bold commanding spirit of the other, and he has been the ladder by which Ranjit Singh has mounted to greatness. He now finds himself, not companion and friend of an equal as formerly, but the nominal favourite of a master... He marches with a considerable force in the train of Ranjit Singh without knowing whither or for what purpose... He is mild and good-natured seemingly simple, and undoubtedly wanting energy."[95] Fateh Singh seems to have been reduced to the level, at the most of a distinguished general of Ranjit Singh.

The beginning of a formal alliance between Fateh Singh and Ranjit Singh was made with the treaty of 1802, solemnised in the presence of *Guru Granth Sahib*, at Fatehbad. As referred to earlier, the *ahd-nama* was accompanied by an exchange of turbans to mark the establishment of perpetual friendship and brotherhood. According to this treaty, Fateh Singh and Ranjit Singh were to join in defence and offence and regard each other's friends and foes as their own. Also they were to share equally in all the conquests made jointly, each bearing the expenses of his respective army in these ventures.[96]

Both the chiefs met frequently and in the meetings the usual formalities and protocol were observed. Besides a formal reception these meetings were particularly marked by exchange of costly presents including horses and riding of an elephant together. Fateh Singh paid *nazaranas* to Ranjit Singh and it was symbolic of an inferior position. The position is further clarified when one finds unintentional evidence furnished by Ram Sukh Rao on this point. Fateh Singh's *vakils* were always stationed at the court of Ranjit Singh while there is no reference to an accredited *vakil* of Lahore Durbar permanently stationed at Kapurthala.

A number of Lahore courtiers including Raja Dhian Singh. Fateh Singh Kalianwala, the Sandhanwalia Sardars, the Attariwala Sardars, Dal Singh Kalianwala, Nand Singh Vakil, Sukh Dayal, Desa Singh Majithia. Mit Singh Bhadhania, Sewa Singh Kumedan and Ghaus Khan received *jagirs* from Fateh Singh.[97]

Even in the status of more or less, a vassal, Feteh Singh seems to have held an important position in the affairs of the Lahore Durbar for a long time. The Maharaja publicly acknowledged Fateh Singh's bravery and diligence in accomplishing many of their joint ventures, Ranjit Singh often told his officers that there was no difference between him and the Ahluwalia chief and that his orders should also be obeyed. The *vakils* of Fateh Singh were generally given a seat in the Durbar of the Maharaja and this was taken as a mark of special favour and distinction.[98] Ranjit Singh always addressed Fateh Singh as 'Bhai Sahib' and consulted him on all important matters.

According to Ram Sukh Rao, Fateh Singh was a powerful and enlightened ruler, a good administrator, a fearless general and a brave warrior. He was a seasoned horse-rider and horse-tamer and *chugan* (a sort of polo) was a game very close to his heart. It continued to be his favourite game throughout his life. He was exceedingly fond of horses and in memory of a black charger, for which he had taken a fancy, he erected a beautiful tomb which exists to this day at the entrance of Kapurthala.[99] He was known for his skill in marksmanship, archery and fencing. Ram Sukh Rao underlines Fateh Singh's valour in the battles of Miani, Duraha, Drauli, Kasur, Kangra, Attock, Hazara, Kashmir, Multan and Peshawar. He would always like to fight in the front line, quite oblivious of the dangers to which he was exposed. But he was always humble in regard to his own acts of bravery. He was a great patron of arts and letters. He was God-fearing, generous charitable and magnanimous and a very dependable and sincere ally.

He started his education under the care of a Persian teacher and acquired workable knowledge of Persian language. He is also said to have written a few books in the traditional style of Punjabi verse.

According to Ram Sukh Rao he was always kind and humane even to the defeated foes. He would provide full protection to the people of the conquered territories. He considered it meanness to plunder the property of the people who were in a state of utter helplessness and misery. He would never allow his people to avail themselves of the deplorable condition of the defeated. At the time of prolonged siege of Multan the parents started selling their children in slavery. Fateh Singh told his men not to purchase the children and, instead, he financially helped those who were found selling their children.[100] He visited the holy places of the Sikhs and the Hindus and gave liberal *Jagirs* to them. He patronised the Muslim institutions also. He was an extremely religious person and performed his *nit-name* (daily prayers) even in the battle-field. He always shared the hardship and the war hazards with his men in the field of battle. During Ranjit Singh's first expedition to Kashmir Fateh Singh placed his elephant at the disposal of the wounded soldiers and he himself trudged some distance on foot.[101]

He had the bad habit of excessive indulgence in liquor. He had marked indifference towards amassing wealth. He was very kind to his officials and was always ready to forgive and overlook even serious lapses on their part. He constructed many buildings in his capital. To promote trade and commerce in Kapurthala he attracted many bankers businessmen and traders from Jagraon, Ludhiana, Phagwara and Sultanpur and settled them there. He once remarked that he would be mightily pleased if the bazars of the capital town were so full of stocks of goods and salable commodities that his elephant might find it difficult to pass through them. He gave *khillats* to the bankers and traders who had outstanding performance to their credit.[102] It eminently displays Fateh Singh's keen interest in the promotion of the economic condition of his state.

Raja Nihal Singh (1836-1852)

After Fateh Singh's death, his elder son Nihal Singh, who was born on March 10, 1817, succeeded him. Amar Singh, the younger brother of Nihal Singh, hatched a conspiracy against his brother. When Nihal Singh was leaving his residence with only one attendant he was attacked by Amar

Singh's men. The attendant threw himself before his master and was cut to pieces by the enemies but the Raja was saved with a few wounds. Ranjit Singh called both the brothers to Lahore and expressed sympathy with Nihal Singh and directed him to allow Amar Singh a separate maintenance allowance of Rs. 30,000, a year. Amar Singh always remained insincere to his elder brother. Nihal Singh would have remained in fear of being dispossessed but for the premature death of Amar Singh.

On the 28th March, 1841, Maharaja Sher Singh went on a boating excursion on the Ravi along with Dhian Singh, Hira Singh, Jamadar Khushal Singh, Bhai Gurmukh Singh, Rai Kesara Singh, Attar Singh Kalianwala and Amar Singh Ahluwalia. The boat was suddenly filled with water. Amar Singh Ahluwalia was drowned and the rest of the party escaped with difficulty by means of their riding elephants which were waiting on the bank and which were driven into the river to their assistance.[103]

Nihal Singh assisted the British in their march to Kabul. In the First Anglo-Sikh war of 1845 Nihal Singh did not side with the British. He was ordered by the British to cross Satluj and join them but he did not comply with the orders. On 31st on November, 1845, news was received by Major Broadfoot to the effect that the Ahluwalia subjects had joined the Lahore forces. They fought against the British at Aliwal and Buddowal.[104] As a punishment for his conduct, Nihal Singh's territories, south of Satluj, estimated at Rs. 5,65,00, a year, were confiscated by the British. In the Second Sikh War, Nihal Singh offered to help the English. After the war was over the Governor-General of the East India Company visited Kapurthala. Nihal Singh died on 13th September, 1852.

"Raja Nihal Singh was popular with his subjects and was of benevolent disposition. He had little strength of character, and was completely in the hands of his favourites, whose influence was rarely for good. His apathy and vacillation were such that he was unable to carry out measures which he acknowledged to be advantageous and he brought on himself and his state troubles which the most ordinary energy and courage might have averted."[105]

Raja Randhir Singh (1852-1870)

Nihal Singh was succeeded by his eldest son, Randhir Singh, who was born in Mach 1831, and was then in his twenty-second year. He was an accomplished ruler. He sided with the British during the Mutiny of 1857. In Jalandhar his troops guarded the civil station, the treasury and the jail. Both in Jalandhar Doab and cis-Satluj he and his brother Bikarma Singh rendered important services to the British who acknowledging the same, remitted a full year's tribute of Rs. 1,23,000 payable by the Raja and also reduced the annual sum by Rs. 25,000. He got the honorary title of *farzand diband*[106] and Prince Bikrama Singh was honoured with the title of 'Bahadur'. In 1858, both the Raja and his brother rendered valuable service to the British government in Oudh. For his services the Raja was given two estates called Boundi and Bithouli in Oudh, which yielded government one lack of rupees per annum on *istimrari* tenure, at half rate. Prince Bikrama Singh received an estate worth Rs. 45,000, a year, in the Baraich district.[107]

After the annexation of the Punjab by the British the position of the Ahluwalia chief, although not strictly sovereign, had yet independent power which had been confirmed to him by the English. The districts in the Jalandhar Doab, "will be maintained in the independent possession of the Sardar." This was in perpetuity, and the government had no right to take away the police jurisdiction from the Raja.[108]

On 17th October, 1864, Randhir Singh was invested with the insignia of the most exalted order of the 'Star of India' at a Durbar held at Lahore which was attended by the rulers of Kashmir, Patiala, Jind, Faridkot and many others.[109]

Randhir Singh had for a long time been 'desirous of paying a visit to England. He left Kapurthala for Bombay on the 15th of March, 1870. When the ship reached Aden he became seriously ill and died there on the 2nd of April. His body was brought to Bombay and handed over to his son, Prince Kharak Singh, who took it to Nasik where the ceremony of cremation was performed.[110]

Randhir Singh was a good scholae of English. He was interested in the promotion of education in the state.

By his first wife, who died in 1853, Randhir Singh had two sons, Kanwar Kharak Singh, born in August 1850, and Harnam Singh, born in November 1852. His only daughter, born in 1851, was married in 1863. His second wife born him one son who died two months after his birth.[111]

Raja Kharak Singh (1870-1877)

Kharak Singh was born in 1850. After his father's death his installation to the *gaddi* took place on the 12th May, 1870. The ceremony was attended by Col. Coxe, Commissioner of Jalandhar and a large number of visitors. On the request of his subjects Kharak Singh announced the opening of a college and a hospital in the name of his father and sanctioned the amount for the construction of the buildings of the college and the hospital.[112] Kharak Singh could not live long. In 1874, on his return from Bhagsu (district Kangra), it was discovered on May 9, 1874, at Hoshiarpur that the Raja was suffering from some brian ailment. Treatment proved of no avail. In order to look after the administrative affairs of the state government, Council of Regency was formed. On April 18, 1875, Lepel Griffin was appointed in charge of this Council. The Raja died at Bhagsu on September 5, 1877.[113] He was cremated at Kapurthala.

Maharaja Jagatjit Singh (1877-1948)

Jagatjit Singh who was born on November 23, 1872, succeeded his father on November 17, 1877. Since he was just a child at the time of his father's death the administration of the state remained in the hands of the British superintendents for a number of years. He attained his majority on November 24, 1890, and was invested with ruling powers, with due ceremony, by Sir James Lyall, the then Lieutenant Governor of the Punjab. He was gifted with a gentle and an amiable disposition and was a just and a considerate ruler of his subjects. He always took keen personal interest in the administration. It was due to this that Kapurthala had ranked as one of the foremost of the well-run states in India.

Jagatjit Singh was among the earliest to sanction free primary education throughout the state. Many High Schools for boys and girls were run in the state. Randhir College, Kapurthala was also built during his regime.

He had full powers of life and death over his subjects and administered justice through properly constituted courts which were run on similar lines as those in British India. Sentences of death and life imprisonment were referred to him for confirmation. He never sanctioned the sentence of death in any case.[114]

For the benefit of the agriculturists, agricultural banks were spread all over the state, providing cheap capital for the *zamindars*. Cooperative societies did a lot of good to the people. Veterinary hospitals were opened at many places.

Besides building a remarkable Gurdwara in his capital, he gave a proof of his broad-minded sympathy with his Muslim subjects by adding a new mosque to Kapurthala. The mosque designed by a French architect is, indeed, a unique building in India, built in a Moorish style and its architectural effect is remarkably beautiful. It cost six lakh rupees and it was consecrated in the presence of Nawab of Bahawalpur and some of the leading Indian Muslims. Kapurthala can, thus, boast of not only the most magnificent palaces and villas but also of the most imposing places of worship for the subjects of all castes and creeds.

The Maharaja was a perfect host and his hospitality was proverbial. He had entertained some of the most prominent personalities of the world at his capital, which included the viceroys, royal princes, governors, Rajas, diplomats, etc.

The Maharaja was a great traveller. It was a hobby with him not only to visit distant lands but also to make personal acquaintances and friendships with the leading personalities of the places he visited. During his time he was not only the most travelled Indian ruler but also one with the widest circle of cosmopolitan friends. He had visited North Africa, Central and South America, China, Japan, Siam, Java, Indo-China, Egypt, Turkey and the Bali islands. Besides Great Britain.

REFERENCES

1. Lepel Griffin, *The Rajas of the Punjab*, Lahore (Second ed, 1873), p. 452. Gian Singh, *Tawarikh Guru Khalsa* II, reprint Patiala, 1970, p. 721.
2. Lepel Griffin, *op. cit.*, p. 452; Gian Singh names the boy as Wadhawa Singh (*op. cit.*, p. 721).
3. Gian Singh, *op. cit.*, p. 721.
4. Lepel Griffin, *op, cit.*, p. 454; Diwan Ramjas, *Tawarikh-i-Riast Kapurthala*, Lahore, 1897, pp. 97-98; Ganda Singh, *Sardar Jassa Singh Ahluwalia* (Punjabi), Patiala, 1969, p. 22.
5. Ramjas. *op. cit.*, pp. 99-100.
6. Lepel Griffin, *op. cit.*, pp. 454-55; Gian Singh, *op. cit.*, p. 722.
7. Khushwaqat Rai, *Tawarikh-i-Sikhan* (1811), (MS., Dr Ganda Singh collection, Patiala), p. 66.
8. Gian Singh *op. cit.*, p. 77; Lepel Griffin, *op. cit.*, p. 455; Ramjas, *op. cit.*, pp. 100-102.
9. Sohan Lal Suri, *Umdat-ut-Tawarikh, Daftar* l, Lahore, 1885, p. 109.
10. Rattan Singh Bhangu, *Prachin Panth Parkash* (1841), Amritsar, 1939, p. 204; Ali-ud-Din Mufti, *Ibratnama*, Vol. 1 (1854), Lahore, 1961, p. 310; cf., M'Gregor, *The History of the Sikhs*, I (1846), Allahabad reprint, 1979, pp. 146-47; Kanaihya Lal, *Tarikh-i-Punjab*, Lahore, 1877, p. 99.
11. Rattan Singh Bhangu, *op. cit.*, p, 204; Ahmad Shah Batalia. Appendix to Sohan Lal Suri's *Umdat-ut-Tawarikh*, I, p. 27; Ali-ud-

Din Mufti, *op. cit.*, p. 310; Bute Shah, *Twarikh-i-Punjab, Daftar* IV, MS., Dr Ganda Singh collection, Patiala, p. 265; Kanaihya Lal, *op. cit.*, 99; Ramjas, *op. cit.*, p. 104.

12. Rattan Singh Bhangu, *op, cit.*, p. 204.
13. *Ibid.*, Gian Singh, *op. cit.*, p. 723; Teja Singh and Ganda Singh, *A Short History of the Sikhs*, Bombay, 1950, p. 123.
14. Ali-ud-Din Mufti, *op. cit.*, Vol. I, p. 311; Khushwaqat Rai, *op. cit.*, p. 66.
15. Muhammad Latif, *History of the Punjab*, Calcutta, 1891, p. 314.
16. Ramjas, *op. cit.*, p. 150; Gian Singh, *op. cit.*, p. 733.
17. Hari Ram Gupta, *History of the Sikhs*, Vol. I, Calcutta 1939, p. 51.
18. Gian Singh, *Panth Parkash*, (5th edition), p. 907.
19. Lepel Griffin, *op. cit.*, p. 457; Gian Singh, *Tawarikh Guru Khalsa*, II, p. 725; Muhammad Latif, *op. cit.*, p. 315; Ganesh Das Badehra, *Char Bagh-i-Punjab* (1855), Amritsar, 1965, p. 93.
20. Gulam Husain, *Syarul Mutakhirin* (1782), Cawnpore, 1897, p. 909, *Haqiqat-i-bina-o-uruj-i-firqa-i-Sikhan*, MS., PUP., p. 19; Sohan Lal Suri, *op. cit.*, I, p. 144; Ali-ud-Din Mufti, *op. cit.*, I, p. 220; Jadunath Sarkar, *Fall of the Mughal Empire*, Vol. II, Calcutta, reprint 1971, pp. 73-74.
21. Ahmad Shah Batalia, *op. cit.*, p. 27.
22. *Ibid.*, Khushwaqat Rai, *op. cit.*, p. 66.
23. *Tazkirah-i-Khandan-i-Rajah-i-Phulkian*, MS., GS., pp. 16-17; Bute Shah, *op. cit.*, IV, p. 260; Lepel Griffin, *op. cit.*, p. 462; Ramjas, *op. cit.*, pp. 194-95.
24. Lepel Griffin, *op. cit.*, p. 463.
25. *Haqiqat-i-bina-o-uruj-i-firqa-i-Sikhan*. MS., PUP., p. 30; Muhammad Latif, *op. cit.*, p. 326.
26. Lepel Griffin, *op. cit.*, p. 464.
27. *Ibid.*, pp. 464-65; Muhammad Latif, *op. cit.*, p. 316.
28. Qanungo, K. R., *History of the Jats*, Calcutta, 1925, p. 176.
29. Hari Ram Gupta, *op. cit.*, IV, Delhi, 1982, p. 35.
30. *Tazkirah-i-Khandan-i-Rajah-i-Phulkian*, p. 19; Lepel Griffin, *op. cit.*, p. 31; Gian Singh, *op. cit.*, II, p. 563; Ramjas, *op. cit.*, pp. 231-32.
31. Ramjas, *op. cit.*, p. 236, cf., *Correspondence of Persian Calendar*, II, 50.

32. Ahmed Shah Batalia, *op. cit.*, p. 28; James Skinner, *Kitab-i-Haqaiq-i-Rajgan* also called *Tazkirah-ul-Umra*, Persian MS., 1830, Dr Ganda Singh collection, Patiala, p. 182; Bute Shah, *op. cit.*, IV, p. 265; Ali-ud-Din Mufti, *op. cit.*, Vol. I, pp. 312-13.

    Formerly Kapurthala was a village in the *taaluga* of Sheikhu pura. It developed into a town under Rai Ibrahim (*Kalfiat-i-Sardaran-i-Ahluwalia*, Persian MS, Dr Ganda Singh collection, Patiala), p. 2.

33. Lepel Griffin, *op. cit.*, p. 467; Ramjas, *op. cit.*, p. 265; Gian Singh *op. cit.*, p. 731.
34. James Skinner, *op. cit.*, p. 182.
35. Khushwaqat Rai, *op. cit.*, p. 73. Ahmad Shah Batalia, *op. cit.*, p. 27; Bute Shah, *op. cit.*, IV, p. 56.
36. Khushwaqat Rai, *op. cit.*, p. 67; Bute Shah, *op. cit.*, IV, p. 58.
37. Ramjas, *op. cit.*, p. 277.
38. Gian Singh, *op. cit.*, p. 730.
39. Gian Singh, *op. cit.*, p. 733; Ganda Singh, *Sardar Jassa Singh Ahluwalia*, Patiala, 1969, p. 210.
40. Ramjas, *op. cit.*, p. 112.
41. Qazi Nur Muhammad, *Jangnama* (1765), ed. Ganda Singh, Amritsar, 1939, p. 50.
42. Lepel Griffin, *op. cit.*, p. 468.
43. Ahmad Shah Batalia, *op. cit.*, p. 27; M'Gregor, *op. cit.*, I, p. 147.
44. Ahmad Shah Batha, *op. cit.*, p. 27; M'Gregor, *op. cit.*, I, p. 147.
45. Lepel Griffin, *op. cit.*, p. 472. According to James Skinner, pulses weighing 10 *maunds pukhta* were cooked in his *langer* daily for the consumption of those who partook food from there (*Tazkirah-ul-Umra*, p. 182); Ramjas, *op. cit.*, p. 110.
46. Ganesh Dass Badehra, *Char Bagh-i-Punjab* (1855), Amritsar, 1965, pp. 130-31; Lepel Griffin holds Ganesh Das Badehra's version as correct (*The Rajas of the Punjab*, p. 461); C. L. Rogers also agrees with Ganesh Das [*Asiatic Society Journal*, 1881-L (1), 71-93].
47. Ahmad Shah Batalia *op. cit.*, p. 27; James Skinner, *op. cit*; p. 182, Ali-ud-Din Mufti, *op. cit.*, Vol, I, p. 313; M'Gregor, *op. cit.*, I, p. 147.
48. Ali-ud-Din Mufti, *op cit.*, Vol. I, p. 313; cf., Bute Shah, *op. cit.*, IV, p. 267.

49. Bute Shah, *op. cit.*, IV, p. 268.
50. Ali-ud-Din Mufti, *op. cit.*, I, p. 313. cf., James Skinner, *op. cit.*, p. 183. Gian Singh, *op. cit.*, p. 733, According to Ahmad Shah Batalia (p. 27) and Bute Shah (p. 267) Bhag Singh was Jassa Singh's nephew.
51. Ramjas, *op. cit.*, pp. 302-03.
52. Muhammad Latif, *op. cit.*, p. 317.
53. Lepel Griffin, *op. cit.*, 473; Ramjas, *op. cit.*, 312.
54. Gian Singh, *op. cit.*, 735; cf., Lepel Griffin, *op. cit.*, p. 473.
55. Ramjas, *op. cit.*, 313, 318-19.
56. *Ibid.*, p. 311.
57. *Ibid.*, pp. 314-17.
58. *Ibid.*, pp. 317-18.
59. Gian Singh, *op. cit.*, p. 735; Bute Shah, *op. cit.*, IV, p. 268; Ramjas, *op. cit.*, pp. 311, 314, 316-18.
60. Lepel Griffin, *op. cit.*, p. 473; Gian Singh, *op. cit.*, p. 735; Ramjas, *op. cit.*, pp. 313-314.
61. Ramjas, *op. cit.*, p. 316.
62. Ahmad Shah Batalia, *op. cit.*, p. 20; Ali-ud-Din Mufti, *op. cit.*, Vol. I, pp. 308-09; Lepel Griffin, *Punjab Chiefs*, pp. 173-74; *The Rajas of the Punjab*, p. 473; Gian Singh, *op. cit.*, p. 238; Ramjas, *op. cit.*, pp. 325-26.
63. Ramjas, *op. cit.*, p. 324.
64. *Ibid.*
65. Lepel Griffin, *The Rajas of the Punjab*, pp. 473-74, Gian Singh, *op. cit.*, p. 736. According to Khushwaqat Rai, Bhag Singh died of great uneasiness and regrets (*Tawarikhi-i-Sikhan*, MS., GS., p. 67).
66. Khushwaqat Rai, *op. cit.*, p. 67; Ahmad Shah Batalia, *op. cit.*, p. 261.
67. Khushwaqat Rai, *op. cit.*, p. 67; Bute Shah, *op. cit.*,p. 268.
68. *Ibid.*
69. Khushwaqat Rai, *op cit.*, p. 67; Ramjas, *op. cit.*, p. 329.
70. Ramjas, *op. cit.*, pp. 342-44.
71. *Kafiat-i-Sardaran-i-Ahluwalia*, MS., GS., p. 16.
72. Khushwaqat Rai, *op. ct.*, p. 67.
73. Bute Shah, *op. cit.*, IV, pp. 268-69.

74. Khushwaqat Rai, *op. cit.*, p. 68; James Skinner, *op. cit.*, p. 185; Bute Shah *op. cit.*, IV, p. 269; Lepel Griffin, *op. cit.*, p. 474; *Kafiat-i-Sardaran-i-Ahluwalia*, p. 21; Ali-ud-Din Mufti, *op. cit.*, Vol. I, p. 313.

75. *Kafiat-Sardaran-i-Ahluwalia*. p. 21.

76. Khushwaqai Rai, *op. cit.*, p. 68; Bute Shah, *op. cit.*, p. 269; Ahmad Shah Batalia, *op. cit.*, pp. 27-28.

77. Ahmad Shah Batalia, *op cit.*, p. 28; M'Gregor, *op. cit.*, I, pp. 147-48.

78. Lepel Griffin, *op. cit.*, pp. 474-75, cf., Prinsep, *Origin of the Sikh Power in The Punjab and Political Life of Maharaja Ranjit Singh* (1834), reprint, Patiala, 1970, p. 46; Cunningham, *A History of the Sikhs* (1849), reprint, Delhi, 1955, p. 120.

79. Sohan Lal Suri, *op. cit.*, II, p. 60; Bute Shah, *op. cit.*, V, pp. 35-36.

80. According to Bute Shah, (*op. cit.*, p. 173), Lepel Griffin (*Rajas of the Punjab*, ed. 1873, p. 45 foot note 2) and Prinsep (*op. cit.*, p. 49), Tara Singh Ghaiba died at Naraingarh.

81. Sohan Lal Suri, *op. cit.*, Daftar II, pp. 72-73; Bute Shah, *op. cit.*, p. 48.

82. Bute Shah, *op. cit.*, IV, p. 269.

83. Sohan Lal Suri, *op. cit.*, II, p. 156.

84. Bute Shah, *op. cit.*, V, p. 171.

85. *Ibid.*, p. 204.

86. Lepel Griffin, *op. cit.*, pp. 482-85; Gian Singh, *op. cit.*, pp. 739-41.

87. Lepel Griffin, *op. cit.*, pp. 485-89; Gian Singh, *op. cit.*, p. 742.

88. Ahmad Shah Batalia, *op. cit.*, p. 28; James Skinner, *op. cit.*, p. 186; Bute Shah, *op. cit.*, IV, pp. 270-71; M'Gregor, *op. cit.*, I, p. 148.

89. Ahmad Shah Batalia, *op. cit.*, p. 28. But according to Bute Shah, Budh Singh Sandhanwalia was appointed to administer the Ahluwalia territory, *op. cit.*, IV, p. 271; Lepel Griffin, *op. cit.*, p. 488; cf., Prinsep, *op. cit.*, p. 114; M'Gregor, *op. cit.*, I, p. 148; Cunningham, *op cit.*, p. 164.

90. Lepel Griffin, *op. cit.*, p. 489; cf., James Skinner, *op. cit.*, p. 185.

91. *Ibid.*, Ram Sukh Rao, Sri *Fateh Singh Partap Prabhakar*, MS., Archives, Patiala, p. 337 b.

92. Ahmad Shah Batalia, *op. cit.*, p. 28; Ramjas, *op. cit.*, p. 439; cf., M'Gregor, *op. cit.*, I, p. 148.

93. Ram Sukh Rao, *op. cit.*, folios 338a-339b; Prinsep, *op. cit.*, p. 114; Ahmad Shah Batalia, *op. cit.*, pp. 28-29; Bute Shah, *op. cit.*, IV,

p. 272; James Skinner, *op. cit.*, p. 187; Ramjas, *op. cit.*, pp. 439-40; Cunningham, *op. cit.*, 164-65; Gian Singh, *op. cit.*, pp. 743-45.

94. Gian Singh *op. cit.*, p. 745; Muhammad Latif, *op. cit.*, p. 318.
95. Lepet Griffin, *op. cit.*, pp. 478-79.
96. Ram Sukh Rao, *op. cit.*, f. 89a-b.
97. *Ibid.*, f. 341b.
98. *Ibid.*, f. 105b.
99. M'Gregor, *op. cit.*, I, p. 149; Muhammad Latif, *op. cit.*, p. 319.
100. Ram Sukh Rao, *op. cit.*, f. 289b.
101. *Ibid.*, f. 265a-b.
102. Ramjas, *op. cit.*, pp. 458-59.
103. Ali-ud-Din Mufti, *op. cit.*, Vol. I, p. 317; Bute Shah, *op. cit.*, IV, pp. 272-73; M'Gregor, *op. cit.*, I, pp. 148-49; Lepel Griffin, *op. cit.*, pp. 492-93. Gian Singh *op. cit.*, p. 746.
104. *Ali-ud-Din Mufti*, *op. cit.*, I, Vol. I, pp. 499-500.
105. Lepel Griffin, *op. cit.*, p. 503.
106. *Ibid.*, pp. 526-28; Muhammad Latif, *op. cit.*, p. 320; Gian Singh, *op. cit.*, p. 760.
107. *Ibid.*, p. 529; Muhammad Latif, *op. cit.*, p. 320; Gian Singh, *op. cit.*, p. 760.
108. Lepel Griffin, *op. cit.*, pp. 510-11.
109. *Ibid.*, p. 535; Gian Singh, *op. cit.*, p. 763.
110. *Ibid.*, pp. 537-38; Gian Singh, *op. cit.*, p. 764.
111. *Ibid.*, p. 504.
112. Gian Singh, *op. cit.*, p. 765.
113. *Ibid.*, pp. 765-66.
114. Raj Kumar, *Modern Kapurthala and its Maker*, p. 12.

4

The Bhangi Misal

The Bhangi Misal was one of the most famous Misals of the Sikhs. Members of this Misal ruled Amritsar, Gujarat, Chinlot and a part of the city of Lahore. This Misal outshined the other Misals in its earlier stages and the Bhangis were probably the first to establish an independent government of their own in their conquered territories. Even in the initial stages of the Misals's history they had nearly twelve thousand horsemen.

Chajja Singh

The founder of the Bhangi Misal, Chajja Singh, a Jat, was a native of Panjwar village, eight *kos* from Amritsar.[1] He was the first companion of Banda Singh to receive Sikh baptism.[2] According to Kanaihya Lal he had taken *pahul* at the hands of Guru Gobind Singh.[3] The Bhangi Misal is said to have its name from its founder's addiction to *bhang*—an intoxicating preparation of hemp.[4] After the death of Banda Singh, Chajja Singh administered *pahul* to Bhima (Bhuma) Singh, Natha Singh and Jagat Singh and made them his companions.[5] Accompanied by many others, he took to vigorous activities and harassing the tyrannical government officials. Chajja Singh's companions whole-heartedly cooperated with him in his armed operations in the face of grave dangers from the all-out effort of the government to liquidate them.

A little later Chajja Singh was joined by Mohan Singh and Gulab Singh of Dnoussa village, six miles north-east of Amritsar, Karora Singh of Choupal, Gurbakhsh Singh a Sandhu Jat of Roranwala, Agar Singh Khangora and Sawan Singh Randhawa. They all took *pahul* from Chajja Singh and formed a strong band of anti-state activists.[6] They carried conviction in their heads that Guru Gobind Singh had destined the *rajor* sovereign power of the Punjab for them. With that mission before them they were vehemently inspired to pursue their activities against the Mughal government of the Punjab.[7] In due course of time Chajja Singh passed away.

Bhima Singh

After Chajja Singh's death Bhima Singh (or Bhuma Singh), a Dhillon Jat of village Hung, in the *pargana* of Wadni, near Moga, became his successor. Bhima Singh's latent genious as an organiser and commander of his men gave a fillip to the Misal. His old associates Natha Singh and Jagar Singh became his subordinates and a large number of Sikhs rallied round them.[8] Nadir Shah's invasion, in 1739, had caused great commotion in the country. Bhima Singh took full advantage of it and turned the small band of attackers, left by his predecessor, into a powerful confederacy.[9] He seems to have died in the *Chhota ghallughara*, in 1746. It is said that Bhima Singh was of so arrogant a disposition that he was called by the Siksh *bala-bash* (a high-head). This, being a Turkoman title, annoyed Bhima Singh so much that he begged his comrades to change it for some other. Accordingly, he was appointed to pound *bhang* for the Sikhs and began to be called Bhangi. This account is popularly believed.[10]

Hari Singh

Since Bhima Singh was childless, he adopted Hari Singh as his son. Hari Singh became the next chief of the Bhangi Misal. He had taken *pahul* from Bhima Singh and had become his close associate from an early life. Hari Singh, the resident of Panjwar village, possessed the qualities of bravery and intrepidity. According to Lepel Griffin. Hari Singh was the son of Bhup Singh, a *zamindar* of Pattoh, near Wadni.[11] He organised a large hand of his followers with which he embarked upon the career of a conqueror. The numerical strength of his followers increased considerably. The fighting strength of the Bhangi Misal at this time was, about 20,000 men who were stationed at different places of his territory.[12]

By the time of Hari Singh's succession to cheifship of the Misal, Natha Singh and Jagat Singh, the close associates of his predecessor, had died. He appointed Jhanda Singh in place of Natha Singh and Ganda Singh in place of Jagat Singh,[13] who made great contributions to his achievements. Hari Singh fought a number of times against Ahmad Shah Abdali.[14] He was fond of keeping good horses in his stable.

Hari Singh had many Misaldars under him. It would not be out of place to differentiate here the respective positions of the Sardar and the Misaldar. A Sardar was the head of the whole Misal whereas there were many Misaldars in a Misal. The Misaldars had parts of the territory of the Misal assigned to them by the Sardar for their services to him in carving out a Misal or a state for him. The Misaldars used to join hands with the Sardar at the time of foreign danger or to fight together against a common enemy. They used to get share from the spoils according to the number of their men.

Hari Singh set-up his headquarters at Gilwali village in the Amritsar district. He captured Sialkot, Karial and Mirowal. He also led his expeditions to Chiniot and Jhang. In 1762, he attacked Kot Khwaja Saeed, two miles from Lahore, where Khwaja Ubaid, the Afghan Governor of Lahore, had kept his large magazine containing ordance, arms and munitions of war, the whole of which was carried away by him. He also took away from there the big gun, later known as *top Bhangian*[15] manufactured by Sardar Jahan Khan. He conquered the fort of Kehlwar in the Sandalbar area. He returned the same to its former masters on the assurance of receiving one lakh rupees annually as a tribute from them.[16] He also subdued the surrounding areas of Bahawalpur.

He next invaded the territories of the Indus and the Derajat. His commanders also conquered Rawalpindi.[17] The Majha and Malwa areas were also subdued. He also took his arms to Jammu at the head of 12,000 horsemen, and made its ruler Ranjit Deo his tributary. On the Jamuna Raj Singh Bhangi, Bhagel Singh Karora Singhia and Hari Singh harassed the old Najib-ud-Daula who wanted to restrain the progress of the Sikh chiefs with the help of the combined forces of the Rohillas and the Marathas. In 1763. Hari Singh joined the Kanaihyas and Ramgarhias in an attack on Kasur and the following year he fought Amar Singh of Patiala but was killed in the action.[18] He died of a gun shot which struck him at Lang-Chalella in Patiala state.[19] He held the Sardari of his Misal for eight years.[20]

Hari Singh had two wives, the first of whom was the daughter of Chaudhari of Panjwar, near Tarn Taran. He had two sons, Jhanda Singh and Ganda Singh from the first wife and Charhat Singh Diwan Singh and Desu Singh from the second.[21]

Jhanda Singh

After the death of Hari Singh, his elders son Jhanda Singh succeeded him. He appointed his younger brother Ganda Singh as the commander-in-chief of the forces of the Bhangi Misal.[22] The army was reorganised and its numerical strength was increased in political power and military resources Jhanda Singh made a remarkable improvement on the position as it obtained under Hari Singh.[23] Jhanda Singh and his brothers, associated by many illustrious leaders like Sahib Singh of Sialkot, Rai Singh and Sher Singh of Buria. Bhag Singh of Hallowal, Bagh Singh Dodia, Nidhan Singh Attu. Tara Singh Chainpuria, Bagh Singh Jalalwalia. Gujjar Singh and Lehna Singh, made great efforts to place the Misal on a very sound footing.[24] Jassa Singh Ramgarhia was one of the close friends of Jhanda Singh.[25]

One of the bravest men under Hari Singh Bhangi was Gurbakhs Singh, an associate of Bhima Singh. He was a great warrior and had about forty villages under him. Being childless he adopted Lehna Singh, son of Dargaha, a Jat of Sadhawala in the Amritsar district, as his son. On Gurbakhsh Singh's death his son Lehna Singh succeeded him. Gujjar Singh was the son of Gurbakhsh Singh's brother. A dispute cropped up between Lehna Singh and Gujjar Singh over the division of the estate left by Gurbakhsh Singh. Ultimately the estate was equally divided between these two Misaldars. These two chiefs, along with Sobha Singh nephew of Jai Singh Kanaihya, accepted the subordination of Jhanda Singh, the Sardar of the Bhangi Misal.

According to Ahmad Shah Batalia, Ahmad Shah Durrani had left behind Kabuli Mal as the Governor of Lahore. Gujjar Singh and Lehna Singh decided to occupy Lahore. They were joined by Sobha Singh. At the head of their forces they marched and besieged Lahore. As a measure of protection Kabuli Mal had bricked up all entrances and when he found it impossible to hold out against the besiegers he escaped from Lahore, leaving it in the hands of the above said trio,[26] in April 1765.

At the head of a large army, Jhanda Singh marched towards Multan in 1766, and declared war against Shujah Khan, the Muhammadan governor, and the Daudputras of Bahawalpur. An indecisive battle was fought on the bank of river Satluj. A treaty was concluded with Bangi chief on one side and Mubarak Khan, the Daudputra chief, and the Multan governor, on the other. Jhanda Singh was acknowledged as the lord of the territories up to Pakpattan.[27] In 1767, he built a fort behind the Loon Mandi in Amritsar which has been known as *Qila*-i-Bhangian.[28]

Jhanda Singh, next, marched towards the Pathan principality of Kasur which was subdued. He made a fresh attack on Multan later in 1771,[29] but it was repulsed by the combined forces of Multan and Bahawalpur.

The following year, a quarrel, arose between the successive governors of Multan, Shujah Khan, Sharif Khan Suddozai and Sharif Beg Taklu. Sharif Beg had been looking after Multan since the days of Ahmad Shah Abdali. When Timur Shah ascended the throne of Kabul he demanded the revenue of Multan from Sharif Beg, who got refractory and asked for help from Jhanda Singh, in return for a *nazarana* of one lakh rupees. The help was readily given.[30] Jhanda Singh accompanied by his brother, Ganda Singh, and Lehna Singh at the head of a well-equipped and strong army, marched to Multan on December 25, 1772, and achieved a complete victory over Shujah Khan and the Daudputras, themselves by Jhanda Singh and Lehna Singh. Diwan Singh Chachowalia was appointed the *qiladar* of Multan, garrisoning the place with the Bhangi forces.[31] Sharif Beg, utterly disappointed, fled to Talamba and then to Khairpur where he died a broken heated man.

On his return form Multan, Jhanda Singh subdued the Baloch territory,[32] captured Jhang and conquered Mankera and Kala Bagh. He failed to capture Shujahbad built by the Afghans after the loss of Multan. He, then, recovered the famous *zamzama* or Bhangi gun from the Chathas of Ramnagar.[33]

According to Ali-ud-Din Mufti, a serious dispute arose between Raja Ranjit Deo of Jammu and his eldest son Brij Raj Deo, in 1770. The heir-apparent was of a dissolute character. The father, a man of great ability and sound judgment, wanted, therefore, his younger son Daler (Dalel) Singh to succeed him. The quarrel developed into an explosive situation. The immature and raw youth, not realising the consequences, sough assistance from Charhat Singh Sukarchakia and Jai Singh Kanaihya, both of whom readily agreed. Raja Ranjit Deo could not fight against this formidable coalition single-handed and invited Jhanda Singh Bhangi to help him.[34]

The united forces of the Sukarchakia and Kanaihya chiefs marched into the Jammu hills and encamped on the Basanter river, a little east of Jammu. Ranjit Deo collected an army of his own, as well as of his allies, such as the chiefs of Chamba, Nurpur and Basoli in addition to the forces of Jhanda Singh.

The contest took place at Dasuha, adjacent to Zafarwal. The fighting dragged on for some days without yielding any result. One day Charhat Singh Sukarchakia was accidently killed by the bursting of his own gun which struck him on the forehead,[35] in 1770.

The loss of Charhat Singh was too great for the allies who found it difficult to maintain their position against the powerful Bhangi chief, Jhanda Singh. It was also felt by Jai Singh that Charhat Singh's son, Mahan Singh, was too young to be a match for Jhanda Singh who was deadly against the Sukarchakias. Jai Singh therefore decided that their safety lay in the murder of the Bhangi Sardar. Consequently he bribed a Rangretta or a Mazhbi Sikh in the service of Jhanda Singh whom he shot dead[36] from behind while he was walking in his camp unattended, soon after Charhat Singh's death.

Under Jhanda Singh the annual income of the Misal was estimated to be one crore rupees.[37] Jhanda Singh was a great organiser and an administrator. The Bhangi Misal made a considerable progress under his able stewardship. He headed his Misal for six years.[38]

Ganda Singh

After Jhanda Singh's death, his brother, Ganda Singh, succeeded to the Sardari of the Misal. Ganda Singh completed the works of improvement which had been undertaken by his deceased brother at Amritsar. He strengthened the Bhangi fort and enlarged and beautified the town many impressive buildings.[39]

Ganda Singh was feeling very uneasy in his mind due to the treachery of the Kanaihyas which had brought about the death of his brother. According to Ahmad Shah Batalia,

Jhanda Singh had conferred Pathankot on one of his Misaldars, Nand Singh, also called Mansa Singh, who died about the same time as his chief, leaving behind him his widow and a daughter. The widow married her daughter to Tara Singh, brother of Hakikat Singh Kanaihya. She also gave away the *jagir* of Pathankot to her son-in-law. Since Ganda Singh was inimical to the Kanaihyas for their nefarious act of arranging the murder of his brother he felt severely annoyed over both the acts of Nand Singh's widow. He asked the Kanahiyas to hand over Pathankot to him but they upon holding it as their rightful possession. Thereupon, Ganda Singh, at the head of a large army, and with the Bangi gun, *Zamzama,* marched to Pathankot via Batala and was joined by the Ramgarhias who were friendly to the Bhangis and hostile to the Kanaihyas. Tara Singh and Hakikat Singh were joined by Gurbakhsh Singh, son of Jai Singh Kanaihya, and Amar Singh Bagga. The two armies faced each other at Dinanagar where fighting continued for several days without any result. Ganda Singh, who was already not keeping good health, suffered from exhaustion due to his military actions and activities. He fell ill and in the course of ten days he passed away,[40] in 1774. Ganda Singh held the Sardari of the Misal for a few years.[41]

After the death of Ganda Singh, in preference to Desu (Desa) Singh, his younger brother Charhat Singh succeeded to the chiefship of the Misal. But shortly thereafter Charhat Singh was killed in an action.[42] These successive deaths of the Bhangi rulers broke the back of the Misal and the Kanaihyas had an upper hand in the contest for power. So, helplessly, Desu Singh was installed to head the Misal.

Desu Singh

Desu Singh, the new Sardar of the Bhangi Misal, appointed one Gujjar Singh as his minister with whose intercession he concluded peace with Kanaihyas and returned to Amritsar.[43] The fort of Pathankot remained in the hands of Tara Singh.[44] Since the Misal came in the hands of the stripping, much could not be expected from him immediately. Many Misaldars who had earlier been giving all the military assistance expected of them, became independent. He was however, repulsed by Diwan Singh the Governor of Multan.

Timur Shah, successor of Ahmad Shah, on the throne of Kabul, was determined to recover his lost territories in the Punjab. He sent his general. Faizullah Khan, to Peshawar to collect forces and attack the Punjab. He assembled a large force of the Afghans, particularly from the Khyber tribes with the avowed object of punishing the Sikhs but entered into a secret conspiracy with Mian Muhammad, son of Sheikh Omar of Chamkanni, a sworn enemy of Timur Shah, to kill the Shah. He marched his forces to the fort of Peshawar on the pretext of parading his troops before the Shah. But on reaching the fort they cut to pieces the Shah's guards at the gate and forced their entry into the fort. The Shah went to the upper storey of the palace and conveyed to his personal body-guards the seriousness of the situation. Shah's body-guards and the Durranis attacked Faizullah's men and there ensued terrible slaughter. Faizullah and his son were also tortured to death.[45]

Now, Timur Shah decided to take vigorous steps in regard to Sind, Bahawalpur and the lower Punjab. In 1777-78, he sent two detachments of the Afghan troops to drive out the Sikhs from Multan but with no success. The Afghans were beaten back with heavy loss and Haini Khan, the commander of the expedition, was tied to a gun and blown off by the Sikhs.[46] But in the end of 1779, the operations of the Shah against Multan were successful. The Shah's troops numbering 18,000, consisting of the Yusafzais, Durranis, Mughals and Kazalbashes, were under the command of Zangi Khan, the Durrani chief. The Sikhs were said to have suffered heavy casualties with 3,000, as killed in the battle-field and 2,000, drowned in the course of crossing the river. After the victory over Multan, it was placed under the governorship of Shujah Khan, father of Muzaffar Khan. The Shah subdued Bahawal Khan, the Abassi chief of Bahawalpur.[47]

The decline of the power started earlier, continued under Desu Singh. Some places got out of the control but he continued receiving revenue to the time of fifty thousand rupees annually from the Sials.[48]

Desu Singh was not on good terms with Mahan Singh of Sukharchakia Misal which was now becoming very powerful. There were occasional skirmishes between the troops of Desu Singh and Mahan Singh. The stars of the Sukarchakias were on the ascendant in those days. Desu Singh could not add any territories to his Misal, rather he lost Pindi Bhatian, Sahiwal Bhera, Isa Khel, Jhang and Takht Hazara to Mahan Singh Sukarchakia and a part of Kasur and some other areas passed into the hands of Nizam-ud-Din Khan of Kasur.[49]

In 1782, Desu Singh marched to reduce Chiniot and had many skirmishes with the Sukarchakia chief, Mahan Singh. He died in action in the same year. He held the chiefship of the Misal for eight years.[50]

Gulab Singh

Desu Singh was succeeded by his minor son. Gulab Singh, who looked after the affairs of the Misal with the help of his cousin, Karan Singh Dulu. Gulab Singh enlarged the city of Amritsar where he lived.[51] During the period of his minority Karam Singh worked as the administrator of Amritsar and on coming of age Gulab Singh dismissed him.[52] A little later, Gulab Singh conquered the Pathan colony of Kasur and Nizam-ud-Din Khan and Kutb-ud-Din joined the service of the conqueror. In 1794, the Afghan brothers recovered Kasur with the help of their countrymen. Gulab Singh, despite his repeated attempts, could not expel the Afghans. He was a weak man and did not possess influence and energy sufficient to keep together the possessions which his father had left for him. Year by year these territories diminished, till at last, the town of Amritsar and some villages including Kuhali, Majitha, Naushehra and Sarhali in the Majha alone remained in his hands.[53] Even the revenue accruing from the Sials got alienated.[54] He had only to live on the income from the city of Amritsar and a few villages.

Ranjit Singh occupied Lahore in July 1799. His successes were creating alarm in the minds of the Punjab chiefs. Gulab Singh called all his Misaldars and supporters to fight against Ranjit Singh. Consequently, an alliance or a cabal was formed with Jassa Singh Ramgarhia, Nizam-ud-Din of Kasur, Sahib Singh and Gulab Singh Bhangi as its members, the last being the leading man behind the whole plan.[55] In 1800, the allies collected their forces at the village of Bhasin, twelve *kos* east of Lahore. Ranjit Singh also advanced and encamped his forces opposite to his enemies. After a minor skirmish the contending armies stood apart waiting for a bigger clash. For some months the things lingered on and none could take initiative in attacking the other. In the meantime mutual jealousies developed in the camp of Gulab Singh. In the midst of confusion Gulab Singh died of excessive indulgence in drinking.[56]

The allies dispersed forthwith, without fighting against Ranjit Singh. It was indeed a great political and psychological victory for Ranjit Singh who now found himself clearly on road to monarchy in the Punjab. The constituent chiefs or the alliance, thus dispersed, could not meet again to challenge Ranjit Singh's power.

Gurdit Singh

After the death of Gulab Singh his ten-year old son, Gurdit Singh, succeeded him. The Misal was on its downward march and the new ruler was in a helpless condition. Gurdit Singh was married to the daughters of Sahib Bhangi and Fateh Singh Kanaihya.[57]

The gun, called *zamzama*, had been taken away by Chahat Singh Sukarchakia from Lehna Singh Bhangi. For some time it remained lying at Ramnagar. When Jhanda Singh Bhangi came back from Multan he removed the gun to his place. Since then the gun remained in the possession of the Bhangis.[58]

At this time, Maharaja Ranjit Singh demanded the famous *zamzama* gun from Gurdit Singh whose mother Sukhan flatly refused to part with it as its possession had assured glory and prestige to the Misal.[59] *Mai* Sukhan got prepared to fight against Ranjit Singh. Jodh Singh Ramgarhia sent a secret reinforcemess to Sukhan to the tune of three hundred soldiers. At the same time he advised her that either she should hand over the *zamzama* gun to the Sukarchakia chief and purchase peace or destroy the gun, *Mai* Sukhan did not accept either of the suggestions and decided to face Ranjit Singh. The Lahore chief, accompanied by his mother-in-law, Sada Kaur, and Fateh Singh Ahluwalia marched upon Amritsar and besieged the town.[60] When the opposing forces were at the point of coming to a severe clash Jodh Singh Ramgarhia and Akali Phula Singh came in between them. *Mai* Sukhan surrendered without much opposition.[61] On the advice of the Ramgarhia chief and the Akali leader the fort and the city of Amritsar were evacuated by *Mai* Sukhan on 14 Phagun, 1861 KB (February 24, 1805).[62] *Mai* Sukhan and her son remained under the protection of the Ramgarhia chief for some time. Then, on the recommendation of the Ramgarhia chief *Mai* Sukhan and her son Gurdit Singh were granted Panjore and five or six villages in *jagir* for their subsistence.[63]

The *top-i-Bhangian* was taken by Ranjit Singh to Lahore and is still lying there. It was manufactured in 1761, by Shah Nazir, a famours mechanic, for Ahmad Shah Abdali. It was composed of brass and copper. Ahmad Shah had left it in the possession of Ubaid Khan, governor of Lahore. In 1762, when Hari Singh Bhangi and the other Sardars plundered the arsenal of the governor of Lahore, they also took away the gun. Ranjit Singh used in the battles of Daska. Kasur, Sujanpur, Waxirabad and Multan.

Gurdit Singh died at his ancestral village of Panjwar in the Tarn Taran *Pargana* of Amritsar district where his descendants, later, lived as simple peasants.

Besides the main House of the Bhangi Misal, there were some Misaldars also who had risen to prominent positions. As mentioned earlier the Sardars of the Misal bestowed a number of villages on their comrades-in-arms who had assisted them in carving out their Misals. These Misaldars, sometimes, by sheer dint of their arms, became as strong in their respective areas as the Sardars of the Misals themselves. The Bhangi Sardars had as their powerful associates in the persons of Lehna Singh Gujjar Singh and Sahib Singh who always stood by them. These men are also known to history as Bhangis.

Lehna Singh

Lehna Singh's grandfather was a *zamindar* of minor consequence. He, in the time of scarcity, left his native village of Sadhawala in the Amritsar district for Mastapur near Kartarpur in the Jalandhar Doab.[64] He belonged to the Kahlon sub-caste of the Jats.[65] Lehna Singh, the son of Dargaha, was a high-spirited youngman. Once he was beaten by his father for allowing cattle to stray into the green fields. He ran away from home and, after wandering for some time, reached the village of Roranwala, one mile from Attari, where a Bhangi Misaldar Gurbakhsh Singh lived.[66] This man was one of the best warriors under Hari Singh Bhangi. He owned about forty villages and helped Hari Singh to maintain law and order in his territory with a band of his horsemen. Gurbakhsh Singh took a fancy to young Lehna Singh and enlisted him among his horsemen and later, having no male issue of his own, adopted him.[67] Gurbakhsh Singh died in 1763, and dissensions arose between Lehna Singh, the adopted son, and Gujjar Singh, the son of Gurbakhsh Singh's brother,[68] each claiming the property.[69]

Jhanda Singh and Ganda Singh came to Vanyeki to settle their dispute but Gujjar Singh was not prepared to listen to the terms of settlement and set out with his followers for Roranwala. Lehna Singh pursued and came up with him. There was a fight between the followers of the two which resulted in the death of a few men on either side. At last the estate was divided by Lehna Singh and Gujjar Singh. The former kept Roranwala and the latter founded a new village between Bharwal and Ranni, which he called Ranghar, in remembrance of his fight with Lehna Singh, with whom he now became the fast friend.[70]

When Ahmad Shah Abdlai left India he appointed a Hindu, named Kabuli Mal, as the governor of Lahore.[71] The governor was a timid and, at the same time, a tyrannical man. Lehna Singh and Gujjar Singh formed a design to expel Ahmad Shah's representative from Lahore and capture the city for themselves. When Kabul Mal obtained secret intelligence of the Bhangi plot he fled from Lahore, leaving it in charge of his nephew (sister's son), Amir Singh (or Amar Singh), Kabul Mal plundered the city before leaving it. He took road to Jammu and on the way he was roughly handled by some of the persons who had left Lahore because of his tyranny. He would probably have been killed, had not some troops, sent by Raja Ranjit Deo as his escort, saved him.[72] the Raja sent him to Rawalpindi where Ahmad Shah's rearguard had halted and there he died shortly afterwards.

Lehua Singh and Gujjar Singh collected their men and decided to surprise Lahore. Bhaia Nand Ram Purbia, who was the *thanedar* of Lahore fort and who had been hostile to Kabul Mal, secretly joined with the Bhangi chiefs. He sent a message to the Sikh Sardars through Dyal Singh that entry into the city by the gates was doubtful and they were asked to enter at night by causing a breach in the wall at a specific point. The Bhangi chiefs agreed and they did likewise[73] and before morning the whole city was in their possession. The occupation of Lahore took place on April 16, 1765. Amir Singh, the deputy governor, was captured and put in irons. Early next day Sobha Singh Kanaihya nephew (brother's son) of Jai Singh Kanaihya arrived.[74] He had been, since the last Afghan invasion staying at his native village Kanah. Though he was late to participate in capturing the city, he was allowed to share the prize. Then came the other chiefs of the bhangis, Kanaihyas, Sukarchakias, etc. But Charhat Singh Sukarchakia would not go away without having got the *zamzama* gun from the Bhangis, which he carried to Gujranwala, the three chiefs then divided Lahore amongst them.[75] Lehna Singh took the fort with the Masti, Khizri, Kashmiri and Roshani gates. Gujjar Singh built for himself a fort without the walls, which he called Qila Gujjar Singh.[76] On the request of a deputation of grandees of the town, the Sardars issued a proclamation that persons who oppressed the people would be severely dealt with. The plundering of the town was stopped forthwith. They took to administering it whole-heartedly.[77]

Lehna Singh and Sobha Singh remained in Lahore in peace till Ahmad shah Abdali made his final descent upon the Punjab in December 1766, when they retired from Lahore.[78] But the Afghan ruler feeling the infirmity and old age creeping opin him and having no such general as should successfully deal with the Sikh chiefs, decided to conciliate them. A deputation of the prominent persons of Lahore, them, upon Ahmad Shah Abdali and told him that Lehna Singh was good ruler and was sympathetic towards his subjects. He made no distinction between Hindus and Muslims. He bestowed turbans on the *qazis, muftis* and *imams* of the mosques in the festival of *id' ul-zuha*.[79] The Muslims of Lahore had no fear of the Khalsa, said the deputationists, and they had started looking upon them as their comrades rather than hostile enemies. This happy circumstance, said they, had made the Muslim leaders of Lahore recommend to Ahmad shah the appointment of Sardar Lehna Singh, as their governor, in preference to a Muslim nominee of his. Ahmad Shah wrote to Lehna Singh offering him the governorship of Lahore and sent him some dry fruit of Kabul. Lehna Singh declined the offer saying that to accept an offer from an invader was against the policy of his community and returned the fruit saying that it was not his food as he lived on parched grams.[80]

Ahmad Shah speedily returned to his country leaving the whole of the territory of the Punjab in the hands of the Sikhs. After Ahmad Shah's departure Gujjar Singh, Lehna Singh and Sobha Singh marched towards Lahore.[81] The nobles of Dadan Khan, the new governor of Lahore, told him plainly that the people were satisfied with the Sikh rule and they might open the city gates and admit the Sikh chiefs into the town. Dadan Khan, therefore, on the advice of his friends, met the Sikh Sardars who treated him with respect and consideration and granted him a daily allowance of twenty rupees and occupied Lahore.[82]

For the next thirty years the Bhangi and Kanaihya Sardars remained in possession of Lahore till 1797, when Shah Zaman, who had succeeded to the throne of Kabul, invaded the Punjab and Lehna Singh again retired from Lahore. On account of the goodness of his heart, the people of the town invited Lehna Singh to _____ shoulder the administration of the place after the departure of the Shah. He came and died the same year[83] Sobha Singh also died the same year and was succeeded by his son, Mohar Singh, while Chet Singh succeeded to Lehna Singh.

Gujjar Singh

Much has been said about Gujjar Singh in the account of Lehna Singh. He was more successful and much more powerful than Lehna Singh or Sobha Singh. Independent of his above said comrades he first occupied Gujarat which was then held by Sultan Mukarrab, a Ghakhar chief. According to Ganesh Das Badehra, Mukarrab was besieged in the town of Gujarat. The fighting raged for a few days. Finding himself insecure in the fortress he came out and recruited a number of citizens of Gujarat in his force. He, then tried to escape to some safe place and planned to flee towards Pothohar. He had hardly covered a distance of half a *kos* from the town when he was surrounded by the Khalsa army. Sultan Mukarrab, riding an elephant, tried to cross a rivulet adjacent to the village of Gheduwal. When the elephant crossed over to the other side it was without its rider. Nothing was later heard about the Sultan[84] and in all probability he was washed away. It is said that the town of Gujarat was given to plunder and its inhabitants went away to different places as Jalalpur Shadipur, Akhnur, etc. A few days later Gujjar Singh reached Gujarat and repopulated the town and since then he firmly established himself there. Charhat Singh Sukarchakia got the fort of Kunjah and the areas upto Miani. The town of Kunjah was given to Sardar Mal Singh and the areas of Kalra and Kuthala were assigned to Sardar Himmat Singh and similarly other Sikh leaders occupied some other territories there.[85] Gujjar Singh made Gujarat his capital and next year, *i.e.*, in 1766, he marched to Jammu, which he overran and held tributary with Jhanda Singh Bhangi and then successfully reduced Punchh, Islamgarh, and Deva Batala.[86] In 1767, Ahmad Shah made his last invasion of India. Gujjar Singh was obliged to leave Gujarat. He went to Lahore and thence as Ahmad Shah advanced to Firozepur, and on the Durrani chief's finally turning his back on the Punjab, he received back his part of the city of Lahore. According to Ganesh Das Badehra, during this invasion Ahmad Shah had occupied areas up to the villages of Daudpur, Patala, Sohian and the areas of Kunjah. Because of their incapacity to content with the heavy horders of Ahmed Shah the Sikhs desisted from confrontation. When Gujjar Singh and Charhat Singh were in the Majha area, Nawab Sarbuland Khan, a relative of Ahmad Shah, occupied Rohtas and launched upon a career of conquest. He took possession of Gujarat. Rehmat Khan Waraich, Chaudhari of the *pargana* of Herat, and the *qanungos* of Gujarat went to Rohtas obviously to make an appeal to Sarbuland Khan to restore Gujarat and the adjoining areas to their Sikh masters. They were imprisoned and Chaudhari Rehmat Khan and Diwan Shiv Nath were done to death on the allegation that it was due to them that the Sikhs had occupied Gujarat.

In the meantime Charhat Singh and Gujjar Singh took a firm resolve that unless the Nawab of Rohtas was not driven out of his possessions they would not be able to set-up their principalities. In order to cement his relations with Gujjar Singh. Charhat Singh engaged his daughter with Gujjar Singh's son, Sahib Singh. Having thus concluded a matrimonial alliance, the two Sardars recrossed river Chenab with a view to fighting against the Nawab of Rohtas. The Nawab's forces, after some initial skirmishes with the Sikhs and defeat at their hands, took asylum in the fort of Rohtas. The Khalsa army besieged the fort and the inmates, including the Nawab, were made prisoners after about four months time. The fort of Rohtas was captured in 1770. The territories of Rohtas, Dhah Baloki, Ghebb and Mukhad fell to the lot of Charhat Singh and the *talluqas* of Wangal, Bharwal, Pindi Rawal and Khanpur, up to the boundary of river Attock, were annexed by Gujjar Singh. But Gujjar Singh gave Rawalpindi to Milkha Singh as a *jagir* and *tapa* of Narli and the fortress of Rutala were conferred upon his brother Chet Singh. Ran Singh Pidah was appointed *tapadar* in Sarai Kala and Jodh Singh Attariwala was made the *thanedar* of (the fort of) Kalar and a *tehsildar* or collector of Pothohar.[87]

For the defence of the holy city of Amritsar Gujjar Singh laid the foundation of Qila Gujjar Singh, Charhat Singh Sukarchakia also built a fort to the north of the Durbar Sahib, while that of Jassa Singh Ramgarhia lay to the east and that of the Bhangis to the south. Gujjar Singh married his eldest son, Sukha Singh to the daughter of Bhag Singh Hallowalia. He married his second son, Sahib Singh, to a daughter of Charhat Singh.

Gujjar Singh divided his territories between his two elder sons, Sukha Singh and Sahib Singh and the youngest son, Fateh Singh, was left out. Sukha Singh and Sahib Singh quarrelled and fought[88] and the younger (Sahib Singh), at the instigation of Mahan Singh Sukarchakia, attacked his elder brother who was killed in the action. Gujjar Singh was much enraged when he heard of the death of his eldest son. He decided to dispossess Sahib Singh of all the territories under his charge. Sahib Singh openly revolted against his father and shut himself upon Islamgarh. But Gujjar Singh did not wish to proceed to extremities and forgave his son the moment he showed a disposition to sue for pardon. Sahib Singh was confirmed in his old possessions and Gujjar Singh made over those which had been held by Sukha Singh to his younger brother Fateh Singh.[89] Another cause of displeasure between Gujjar Singh and his son, Sahib Singh, cropped up. Mahan Singh Sukarchakia was besieging Rasul nagar, the capital of his enemies, the Chathas. A principal officer of the Chathas, escaping from the town, took shelter in Gujjar Singh's camp. Mahan Singh asked for his surrender which was refused. In order to oblige his brother-in-law, Sahib Singh handed over the demanded person to the Sukarchakia chief. Gujjar Singh felt very much annoyed with Sahib Singh's conduct. It so deeply preyed upon his mind that he fell ill. He retired to Lahore where he died in 1788.[90] His tomb is situated near the Samman Burj. He ruled his territory for twenty four years.[91]

Sahib Singh

Despite the utter displeasure of his father, Sahib Singh took possession of the family estates without active opposition form his younger brother, Fateh Singh, who went to Gujranwala to live with Mahan Singh. For some time there was peace between the brothers-in-law, Mahan Singh and Sahib Singh. Shortly thereafter, Mahan Singh demanded *haq-i-hakmana* or succession money or tribute from Sahib Singh who refused to give any. The famous maxim that "kingship knows no kinship" so aptly applied to the situation. To promote the interests of ones principality even close-blood relationship was disregarded. Sahib Singh was the husband of Mahan Singh's real sister. In 1789, they quarrelled and remained in constant hostility for some time. At last in 1790, Mahan Singh besieged Sahib Singh in the fort of Sodhra and reduced him to great straits.[92] Sahib Singh sought the help of Lehna Singh of Lahore and Karam Singh Dulu. Lehna Singh did not move but Karam Singh came with a large force. There was some fighting but the Sukarchakia chief was not keeping good health at this time. When Mahan Singh put Sahib Singh in a tight corner at Sodha the former's sister (Raj Kaur), who was the latter's wife, came to see her brother and sue for peace. The meeting could not take place as due to ill-health Mahan Singh had fainted on the elephant outside Sodhra and the *mahabat* had turned back and carried his master to Gujranwala where he died three days later on the 5th Baisakh, 1847 BK., April 15, 1790.[93] He had deeply taken to mind the desertion of his old friend, Jodh Singh Wazirabadia.

In 1797, Shah Zaman invaded the Punjab and Sahib Singh was obliged to retire to the hills. The Shah remained only a few day in the Punjab and then returned to Afghanistan. According to Bute Shah the Shah left behind him an officer, named Ahmad Khan Shahanchi, with 8,000 Afghan troops. The Shahanchi forcibly took a Brahman woman to his *harem*. There was wide resentment against him. Sahib Singh came back to Gujarat and marched against the Shahanchi. Sahib Singh in collaboration with Nihal Singh and Wazir Singh Attariwala, Jodh Singh Wazirabadia and Karam Singh Dulu completely defeated the Afghan forces killing the Shahanchi. The Sikhs plundered the Afghan camp and Sahib Singh gathered huge booty.[94]

Since Sahib Singh was very humble and docile by disposition the Sikhs addressed him as if he were an effeminate character. But as he emerged victorious against the Afghans twice he began to be treated as a manly and masculine character.[95]

Zaman Shah, the ruler of Kabuul, again marched to the Punjab in the beginning of the winter of 1798, and reached Lahore on November 27. The chiefs of Lahore lefts the town before the Shah entered it. Every night Ranjit Singh visited, with a few *sawars*, the suburbs of the city of Lahore and attacked the forces of the Shah at night with a view to harassing him.[96] According to Sohan Lal Suri,[97] Ranjit Singh, at this time thrice rushed upon the Samman Burj of the Lahore fort with a few men, fired a number of shots, killed and wounded a number of Afghans, and on one occasion challenged the Shah himself to a hand to hand fight. "Come out you, o grandson of Ahmad Shah", shouted Ranjit Singh to him, "and try two or three hands with the grandson of the great Sardar Charhat Singh." But as there was no response from the other side Ranjit Singh had to retire without a trial of strength with the Durrani. At this time the Shah was receiving disquieting news from Qandhar and Herat. Under the circumstances he thought it proper to retire from the Punjab.

According to Ali-ud-Din Mufti, Zaman Shah left for Kabul after a month's stay a Lahore as Mahmud Shah, in collaboration with Baba Qachar, had attacked Kabul. Diplomatically enough, Ranjit Singh did not harass Zaman Shah on his return march rather facilitated his return so that he might not get annoyed with him and think of hitting back at him at the earliest opportunity. Since the Shah had to go back hurriedly 12 of his guns sank in river Jhelum, that was in spate because of rainy season. On the Shah's request Ranjit Singh extricated all the 12 guns from the river. He despatched 8 of them to Kabul and retained the four with him in his arsenal, one of which was of iron and three of brass.[98]

Bhangis Lose Lahore

Twenty six days after Zaman Shah's exit from Lahore on January 4, 1799, the Bhangi Sardars re-entered it. The three rulers of Lahore were not functioning in collaboration with one another. There mutual dissensions adversely affected the law and order situation in the city. The people were feeling insecure and unhappy about the condition created by their rulers. Finding the situation in Lahore fluid, Nawab Nizam-ud-Din of Kasur started toying with the idea of possessing it. But in view of Ranjit Singh's growing power the Nawab of Kasur was obliged to drop the idea of occupying Lahore. According to Ali-ud-Din Mufti some of the Arains of Lahore were imprisoned and deprived of their belongings by its rulers. They invited Nizam-ud-Din Khan to deliver them of the bondage. The Nawab got ready for Lahore but he shortly realised that it would not be possible for him to keep Lahore in his hands for long. So he did not dare to come.[99] According to Munshi Sohan Lal Suri, the people of Lahore were suffering hardship under the misrule of their chiefs.[100] The respectable people of Lahore including the Hindus, Muslims and Sikhs met secretly and decided to address an invitation to Ranjit Singh to come to Lahore and arrange its occupation. Ranjit Singh accepted the invitation.[101] The letter of invitation sent to him was signed by Muhammad Ashaq, Gurbakhsh Singh, Hakim Rai, Mufti Muhammad Mukarram, Muhammad Bakkar, Mir Shadi and Mehr Mohkam Din. It was sent through Hakim Rai.[102]

Ranjit Singh started from Rasulnagar, reached Batala and discussed the matter of occupation of Lahore with his mother-in-law, Rani Sada Kaur.[103] She accompanied him to Lahore. They had, at their command, an army of about twenty-five thousand horsemen and foot-soldiers. The people of Lahore had earlier promised Ranjit Singh to open the Lohari Gate at his arrival there. On the day Ranjit Singh reached Lahore, Lohari Gate could not be opened as it was strongly defended by Chet Singh, Ranjit Singh repaired to Wazir Khan's garden and Anarkali's mausoleum in the south of Lahore.[104] He was told by the people who had invited him that he should come to Lohari early next morning.

The rulers of Lahore were not aware of the intentions or plans of Ranjit Singh. Sweets were sent to Ranjit Singh by Mohar Singh—one of the chiefs of Lahore.[105] In order to put them off their guard Ranjit Singh went to river Ravi in the evening and made arrangements for the boats to be available to him next morning.[106] He just wanted to give an impression that he was on his way to Gujranwala. Next morning, that is, on July 6, 1799,[107] he led his men to Lohari Gate which was opened unto him. He entered the city triumphantly. First, the victors repaired for the *haveli* of Lakhpat Rai where Sardar Mohar Singh son of Sardar Sobha Singh Kanaihya, was residing.[108] Mohar Singh fled from the *haveli* and concealed himself in the house of a hay-seller.[109] Ranjit Singh entered the Badhashi Masjid adjoining the fort. His army started plundering the city but as soon as he came to know of it he announced with the beat of drum that complete peace should be restored in the town and people's fears from his side should be put to rest and all the plunderers and robbers should keep their hands off the town.[110]

Mohar Singh was captured and produced before Ranjit Singh. He allowed him to proceed to his *jagirs* along with his goods.[111] Chet Singh Bhangi, who was in possession of the fort of Lahore, continued exchanging fire from within the fort with Ranjit Singh's men. On Sada Kaur's suggestion negotiations were conducted and Chet Singh was asked to vacate the fort. He was offered to be treated kindly and permitted to take all his movable property with him to his *Jagir* at Vanyeki (in the *pargana* of Ajanala) where he could live in peace and comfort.[112] Chet Singh accepted the offer and evacuate the fort next morning, that is, on July 7, 1799 (29th of the month of Har, Samat 1856), and Ranjit Singh occupied the fort the same day.[113] Chet Singh held the annual *jagir* of 60,000 rupees in Vankeki till his death in 1815. He left no son by any of his eight wives, but four months after his death Hukam Kaur gave birth to a son, named Attar Singh. In favour of whom Ranjit Singh released an estate of 6,000 rupees at Vanyeki and the same was, afterwards, much reduced.[114]

Sahib Singh Bhangi was not in the town at the time of Ranjit Singh's attack and occupation of Lahore. None of the contemporary or semi-contemporary writers including Khushwaqat Rai, Bute Shah, Amar Nath, Sohan Lal Suri, Ali-ud-Din Mufti and Ganesh Das Badehra had made a mention of him. In Ranjit Singh's career the capture of Lahore was of the greatest significance and this possession made him the most powerful chieftain in northern India. Lahore had always been a provincial capital and it gave Ranjit Singh an edge over the other chiefs in the Punjab and enhanced his political prestige considerably at the cost of the Bhangis.

Sahib Singh's brother, Fateh Singh Bhangi, joined Ranjit Singh and the latter got from the former the possession of Fatehgarh and Sodhra. When Sahib Singh heard of the fall of Lahore, he moved with a large force against Ranjit Singh. The Ramgarhias and the Kasur troops marched from the east and the south to Bhasin but nothing came out of that assemblage of forces. Fateh Singh became reconciled to his brother Sahib Singh but this friendship did not last long. Fateh Singh favoured Raj Kaur, wife of Sahib Singh, who disgusted at her husband's third marriage, held the of Jalapur against him. Fateh Singh went back to Ranjit Singh who would not do any thing for him as he had left the Maharaja in the middle of a campaign. Fateh Singh remained at Lahore in poverty for an year and then he was compelled to return to his brother at Gujarat who gave him Daulatnagar and other estates.[115]

In the later part of his life Fateh Singh was given to excessive drinking which sapped his energy. He quarrelled with Nihal Singh Attariwala and his Diwan, Mohkam Chand, afterwards so celebrated a courtier of Ranjit Singh.

Bhangi Sardar Sahib Singh Gujarati and Dal Singh of Akalgarh started their preparations for an invasion of Lahore. Ranjit Singh got enraged and, accompanied by Sada Kaur, led ten thousand soldiers to Gujarat, in 1801. The Bhangis started firing from within the fort. Ranjit Singh had also carried 20 guns with him to Gujarat. Bhangis, finding themselves no match for Ranjit Singh, sued for peace through Baba Sahib Singh Bedi, and fighting was stopped.[116]

Although Sahib Singh accepted the overlordship of Ranjit Singh, he exercised great influence in his territories which had strong forts at Jalalpur, Manawar and Aslamgarh.[117] He had a lot of wealth and war material also. About 1809, he developed strained relations with his son, Gulab Singh,[118] who occupied a couple of forts against the wished of his father. Ranjit Singh availed himself of this opportunity and, in the course of two or three months, he occupied the whole of Gujarat including the towns of Gujarat, Aslamgarh, Jalalpur, Manawar, Bajwat and Sodhra.[119] Sahib Singh escaped to the hilly areas,[120] and took refuge in Deva Batala.[121] In 1810, when Ranjit Singh was engaged in the siege of Multan, *Mai* Lachmi, mother of Sahib Singh, proceeded thither and interceded for her son with such effect that the *ilaqa* of Bajwat, with an annual income of one lakh rupees, was released in his favour.[122] This *jagir* was held by him till his death which took place in 1814. His mausoleum was built at Rajwat.[123] Sahib Singh ruled Gujarat for a period of twenty two-years.[124] Ranjit Singh took two of Sahib Singh's widows, Daya Kaur and Rattan Kaur, into his *harem*, marrying them by the ceremony of *chadar pauna*. Daya Kaur was the mother of Prince Peshaura Singh and Kashmira Singh and Rattan Kaur was the mother of Multana Singh.[125] Faqir Aziz-ud-Din was appointed to look after the administration of Gujarat[126] and he was succeeded by Faqir Nur-ud-Din.

Fateh Singh Gujratia, after the death of his brother, went to Kapurthala where he remained in the service of the Ahluwalia chief[127] for two years till, on the death of his mother Mai Lachmi, he received a grant of Rangher and some other villages in the Amritsar district. He entered the service of Sham Singh Attariwala, in whose contingent he served for many years. He was killed in Bannu in 1832, during the siege of the fort of Malik Dilasah Khan. About the same time Sahib Singh's son, Gulab Singh, also died and his *jagirs* were resumed.[128] Fateh Singh's son, Jaimal Singh, was, for some time, in Sham Singh Attariwala's force and served on the frontier and at Peshawar. Through his enmity with Sham Singh he lost his *jagir*. When the British occupied the Punjab Jaimal Singh, was in great poverty. This representative of the great Bhangi house, which possessed more power and ruled over a larger territory than any other family between the Satluj and the Indus, lived without pension or estate.[129]

REFERENCES

1. Ahmad Shah Batalia, Appendix to Sohan Lal Suri's *Umdat-ut-Tawarikh*, Daftar I, Lahore, 1885, p. 15; Bute Shah's *Tawarikh-i-Punjab*, Daftar IV, (1848), (MS, Ganda Singh's personal collection, Patiala), p. 6; Kanaihya Lal, *Tarikhi-i-Punjab*, Lahore, 1877, p. 88; Ali-ud-Din Mufti, *Ibratnama*, Vol. I, (1854), Lahore, 1961, p. 244. Muhammad Latif *History of the Punjab* (1891), Delhi, 1964, p. 296.
2. Ahmad Shah Batalia, *op. cit.*, p. 15; Bute Shah, *op. cit.*, p. 6.
3. Kanaihya Lal, *op. cit.*, p. 89.
4. Ahmad Shah Batalia, *op. cit.*, p. 15; Bute Shah, *op. cit.*, p. 6; Kanaihya Lal, *op. cit.*, p. 89; Ali-ud-Din Mufti, *op. cit.*, pp. 244-45; Muhammad Latif, *op. cit.*, p. 298.
5. *Ibid.*
6. Ali-ud-Din Mufti, *op. cit.*, p. 245; Kanaihya Lal, *op. cit.*, p. 89.
7. Rattan Singh Bhangu, *prachin Panth Parkash* (1841), Amritsar, 1939, p. 199; Kanaihya Lal, *op. cit.*, p. 89.
8. Ahmad Shah Batalia, *op. cit.*, p. 15; Bute Shah, *op. cit.*, p. 6.
9. Ahmad Shah Batalia, *op. cit.*, p. 15; Muhammad Latif, *op. cit.*, Calcutta, 1891, p. 296.
10. Lepel Griffin, *The Punjab Chiefs*, Lahore, 1865, pp. 385-86.
11. *Ibid.*, p. 385.
12. Muhammad Latif, *op. cit.*, p. 296.
13. Ahmad Shah Batalia, *op. cit.*, p. 15; Bute Shah, *op. cit.*, p. 6.
14. *Ibid.*
15. *Ibid.*
16. Bute Shah, *op. cit.*, p. 10.
17 *Ibid.*
18. Lepel Griffin, *op. cit.*, p. 386; Muhammad Latif, *op. cit.*, pp., 296-97; cf., Ahmad Shah Batalia, *op. cit.*, p. 15; Bute Shah, *op. cit.*, pp. 7, 10; Ali-ud-Din Mufti, *op. cit.*, I, p. 246.
19. Bute Shah, *op. cit.*, p. 10.
20. *Ibid.*
21. Muhammad Latif, *op. cit.*, (ed. 1964), pp. 296-97; Gian Singh, *Tawarikh Guru Khalsa*, Part II, reprint, Patiala, 1970, p. 227.
22. According to Bute Shah, Jhanda Singh was one the illustrious followers of Hari Singh Bhangi. He was a Dhillion Jat of Majitha village. (*Tawarikh-i-Punjab*, IV, p. 10.)

23. Ahmad Shah Batalia, *op. cit.*, p. 16; Bute Shah, *op. cit.*, p. 7; Cunningham, *A History of the Sikhs* (1849), Delhi, 1955, p. 103.
24. Bute Shah, *op. cit.*, pp. 10-11; Lepel Griffin, *op. cit.*, p. 386; Muhammad Latif, *op. cit.*, p. 285; Gian Singh, *op. cit.*, p. 386; Muhammad Latif, *op. cit.*, p. 285; Gian Singh, *op. cit.*, part II, p. 228.
25. Bute Shah, *op. cit.*, p. 11.
26. Ahmed Shah Batalia, *op. cit.*, pp. 15-16; Bute Shah, *op. cit.*, p. 7; cf., *Haqiqat-i-bina-o-uruj-i-firqa-i-Sikhan*, MS., PUP., p. 31; M'Gregor, *The History of the Sikhs*, I (1846), Allahabad reprint, 1979, p. 122.
27. Lepel Griffin, *op. cit.*, p. 386.
28. *Ibid.*
29. *Ibid.*, p. 387.
30. *Ibid. op. cit.*, p. 387.
31. Ahmad Shah Batalia, *op. cit.*, p. 16; *Haqiqat-i-bina-o-uruj-i-firqa-i-Sikhan*, MS., PUP., p. 21; Bute Shah, *op. cit.*, pp. 7, 11; Ganesh Das Badehra, *Char Bagh-i-Punjab* (1855), Amritsar, 1965, p. 132; Ali-ud-Din Mufti, *op. cit.*, Vol. I, p. 248; M'Gregor, *op. cit.*, I. pp. 122-23; Lepel Griffin, *op. cit.*, p. 387, Muhammad Latif, *op. cit.*, ed. 1916, p. 86.
32. Muhammad Latif, *op. cit.*, p. 86.
33. Lepel Griffin, *op. cit.*, p. 387.
34. Ali-ud-Din Mufti, *op. cit.*, Vol, p. 246; Lepel Griffin, *op. cit.*, p. 387.
35. *Ibid.*
36. Ali-ud-Din Mufti, *op. cit.*, Vol. I, p. 247; cf., Ahmad Shah Batalia, *op. cit.*, p. 16; M'Gregor, *op. cit.*, I, p. 123.
37. Gian Singh, *op. cit.*, part II, p. 228.
38. Bute Shah, incorrectly believes that Jhanda Singh ruler for fifteen years (*op. cit.*, p. 14).
39. Ahmad Shah Batalia, *op. cit.*, p. 16; M'Gregor, *op. cit.*, I, p. 123.
40. Ahmad Shah Batalia, *op. cit.*, p. 16; cf., Bute Shah, *op. cit.*, IV, pp. 14, 40; cf., Ali-ud-Din Mufti, *op. cit.*, Vol. I, p. 250; M'Gregor, *op. cit.*, I, pp. 123-24; Lepel Griffin, *op. cit.*, p. 338-39.
41. Bute Shah wrongly writes that Ganda Singh ruled for ten years, *op. cit.*, IV, p. 14.

42. Bute Shah, *op. cit.*, IV, p. 14; Ahmad Shah Batalia, *op. cit.*, p. 16; M'Gregor, *op. cit.*, I, p. 124; Bute Shah writers that Desu Singh was Ganda Singh's son and Charhat Singh was his nephew (Bute Shah, *op. cit.*, p. 10).
43. Ahmad Shah Batalia, Appendix, *op. cit.*, p. 16.
44. *Ibid.*
45. *Tarikh-i-Ahmadi*, p. 19, cited by S. M. Latif, *History of the Punjab*, (1891), p. 299.
46. Muhammad Latif, *op. cit.*, p. 299.
47. *Ibid.*
48. Bute Shah, *op. cit.*, IV, p. 15.
49. Ali-ud-Din Mufti, *op. cit.*, Vol. I. p. 251.
50. Bute Shah, *op. cit.*, p. 15; Lepel Griffin, *op. cit.*, p. 389.
51. Ahmad Shah Batalia, Appendix, *op. cit.*, p. 16.
52. *Ibid.*
53. Bute Shah, *op. cit.*, p. 15; Gian Singh, *op. cit.*, p. 231.
54. *Ibid.*, Lepel Griffin, *op. cit.*, p. 390; Gian Singh, *op. cit.*, p. 231.
55. Ahmad Shah Batalia, *op. cit.*, p. 16; Bute Shah, *op. cit.*, p. 16.
56. Khushwaqat Rai, *Tawarikhi-i-Sikhan* (1811), (Ms., Dr Ganda Singh private collection, Patiala), pp. 82a-b; Bute Shah; *op. cit.*, IV, p. 16; Ganesh Das Badehra, *op. cit.*, p. 142; Lepel Griffin, *op. cit.*, p. 390. According to Ahmad Shah Batalia, Gulab Singh fell ill at Bhasin. He came back to Amritsar where he passed away (*op. cit.*, pp. 16-17); cf., Ali-ud-Din Mufti, *op. cit.*, Vol. I, p. 404.
57. Bute Shah, *op. cit.*, IV, p. 16; Lepel Griffin, *op. cit.*, p. 390.
58. Bute Shah, *op. cit.*, IV, p. 16.
59. *Ibid.* Lepel Griffin, *op. cit.*, p. 390.
60. Bute Shah, *op. cit.*, IV, pp. 16-17.
61. Ali-ud-Din Mufti, *op. cit.*, I, p. 404; Ganesh Das Badehra, *op. cit.*, p. 146; Khushwaqat Rai, *op. cit.*, f. 142.
62. Sohal Lal Suri, *op. cit.*, II, pp. 56-57. The date of occupation of Amritsar by Ranjit Singh has been given differently by different authors. According to Ali-ud-Din-Mufti, (*op. cit.*, Vol. I, p. 404) and Ganesh Das Badehra (*op. cit.*, p. 146), Ranjit Singh conquered Amritsar in 1803, and according to Amar Nath, the occupation of Amritsar took place in 1802 [(*Zafarnama-i-Ranjit Singh*, (1836), Lahore, 1928, p. 27)]. Though these three writers had the

privilege of being Ranjit Singh's contemporaries their dates of the occupation of Amritsar do not seem to be correct. In this regard Sohan Lal Suri is accepted to be correct.

63. Sohhan Lal Suri, *op. cit.*, II, p. 57; Muhammad Latif, *op. cit.*, p. 359.
64. Bute Shah, *op. cit.*, p. 17; cf., Ali-ud-Din Mufti, *op. cit.*, I, p. 207.
65. Lepel Griffin, *op. cit.*, p. 391; cf., Bute Shah, *op. cit.*, p. 17.
66. Bute Shah, *op. cit.*, p. 17.
67. *Ibid.*
68. Ahmad Shah Batalia, *op. cit.*, p. 85; Bute Shah, *op. cit.*, p. 19; Lepel Griffin and Muhammad Latif write Gujjar Singh to be the son of Gurbakhsh Singh's daughter.
69. Lepl Griffin, *op. cit.*, p. 391.
70. *Ibid.*, Bute Shah, *op. cit.*, p. 18.
71. Bute Shah, *op. cit.*, p. 18; Ali-ud-Din Mufti, *op. cit.*, Vol. I, p. 255; Sohan Lal Suri, *op. cit.*, I, p. 165; Ahmad Shah Batalia, *op. cit.*, p. 15. Muhammad Latif, *op. cit.*, p. 300.
72. Sohan Lal Suri, *op. cit.*, I, p. 164; Mohammad Latif, *op. cit.*, p. 300.
73. Ali-ud-Din Mufti, *op. cit.*, p. 255; Bute Shah, *op. cit.*, p. 18.
74. *Ibid.* pp. 237-38; Gian Singh, *op. cit.*, p. 217.
75. Bute Shah, *op. cit.*, p. 18; Muhammad Latif, *op. cit.*, p. 300.
76. Lepel Griffin *op. cit.*, p. 392.
77. Ali-ud-Din Mufti, *op. cit.*, p. 239; Sohan Lal Suri, *op. cit.*, pp. 163-64; Mian Ahmed Yar Maulvi, *Shahnama-i-Ranjit Singh* (ed. Ganda Singh), Amritsar, 1951, p. 52.
78. Ali-ud-Din Mufti, *op. cit.*, I, pp. 239-40.
79. *Ibid.*, p. 240; cf., Khushwaqat Rai, *op. cit.*, p. 85.
80. Ali-ud-Din Mufti, *op. cit.*, Vol. I, p. 240.
81. *Ibid.* pp. 240-41; Bute Shah, *op. cit.*, p. 18.
82. *Ibid.* cf., Sohan Lal Suri, *op. cit.*, I, p. 165.
83. Bute Shah, *op. cit.*, p. 18; Muhammad Latif, *op. cit.*, ed. Lahore, 1916, p. 93.
84. Ganesh Das Badehra, *op. cit.*, pp. 129-30.
85. *Ibid.*, p. 130.

86. Lepel Griffin, *op. cit.*, p. 394.
87. Ganesh Das Badehra, *op. cit.*, pp. 130-31.
88. Ahmad Shah Batalia, *op. cit.*, p. 17.
89. Lepel Griffin, *op. cit.*, p. 395.
90. *Ibid.* p. 396; Ganesh Das, *op. cit.*, p. 133.
91. Ganesh Das Badehra, *op. cit.*, p. 133.
92. Sohan Lal Suri, *op. cit.*, II, p. 27; Bute Shah, *op. cit.*, IV, p. 16.
93. Sohan Lal Suri, *op. cit.*, II, p. 28; Bute Shah, *op. cit.*, p. 17; cf., Ahmad Shah Batalia, *op. cit.*, p. 17.
94. Bute Shah, *op. cit.*, IV, p. 20; Ganesh Das Badehra, *op. cit.*, pp. 133-34.
95. Ganesh Das Badenra, *op. cit.*, p. 133.
96. Sohan Lal Suri, *op. cit.*, II, p. 39; Ganesh Das Badehra, *op. cit.*, p. 140.
97. *Ibid.* cf., Bute Shah, IV, *op. cit.*, p. 22; Ganesh Das, *op. cit.*, p. 140.
98. Ali-ud-Din Mufti, *op. cit.*, Vol. I. p. 397.
99. *Ibid. op. cit.*, pp. 397-98.
100. Sohan Lal Suri, *op. cit.*, II, p. 40; f., Bute Shah, *op. cit.*, IV, p. 22.
101. *Ibid.*
102. *Ibid.* p. 41; Bute Shah, *op. cit.*, p. 23; Muhammad Latif, *op. cit.*, p. 349.
103. *Ibid.* Muhammad Latif, *op. cit.*, p. 349; Gian Singh, *op. cit.*, p. 290.
104. *Ibid.* Gian Singh, *op. cit.*, p. 290; Muhammad Latif, *op. cit.*, p. 350.
105. Bute Shah, *op. cit.*, , p. 23.
106. *Ibid.*
107. *Ibid.* p. 24.
108. Ali-ud-Din Mufti, *op. cit.*, Vol. I, p. 400.
109. Sohan Lal Suri, *op. cit.*, II, p. 42; Ali-ud-Din Mufti, *op. cit.*, Vol, I, p. 400.
110. Sohan Lal Suri, *op. cit.*, II, pp. 42-43.
111. Bute Shah, *op. cit.*, p. 19.

112. Sohan Lal Suri, *op. cit.*, II, p. 43; Bute Shah, *op. cit.*, p. 19; Muhammad Latif, *op. cit.*, pp. 350-351; Gian Singh, *op. cit.*, p. 291.
113. *Ibid.*, pp. 42-43.
114. Lepel Griffin, *op. cit.*, p. 394.
115. Lepel Griffin, *op. cit.*, p. 397.
116. Sohan Lal Suri, *op. cit.*, II, pp. 48-49; Ganesh Das, p. 163; Amar Nath, *Zafar-nama-i-Ranjit Singh*, p. 18.
117. Sohan Lal Suri, *op. cit.*, II, p. 95.
118. Ganesh Das Badehra, *op. cit.*, p. 152; Bute Shah, *op. cit.*, IV, p. 21.
119. *Ibid.*, Ahmad Shah Batalia, *op. cit.*, p. 17.
120. Sohan Lal Suri, *op. cit.*, II, pp. 100-01.
121. Ganesh Das, *op. cit.*, p. 152.
122. Ahmad Shah Batalia, *op. cit.*, p. 17; Bute Shah, *op. cit.*, p. 21; Lepel Griffin, *op. cit.*, p. 398; Muhammad Latif, *op. cit.*, p. 306.
123. Ganesh Das Badehra, *op. cit.*, pp. 168-69.
124. *Ibid.*
125. Muhammad Latif, *op. cit.*, p. 306.
126. Ahmad Shah Batalia, *op. cit.*, p. 34.
127. Muhammad Latif, *op. cit.*, p. 306.
128. Lepel Griffin, *op. cit.*, p. 98.
129. *Ibid.* cf., Muhammad Latif, *op. cit.*, p. 306.

5

The Ramgarhia Misal

The founder of the Ramgarhia Misal was a Jat Sikh, named Khushal Singh,[1] of Guga village, near Amritsar. He received *pahul* (baptism) from the hands of Banda Singh. During the Sikh revolt against the Mughal tyranny he came into prominence through his daring adventures. Khushal Singh was succeeded by another Jat, Nand Singh, who belonged to village Sanghani, near Amritsar.[2] Under Nand Singh's command the band grew more powerful and they expanded their activities considerably. Nand Singh, after his death, was succeeded by a much more enterprising and a valiant man, named Jassa Singh, under whose stewardship the band assumed the status and the name of the Misal.

Hardas Singh, the grandfather of Jassa Singh, a carpenter by caste, was the resident of Sur Singh[3] which is situated about nineteen miles east of Khem Karan, in the present district of Amritsar. Hardas Singh was initiated into the Khalsa faith by Guru Gobind Singh himself from whose hands he took *pahul* and fought some battles from the Guru's side. When the Guru proceeded towards the Deccan Hardas Singh retired to his village. When Banda Singh organised the Sikhs to fight against the Mughals Hardas Singh joined his followers and participated in most of the battles fought by him. He died in the battle of Bajwara in A.D. 1715 (B.K. 1772).[4]

Jassa Singh (1723-1803)

Bhagwan Singh, the only son of Hardas Singh, was of a still more adventurous disposition. He had also mastered, the *Adi Garnth,* he Sikh scripture, and was called *Gyani.* He shifted to village Ichhogil which lay about twelve miles east of Lahore.[5] He preached the Sikh faith in the neighbouring villages. He was an intrepid soldier. Bhagwan Singh had five sons, named. Jai Singh, Jassa Singh, Khushal Singh, Mali Singh and Tara Singh.[6] Bhagwan Singh, who was in the service of Adeena Beg Khan, commanded a contingent of one hundred horsemen. In 1739, during the invasion of Nadir Shah, Bhagwan Singh saved the life of the governor of Lahore at the cost of his own. To reward his brave deed the governor gave a village each to all of his five sons. The villages gifted were: Valla, Verka, Sultanwind, Tung and Chubhal.[7] Of these villages Valla came to the share of Jassa Singh.

In the battle fought between Nadir Shah and Zakariya Khan, at Wazirabad, Bhagwan Singh fought very bravely but lost his life. Jassa Singh and his two brothers Mali Singh and Tara Singh are also said to have fought against Nadir Shah.

Adeena Beg, the *faujdar* of Jalandhar Doab, was strengthening his position in the territory under his control, despite the rising power of the Sikhs. The Sikhs were determined to restrain Adeena Beg's power under all circumstances. As a conciliatory measure, the Sikhs sent Jassa Singh to Adeena Beg as their representative for negotiations. Adeena Beg was very much impressed by the sharp intelligence, winning eloquence and brave and manly bearing of Jassa Singh. He persuaded him to join his service as an officer.[8] He was appointed tehsildar of a sizeable territory.[9] He gained a lot of administrative experience while in the service of Adeena Beg.

A little later, Jassa Singh, along with his two brothers, Mali Singh and Tara Singh, joined the band of Nand Singh. He soon earned the distinction of being the most paring and fearless of the band. After Nand Singh's death he was acknowledged as the leader of the band.

After some time, Jassa Singh was again invited by Adeena Beg, *faujdar* of Jalandhar Doab, to join his service as an important officer which he did. Jassa Singh, along with his two brothers, fought on the side of Adeena Beg when the latter launched upon hostilities against Ahmad Shah Abdali. Jassa Singh's gallantry was so conspicuous that Adeena Beg gave him the command of his own troops.

Besieged Ram Rauni

In October 1748, when the Sikhs assembled at Amritsar to celebrate Diwali, Adeena Beg was ordered by Muin-ul-Mulk, popularly known as Mir Mannu, the Governor of Lahore, to march against them. The fort of Ram Rauni at Amritsar, where 500 Sikhs were staying, was besieged by Jassa Singh, accompanied by Adeena Beg and Aziz Khan. The siege lasted nearly for three months[10] and two hundred of the besieged Sikhs laid down their lives fighting against the besiegers. Since all supplies of foodstuffs, etc., from outside had been cut-off and the inmates of the fort were pushed into the state of stark starvation, the Sikhs saw death staring them in the face.[11] Jassa Singh, who was fighting against the Sikhs from outside, was feeling very sore about the plight of his co-religionists inside the fort. The besieged Sikhs wrote a letter to Jassa Singh that if he joined them in their hour of difficulty he would be excused of his previous lapses and readmitted into the fold of Sikhism otherwise he would stand excommunicated for all time to come. Honouring the invitation from the Sikhs he joined the inmates of the fort of Ram Rauni.[12]

From within the fort Jassa Singh addressed a personal letter to Diwan Kaura Mal at Lahore, requesting him to save the lives of the besieged Sikhs. Kaura Mal, who was sympathetically disposed towards the Sikhs, prevailed upon Mir Mannu, the Governor of Lahore, to order to withdrawal of the forces be sieging Ram Rauni. Jassa Singh's appeal to Kaura Mal had the desired effect. The Punjab was, just at this time, threatened with an invasion of Ahmad Shah Durrani. Under Kaura Mal's advice, Muin-ul-Mulk agreed to lift the siege and grant the Sikhs a *jagir* to settle down as peaceful citizens.

Jassa Singh remained in the fort of Ram Rauni or Ramgarh for quite sometime. He repaired it after its destruction and his Misal took its name from the name of this fort. And he began to be called Jassa Singh Ramgarhia. It is amusing to note that the whole of the carpenter community began to call itself Ramgarhias which is a misnomer.

In due course of time, the relations between the Sikhs and Mir Mannu again got strained. Mir Mannu commissioned Adeena Beg and Sadiq Beg to attack Ramgarh and give a crushing blow to the Sikhs. Jassa Singh fought valiantly against his foes and finding further resistance to the Mughal forces extremely difficult he managed to escape to a place of safety. The fort was destroyed by the Mughals. Availing himself of the disorder caused in the Punjab after the death of Muin-ul-Mulk in 1753, Jassa Singh rebuilt the fort of Ramgarh.[13] It was again destroyed in 1757, now by Timur the Durrani Governor of Lahore. But after the expulsion of Timur in 1758, by the combined forces of the Sikhs, the Marathas and Adeena Beg, the fort was again rebuilt by Jassa Singh.

Territorial Acquisitions of Jassa Singh

Jassa Singh actively participated in the battles against Jahan Khan of Lahore and Zain Khan of Sirhind. He joined the Sikhs in their incursion of Bharatpur. Accompanied by his brother Mali Singh, he launched upon a career of conquests in the Shivalik hills and the Majha areas. He placed under his control the *parganas* of Batala, Kalanaur, Mastiwal, Dasuha, Talwara Lakhpur, Sanguwala, Sharif Chak, Miani, Begowal, etc. These territories fetched him an annual income of seven lakh rupees.[14] Jassa Singh also subordinated Raja Ghumand Chaud Katoch of Kangra and the Rajas of Haripur, Jaswan, Datarpur and many other petty hill chiefs that yielded him a revenue of two lakh rupees.[15] Jassa Singh entrusted Batala and its surrounding areas to his brother Mali Singh and Kalanaur and its adjoining territories to his other brother, Tara Singh. He himself would not confine himself to one place. He kept on visiting regularly the various places under the Misal's control.[16] If on a certain day he was at Rahilla, next day he would be at batala and on the third day he would go to Meghaowal. Most of their relatives lived at Meghowal where they had *pucca havelis*. He constructed a fort at Talwara on the bank of river Beas so that he could keep the bill chiefs under awe. He also realised one-fourth of the produce from the *zamidars* of Phagwara. His influence increased considerably. He had under his command ten thousand horsemen.[17] The Ramgarhias reduced Batala to submission in February-March 1763. All the *Zamindars* of the *taaluqa* of Batala, including Saran das of Jadiala, Dharam Das of Toli and Mirza Nur Muhammad of Qadian, accepted the overlordship of Jassa Singh and started paying revenue to him.[18] He had also captured Urmar Tanda, Yahyapur and some territories in the neighbourhood of Hoshiarpur. The new additions referred to above, brought him an additional income of about ten lakh rupees. In due course of time, his possessions including almost the whole of Shivalik territories between the Ravi and the Beas and the territories of the Jalandhar Doab in the plains. Now Ramgarh could not serve as his ideal headquarters, so he made Sri Hargobindpur, near Batala, on the river Beas, his capital.[19] He built many forts at strategic places within his territories, and extended full protection to his subordinate principalities. For example, Chamba was protected against Ranjit Deo of Jammu. Jassa Singh established his reputation as one of the strongest chiefs of the Punjab.[20] He had been actively participating in all the Sikh incursions and displaying deeds of gallantry in all the battle-fields wherever he fought.

Differences with Kanaihyas

The rising power of Jassa Singh ramgarhia could not remain unchallenged even from his best friends. He had very friendly and cordial relations with Jai Singh Kanaihya. They had jointly led many expeditions against their enemies. Jassa Singh joined by his ally, Jai Singh, had subjected the territories, north of Amritsar, and those in the neighbourhood of Batala, to his rule. Jai Singh had also participated on the side of Jassa Singh in the protection and later reoccupated of the fort of Ramgarh, at Amritsar. They had also jointly attacked Kasur. Their relations remained smooth and unruffled till 1763. It is said that during their joint attack of Kasur they got huge amount of booty. Mali Singh, brother of Jassa Singh, was alleged to have concealed a valuable part of the booty against Jassa Singh's wishes. When this fact was discovered later the friendship between the Ramgarhia and Kanaihya chiefs came to an end.

It is said that Ghumand Chand Katoch, who was one of the subordinates of Jassa Singh Ramgarhia, once remarked that the Ramgarhia chief's influence in the hills was due to him. Jessa Singh told him that it was because of the grace of Lord and not because of him. He asked the Katoch chief to be careful in future, in respect of such remarks. Raja Ghumand Chand got enraged and decided to shed off the overlordship of Jassa Singh, by fighting against him. The Raja, who was defeated, solicited the help of Jai Singh Kanaihya by offering to pay the expenses. The Kanaihya chief gave assistance to the Katoch Raja. Jassa Singh defeated both of them and plundered the *derahs* of Ghumand Chand and jai Singh. From that day onwards, Jai Singh nursed a deep-seated hostility against Jassa Singh.[21]

When Jassa Singh happened to fight against Charhat Singh Sukarchakia the latter was defeated and his power was shattered. His *zamburks* and other goods were taken away as booty by the Ramgarhia chief. So, Ghumand Chand, Jai Singh and Charhat Singh turned hostile to Jassa Singh to the extent that they decided to completely crush his power and turn him out of the Punjab.[22]

In the meantime Ghumand Chand died and he was succeeded by his son Nek Chand. The allies, referred to above, jointly continued their hostilities for a period of four years with indecisive skirmishes between the contents. This resulted in the loss of revenue accruing to Jassa Singh from the hill areas.[23] But the Ramgarhia chief's power remained unbroken. He stood the strain caused by the allies.

In 1774, Jai Singh Kanaihya occupied the fort of Kangra by a clever strategem. This impaired the supremacy of Jassa Singh in the Shivalik hills. The widow of Nand Singh, a Bhangi Misaldar, gave away Pathankot as *jagir* to her son-in-law, Tara Singh, the brother of Hakikat Singh Kanaihya. Ganda Singh, Bhangi Sardar, asked the Kanaihyas to return him Pathankot which, he said, had been bestowed by his brother Jhanda Singh on Nand Singh. Kanaihyas refused to accept the proposal and, assisted by Jassa Singh Ahluwalia, prepared for a battle. Jassa Singh Ramgarhia came to the help of Ganda Singh. The two armies met each other at Dinanagar. Ganda Singh fell ill in the course of fighting and died,[24] Jassa Singh also met with an accident though not seriously hurt. The Bhangis dispersed from the battle-field, and it served as a big blow to the prestige of the Ramgarhia chief also. Jassa Singh Ramgarhia's enmity with the Kanaihyas was now extended to that of the Ahluwalia also.

Relations with Ahluwalias

Till 1766, the relations between the Ramgarhias and the Ahluwalias remained very cordial and friendly. They jointly fought against the internal enemies and foreign or external invaders. They had cooperated with each other against Ahmad Shah Abdali. In the battle-field of Dinanagar they found themselves arrayed in the opposite camps. The escalation of hostilities between the two resulted in their open warfare.

Jassa Singh Ramgarhia was wounded by a gun-shot fired by Jassa Singh Ahluwalia in the battle fought between the two at Zahura, on the river Beas. A little later, in 1775, Jassa Singh Ahluwalia was passing near Gurdaspur on his way to Achal, a place of pilgrimage, or, as some say, he was hunting somewhere around Batala when he was attacked by Jassa Singh Ramgarhia's brothers—Khushal Singh, Mali Singh and Tara Singh. The troops of the Ahluwalia chief were dispersed and he was taken prisoner.[25] Since Ahluwalia Sardar was a very revered Sikh leader he was duly honoured by Jassa Singh Ramgarhia and released with rich gifts, including a robe of honour (*a khillat*) and a palanquin in which he was sent back.[26] As Lepel Griffin puts it, 'the old Sikh barons had much of the spirit of chivalry.' But Jassa Singh harboured a deep animosity against the Ramgarhias for the indignity suffered by him on account of his imprisonment at their hands.[27] He was not going to be appeased. Jassa Singh Ahluwalia, whose followers called him *sultan-ul-qaum* (the Sikh king), felt deeply wounded in prestige and insulted in self-respect by the Ramgarhia youth. He swore an oath to seize all the possessions of the Ramgarhia and drive them out of the Punjab. Many chiefs came to Ahluwalia Sardar's aid. They included Ganda Singh and Jhanda Singh Bhangis and Jai Singh and Hakikat Singh Kanaihyas who were the old friends of the Ramgarhias. Charhat Singh Sukarchakia, Nar Singh Chamiariwala and many others.[28]

Gurbaksh Singh son of Jai Singh Kanaihya, attacked Dasuha and the adjoining areas on the other side of river Beas and occupied the same. Then, he attacked Batala, in 1780, which was under Jassa Singh's brother, Mali Singh. Mali Singh had been branded as a cruel man and had earned the displeasure of the people of the town. To the chargin of Mali Singh, and relief of the people, Gurbakhsh Singh secured an easy entry into the town.[29] Raja Singh, Deva Singh and Mansa Dhari *qanungos* and Tara Singh Brahman, Kala and other *muqadams* and *zamindars*, by a joint decision, opened the gate of the fort.[30] Hakikat Singh Kanaihya forcibly snatched Kalanaur from Jassa Singh's brother, Tara Singh.[31]

Gradually, the Ramgarhias lost all their possessions, one by one, until not a village was left with them and were forced into exile in the territory of Malwa.[32] He had four thousand horsemen with him. Raja Amar Singh of Patiala gave away Hisar and Hansi to Jassa Singh as a *jagir*. His son, Jodh Singh, stayed with Amar Singh and the Ramgarhia chief crossed river Jamuna and realised revenue from the *parganas* of Sambhal, Chandausi, Kash Ganj, Khurja, Sikandra, Meerut, etc.[33] Zabita Khan, the Nawab of Meerut, paid a tribute of 10,000 rupees, a year, to save his territory from the occupation of Jassa Singh.[34] The Ramgarhia chief entered Delhi and plundered Mohalla Mughlan and some places were set on fire. He carried off four guns from the Mughal arsenal and many other things from there. The Mughal Emperor Shah Alam, in uttar helplessness, sent message to Jassa Singh that he would gain nothing by burning down the city of Delhi and implored that he should not do it. The people of Delhi made an offering of five hundred rupees to him and escaped the ruination.[35] He remained in the cis-Satluj areas for nearly five years.[36]

It is said that one day a Brahman complained to Jassa Singh that the Governor of Hisar had carried off his two daughters by force. Jassa Singh collected his men and marched against Hisar, recovered the girls and restored them to their father.[37]

At times, the Ramgarhia chief was reduced to great straits. There is a story which may be true as Lepel Griffin believes, that at Sirsa, a servant of the Sardar happening to drop his vessel down a well, a diver was sent to fetch it. He discovered at the bottom four boxes full of gold *mohurs,* to the value of five lakhs of rupees enabling Jassa Singh to pay his troops and enlist new followers.[38]

In the year 1785, Mahan Singh came to Amritsar, on the occasion of Diwali. Most of the chiefs of the Misals, including Jai Singh Kanaihya, had assembled there.[39] Jai Singh was held in high esteem by all other Sardars of the Misals. Mahan Singh visited Jai Singh to pay his regards to him. In the course of the meeting Jai Singh, who was jealous of the growing power of the Sukarchakias, insulted Mahan Singh by his remarks, "Go away you *bhagtia* (dancing boy); I do not want to hear your sentimental talk." "This was too much to be borne in silence by so haughty and impervious a young chief as Mahan Singh was."[40] Jai Singh demanded a share from the booty which Mahan Singh had brought from Jammu.[41]

Mahan Singh felt highly enraged at the rude treatment meted out to him by the Kanaihya chief, but he was not in a position to proceed against him single-handed. Mahan Singh knew that without Jassa Singh Ramgarhia's help he could not have success against Jai Singh. Mahan Singh sent him a word that in case of his cooperation and support his former possessions would be restored.[42] Jassa Singh availed himself of the invitation from his exile into which he had been driven by Jai Singh.[43] Sansar Chand Katoch, the ruler of Kangra, was called by Mahan Singh to join him. The there chiefs, with their combined forces, marched against the Kanaihyas. The battle was fought at Batala and Jai Singh's son Gurbakhsh Singh was killed[44] in the course of fighting and the Kanaihyas were routed, thus humbling the old Kanaihya chief. The Ramgarhia and the Katoch chiefs got back their territories already captured by the Kanajhyas. Jassa Singh occupied the *parganas* of Rahilla, Sri Hargobindpur, Kalanaur, Mastiwal, Wadyal, Dhoot and Hajipur, which fetched him an annual revenue of three lakh rupees.

According to Khushwaqat Rai, when all the possessions of Jai Singh Kanaihya had gone out of his hands he retained the occupation of the fort of Kangra.[45] Jassa Singh was of the opinion that with the fort of Kangra in his hands Jai Singh would again strengthen his possessions. So, in order to subdue him completely the Ramgarhia chief suggested to Sansar Chand, ruler of Kangra, that he (Jassa Singh), along with his allies, would harass Jai Singh, and on the other hand he, the Katoch chief, should get closer to the Kanaihya chief and get the fort of Kangra from him. That was the most opportune time for the same. The strategy worked and Jai Singh handed over the fort of Kangra to Sansar Chand. But soon after it Jai Singh engaged his son Gurbakhsh Singh's daughter to Ranjit Singh, son of Mahan Singh. Thus Jai Singh won over to him Sansar Chand and Mahan Singh.[46]

Shortly thereafter, the towns of Batala and Kalanaur went out of the hands of the Ramgarhias. Due to the oppressive rule of the Ramgarhias the Bhandaris, Khatris of Batala, joined Sada Kaur, the widow of Gurbakhsh Singh Kanaihya. They made an opening in the outer wall of the town and admitted the Kanaihyas into it. For two or three days the Ramgarhia contingent remained entrapped in the *haveli* of Dasondhi Mal, inside the fort. When they lost all hope of reinforcement from outside they escaped from the fort and joined Jassa Singh who had gone to subdue Haqiqat Singh's son, Jaimal Singh.[47]

Jassa Singh's last and most severe struggle with the Kanaihyas took place in 1796. Sada Kaur, widow of Gurbakhsh Singh Kanaihya, was, then, heading the Misal. With all her own forces and those of her young son-in-law, Ranjit Singh, she besieged the Ramgarhia chief in the Miani fort, in the Hoshiarpur district, near river Beas. Jassa Singh defended himself for some time but his provisions ran short and he sent a word to Sada Kaur and Ranjit Singh asking them to raise the siege of Miani. But Sada Kaur was intent upon taking revenge for her husband's death. So, she took no notice of Sahib Singh's advice. Again, Jassa Singh sent a messenger, and Sahib Singh said, "they will not mind me; but God Himself will aid you." The messenger returned to Miani and that very night river Beas came down in flood and swept a large portion of the Kanaihya camp, men, horses and camels. Sada Kaur and Ranjit Singh escaped with difficulty and retired to Gujranwala.[48]

After Ranjit Singh occupied Lahore, many chief of the Sikh Misals and others became apprehensive of his rising power. They joined hands to restrain Ranjit Singh from his policy of territorial aggrandisement. After the festival of *Holi,* in 1800. Sahib Singh of Gujarat, Gulab Singh Bhangi, Jassa Singh Ramgarhia and Nizam-ud-Din of Kasur assembled their forces at the village of Bhasin, about 9 *kos* on the cast of Lahore.[49] Ranjit Singh came from Lahore. Both sides arrayed themselves in the battle-field and no action took place between the contending forces for two months.[50] Gulab Singh Bhangi drank himself to death.[51] The leaders of the confederacy dispersed without achieving anything. During the next couple of years the Ramgarhia chief lived at Sri Hargobindpur. He continued having friendly relations with the Bhangis till his death.[52]

Jassa Singh died on April 20, 1803, at the ripe age of 80, after having led his band and later his Misal for 60 years.[53] No recorded contemporary evidence is available about Jassa Singh's date of birth. But the contemporary records are unanimous about his death in 1803, at the age of 80. From this, it can be deduced that he was born in 1723.

According to Khushwaqat Rai, Jassa Singh possessed winning manners. He was bounteous to the strangers as well as his officials who sought his protection even after committing crimes. He helped the needy even at heavy costs to him. He provided asylum to the strangers even for years together. Nawab Bhambu Khan, grandson of Najib-ud-Daulah, the dictator of Delhi (1761-70), after having been charged with a murder, took protection under Jassa Singh who bestowed upon him the needed care. The position and honour due to the Nawab, on the basis of his earlier status, were maintained. The Sikhs told the Ramgarhia chief that Bhambu Khan was a robber in the eyes of the Emperor of Delhi, therefore, he should not be given an asylum. The Sardar told them that they were also considered robbers by the Delhi rulers. This country had not been under the Mughal rulers for ever. Once a Brahman, named Lal Singh, earning the displeasure of Ranjit Singh, sought asylum with Jassa Singh. Ranjit Singh expressly demanded the restoration of the Brahman to him but he was not repatriated though the Ramgarhia chief had to face hostilities from the Sukarchakia ruler.

Khushwaqat Rai further writes that in the event of fighting, with his small numbers against the heavy odds of the enemies he would display extraordinary bravery and intrepidity. He would jump into the battle-field amidst booming guns, totally indifferent and insensitive to the grave hazards to his life.[54] Out of deep regards Jassa Singh was addressed by his followers as 'Baba ji'. At times, his generosity and magnanimity knew no bounds. He was a staunch Sikh and was always ready to lay down his life for the cause of Sikhism. During Ahmad Shah's invasions of the Punjab Jassa Singh always fought in the front ranks against the foreign invader.

Jodh Singh (1803-1815)

Jassa Singh Ramgarhia had two sons, Jodh Singh and Bir Singh. Jodh Singh succeeded to his father after his death. He contracted friendship with Raja Sansar Chand of Kangra with whose help he occupied *Parganas* of Batala, Bhunga. Hoshiarpur and the surrounding areas.[55]

When Maharaja Ranjit Singh demanded the *zamzama* gun from Mai Sukhan, the widow of Gulab Singh Bhangi, in 1805, she gave a flat refusal to hand over the gun and prepared to fight against the Maharaja. Jodh Singh sent a secret reinforcement of three hundred soldiers to Sukhan. At the same time he advised her either to hand over the bone of contention—the *zamzama* gun, to Ranjit Singh or destroy the gun. She did not accept either of the suggestions. The Maharaja, accompanied by his allies, Sada Kaur and Fateh Singh Ahluwalia, besieged Amritsar. When the opposing forces were at the point of severely clashing, Jodh Singh and Akali Phula Singh intervened and persuaded Sukhan to surrender. Thus, they were able to avert the bloodshed.[56] Mai Sukhan and Gurdit Singh accepted the hospitality of Jodh Singh and stayed with him for some time.[57] In earlier stages, Jodh Singh was very friendly towards Sansar Chand Katoch but later their relations get strained due to the former's inability to help the latter against the Gurkhas.

Maharaja Ranjit Singh felt that unless Ramgarhias were befriended he could not occupy the whole of the Punjab. So, with this thing in view, Ranjit Singh wrote a letter to Jodh Singh, soliciting his friendship and cooperation. After the things were settled the Maharaja sent Bishan Singh Munshi, Mehar Singh Lamba and Fateh Singh Kalianwala to conduct Jodh Singh to Lahore. Jodh Singh told them that he would join Maharaja Ranjit Singh on the acceptance of two conditions. First, that Batala, Kalanaur, Bajwara, and Sangowal which previously belonged to them and, of late, were in the hands of their opponents, should be restored to them. Second, Gurdit Singh Bhangi, who was lying at his door, should be provided with a *jagir* for his subsistence. The maharaja accepted both the conditions. Jodh Singh, accompanied by his close associates, came to Amritsar and met Ranjit Singh at Harmandir Sahib and he was duly honoured by the letter.[58]

The demanded territories were restored to Jodh Singh and Panjore and five or six villages were given in *jagir* to Mai Sukhan and her son, Gurdit Singh.[59] Jodh Singh was very much known for his magnanimity of heart and lavish generosity. Any defeated chief or improverished person could go to him and enjoy his hospitality. He always sympathised with those on whom the fortunes frowned. In his Misal, he had introduced strict discipline and anybody found guilty of theft or any other crime was strictly dealt with. He would never sell justice but administer it with utmost honesty.[60] He was very keen to give neat and clean administration to his people and there was nothing nearer his heart than the welfare of his subjects.

Jodh Singh participated in the battle of Kasur on the side of Ranjit Singh. After the occupation of Kasur the Maharaja gifted an elephant to the Ramgarhia chief. Later Jodh Singh always sided with Ranjit Singh in his expeditions against Multan and his other adversaries.[61]

Maharaja Ranjit Singh gave away in *jagir* the *pargana* of Ghuman to Jodh Singh. It gave an annual revenue of twenty five thousand rupees. Formerly, this area belonged to the Ramgarhias and at that time it was in the hands of Gulab Singh Bhangi.[62]

In 1811, Ranjit gave to Jodh Singh eleven villages from the *pargana* of Sikhowala (Sikhorwala, according to Khushwaqat Rai, and Sheikhupura, according to Gian Singh) which was in the possession of the sons of Fateh Singh Kanaihya, which fetched an annual revenue of twelve thousand rupees.[63] Of all the Sikh Sardars the Maharaja had the greatest regards for Jodh Singh Ramgarhia and addressed him as 'Baba Ji.' When he came to see Maharaja Ranjit Singh the latter would go out a few steps to receive him and seated him by his side.[64] Jodh Singh, mostly, lived at Lahore or Amritsar and he always mobilised his forces according to the instructions of the Maharaja.[65] Because of his unstinted loyalty to the Maharaja the Ramgarhia chief retained his possessions intact till his death on August 23, 1815. He remained hostile to the Ahluwalias and Rani Sada Kaur.[66]

Jodh Singh's Successors

After Jodh Singh's death, the members of his family began to quarrel for the division of the Misal's possessions. Diwan Singh (son of Tara Singh), cousion brother of Jodh Singh, Vir Singh (brother of Jodh Singh) and widow of Jodh Singh were all claimants to the principality. Maharaja Ranjit Singh, hearing of their dispute, called the three claimants: Vir Singh, Diwan Singh and Musftah Singh (son of Khushal Singh and cousin brother of Lodh Singh) to him at Nadaun, with a view to setting their dispute by arbitration. The Maharaja received them with courtesy but they misbehaved towards one another so rudely that Ranjit Singh was obliged to keep them in detention.[67] Then, the Maharaja marched on Amritsar and after some fighting took the fort of Ramgarh. He seized all the Ramgarhia *jagirs* and, in a short time, reduced all their forts, upwards of a hundred and fifty in number. They contained abundant provisions in them. Almost all of them were pulled down.[68]

On the intercession of Sardar Chanda Singh Kanaihya the Ramgarhia Sardars were released from the jail and an annual *jagir* of 35,000 rupees was granted to them. Diwan Singh refused to accept his share. He fled to Patiala where he was well received. He also left that place and moved about for some time. Maharaja Ranjit Singh sent a word to Diwan Singh, through Desa Singh Majithia, assuring him the grant of a big *jagir*. He was respect fully received by the Maharaja at Lahore and was given command of 700 men in the expedition then setting out for Kashmir. There, he remained in charge of Baramula, a difficult bill post, till his death in 1834.[69] The widows of Jodh Singh were given *jagir* of four villages for their maintenance. Vir Singh was given Dharmkot Randhawa in *jagir*. These were service-free *jagirs*.[70] Vir Singh had died six years earlier, in 1828, when two-third of his *jagirs* were resumed by the Maharaja.[71]

After Diwan Singh's death his son Mangal Singh, who was born in 1800, succeded to his father's estate. During his younger days he served Ranjit Singh on his personal staff. The Maharaja gave him *jagirs* in Dharmkot, Kalowala, Tibrah and Kundilah worth 9,000 rupees of which 3,600 rupees were personal, and 5,400 rupees for service.[72]

After his father's death Mangal Singh was sent to Peshwar in a command of 400 foot and 110 *swars*. There, he did commenable service under Hari Singh Nalwa and Tej Singh and fought in the famous battle of Jamrud in April 1837, where the brave Hari Singh Nalwa laid down his life.[73]

In 1839, Mangal Singh was recalled and sent to the hill territories between the Beas and the Satluj under orders of Lehna Singh Majithia and during the absence of that chief at Peshawar he was placed in charge of the hill forts, and was active in the suppression of the insurrection of 1840.[74] During the reign of Maharaja Sher Singh he was employed under Lehna Singh in Suket, Mandi and Kulu and he remained there till the close of the Satluj Anglo-Sikh war in 1846. During the second Sikh war, Mangal Singh remained loyal to the British and served them in guarding the roads and maintaining order in the Amritsar and Gurdaspur districts. Latter, he worked as a manager of the affairs of Harmandir Sahib, Amritsar.

Mangal Singh was a man of education and liberal ideas. It was mostly owing to his influence that the cause of female education was systematically taken up in Amritsar.[75] Mangal Singh's two sons, Gurdit Singh and Mitt Singh, served the British government in the police and civil departments respectively.

REFERENCES

1. Ahmad Shah Batalia, Appendix. Sohan Lal Suri's *Umdat-ut-Tawarikh,* Lahore, 1885, p. 18; Muhammad Latif, *History of the Panjab* (1891), Delhi, 1964, p. 306. According to M'Gregor Khushal Singh belonged to Guga village (*A history of the Sikhs,* I,) (1846), Allahabad reprint, 1979, p. 130. According to Ahmad Shah, Khushal Singh belonged to Kukarpur (p. 18).
2. *Ibid.,* M'Gregor, *op. cit.,* I, p. 130.
3. Lepel Griffin, *Panjab Chiefs,* Lahore, 1865, p. 170; Gian Singh, *Tawarikh Guru Khalsa,* Part II, reprint, Patiala, 1970, pp. 233-34; Muhammad Latif, *op. cit.,* p. 306.
4. Gian Singh, *op. cit.,* II. 334.
5. Ali-ud-Din Mufti, *Ibratnama* (1854), Vol. I, Lahore, 1961, p. 304; Lapel Griffin, *op. cit.,* p. 171; Kanaihya Lal, *Tarikh-i-Punjab,* Lahore, 1877, p. 91.
6. Lepel Griffin, *op. cit.,* p. 171; Gian Singh, *op. cit.,* p. 234. According to some writers Bhagwan Singh had three or four sons. See Bute Shah *Tarikh-i-Punjab,* IV, Dr. Ganda Singh's private collection, Patiala, p. 55. Ahmad Shah Batalia names three sons. He excludes Jai Singh and Khushal Singh, *op. cit.,* p. 18. It is probable that only three or four of them actively participated in the Sikh movement.
7. Gian Singh, *op. cit.,* II, p. 234; Hari Ram Gupta, *History of the Sikhs,* IV, Delhi, 1982, p. 276.
8. Kanaihya Lal, *op. cit.,* p. 94; Gian Singh, *op. cit.,* II, p. 234; cf., Ahmad Shah Batalia, *op. cit.,* p. 18; Ali-ud-Din Mufti, *op. cit.,* Vol. I, p. 304.

9. Kanathya Lal, *op. cit.*, p. 94; Suraj Singh and Darbara Singh, *Ithas Ramgarhian*, Vol. I, Lahore, 1915, p. 411.
10. Khushwaqat Rai, *Tarikh-i-Sikhan* (1811), MS., Dr. Ganda Singh, private collection, Patiala, p. 72; Bute Shah, *op. cit.*, IV, p. 55.
11. Ali-ud-Din Mufti, *op. cit.*, Vol. I, pp. 304-05; Gian Singh, *op. cit.*, II, pp. 163, 234.
12. Khushwaqat Rai, *op. cit.*, p. 72; Bute Shah, *op. cit.*, IV, p. 55. The Sikh writers believe that Jassa Singh's conscience smote him for having deserted his brethren. He decided to rejoin them. A message was sent in the fort by him, requesting his comrades-in-faith to forgive him and to have him back. They welcomed him with open arms and he came in with a hundred followers. [Rattan Singh Bhangu, *Prachin Panth Parkash* (1841), Amritsar, 1939, pp. 311-15; Teja Singh and Ganda Singh, *A Short History of the Sikhs*, Bombay, 1950, p. 139; Gian Singh, *op. cit.*, II, p. 163].
13. Khushwaqat Rai, *op. cit.*, p. 72, Bute Shah, *op. cit.*, IV, p. 56.
14. *Ibid.*, pp. 72-73; Ahmad Shah Batalia, *op. cit.*, p. 19; Bute Shah, *op. cit.*, IV, p. 56; Ali-ud-Din Mufti, *op. cit.*, Vol. I, p. 305; Gian Singh, *op. cit.*, II, p. 235.
15. *Ibid*, p. 73; Bute Shah, *op. cit.*, IV, p. 56; Gian Singh, *op. cit.*, p. 235.
16. Ahmad Shah Batalia, *op. cit.*, p. 19; M'Gregor, *op. cit.*, I. p. 134; cf., Gian Singh, *op. cit.*, II. p. 235; Muhammad Latif. *op. cit.*, p. 308.
17. Khushwaqat Rai, *op. cit.*, p. 73; Bute Shah, *op. cit.*, IV. p. 56.
18. Ahmad Shah Batalia, *op. cit.*, p. 19.
19. Gian Sing, *op. cit.*, II. 235.
20. *Ibid.*
21. Khushwaqat Rai, *op. cit.*, p. 73; Bute Shah, *op. cit.*, IV, pp. 56-57.
22. *Ibid.*, Bute Shah, *op. cit.*, IV, p. 57.
23. *Ibid.*
24. Ahmad Shah Batalia, *op. cit.*, p. 16; Bute Shah, *op. cit.*, IV, p. 14; Ali-ud-Din Mufti, *op. cit.*, Vol. I, p. 250.
25. Lepel Griffin, *op. cit.*, p. 172; Ahmad Shah Batalia, *op. cit.*, p. 27.
26. Khushwaqat Rai, *op. cit.*, p. 73; Bute Shah, *op. cit.*, IV, p. 56.
27. *Ibid.*
28. Lepel Griffin, *op. cit.*, p. 172; cf., Khushwaqat Rai, *op. cit.*, p. 67.

29. Ahmad Shah Batalia, *op. cit.*, pp. 19-20.
30. *Ibid.*, p. 20.
31. *Ibid.*
32. Khushwaqat Rai, *op. cit.*, p. 74; Bute Shah, *op. cit.*, IV, p. 58; Muhammad Latif, *op. cit.*, p. 308.
33. Khushwaqat Rai, *op. cit.*, p. 74; Bute Shah, *op. cit.*, IV, p. 58.
34. *Ibid.*, Lepel Griffin, *op. cit.*, p. 172; Gian Singh, *op. cit.*, II, p. 237.
35. Khushwaqat Rai, *op. cit.*, p. 74; Bute Shah, *op. cit.*, IV, p. 58; Gian Singh, *op. cit.*, II, p. 237.
36. *Ibid.*, Gian Singh, *op. cit.*, p. 237.
37. Lepel Griffin, *op. cit.*, pp. 172-73; cf., Gian Singh, *op. cit.*, II, p. 236.
38. *Ibid.*, p. 173; Gian Singh, *op. cit.*, II, pp. 236-37; Suraj Singh and Darbara Singh, *op. cit.*, p. 423-24.
39. Sohan Lal Suri, *op. cit.*, II, p. 21.
40. Muhammad Latif, *History of the Panjab,* New Delhi, reprint 1964, p. 343.
41. Bute Shah, *op. cit.*, V, p. 10.
42. *Ibid.*, IV, p. 59; Ali-ud-Din Mufti, *op. cit.*, p. 307; cf., Ahmad Shah Batalia, *op. cit.*, p. 24.
43. Sohan Lal Suri, *op. cit.*, , II. p. 22; Bute Shah, *op. cit.*, V, pp. 11-12.
44. *Ibid.*, Ali-ud-Din Mufti, *op. cit.*, I. p. 308; Ahmad Shah Batalia, *op. cit.*, p. 20; Muhammad Latif, *op. cit.*, p. 308.
45. Khushwaqat Rai, *op. cit.*, p. 75; Bute Shah, *op. cit.*, IV. p. 60.
46. *Ibid.*
47. Ahmad Shah Batalia, *op. cit.*, p. 20; Khushwaqat Rai, *op. cit.*, p. 76.
48. Ahmad Shah Batalia, Appendix, *op. cit.*, p. 20; M'Gregor, *op. cit.*, I, pp. 135-36; Ali-ud-Din Mufti, *op. cit.*, I, pp. 308-09; Lepel Griffin, *op. cit.*, pp. 173-74; Gian Singh *op. cait.*, II, p. 238.
49. Khushwaqat Rai, *op. cit.*, p. 76; Amar Nath, *Zafarnama-i-Ranjit Singh* (1836), Lahore, 1928, p. 11; Sohan Lal Suri, *op. cit.*, II, p. 46.
50. Khushwaqat Rai, *op. cit.*, p. 139; Amar nath, *op. cit.*, p. 12.
51. *Ibid.*, p. 140; Sohan Lal Suri, *op. cit.*, II, p. 46; Ganesh Das Badehra, *Char Bagh-i-Punjab* (1855), Amritsar, 1965, p. 142.

52. Khushwaqat Rai, *op. cit.*, p. 76; Bute Shah, *op. cit.*, IV, p. 56.
53. *Ibid.*
54. Khushwaqat Rai, *op. cit.*, p. 76.
55. Khushwaqat Rai, *op. cit.*, p. 77; Bute Shah, *op. cit.*, IV, p. 61.
56. *Ibid.*, p. 142; Ganesh Das, *op. cit.*, p. 146; Ali-ud-Din Mufti, *op. cit.*, I, p. 404.
57. Bute Shah, *op. cit.*, IV, p. 17.
58. *Ibid.*, pp. 78-91; cf., Ahmad Shah Batalia, *op. cit.*, 20.
59. Sohan Lal Suri, *op. cit.*, II, p. 57.
60. Bute Shah, *op. cit.*, IV, pp. 62-63.
61. Khushwaqat Rai, *op. cit.*, p. 79; Bute Shah, *op. cit.*, IV, p. 62.
62. *Ibid.*, Gian Singh, *op. cit.*, II, p. 24.
63. Khushwaqat Rai, *op. cit.*, p. 79; Bute Shah, *op. cit.*, IV, p. 62; Gian Singh, *op. cit.*, p. 240.
64. Khushwaqat Rai, *op. cit.*, p. 79; Bute Shah, *op. cit.*, IV, p. 62; *Ibid.*, Singh, *op. cit.*, p. 240.
65. Ahmad Shah Batalia, *op. cit.*, p. 21; Bute Shah, *op. cit.*, IV, p. 62.
66. Bute Shah, *op. cit.*, IV, p. 63.
67. Lepel Griffin, *op. cit.*, 174; cf., Ahmad Shah Batalia, *op. cit.*, p. 21; M'Gregor *op. cit.*, I, p. 136; Gian Singh, *op. cit.*, p. 240; cf., Bute Shah, IV, p. 63; cf., Ali-ud-Din Mufti, *op. cit.*, p. 404.
68. Ahmad Shah Batalia, *op. cit.*, p. 21, M'Gregor, *op. cit.*, I, pp. 136-37; Muhammad Latif, *op. cit.*, p. 309.
69. Lepel Griffin, *op. cit.*, p. 175; Gian Singh, *op. cit.*, p. 240; cf., Ahmad Shah Batalia, *op. cit.*, p. 21; M'Gregor, *op. cit.*, I, p. 137.
70. Ali-ud-Din Mufti, *op. cit.*, Vol. I, p. 310.
71. Ahmad Shah Batalia, *op. cit.*, p. 21.
72. Lepel Griffin, *op. cit.*, p. 175; Gian Singh, *op. cit.*, pp. 240-41.
73. *Ibid.*
74. *Ibid.*
75. Lepel Griffin, *op. cit.*, pp. 175-76.

6

The Maharaja of Punjab

Lahore was the most important and biggest city of Punjab. After Amritsar, it was next in importance to Sikhs, as it was not only the capital of the province but also the birth-place of the fourth Guru of the Sikhs, Guru Ram Das. It was the central place from where the entire province could be ruled. Its capture would have certainly meant increase in Ranjit Singh's strength and would have made him the ruler of the land of five rivers. It would also have invested him with the semblance of a title to the rest of Punjab. Ranjit Singh turned his eyes towards Lahore.

Lahore at that time was ruled by Bhangi Sardars. It was captured earlier by them and remained under their control till it was reoccupied by Shah Zaman in 1797. Shah Zaman had to leave for Afghanistan and the Bhangi Sardars Chet Singh, Sahib Singh and Mohar Singh who had field were back in their possession. They had no talent and ability to rule. These incapable Sardars did not take any interest in the welfare of the people and were inept and imbecile. They had no control over the people. They were "unscrupulous, drunken, profligate and tyrannical."

The Muslims too had a considerable influence in the town. Mian Ashak Mohammad and Mian Mukkam Din were very powerful and exercised a lot of hold on the people. They were called the *Chaudhries* and were often consulted in most of the affairs of the city. Main Ashak Mohammad's daughter was married to Badar-ud-din. He was also a very influential man. Due to some unknown reason, he had some dispute with *Khatries* of the town.

By this time the people of the country had become aware of the rising strength of Ranjit Singh, the rising star on the horizon. He was the most popular leader of Punjab and was already yearning to enter Lahore. In the words of Resident Collins: "At present this Chief is regarded throughout Hindustan as the protector of the Sikh nation, it being generally believed that were it not for the fortitude and excellent conduct of Ranjit Singh, the whole of Punjab would were this have become a desert waste since it is the boast of these northern savages (the Afghans) that the grass never grows where their horses have once trodden."[1]

The People of Lahore being extremely oppressed, raised their voices of wailing to the skies and were looking towards their liberator. Nawab Nizam-ud-Din of Kasur had also an eye on Lahore and he sent his emissaries to the *Chaudhries* of Lahore seeking their help in case he attached Lahore but his offer was rejected and the Muslims joined the Hindu and Sikh residents of Lahore in making an appeal to Ranjit Singh to free them from the tyrannical rule.

A petition was written and was singed by Mian Ashak Mohammad, Mian Mukkam Din, Mohammad Tahir, Mohammad Bakar, Hakim Rai and Bhai Gurbaksh Singh. It was addressed to Ranjit Singh and read: "We are being oppressed. There is no rule of law. The people are ill treated. The Sardars are drunkards and do not take interest in the welfare of the people. The few troops are insufficient for the defence of the town. The suburbs of the town have been completely devastated. The houses have been burnt and property looted. The city presents a deserted look. Many people have fled to safer places. The life and honour of the people are not safe and the Sardars are habitually carousing and are plundering the residents for their own personal ends."

Ranjit Singh was invited to liberate Lahore as early as possible. He was told that his mere presence in the town would create terror and the rest of the things would be done by the citizens themselves in achieving their objective. A special messenger was sent to Ranjit Singh to deliver the petition.

Ranjit Singh was at Rasulnagar when the citizens of Lahore approached him with a request. Ranjit Singh patiently listened to the pathetic tale of the residents of Lahore, but remained non-committal. He was shrewd enough to judge the whole situation. He deputed his confidant, Abdul Rehman to Lahore to start negotiations with the people of Lahore headed by their leaders who had sent the representation. Ranjit Singh went to Amritsar on the plea of taking a dip in the holy tank. From Amritsar, Ranjit Singh proceeded to Batala to consult his mother-in-law, Rani Sada Kaur. Abdul Rehman met Ranjit Singh at Batala and informed him that the people of Lahore were really tired of the misrule of Bhangi leaders and wanted Ranjit Singh to liberate them. He further informed Ranjit Singh that the Sardars were busy with wine and women and he would meet with nominal resistance. The time to strike had come, Sada Kaur advised him not to lose any time. Ranjit Singh mobilised a 25,000 strong army and marched towards Lahore on July 6, 1799.

The time for any major campaign was most in opportune. The plains were burning with scorching heat and the *loo* pierced into the veins. Rainy season was about to set in and in case the campaign was a prolonged one, the plains would look like a big lake. The roads would become inaccessible. But Ranjit Singh decided to proceed and took the Sardars by surprise. Ranjit was received at the Shalimar Gardens by the petitioners who promised to open the city as and when required.

It was the last day of the Muslim festival of Muharram when a big procession was to be taken out in the town in the memory of the two grandsons of Prophet Mohammad who were martyred in the battlefield without having a drop of water. The procession started with the people beating their breasts with hands and chains and chanting, Hassan ! Hussain ! Hussain ! Hussain !" The procession passed through the main streets of the town. They carried with them the effigies of the martyrs' tombs for burying them with reverence. Although, the occasion was celebrated only by the Shia section of the Muslims, yet it was watched by several hundred people of all religions. It was expected that the Bhangi sardars would also participate in the festival and mourn with their Shia brethren. By the time the procession was over, Ranjit Singh had already reached the outskirts of the town.

Early next morning on July 7, 1799, at the time of sunrise, Ranjit Singh's men had taken their positions. Guns glistened and the bugles were sounded. Rani Sada Kaur stood outside the Delhi Gate and Ranjit proceeded towards Anarkali. Ranjit Singh rode along the walls of the city and got the wall mined. A breach was blown. It created panic and confusion. Mukkam Din, who was one of the signatories of the petition made a proclamation with the beat of the drum that the administration of the town had been taken over by him and he was now the head. He ordered all the city gates to be opened. Ranjit Singh entered the city with his troops through the Lahori Gate. Sada Kaur with a detachment of cavalry entered, through Delhi Gate. Before the Bhangi Sardars had any inkling of it, a part of the citadel was occupied without any resistance. The news spread and the two Bhangi Sardars Mohar Singh and Sahib Singh left the town and sought shelter at some safer place. Only Chet Singh was left either to fight, defened the town or to flee as he liked. Chet Singh shut himself in Hazuri Bagh. Ranjit Singh camped in—Wazir Khan's *Baradari.* Chet Singh had only 500 men with him who obviously could not offer any resistance. Ranjit Singh's cavalry surrounded Hazuri Bagh, but after some desultory firing, the fort surrounded and Chet Singh was given permission to leave it alone with his family. Orders were issued to the army not to plunder the town or molest women. Whosoever disobeyed there orders would be given death penalty.

Ranjit Singh was well-entrenched in the town now. Immediately after taking possession of the town, he paid a visit to Badshshi mosque, built by Emperor Aurangzeb. This gesture increased his prestige and his status was raised in the eyes of the people. He won the hearts of the subjects, Hindus, Muslims and Sikhs alike. It was July 7, 1799 when victorious Ranjit Singh entered Lahore. Guns fired the royal salute and "trumpets of happiness were blown and kettle drums of victory beaten in every direction."[2]

The occupation of Lahore by Ranjit Singh is a landmark in the history of the Sikhs. It wiped out the remnants of the powerful Bhangi *Misal* and created panic in the minds of other Sardars. Ranjit Singh got the historic capital which paved the way for a sovereign Sikh State in the land of five rivers.

By this time, Shah Zaman was backs in Afghanistan, but he still nourished the idea of capturing India. His heart throbbed with the very idea of laying Hindustan under his feet, but his dream remained unfulfilled because Ranjit Singh stood like a rock between Shah Zaman and the throne of Delhi. Ranjit Singh's power and prestige had increased tremendously by now and he had become a force to be reckoned with. Shah Zaman sent Ranjit Singh feelers along with presents of horses of good breed and *Khillats*. Ranjit Singh reciprocated but forgot that once the Shah was his arch adversary.

The jealousy of the leading sardars surfaced with increase in Ranjit Singh's fame. Shah Zaman no longer posed any threat. Earlier, the Sikh Chiefs joined hands and collaborated to meet the Afghan menace. The bonds of unity were cut into pieces now and the potential Sikh chiefs Sahib Singh Bhangi of Gujarat, Jassa Singh Ramgarhia, Jodh Singh of Wazirabad and Gulab Singh Bhangi of Amritsar joined hands to wrest Lahore from Ranjit Singh. They sought the help of Nizam-ud-Din of Kasur, who was an aspirant to the Subedari of Lahore. They combined their forces and early in 1800 marched towards Lahore. They camped at Bhasin, about 16 kilometers from Lahore where Ranjit Singh faced them with his troops reinforced by the Kanahayias. The attackers lacked unity and could not launch a combined onslaught. Jassa Singh Ramgarhia fell ill at the last moment and could not join the combined forces. Gulab Singh Bhangi spent his time in enjoying wine and women and was incapable of taking any action. The forces faced each other without firing a shot for two months. Gulab Singh Bhangi breathed his last while drinking excessively. The presence of Nawab of Kasur created suspicion in the minds of the forces and the allies broke away without taking any action. They started dispersing as they were demoralised and lost all hopes of conquering Lahore of which Ranjit Singh was the ruler now. Meanwhile, Rani Sada Kaur with a detachment of Kanahayias routed the Ramgarhias in a lightening action at Batala. These *Misal* Sardars were unable to dislodge Ranjit Singh from his citadel.

Ranjit Singh hastened back to Lahore triumphantly. He was given a royal reception by the citizens. Flowers were showered on him and he was taken in a procession. However, Ranjit Singh had to incur a lot of expenditure on the battle without action. His army remained inactive but he had to pay them. His treasure was almost empty but once again the luck favoured him. He had planned to take a loan from the town's money-lenders but suddenly he got a chest containing 20,000 gold mohars from an old ruin of *Budhu-Ka-Ava,* outside the walls of Lahore, which replenished his treasury.

Ranjit Singh's expansionist designs now knew no bounds. He marched on to Jammu. On the way he annexed Narowal and Verowal. *Nazrana* worth Rs. 8000 was presented to him. Then the fort of Jassowal was attacked and seized. His forces marched further and came 6 km. Away from

Jammu. The Raja of Jammu had neither any intention nor was capable of fighting. He along with his courtiers came and presented Ranjit Singh elephants worth Rs. 20,000. Ranjit Singh presented him a *Khillat* too. Now Ranjit Singh marched towards Sialkote, accepted *Nazrana* and captured Dilawargarh. On the way he accepted *Nazranas* from several petty chiefs and returned to Lahore.

Bhangi Sardars nourished a revengeful spirit in their hearts, after losing Lahore. They were intriguing to drive out Ranjit Singh from his citadel. By that time Ranjit Singh had fortified Lahore further to meet any eventuality. The forces stationed at Gujranwala were also recalled to Lahore. Sahib Singh Bhangi of Gujarat got the opportunity, joined hands with Dal Singh of Akalgarh and made preparations to attack Gujranwala. Ranjit Singh's father, Charat Singh and bestowed a *Jagir* of Akalgarh to Dal Singh. Ranjit Singh was informed of the conspiracy and in a spate of anger, he attacked Gujarat with his 20,000 strong army and 20 guns. Sahib Singh closed the gates of the fort and started firing on Ranjit Singh's army from the ramparts of the fort. Ranjit Singh's artillery fired back. Sahib Singh Bhangi could not face the strong army of Ranjit Singh and sent his emissaries to Sahib Singh Bedi to mediate a compromise with Ranjit Singh. A treaty was made and the city was saved from devastation.

Ranjit Singh marched towards Akalgarh. Dal Singh was arrested and imprisoned in the Lahore fort but later on he was released at the instance of Sodhi Kesra Singh but was reprimanded for betrayal. Dal Singh apologised and Ranjit Singh restored him his estate. Soon afterwards Dal Singh died. Ranjit Singh personally went to Akalgarh for offering condolence and bestowed *Jagir* on his widow after annexing Akalgarh.

However, the open rift between Sahib Singh Bhangi and Ranjit Singh and some of the other Sardars invited interference from other powers. Shah Zaman of Afghanistan did not remain inactive and sent feelers to various Sardars. Ranjit Singh was told that some of the Sardars had openly promised support to the Afghan ruler. They wanted to let down Ranjit Singh and put him in trouble at any cost. They were even prepared to accept the foreign yoke in order to teach Ranjit Singh a lesson. However, Ranjit Singh made a diplomatic move and accepted gracefully the gifts sent by the Afghan ruler and in turn sent valuable gifts to him. This mutual trust and faith soothed the pent-up feelings and when the Sardars came to know of this, they became disheartened. They had lost the game. The Shah's men did not negotiate with them at all and returned to their capital. It was a diplomatic victory of Ranjit Singh. In the meanwhile, the British Government was also much perturbed. Their concern was the rising power of Ranjit Singh who could pose danger to them one day. In April 1800, the Governor-General made up his mind to show Ranjit Singh his place and counteract Shah's influence on Ranjit Singh. He issued instructions that Mir Yusuf Ali be sent to Lahore to hold negotiations with Ranjit Singh and he should impress upon the young ruler that it would be detrimental to enter into any treaty with the Shah and Shah's proposals if any could not be accepted. Ranjit Singh should have no link with the Shah.

Yusaf Ali called on Rani Sada Kaur at Amritsar. Ranjit Singh was sent for. The city was in the hands of Bhangis and Ranjit Singh's life could also be threatened. Ranjit Singh had to take a chance as he had a great desire to apprise himself of the feelings of Britishers on the subject of dealing with the Afghans.

This historic meeting was held at the residence of Rani Sada Kaur on October 22, 1800. Present in the meeting were Ranjit Singh, Rani Sada Kaur, Fateh Singh Ahluwalia and Misr Ram Dayal. Yusaf Ali gave a long sermon on the treachery of the Afghans and how Abdali was cruel to the Sikhs; how he did not spare even the holy places of worship of the Sikhs including the holy shrine at Amritsar. The Afghans could never be faithful; treachery was in their blood. Ranjit Singh, a greater diplomat as he was, remained silent throughout and listened to the sermon patiently without even winking his eyes. Finally he broke the silence by retorting that the Afghans could not be relied upon as they never adhere to their promises and he had no faith in Durranis. However, Fateh Singh Ahluwalia did not agree with Ranjit Singh and felt that the Shah seemed to be sincere in his efforts to remain friendly with Ranjit Singh and that he had already sent valuable gifts to him. If he had any evil intention, he would not have sent any emissary to Lahore. Ranjit Singh was advised to hold the hand of friendship raised by the Shah. The meeting remained indecisive. Ranjit Singh invited Yusaf Ali to Lahore.

Yusaf Ali had no alternative but to visit Lahore immediately. He met Ranjit Singh and once again expressed the fears of the British Government that Ranjit Singh was trying to be friendly with the Afghans and it could pose a danger to the British Government. Ranjit Singh again listened to Yusaf Ali patiently and did not give him any reply. He thought it proper only to send a communication to the British Government stating that he had fought the Afghans during their last invasion to Punjab with full vigour and strength; he had challenged Shah Zaman personally for a hand to hand fight and the Afghans were forced to leave Lahore. Shah hurried back to Kabul leaving his cannon while crossing the Jhelum river. This explanation pacified the British Government for the time being.

Ranjit Singh was now considered a great force. His reputation spread far and wide. Many youngmen, sons of the chieftains offered their services to Ranjit Singh in the army. Many scholars and physicians sought services under him. Poets, artists and artisans begged for royal patronage. Ranjit Singh held regular *darbars* and received visitors. He appointed Misr Ram Dayal to look after the day-to-day affairs of the State. Fateh Singh Ahluwalia guided him on army matters.

During the same period the *darbar* attracted the *Fakir* brothers who held high offices under Ranjit Singh. Fakir Aziz-ud-Din was the most prominent among them. He came along with his father, Ghulam Mohiud-din, when he was summoned for treatment of the Maharaja for an eye ailment. Then came Nur-ud-din and last of all Imam-ud-din. The family originally belonged to Arabia and their elder *Fakir* Jalal-ud-din was a holyman of religious disposition. It was he who had converted Halaku Khan of Bokhara to Islam, married one of his daughters and travelled with her to Punjab, where he finally settled down. From Jalal-ud-din's residence in Bokhara the family acquired the name of Bokhari but since Ranjit Singh's time that name has yielded place to the title of *Fakir*. The title was first assumed by Ghulam Mohi-ud-din by popular acclaim because of his piety and large-heartedness but it was Aziz-ud-din who was given an official recognition. He later became the foreign minister of the Maharaja. In the beginning. Ranjit Singh used to address Aziz-ud-din as Shahji. One day, when the Maharaja was particularly pleased with Aziz-ud-din, he said to the latter, "Shahji, I wish to give you some new title. Please suggest one." "Maharaja, if it is you highness's pleasure to do so, then be gracious enough to grant me a title which will not sound too big for future generations of my family should they become poor and will have an added grace if they should remain rich or become richer still." What about *Fakir?* asked the Maharaja, "Your father has this title already." "There could be no better title than that for me and my family," agreed Aziz-ud-din. So the title was formally confirmed. A gift of two shawls was presented to *Fakir*.

Aziz-ud-din had a place of his own in Maharaja's esteem and enjoyed his confidence. The Maharaja never undertook any important operation without consulting him or against his advice. "It was due to his wise counsel that the Maharaja maintained friendly relations with the British Government; and the fact that these relations were on a footing of equality and mutual respect was largely an outcome of his ardent loyalty to Ranjit Singh, his inborn tact and his great skill in negotiation."[3]

Then there was *Fakir* Nur-ud-din, who did host of duties as the Maharaja's Home Minister. He was a physician, Director of the Royal Palaces and Gardens, one of the custodians of the keys of the royal treasury, commandant of the arsenal of the fort and a judge. These multifarious duties brought him into constant personal contact with the Maharaja who respected him for his integrity and sincerity.

The third of the *Fakir* brothers, Imam-ud-din held many important administrative and military posts. He was the custodian of the Gobindgarh Fort at Amritsar.

By now, Ranjit Singh had become the leader of the people of Punjab but he had not taken as yet the title of the Maharaja because he did not want to give any chance to other Sardars to conspire against him on this account.

But the time had now come that Ranjit Singh should declare himself as the Maharaja of Punjab and treat all his subjects Hindus, Muslims and Sikhs equally. The semblance of a title would have certainly enhanced his status. So on April 12, 1801, on the auspicious day of the Baisakhi, when the Khalsa was founded by Guru Gobind Singh to fight against tyranny and injustice and to uplift the down-trodden, Ranjit Singh was crowned as the Maharaja of Punjab. The coronation took place amidst great festivities and public rejoicings, proclaiming the investiture of sovereignty in the *Sarkar Khalsa*. A commemorative coin, *Nanakshahi* was issued. The inscription on it read:

Degh-o-Tegh-o-Fateh-o-Nusrat be-darang
Yaft-az-Nanak-Guru Gobind Singh.

The investiture ceremony was performed by reversed Sahib Singh Bedi who put saffron paste on Ranjit Singh's forehead and proclaimed him the Maharaja of Punjab. A royal salute was fired from the fort. In the evening, the Maharaja rode on the elephant and passed through the streets of Lahore. It was a grand gala occasion. People showered flowers on him and in turn Ranjit Singh showered good and silver coin on his subjects. He won popular acclaim and earned a lasting place in the hearts of the people. At night the town was illuminated with oil lamps and there was display of fire works.

Many chiefs and Sardars offered *Nazays* and in return received *Khillats*. Immediately afterwards, important offices of the government were assigned to various persons. The fort was garrisoned. The city which had suffered for 30 years under the Bhangi misrule, needed peace and rule of law. Normal life had to be restored. The Maharaja ordered that no interference be made with the personal and public law of the Muslims. They were given the equal rights with other subjects. No discrimination was made on the basis of caste or creed. Courts presided over by the *Qazis* and *Muftis* were confirmed. Imambaksh was appointed the city Kotwal. Prominent citizens were designated as the *chaudhries* of the *mohallas*. They were made responsible for the maintenance of law and order in the town. A sense of security was given to the people. Trade and business were established on a sound basis.

Meanwhile, reports were received from Batala that Rani Sada Kaur's territory had been attacked by the Kangra Raja, Sansar Chand who had descended into the plains of Punjab and plundered some of the villages under the Rani's control. Ranjit Singh ordered his troops to march to Batala. Fateh Singh Ahluwalia was requested to join the main body of troops at Batala. The Maharaja himself followed them. Raja of Kangra's men fled in fear and all territory of the Rani was restored to her. The Maharaja occupied Noushera, part of Sansar Chand's dominion and put it under Sada Kaur with the power to collect all its revenue. The Maharaja them marched towards Nurpur. Sansar Chand fled to the Kangra hills on hearing the arrival of the Maharaja.

The Maharaja's power went on uncreasing. On return from the hills, he razed to the ground the Sujanpur fort near Pathankote where two Sikh Sardars, Budh Singh and Sangat Singh had resorted to aggressive activities. The Sardars were made to hand over the ammunition to Ranjit Singh and a police post was established at Sujanpur. The Maharaja also occupied the neighbouring territory of Dharmkot, Sukalgarh and Bahrampur. He then, proceeded to Pindi Bhatian, occupied it and handed it over to Fateh Singh Ahluwalia.

The Maharaja marched further, crossed the Jhelum river and annexed *Dhanni-Pothohar illaqa.* It was made the Maharaja's tributary. Maharaja returned to Lahore with 400 horses of good breed.

When the Maharaja was at Lahore, he received the news of the rebellion of Uttam Singh Majitha, officer-in-charge of Sitapur fort. The Maharaja sent troops to quell the rebellion, the fort was seized and the Sardar was arrested, put in chains and brought to Lahore. He was fined heavily, reprimanded and forgiven.

The Maharaja now went to Tarn Taran to take bath in the holy tank built by Guru Arjan Dev, the fifth Master. It was usual with the Maharaja to take dip in the holy tanks at Amritsar and Tarn Taran whenever he could get time and was free from campaigns.

The shrewd Maharaja had already entered into alliances with the powerful Kanahaiya and Nakai *Misals*. Another powerful *Misal* was Ahluwalia, whose founder Jassa Singh had once formed the *Dal Khalsa*. His son, Fateh Singh Ahluwalia, was the head of the *Misal* now. The Maharaja thought it proper to befriend him and when he reached Tarn Taran in 1802, he sent a message of goodwill to Fateh Singh Ahluwalia and expressed desire to meet him. Fateh Singh Ahluwalia gladly came and in the presence of *Sri Guru Granth Sahib,* both of them exchanged turbans and swore to become *dharmbhais.* An agreement of perpetual friendship was signed and it was declared that the enemy of one would be the enemy of the other. No *nazrana* would be charged while passing from each other's territory and Fateh Singh would assist Ranjit Singh in all his campaigns and whenever any new territory was occupied, a *Jagir* would be bestowed on the Ahluwalia Sardar. Thus the Maharaja made a powerful

Sardar as his friend who stood by him in all his adversities. It was a grand alliance which proved very useful in building up of the Sikh empire.

1802 proved to be an auspicious year for the Maharaja. His Rani Raj Kaur, daughter of the Nakai Sardar Khazan Singh gave birth to a son. He was named Kharak Singh. The happy event was celebrated with great rejoicings. Valuable *Khillats* were bestowed on the Sardars of the *darbar* and each soldier in the army was presented with a gold necklace. A large amount was distributed among the poor and the needy and the capital witnessed the festive merriment for many days. The Maharaja was over-joyous in getting the heir-apparent.

When the celebrations were over, the Maharaja along with his ally, Fateh Singh Ahluwalia marched on to Daska. The fort was seized, the incharge fled in fear and it was plundered. A police post was set up and the victorious Maharaja returned to Lahore. Now a message was received from Pindi Bhatian, that Jassa Singh Bhangi was committing excesses on the local *Zamindars*. He held the Chiniot fort. The Maharaja reached there with his army. Jassa Singh hid himself in the fort which was seized by the Maharaja's army. Some resistance was offered before the fort fell to Ranjit Singh's army. Some money was provided for the subsistence of the Sardar.

However, all was not quiet. The Pathan Chief of Kasur, Nizam-ud-Din created fresh trouble. He had collected a large force of Afghans and plundered few villages under the Maharaja and was making further preparations to create more trouble. The Maharaja was enraged. He directed Fateh Singh Ahluwalia to proceed to Kasur as the Nawab had broken the terms of the treaty. He should be severely punished. Ranjit Singh himself followed along with his troops. The Nawab offered stout resistance as he was well-prepared. A fierce battle ensued. The Sikhs showed their valour under the command of their able generals. The Pathans entered the fort as they were unable to fight the Sikh army in the open. Many were slain. At last the fort was seized and remaining soldiers were put to death. The town was plundered. A large number of people were made prisoners. The Nawab surrendered with humility. He was forgiven, reinstated and he promised to remain submissive. He paid a huge sum of money as *nazrana* and was made to pay war reputations. The victorious Maharaja returned to Lahore. Money was distributed among the poor and the needy to celebrate the victory.

Then, after a brief spell, the Maharaja marched into Jullunder Doab. He annexed several places on the way. A rich widow of a Khatri Chuhar Mal was in possession of the Phagwara town. Ranjit Singh attacked Phagwara, seized the town and forced the widow to retire to Hardwar. Her property was confiscated and handed over to Fateh Singh Ahluwalia along with the town.

The Maharaja visited Kapurthala and there he came to know that Raja Sansar Chand of Kangra had entered Bijwara and Hoshiarpur. The Maharaja hastened back, turned out Raja Sansar Chand and established his army posts at these two places. Sansar Chand fled to Kangra and Ranjit Singh captured many villages in the foot of the hills.

By this time Ranjit Singh had become a great force. While returning from the hills, the Maharaja subdued old Sikh chiefs and Sardars, Tara Singh Gheba, Dharm Singh of Amritsar and Budh Singh of Fyzulapur.

And now came the engagement of his son Kharak Singh to Chand Kaur, daughter of Jaimal Singh of Kanahaiya *misal*. There were rejoicings throughout the kingdom. Celebrations continued for several days. *Nauch* parties were arranged and money was spent lavishly. In one of such parties, the Maharaja fell in love with a very beautiful Muslim dancing girl, Moran, whom he ultimately married. The marriage was celebrated with great splendour and gaiety. She had great influence over the Maharaja and money was coined with the inscription of *Mor;* Peacock on it in commemoration of the marriage. The Maharaja performed a pilgrimage to Hardwar, accompanied by Moran. The Chiefs presented him *Nazranas* and at Hardwar, the Maharaja distributed a lakh of rupees to the poor.

However, this marriage with Moran raised a storm in the kingdom. Sikh public opinion received a rude shock. The Maharaja was summoned to the *Akal Takht*. The Maharaja sought forgiveness with all humility. He offered gifts to the *Panj Payaras,* under whose orders he was called. They pronounced punishment which the Maharaja gladly accepted. He was to be flogged publicly. *Panj Payaras* were gratified at the submission of the Maharaja and took a lenient view and accepted a fine of Rs. 1,25,000 from the Maharaja.

Moran's influence over the Maharaja remained only for a short while. The Maharaja sent Moran away to Pathankote, where she spent many years of her life in peace.

The Maharaja established a secular state in which all the subjects, Hindu, Muslims and Sikhs were treated alike. Many talented Hindus and Muslims joined his service and the Maharaja gladly participated in the religious festivals of all the communities. Festivals like Dussehra, Diwali, Holi and Basant were celebrated with splendour and gaiety. The Maharaja participated in them along with his subjects and on the occasions of *Amavas* and *Baisakhi* took a dip into the holy tank at Amritsar. By his secular outlook, the Maharaja earned great respect from his subject and also their loyalty.

REFERENCES

1. Collins S.C., June 24, 1800.
2. Sohan Lal, Udmat-ut-Twarikh, Daftar II, p. 43.
3. Syed Maheduddin, The Real Ranjit Singh, p. 40.

7

Amritsar Conquered

Amritsar is the spiritual capital of the Sikhs. A holy tank was got dug by Guru Ram Das and the temple was built by Guru Arjan Dev, who installed *Guru Granth Sahib* in it. Akal Takht was built by Guru Hargobind. It was the seat of temporal Authority. The Guru himself sat there and held a Court of Justice. Many Sikhs used to gather there for the redress of their garievances. *Gurmattas* were passed which were binding on the Sikhs.

Guru Arjan Dev proclaimed the benefits of the holy tank at Amritsar:

> "All the sins that a man committeth are washed away by bathing in the Tank of Ram Das."

It was must for every true Sikh to take a dip in the holy tank. Moreover, Amritsar was the biggest trade centre of Punjab. Goods from Central Asia were exchanged here for the local goods. Silk, muslin, spices, tea, hides and several other articles were bought and sold here. For the Sikhs, Amritsar was the Mecca. It is almost obligatory for every Sikh to take a dip in the holy tank once or twice a year.

Amritsar was divided among a dozen families manning different parts of the city. In each of these parts they had built for themselves small fortresses and maintained a task force of tax collectors who sometimes forcibly collected money form the trading community. These tax collectors very often quarrelled among themselves and sometimes even created scenes in the streets to the amazement of the residents. The citizens could not stand such a situation for long and secretly approached Maharaja Ranjit Singh to invite him to attack the city. It was reported to Ranjit Singh that there was hardly any unity among these Sardars. The only formidable family was that of Mai Sukhan, widow of the Bhangi chief, Gulab Singh. She was in possession of the Gobindgarh fort. According to Lepel Griffin, Ranjit Singh demanded from Mai Sukhan the famous Bhangi gun, *Zamzama,* made of copper and brass, which had caused disaster among the rank and file of the Marathas in the battle of Panipat. It was captured from the Durranis in 1764 by the Bhangis and it was because of this reason that it was known as *Bhangian di tope.*

Earlier, Maharaja Ranjit Singh had joined hands with the Ahluwalia chief, Fateh Singh. Before Amritsar was attacked, he exchanged turbans with him, thereby binding himself to an alliance with him. Sada Kaur, Maharaja's mother-in-law also rendered him the desired help and assistance.

Thus, in 1802, Maharaja Ranjit Singh marched towards the city of Amritsar at the head of the force consisting of Kanahaiya, Nakkai and Ahluwalia troops in addition to his own force in strength. Sada Kaur also accompanied the troops. When the combined army reached Amritsar, the Rani closed the gates of the town, mounted the ramparts of the city with arms and ammunition in considerable quantity and gave the attacking army a very good reception. Fateh Singh Ahluwalia, commenced his operations in front of the Bridge Gate and the Maharaja on the other end of the Lohgarh fort. A fierce fighting took place but in the end the gates could not stand the heavy cannonade and the marching army entered the city in triumph, with the Maharaja at the head. Ranjit Singh ordered that the city should not be plundered as the place was too sacred with the memory of the Gurus. The fort of Lohgarh was besieged without any difficulty. As a coincidence, there was heavy rain during the day and the Rani and her son had no place to take shelter. They went to the *haveli* of Sardar Jodh Singh Ramgarhia, who took pity on them and gave them shelter. Ranjit Singh sanctioned a small *jagir* for them for their maintenance. The confederacy collapsed. Ranjit Singh occupied the fort and captured considerable war material, including the *Zamzama* and the area which yielded a handsome revenue.

More important than the capture of the fort was the acquisition of the services of the gallant warrior, Akali Phula Singh. He belonged to the militant order of the Nihangs and had devoted his life to the protection of the Sikh shrines. He rendered necessary help to the Maharaja in capturing the city of Amritsar. With him were about three thousand Nihangs who wanted to join the army of the Maharaja. The Akali proved to be a great asset to the Maharaja in capturing other territories later on. He died a heroic death in the battle of Naushera. He was a man of such a forceful will and character that at one time he decoyed even Maharaja Ranjit Singh to undress and get flogged on his naked body before the holy Akal Takht. With a person of such a high stature as the Maharaja himself accepting the punishment awarded, the Akal Takht gained a dignity and prestige among the Sikhs who henceforth came to seek a pardon here.

Akali Phula Singh, though a soldier of zeal and valour, sometimes acted according to his own whims. Since 1800, the management of the holy shrines passed into the hands of the Akalis under the supervision of Akali Phula Singh. In 1815 he reached Amritsar with some of his devotees and out of Rs. 1,100 collected as contribution at *Darbar Sahib*, he claimed Rs 1,000. It was Baisakhi day. He picked up quarrel with his rivals and in the ensuing encounter there were three casualties. The matter was reported to Ranjit Singh who ordered Hakim Imam-ud-Din to settle the dispute. Phula Singh was directed to take the quantum of the offering already fixed in such cases.

Ranjit Singh, the victor, paid a visit to Hari Mandir as a humble man and performed his ablutions in the holy tank. While passing through the streets of Amritsar, he distributed a large sum of money as alms to the poor and the needy.

The capture of Amritsar brought fame and honour to Ranjit Singh. Many Indians from the force of the East India Company started joining the ranks of his army. As many Sardars of the Bhangi family had joined the Maharaja's army, they were required to furnish well-equipped soldiers at times of war. There could be as many as 10,000 men in the field. The other section consisted of the militants of the *Misals* which were allies of Ranjit Singh. The total fighting force which could be utilised on any occasion was 31,000 men. Ranjit Singh appointed Misar Chhhajju Mal as the Collector of Customs as Amritsar. The Misar was extremely loyal to the Maharaja and rendered him useful service. Ranjit Singh took keen interest in the management of the holy shrine. He appointed Surat Singh as its Manager. He gave the shrine its marble face and its golden look from which the name Golden Temple or *Swarn Mandir* is derived. Marble and fresco paintings were also added. The eastern loggia of the shrine was gilded by Rani Sada Kaur at a cost of Rs. 1,75,300, while the other sides were done by the Maharaja at a cost of Rs. 5,35,332. Amritsar's gaiety and splendour increased. It was inhabited by aristocracy and many high dignitaries often visited the town. It was illuminated on special occasions. There were rejoicings in the city and it gave a festive appearance and whenever the Maharaja was victorious in any campaign, large scale celebrations were held.

By that time, civil war had started in Afghanistan. The four sons of Taimur Shah quarelled among themselves for ascendancy. This ugly situation brought ruin to the once powerful Afghan empire. It was looked upon with contempt. The power which once created terror was now helplessly looking for other's help. The time was thus opportune for Ranjit Singh to strike. He could extend his frontiers east of the Indus.

The Dussehra festival came. It was celebrated with great pomp and show. And then came the season for campaigns. Ranjit Singh sent his emissaries to Ahmad Khan, the Sial Chief of Jhang, who was the most powerful ruler. A tribute was demanded and the Khan was asked to remain loyal and submissive in future. The Khan was left with option either to agree on these terms or be embroiled in a battle. Ranjit Singh had already made preparations to attack Jhang in case of any eventuality. He had equipped his army with the latest weapons. The emissaried contacted the Khan, whose pride did not allow him to surrender. Ranjit Singh had no alternative but to attack.

It was 1803 when Ranjit Singh marched towards Jhang at the head of a strong army. The Ahluwalia Chief Fateh Singh accompanied him. The newly established battalion, Najibwala formed part of the expedition. In the way, the towns and villages were plundered. Some resistance was offered by the local zamindars but they were too weak to hold up Ranjit's army. However, when the Maharaja was informed of the behaviour of his soldiers, he immediately prohibited them from indulging in such activities which brought bad name to his army. Coming to know of the impending attack, Ahmad Khan had collected a large number of tribesmen to give Ranjit Singh's army a befitting reply. He also had two artillery guns with him. The battle started in the noon and ceased by evening. Ahmad Shah could not stand the onslaughts of the Sikh army and retired to the town. Many soldiers of both the sides were killed. The town was besieged by the Khalsa army and all the supply lines were cut off. But again on the next day, the fighting started, more fiercely this time. Ahmad Khan himself controlled the artillery fire and once was able to fire inside the Maharaja's tent, but it could not do any harm to him. The siege continued for 3 days. Many people deserted the Nawab and his army was getting depleted. The Nawab looked a helpless creature.

Even Nawab's personal attendants deserted him and fled the town. Only Nasrat Khan stood by the Nawab but it was a desperate situation for the Nawab and he had no alternative but to leave his territory along with his family to Multan. At this juncture the local citizens, mostly Hindus sent a petition to the Maharaja, assuring him all help, if he entered the town. The Maharaja entered the town at the head of the victorious army and took possession of the large wealth accumulated by the Jhang chief. Although the Maharaja had issued strict orders not to plunder the town, his soldiers enjoyed the booty full well. Ahmad Shah had agreed to pay a tribute of Rs. 60,000 a year to the Maharaja and was allowed to return to his capital. Peace was restored, but the amount of tribute was raised to Rs. 1,20,000 after two years.

The Maharaja now attacked Uch and asked for a tribute from the chief of Uch, Nag Sultan. It was paid. After that the Maharaja's army entered Sahiwal and Garh. The Baluch chiefs offered the Maharaja money and horses.

Now came Jammu, Bhimber, Rajauri and Kotla. Since the death of Raja Ranjit Deo of Jammu in 1780, the new ruler, Brij Raj Deo had lost his strength and had become very weak and inactive. The Sikhs attacked Jammu several times. Brij Raj Deo agreed to pay *nazrana* of Rs. 60,000 to the Sikhs and they were kept away from the territory. Things went smoothly for some time but with the death of Brij Raj Deo, the situation again changed. Sampuran Singh became the ruler, who was a minor and Mian Mota acted as his regent. As ill-luck would have it, the Raja died within two years of becoming a ruler. The war of succession started and in course of time Chet Singh became the new ruler.

Chet Singh was a weak ruler. His territory disintegrated and the weak army could hardly deaf end the town from any outside invasion. Ranjit Singh sent a strong contingent of his army in 1806 to annex the territory, which after extracting the *nazrana* returned back to the capital.

The Sikhs again marched to Jammu in 1807 under the command of Misar Dewan Chand. All the hill chiefs joined hands and offered stout resistance. The Sikh general returned after accepting the *nazranas*. In 1809, when Jai Singh, the ruler of Jammu passed away, Ranjit Singh's forces attacked Jammu under the command of Dewan Bhawani Das. The family of the deceased Raja fled across the Sutlej and the Sikhs captured Jammu. Jamedar Khushal Singh was appointed the first Governor to manage the affairs of the territory. However, stiff opposition was offered by the local zamindars and they refused to pay the land revenue. Ranjit Singh was annoyed with Khushal Singh and Gulab Singh obtained a *Jagir* of Rs. 40,000. In 1818, Gulab Singh was made the Raja of Jammu and he promised to pay an annual tribute of Rs. 4,00,000 to the Lahore *darbar*.

When things settled down, the Maharaja took the first major step towards the annexation of Kashmir. In 1811, Ranjit Singh sent a strong force under Desa Singh Majitha to capture Kotla which was between Nurpur and Kangra. It was under Raja Dhian Singh. The fort was captured without much resistance.

Meanwhile, one victory followed another. The Sikh empire was expanding. Raja Sultan Khan of Bhimber joined hands with Sahib Singh Bhangi of Gujarat. It was not liked by the Maharaja. In his spate of anger, the Maharaja summoned Sultan Khan to Lahore, which he refused. Ranjit Singh despatched two battalions under the command of Fakir Aziz-ud-din to march to Bhimber. The Khan offered stout resistance and in a battle that ensued, the Sikh army had to retreat. The force was strengthened and more troops reached under Dewan Mukham Chand. 5,000 horsemen invaded the fort, the Khan finally had to surrender and agreed to pay a tribute of Rs. 40,000. Ismail Khan was appointed the ruler of Bhimber. In 1812, Sultan Khan murdered Ismail Khan. Again, the Sikh forces marched under the command of Dewan Mukham Chand and Bhai Ram Singh. The battle could not decide the fate of two armies and negotiations were started. Sultan Khan was brought to Lahore and was promised full protection. But later, he was imprisoned and his territory was annexed to the Lahore *darbar*. This sealed the fate of Sultan Khan.

Now Rajauri remained. It was attacked in 1812 and Agar Khan was given all help by Ata Mohammad Khan of Kashmir and the Raja of Poonch. The Khalsa forced withdrew but during the beginning for next year Rajauri was again attacked by Bhai Ram Singh and made Agar Khan to flee but soon afterwards was called back and Rajauri was made the tributary of the Sikh ruler.

In 1804, Kangra again rose in revolt. Raja Sansar Chand left the hills and plundered Bijwara and Hoshiarpur. When Ranjit Singh came to know of the incident, he marched towards these places and Raja Sansar Chand was made to retreat. After that the Kangra chief had involved himself with the Gorkhas, who had aspired to rule over the entire country. He had no time to attack Ranjit Singh's territory.

Things went on like this. The Maharaja once fell ill and rested in the famour Shalimar Garden, built by the Emperor Shahjahan. Some of the Maharaja's courtiers accompanied him to look after his requirements. Once an animated discussion started between the Maharaja and his courtiers regarding name of the Garden. The Maharaja opined that the literal meaning of the word *Shala* was God's and *Mar* means a curse. It was, therefore appropriate that the name of the Garden should be changed to some other name. The courtiers told the Maharaj that *Shala* was a Turki word which means pleasure and the *mar* means the place to live in. So Shalimar means the place of pleasure and this name was given to many such Gardens by the Muslim rulers of India. But Ranjit Singh was not convinced at all. He argued with his courtiers further and asked them if the word really meant the place of pleasure, then how it was that Mirza Mahdi called it *Shaha mah* in the biography of Nadir Shah which meant 'A moon's blaze'. The courtiers once again explained that the word actually meant a place of pleasure, but the Maharaj did not agree and named the Garden an 'Shahla Bagh'. Shahla means in Persian a beloved whose eyes are dark grey with a reddish streak and the *Bagh* means garden. Orders were issued that in all future correspondence the name *Shahla Bagh* should be used.

Ranjit Singh paid a visit to Hari Mandir at Amritsar. He fortified and renovated the Gobindgarh fort. The fort had an imposing appearance. The fort was built by Gujjar Singh Bhangi. The Maharaja got it repaired under the supervision of Iman-ud-Din, who was later on appointed the Governor or the Fort, the post which he held for many years. It is said that Ranjit Singh got the fort built on the plea of protecting the holy tank and the pilgrims visiting it but mainly it was constructed to keep the treasure in the fort for safe custody. Earlier the treasure was kept with the local bankers, which, of course, was not safe.

The fort was built of lime and brick with several bastions and strong iron gates. Twenty-five cannons were mounted on its ramparts. Its structure was further improved and a lot of expenditure was incurred. It was described as "the most striking edifice which held the wealth of the Government in Ranjit Singh's time".[1]

Many house were built on the bastions. Generally foreign visitors were not allowed inside the fort. They were allowed to have a glimpse from outside only. An exception was made in the case of a distinguished visitor, W. G. Osborne who was taken round the fort. He was immensely impressed and mentioned that the fort contained the treasure of Ranjit Singh amounting to twelve missions in gold.

Ranjit Singh also got extended the Hansli Canal, constructed by Shahjahan in 1633 from Lahore to Amritsar to fill the tank surrounding the Goden Temple at Amritsar. It solved the water problem.

During his visit to Amritsar in 1804, the Maharaja held a grand *darbar*. Some of the Hindustani soldiers presented themselves to the Maharaja and showed him their feats of warfare, learnt by them in the British army. They had once served the East India Company but had now left the jobs. The Maharaja gave them employment but the Sikh soldiers were reluctant to learn anything from them. The Sikh soldiers were the best horsemen and did not want to fight while marching on foot. It was considered below their honour.

The Maharaja called for a general muster of his forces at Amritsar so that he could watch the various units parading and ultimately settle their Divisions and Commands. The Maharaja bestowed the honours and awards on his Sardars:

Sardar Desa Singh Majitha, command of 400 horsemen. Hari Singh Nalwa 800 infantry and cavalry. Hukma Singh Chimni Daroga of 20 artillery; Gouse Khan commandant of artillery with 2000 horsemen; Roushan Khan and Sheikh Ibadulla, Commandant 2000 najibs, Babu Bhag Singh Moraliwala, Commander of 500, Milka Singh to command 700, Nodh Singh Commander of 400, Attar Singh to be Risaldar of 500 infantry, Mit Singh to command 1500 Cavalry. Kurma Singh to command 1000, Nihal Singh Attariwala to be commander of 500. The total came to about 13000 active troops.

They were made Sardars and *Jagirs* were bestowed on them. Some of the Sardars were made honorary commanders of the troops given against each name. They were to help the Maharaja in the war time only along with their men. They were: Jassa Singh son of Karan Singh (10000): Sahib Singh son of Gujjar Singh Bhangi (10000); Chet Singh son of Lehna Singh Bhangi (10000); Bhag Singh Ahluwalia 10,000; Nahar Singh of Chamiari (10000); Kanahaiya Sardar (5000) Nakais (4000); Hill Rajas (5,000); Doaba Sardars (10000). The grand total was about 31000 troops.

In 1805, Ranjit Singh entered into treaties with the Muslim chiefs of Chenab and Jhelum. The Afghan empire was cracking and Ranjit's Singh power was increasing. The chiefs started looking towards the Maharaja than to Kabul. They paid homage to him and rallied around him in case of any attack. The Maharaja continued to advance and went as far as Rawalpindi in the north-west. The area between the Ravi and Chenab and the Sahiwal between the Chenab and Jhelum were made his tributories. He levied contributions on Ahmedabad and Khushab.

The Maharaja returned to Lahore and celebrated the Holi festival with great pomp and grandeur. He then proceeded to Hardwar to take bath in the holy Ganges. The Maharaja returned to Lahore in June and organised the financial matters, which had remained in jeopardy for sometime. Land revenue system was changed and new collectors were appointed.

REFERENCE

1. Steinbach, The Punjab, p. 5.

8

The Maratha Chief Visits Punjab

By now, the situation had changed. Ranjit Singh was the acknowledged leader of his people. However, there were other powers around his empire which could not be ignored and who exercised considerable influence in their respective territories. They were George Thomas at Hansi, the Scindia at Delhi and beyond Delhi, the British.

In 1979, George Thomas tried unsuccessfully to enter into a compromise with the chiefs of Malwa, to crush the Maratha power which was already waning in the northern India. The Malwa chiefs had joined hands temporarily setting aside their mutual ill-will to fight against Shah Zaman of Afghanistan who had reached Lahore. It was said that he was about to cross Sutlej and if that happened. They sent forces towards the north to face the impending danger. George Thomas thought that he should avail this golden opportunity. He attacked and seized Jind. But the Malwa chiefs united themselves and gave Thomas a befitting reply. The joint forces of Patiala, Jind, Ladwa, Kaithal and Thanesar reached Jind and repulsed George's forces. He withdrew but it was a tactical withdrawal ang again at night, he attacked the chiefs' forces and routed them. They were forced to surrender and a humiliating treaty of peace and friendship was imposed on them.

But hardly two years had passed when in 1799, he attacked the Malwa chiefs. A fierce battle was fought at

Dibrah but it could not decide the fate of anybody. However, George plundered Bhawanigarh, Narangwal and Sunam and invaded Kaithal and Safidon. He was able to capture Safidon. Bhag Singh of Jind came to the rescue of chiefs' forces. George's forces were turned out of Safidon. George went back to Hansi, plundering so me towns and villages en route.

George Thomas remained quiet for some time. He reorganised his forces and equipped them well. But the Malwa chiefs were rired of George's frequent invasions and approached the French General Perron, who was the Maratha Deputy at Delhi. He represented Daulat Rao Scindia. In 1801. A delegation consisting of Raja Bhag Singh of Jind, Lal Singh of Kaithal and Chain Singh, representative of Raja of Patiala reached Delhi to meet Perron. These chiefs solicited help of the Maratha and in liquidating George's power. Perron was already aware of the George's activities and desired to put a curb on them. He willingly extended his hand of friendship towards the Malwa chiefs. He exchanged turbans with them and exploited the situation to the maximum extent possible. Perron desired to extend Maratha influence in the region. A Maratha paramountcy was accepted by the Malwa chiefs. An army of 12000 strong under the command of Louis and assisted by the forces of Jind and Kaithal marched towards Chinagarh. Thomas was forced to retire to Hansi. Hansi was sieged which continued for some time. Meanwhile Louis' forces were further reinforced from Delhi and their number increased to 20,000. George was bewildered and lost his wits. He was ordered to surrender and offered a post in the Maratha army. He was assured a monthly subsidy of Rs. 30,000 for his forces, provided he dissolved his small empire.

The terms were not accepted by George. He made up his mind to fight the Maratha general and his allied forces. George had an army of 10,000 men and 500 horsemen. He marched towards the north to wipe out the Jind and Kaithal detachments. He reached Georgegarh and pushed off a detachment of Bourquin's troops from the place and firmly entrenched himself there. He was flanked by a small fort on his right side and on his left were sand dunes and hillocks. A fierce fight took place. The Marathas opened up their guns and 4000 men of Bourquins force were killed. George Thomas lost the ground and retired to Hansi and on Januar 1,1802 was forced to surrender. He was allowed to proceed towards the British territory where he died later on.

Now came the turn of Sikh chiefs to Cis-Sutlej who earlier sought the Maratha Chiefs' help against George Thomas. The Maratha general Perron imposed heavy tributes on them which they were unable to pay. They actually did not gain anything in George's defeat and their position remained the same. The slavery of the Marathas was as bad for them as that of George Thomas. They had to pay an annual tribute of 1/3 of their revenue which was too heavy. The Raja of Patiala who had earlier exchanged turbans with the Maratha general Perron, had to pay an annual tribute of Rs. 38250, Jind had to pay Rs. 7250, Nabha Rs. 9500 and Kaithal Rs. 15000.

Besides the payment of these heavy amounts the Cis-Sutlej chiefs were treated as dependents to the Marathas. The chiefs suffered humiliation and led a life of indignity and dishonour. The Marathas were overjoyous. The chiefs had suffered for no gain. They had only self-interest before them. Opportunism did not pay them. Then came the Maratha war with the British in 1802. All the chiefs except those of Ladwa and Thasesar remained aloof and did not render any assistance to the Marathas. The Cis-Sutlej chiefs changed sides. A treaty was signed at Surjiarjan gaon according to which the Marathas surrendered Delhi, Sirsa, Hansi, Rohtak, Agra and Hissar to the British who became the masters of this part of the country. The sun of Maratha empire had set. Delhi was occupied by the British and with it their strength increased considerably. The Cis-Sutlej chiefs looked towards them for protection. Sahib Singh of Patiala himself sent the offer of help and Bhag Singh of Jind and Lal Singh of Kaithal joined the campt of Col. Burn at Panipat.

The treacherous role played by the Cis-Sutlej chiefs by declaring their allegiance to the British changed the course of history. In March 1805, General Lake proclaimed general anmestly and occupied Karnal and Jinjanna. They granted sanads for the estates of Faridpur, Gohana and Barsat to Bhag Singh of Jind and Lal Singh of Kaithal.

This was not the time for Ranjit Singh to sit idle. He was too shrewd a Maharaja who could not take any chance. While the Cis-Sutlej chiefs were busy intriguing and fighting amongst themselves, Ranjit Singh preoccupied himself in increasing the strength of his army and equipping it with the latest weapons. "He was reported to be daily increasing his cavalry with a view to subduing all the chiefs on the other side of the Sutlej."[1] He cherished in his heat to further expand his empire and fulfil his dream of establishing a *Khalsa raj* in all parts of Punjab.

On the other hand, the British were in no mood to relax and their intelligence agencies were more active than before. On December 18, 1804, the British agent received a report that Ranjit Singh had crossed the Sutlej with his large army to capture Ludhiana. Holkar, the Maratha chief was already on his side and was inviting Ranjit Singh to join hands with him. The British Resident at Delhi was aware of the prevailing situation. He had a lurking fear in his mind that Ranjit Singh might be tempted to join hands with the Maratha chief, thinking that the British possessions were vulnerable.

Sahib Singh of Patiala became nervous. He was afraid of losing his State, as Ranjit Singh had already taken possession of Phagwara. He sent an appeal to the Resident at Delhi and sought his help and assistance, as he was afraid of an open rupture with the Maharaja. It was confirmed by the news-writer of Patiala, who informed the Resident that Ranjit Singh intended to capture the Patiala State. Sahib Singh sent his *vakil* to Delhi to obtain British aid at the cost of his self-respect and against national interests. But the British Government did not pay any heed to his request and simply ignored it. They felt that Sahib Singh of Patiala was very weak and feeble-minded person who had no judgement of his own. He might have been instigated by his counsellors. The British refused to indulge in these internal matters and they did not want to pick up quarrel with Ranjit Singh on this account.

When Ranjit Singh arrived at Patiala, Sahib Singh realised his mistake of inviting the Maharaja and locked himself up in his fort. A few rounds of fire made him to come in the open. He welcomed the Maharaja and he was lavishly entertained and was assured that he was the recognised Maharaja of Punjab. A meeting of the chiefs took place on a bank with precautions on both sides. Great respect was paid to Ranjit Singh. Sahib Singh (Patiala) said to him: "Jaswant Singh (Nabha) has acted towards me in a very extraordinary manner." Ranjit Singh replied, "He is your brother; all of you are alike to me. I have only come to settle your disputes." Raja Sahib Singh observed: "If you had considered me in the same light as Bhag Singh (Jind) and Jaswant Singh you would not have fired at me so furiously. "Ranjit replied: "This took place at the request of your brother and uncle, otherwise I consider you greater than myself." Sahib Singh said: "I am yours." Bhai Lal Singh (Kaithal) said to Ranjit Singh: "You are the chief and the light of our tribe. Now that you have come into this country, you will act according to your goodness and excellence." Sahib Singh did not get rid of his suspicions. After this Sahib Singh in conversation with the Ranee said Ranjit Singh is a great villain."[2]

The political situation was very fluid and was changing rapidly. Within two years of the defeat of Scindia, Jaswant Rao Holkar, a Maratha chief, picked up a dispute with the British. Holkar could not face the might of the British and the initiative passed into the hands of the British commander,

Lord Lake. Holkar was defeated at Deeg and he and his Rohilla ally, Amir Khan, escaped and tried to seek help from wherever it was available. They came to Patiala, stayed for quite some time and held discussions with the Malwa chiefs. Holkar also sent an invitation to the Afghan chief to attack India again. On the other hand, Lord Lake resumed his activities. Holkar and Amir Khan reached Amritsar. Lake followed them to Beas. Both of them sent urgent communications to Ranjit Singh. Lord Lake wrote that if Ranjit Singh helped Holkar, he would be responsible for the consequences. Holkar begged Ranjit Singh to help him to face the challenge of the British. Ranjit Singh realised the gravity of the situation but could not make up his mind at such a short notice.

Although a shrewd Politician, Ranjit Singh did not want to decided anything in haste. Such a decision might endanger the interests of his empire. Therefore, in order to seek the benefit of their advice, he sent a word to all his principal Sardars to come to Amritsar and give their counsel. An assembly of *Sarbat Khalsa* was called in which the leading Sikh chiefs and other dignitaries participated. An open discussion was held and pros and cons of both the situations were considered. Holkar and Amir Khan had come to Amritsar to take shelter and it was the noble duty of the Maharaja to give them protection. Holkar paid a visit to the Golden Temple and made a handsome offering. He almost begged help from Ranjit Singh and said that it was only he who could save the situation and protect the Hindus of India. On the other hand, there was a grave threat from the British who could even go to the extent of bringing the war into the territory of Ranjit Singh. The Maharaja was perplexed. Both the alternatives were dangerous. Ultimately he decided to move among the Holkar troops and found that they were not match to the British forces fully equipped with the latest war weapons.

As was usual with the Maharaja, in such circumstances and difficult situations he took guidance from *Sri Guru Granth Sahib*. He wrote names of Holkar and Lord Lake on two slips of paper and placed them before the holy book. He offered prayers before the before the *Granth Sahib*, and then picked up one of the slips. The name of Lord Lake was written on it. Moreover, Fateh Singh Ahluwalia advised Ranjit Singh not to strain his relations with the British and the advice was accepted by the Maharaja.

Ranjit Singh decided not to be drawn into British and Maratha dispute and tried to mediate for an amicable settlement. At the same time, orders were received from London by Lord Lake that no more accexations be made and Holkar be allowed to take possession of his territory. Ranjit Singh heaved a sigh of relief. Holkar and Rohillas left the Punjab for ever.

In 1827, Ranjit Singh told Wade: "I well tell you a story. Holkar pressed by the British solicited my assistance and made temporary offers to secure my cooperation. Uncertain as to what part I should take, I resorted to a measure I have often adopted to determine my decision in doubtful cases. I took two slips of paper and writing on one the propositions of Holkar and on the other whether I should preserve peace with the Britishers, I put them into the leaves of the Granth, and desired a boy of innocent years to bring one of the papers to me. He brought that one on which the last was written and I acted accordingly."[3]

The Maharaja thus made up his mind to help Holkar and remain friendly with the British. The Maharaja further said: "Vexed at my refusal to help him, Holkar began to reproach the Sikhs as worthless and spiritless set of people saying, "I have heard a great deal of your enterprise, but find on coming among you, you have none. If you won't join me against the British, I shall go to the Afghans and seek the aid of foreigners." To which I said, "you talk tauntingly of the Sikhs, yet here you are with an army of

1,00,000 men flying before the troops of Lord Lake which hardly exceed 5,000." He made no reply.[4]

Besides, the reasons offered by Ranjit Singh for his refusal to help Holkar in his fight against the British, it can be said that he thought that it would be disastrous and an exercise in futility for him to ally himself with the setting star. "Moreover, Raja Bhag Singh of Jind, an uncle of Ranjit Singh advised him not to enter into a conflict with the British. The Maharaja took the sanest course and saved his infant kingdom from destruction. However there is other side of the picture. It is reported that the Maharaja's decision was disagreeable to the Sardars and generals, who murmured among themselves that their royal master had broken faith and had allied himself with that hated *firangis*, who were the enemies of the faith."[5]

The Maharaja, thus entered into a treaty with the British government known as the first Anglo-Sikh treaty of friendship and unity signed on January 1, 1806 by Sardar Fateh Singh Ahluwalia for himself and on behalf of Maharaja Ranjit Singh on the one hand and East India Company on the other which said:

Sardar Ranjit Singh and Sardar Fateh have consented to the following articles of agreement, concluded by Lieutenant Colonel John Malcolm, under the special authority of the Right Honourable Lord Lake, himself duly authorise by the Honourable Sir George Hilaro Barlow, Bart., Governor-General and Sardar Fateh Singh, as principal on the part of himself, and plenipotentiary on the part of Ranjit Singh:

One: Sardar Ranjit Singh and Sardar Fateh Singh Ahluwalia hereby agree that they will cause Jaswant Rao Holkar to remove with his army to the distance of thirty coss from Amritsar immediately, and will never hereafter hold any further connection with him, or aid or assist him with troops, or in any other manner whatsoever; and they further agree that they will not in any way molest such of Jaswant Rao Holkar's followers or troops as are desirous of returning to their homes in the Deccan, but, on the contrary, will render them every assistance in their power for carrying such intention into execution.

Two: The British Government hereby agrees, that in case a pacification should not be effected between the Government and Jaswant Rao Holkar, the British army shall move from its present encampment, on the banks of the river Beas, as soon as Jaswant Rao Holkar, aforesaid shall have marched his army to the distance of thirty coss from Amritsar; and that, in any treaty which may hereafter be concluded between the British and Jaswant Rao Holkar, it shall be stipulated that, immediately after the conclusion of the said treaty, Holkar shall evacuate the territories of the Sikhs, and march towards his own, and that he shall in no way whatever injure or destroy Government such parts of the Sikh country as may lie in his route. The British Government further agrees that, as long as the said Chieftains, Ranjit Singh and Fateh Singh, abstain from holding any friendly connection with the enemies of the Government or from committing any act of hostility on their own parts against the said Government, the British armies shall never enter the territories of the said Chieftains, nor will the British Government form any plans for the seizure or sequestration of their possessions or property.

"The treaty was signed and the evil which Ranjit Singh dreaded was averted. Friendly relations were further strengthened between the British Commander and Ranjit Singh, and the Ahluwalia chief, and in course of the same month, the armies which had inspired so much alaram in the Punjab retraced their steps to Hindostan. Ranjit Singh had heard many particulars regarding the British from the Maratha chief, Jaswant Rao, and expressed his astonishment at their warlike exploits. Even after this, Ranjit dreaded the power of that Government and determined to be at peace with it."[6] The chief interest of the treaty lies in the fact that it was Ranjit Singh's first transaction with the British Government, and brought him for the first time into personal contact with British political and military officers and troops trained and disciplined on Western lines.[7]

After the treaty was signed, the festival of Holi was celebrated at Lahore and the city presented a colourful picture. Men, women and children, both high and low participated in the celebrations and Ranjit Singh mixed with the people as freely as he could. He indulged in all kinds of excesses which resulted in creating tension in his mind and above all the hectic days he passed made him ill. He went to take a bath in holy tank at Katas in the Jhelum district. Again on his return, he fell dangerously ill and was forced to break his journey at Miani and stayed there till he was fully recovered.

In the same year, 1806, Ranjit Singh appointed Mukham Chand as the chief of the army much to the annoyance of his Sardars. Mukham Chand was Khatri by birth and was proud to be one of Ranjit Singh's ablest generals. Earlier he was in the employ of Sahib Singh of Gujarat. Ranjit Singh did not care for any opposition and true to his secular character, showed full confidence in Mukham Chand, who in turn remained loyal to his Master till the end.

Then, Ranjit Singh captured Zira, expelling the widow of Mohar Singh Nishanwala. Ranjit Singh also seized Muketsar and Kot Kapura, possessions of Jagat Singh. He then fell on Dharmkot, reduced it and marched to Faridkot. The ruler of that place proved shrewd enough and avoided any destructive confrontation by agreeing to pay a handsome tribute.

Luck favoured Ranjit Singh. He achieved success after success and was now the most powerful ruler. A dispute arose between Raja Sahib Singh of Patiala and his wife, Rani Aas Kaur, both claiming of the regent prince, Karam Singh. Rani Aas Kaur was an ambitious and intriguing woman. She chalked out a plan to dislodge her husband from the *Gaddi*, and put her son on it. She conspired with the Maratha chief, Jaswant Rao Holkar, when he was on a brief visit to Patiala,

He too wanted to try his luck and got benefit out of the quarrel. However, when Lord Lake appeared on the scene, the Maratha Chief crossed the Sutlej. The matter did not end here, the Raja of Patiala also had a dispute with the Raja of Nabha. They had differences on the possession of the village Doladhi, 32 km. from Patiala and 3 km. from Nabha. It was claimed by the Raja of Nabha which was disputed by the Raja of Patiala. The incharge of the village, Bhai Bhag Singh of Jind took side of the Nabha Raja and the Raja of Patiala was helped by the Thanesar Chief, Bhanga Singh and his nephew Mehtab Singh and Lal Singh of Kaithal. The situation became critical and several skirmishes took place between the armies of both the sides and in one of these fights Sardar Mehtab Singh was killed. The Patiala Raja was infuriated and attacked Narwana, where a bloody battle took place, the Raja of Nabha, Jaswant Singh was given a crushing defeat and he fled to Nabha. About 150 persons from both sides were killed. There seemed to be no end to the dispute. Then, both the parties invited Ranjit Singh to mediate between them. This gave Ranjit Singh an opportunity to enforce his will.

Thus on July 26, 1806 Ranjit Singh crossed the Sutlej with 200,00 horsemen. Fateh Singh Ahluwalia and Gurdit Singh of Ladwa accompanied him besides many other Sardars. On the way the Maharaja realised handsome tributes and *nazranas* from Budh Singh of Jullunder and Dharam Singh of Phillaur. He entered the Patiala territory the third day.

The Maharaja took possession of the Doladhi town, the disputed place between the Raja of Patiala and Nabha. The Patiala forces were driven out from Doladhi, the Maharaja reached Mansurpur in the Patiala State and invested it. The Rajas of Nabha and Jind accompanied him. However, the Patiala forces were much more in strength than the Maharaja's and Mir Zulfikar Ali, Commandant of the Patiala artillery, who was most perfect in his art personally supervised the ordnance. He sent a shot through the *howdah* of the elephant on which Raja Bhag Singh of Jind was seated. Ranjit Singh witnessed the scene from the distance, and noticed the overwhelming number of the enemy's troops. In the meantime Sahib Singh of Patiala sent a message to the Maharaja and peace was restored the next day. Doladhi was restored to the Patiala chief. Raja Jaswant Singh of Nabha paid a *nazrama* of Rs. 50,000 to the Maharaja whose objective was achieved by implication.

On his return the Maharaja celebrated the Diwali at Thaneasar. After performing ablutions in the holy tank, he reached Sutlej. He did nothing to settle the dispute between Sabib Singh of Patiala and his wife, though both of them presented him with huge sums of money and precious jewellery to obtain his goodwill. However, the Maharaja advised Sahib Singh of Patiala not to nominate his son to the throne in his lifetime. Karam Singh was to be paid a Jagir of Rs. 50,000 a year. Both the parties thanked the Maharaja.

Amritsar's gaiety and splendour was increasing day by day. It was inhabited by aristocracy and many high dignitaries often visited the town. It was illuminated on special occasions. There were rejoicings and the city gave a festive appearance and whenever, the Maharaja was victorious in any campaign, large scale celebrations were held.

The Maharaja also constructed at Amritsar a palace costing Rs. 125,000 in those days. In this beautiful palace Ranjit Singh used to spend his summer months. There were underground apartments for use in the summer season. A swimming tank constructed nearby was used by the ladies of the household. There were tiny palaces for the chiefs.

The Garden and the buildings were constructed under the direct supervision of the Fakir Aziz-ud-din, in collaboration with Sardar Desa Singh and Lehna Singh Majithia. The red stone work was executed by workers specially brought from Delhi.

The area of the Garden is about 84 acres. The central hall and the ante-chamber of Maharaja Ranjit Singh's palace were renovated several times.

REFERENCES

1. Ochterlony to Commander in-Chief, Dec. 7, 1804.
2. Letter No. 4, SC 7 of November 27, 1806.
3. Wade to Metcalfe, Aug. 1, 1827.
4. Wade to Metcalfe, Aug. 1, 1827.
5. Suri, Sohan Lal, Umdat-ut-Tawarikh II, pp. 57-60.
6. Latif Mohd, History of the Panjab, p. 363.
7. Payne C.H., A Short History of the Sikhs, p. 77.

9

Capture of Hills

Ranjit Singh proceeded towards Lahore, his capital. In the way, he hunted and spent some time enjoying the bounties of nature. As was usual with him, he spent some care-free days after each victory. While he was still away from the Capital, his help was sought by Sansar Chand Katoch against the Gurkhas who had occupied the hill area between Jammu and the Sutlej and had surrounded the Kangra fort.

The Gurkhas had extended their frontiers to the Mechi river in the east by capturing the territories of the Kiratas and the Dimbus; in the west all the Rajput States. Doti, Kumaon and Almora, Garhwal and Srinagar had fallen to the Gurkha arms. By 1804, they had entered the small Simla Hill States. The Nepalese General Amar Singh Thapa had swept the Himalayan foothills and had established Nepalese authority over Chamba, Kotla, Nurpur, Basohli, Kulu, Mandi and Saket. He then attacked Kangra. The Sikhs intervened and his further march was halted. Earlier, Ranjit Singh had routed Sansar Chand Katoch from Hoshiarpur and Bijwara; dissatisfaction prevailed among the hill chiefs who were harassed by Sansar Chand. They approached the Gurkha Commander and sought his help against Sansar Chand. The combined forces of the Hill rajas and the Nepalese general defeated Sansar Chand at Mahal Mori. He was badly beaten and took shelter deep into the hills. Amar Singh Thapa advanced towards Kangra and laid its siege.

Raja Sansar Chand was defeated. However, he did not rest and made efforts to regain his lost territory. He regrouped his forces. The hill areas continued to be the base for power struggle between the Katoch and the Gurkhas. The hill chiefs went against the Katoch raja and took side by the Gurkhas. In the process, the whole country-side was devastated. Crops were destroyed, houses were burnt and cattle were killed, Not a blade of grass grew, fields were not cultivated, the towns wore a deserted look and tigers roared in the streets of towns and villages.

The struggle between the Gurkhas and the Kotach chief has been described thus: "The memory of the disastrous days which then followed stands out as a land mark in the annals of the hills. Time is computed with the reference to that period and every misfortune is justly and unjustly ascribed to that prolific source of misery and distress. The Gurkhas prepared to establish their success. Certain portions of the country were subdued and held by them. Other portions including the fort of Kangra and the principal strongholds remained in the hands of Katochs. Each party plundered the districts held by the other to weaken his adversary's resources. The people, harassed and bewildered, fled to the neighbouring kingdoms, some to Chamba, some to the plains of the Jalandhar Doab, other hill chieftains incited by Sansar Chand's former oppressions, made inroads with impunity and aggravated the general disorder. For three years this state of anarchy continued in the fertile valleys of Kangra."[1]

The situation was grim. Sansar Chand sent messengers to Ranjit Singh and met him personally. Ranjit Singh was already looking for an opportunity to capture the hills and establish his authority over this part of the country. He had a special yearning to possess the Kangra fort. He laid down a condition that he could help Sansar Chand against Gurkhas, provided the fort of Kanagra was handed over to him. Sansar Chand agreed to this demand, but the Maharaja asked him to give some guarantee the that he would fulfil his promise as he could not rely upon the hill chief. Sansar Chand agreed to leave his son Anurudh Chand as hostage with the Maharaja. But this was a mere act of hypocrisy. On the one hand, he promised the fort to Ranjit Singh and on the other, he made up his mind to surrender the same to the Gurkha chief. He hoped that the Sikhs and the Gurkhas would clash among themselves and in the clash of arms the strength of both would be reduced considerably. The Raja hid himself in the Kangra fort and made all the preparations for a long siege.

The news reached Ranjit Singh. He was upset at the duplicity of Sansar Chand and put his son Anurudh Chand under surveillance and started preparations to attack the Kangra fort. He was also keen that Kangra and other hill areas should not fall under the Gurkhas. He pitched his campt at Jawala Mukhi—a holy place where thousands of people go every year to seek the blessings of the *Mata*. Here, Ranjit Singh mustered his forces under the command of his mother-in-law Rani Sada Kaur. A fierce battle took place, Amar Singh Thapa was made to flee towards the Malakra fort. The Sikhs pursued him, the fort was besieged. The Gurkha chief surrendered and started peace negotiations. He paid *nazrana* of Rs. 100,000 to the Maharaja and showed willingness to leave the hills.

It is believed that the Gurkha chief had proposed to the Maharaja a joint enterprise against the Rajputs and the hills, offering the fortress of Kangra to the Sikhs. The Maharaja did not agree to this suggestion. The Gurkha chief also tried to negotiate with the British through David Ochterlony and proposed that a joint march be made to the Indus after overcoming the Sikh resistance. These overtures did not find favour with the British as they had already entered into a treaty with Ranjit Singh as Amritsar.

The Gurkhas were cleared out of the Kangra. The Sikhs decided to enter the fort. Sansar Chand coult not help it. The Maharaja's forces occupied the Kangra fort on August 24, 1809. It was Maharaja's triumphant entry into the citadel of the hill chief. Desa Singh Majitha was appointed the Governor of Kangra Sansar Chand paid tribute to the Sikhs—Rs. 200,000 annualy equal to one-fourth of the total revenuce of his possessions.

Sansar Chand's heart burnt with vengeance. He tried to create mischief and intrigued against the Sikhs. He made efforts to seek help of the British to regain control over the Kangra fort, but he failed in his effort.

The fort of Kangra fell and Sansar Chand sank into the position of an obsequious dependent. "His country's revenue was valued at six lakhs, yielded eight and he paid to Ranjit Singh two lakhs of rupees, used to keep two disciplined sepory battalions under the command of a European officer, a deserter from the company's artillery, named Jackson."[2]

Sansar Chand could not seek British help, as stated earlier. However, his anxiety to remain under the British protection continued. "He has sought the protection of the British Government and has declared his attachment to it and is ready with a body of 10/12 thousand men to devote himself to its cause." Sansar Chand stated: "My object is to get my former possession with the fort of Kangra restored to me and the administration of justice left in my hands. I am continuously putting up my prayers that the auspicious day may arrive when I shall be favoured with an interview which will be a source to me of temporal and eternal happiness."[3]

The fall of Kangra ended the Katoch domination in the hills. The Gurkha menace in Punjab was ended once for all. The chiefs of Kangra, Chamba, Nurpur and Kulu paid homage to Ranjit Singh.

Maharaj returned to Lahore. In December 1807, Rani Mehtab Kaur, daughter to Rani Sada Kaur gave birth to a twin sons. Sher Singh and Tara Singh. There were large scale rejoicing. Ranjit Singhs gave large sums of money in charity and Lahore was illuminated for many nights.

From wherever Ranjit Singh passed, he was given a royal reception. Flowers were showered on him and streets and bazars were decorated profusely. When the Maharaja reached Amritsar, the guns were fired. The city and the Golden Temple were illuminated. The Maharaja rode through the streets, sitting on an elephant and showered silver coins on the people.

In 1811, the Kotila fort fell into the Sikhs's hands. In 1813, Desa Singh annexed Haripur the territory of Raja Bhup Singh. In 1815, Rajas of Nurpur and Jaswar were ousted from their territories. In 1818, Datarpur Raja surrendered his territory and became a Jagirdar of the Maharaja. In 1825 the Sikhs sieged the fort of Kotlehr and the Raja accepted the Jagir of Rs. 10,000.

Till his death, Raja Sansar Chand lived at Nadaun as a tributary of the Maharaja. William Moorcroft, who visited Kangra in 1823 writes: "Raja Sansar Chand is a tall, well-formed man, abut sixty. His son Rai Anirudh Singh has a very handsome face and rudy complexion, but is remarkably corpulent. He is now poor, and in danger of being wholly subjected to Ranjit Singh. His misfortunes are mainly owing to himself and his decline presents remarkable contrast to the rise of neighbour and now paramount Lord, Ranjit Singh."[4]

In 1828, Anurudh Chand visited Lahore and Ranjit Singh asked him to marry his sister to Raja Hira Singh, son of Raja Dhian Singh. He agreed in the spur of moment but on returning to Nadaun, he backed out and refused. He did not want to marry the Katoch princess to the Jammu Dogra. But he was afraid of the Maharaja and apprehended trouble from him. He crossed the Sutlej and sought the protection of the British. He took refuge at Hardwar and married his sister to the Garhwal raja. While Anurudh chand was away, Ranjit Singh sent his forces to Nadaun and annexed it to his empire. The forts of Tirah, Riah and Palhiar were sieged. Jagirs were granted to the brother of the raja and other heirs of the Katoch family. Later, the Maharaja himself reached Kangra, when

Anurudh Chand had died. He reached the holy place of Jawalamukhi to pay his respect to eternal natural flames. Ranjit Singh now married two daughters of Raja Sansar Chand and took them to Lahore. One of the Ranis, Kotochan was cremated with Ranjit Singh when he died. The Maharaja got himself fully entrenched in the hills. He appointed Desa Singh Majithia and then his son Lehna Singh Majitha as Governors. They controlled the area between the rivers Ravi and Sutlej which included Chamba, Nurpur, Mandi, Kulu Datarpur and other hill tributaries. The Government was carried by their *Nazirs* and *Kardars* . All revenue was collected by these officials and after meeting the expenditure on army and administration the balance was sent to the Lahore *darbar*. It was a just rule, the people were happy and content. There was no interference in the day-to-day life of the people and their customary law remained intact like the earlier tradition of paying one-half of the produce on good land, two-fifth, one-third and one-fourth on the inferior land.

In 1807, while returning from Patiala, the Maharaja halted at Ambala, where Rani Dia Kaur, widow of Gurbaksh Singh presented him with a *nazrana*. The Maharaja was paid tribute by Lal Singh of Kaithal, Gurdit Singh and Karam Singh of Shahabad, Bhagwan Singh of Buria, Jodh Singh of Kalsia and all the Sikh Sardars of Sirhind. He bestowed *Khillats* on all of them.

The Maharaja then marched towards Naraingarh, held by Kishan Singh of Nahan. The fort was invaded. The besieged held out bravely for three weeks and repulsed the invading forces several times. However, the fort ultimately fell to Fateh Singh, the general in the army of Maharaja Ranjit Singh.

The general, however was killed in the encounter. 400 men of the Maharaja's army were also either killed ro wounded. After the victory, the Maharaja handed over the territory to Fateh Singh Ahluwalia who paid him a *nazrana* or Rs. 40,000.

Tara Singh Gheba, the old chief who had followed the Maharaja's forces during the siege of Naraingarh died before he reached there. His dead body was sent to Lahore for cremation where his wife and sons lived. While the body of the Gheba Sardar was still burning on the pyre and the other obsequies were being performed, a body of Ranjit Singh's troops, who got the secret information, appeared on the scene and instantly demanded the Gheba's wealth and possession of his estates. The widow of the deceased refused bluntly and appeared with a sword in her hand and challenged Ranjit's troops to face her in the battle-field. She defended the fort of Rahon with all her might but the mudwalls of the fort could not stand against the onslaught of the invaders. The fort was seized and a handsome amount was fixed for the maintenance of the widow and her children but later on this was also discontinued.

Ranjit Singh now turned his attention towards the petty chieftains. First of all he took into possession the estate of Tara Singh Gheba, Naughera. He expelled all the officials. Then he seized Morinda, Jagir of Dharam Singh from his son, who had earlier refused to pay *nazrana*. Ranjit Singh annexed Bahlopur and Bharatgarh from Bhag Singh's widow.

The campaigns continued and Ranjit Singh's general Mukham Chand, conquered Wadni in Ferozepur. However, the territory was later presented to Rani Sada Kaur, Ranjit's mother-in-law. A tribute of Rs. 20,000 was levied on Ranjit Singh, a big Zamindar or Manauli, Rs. 30,000 on Gopal Singh of Mani Majra, Rs. 15000 on Hari Singh of Ropur and Rs. 80,000 on the Zamindars of the Doaba.

In 1808, Ranjit Singh attacked Pathankote, at the foot of Kangra hills which was in possession of Jai Singh Kanahaiya. The incharge of the fort fled to the hills. Ranjit Singh next marched to Jasrota, the raja surrendered without offering any resistance, became his tributary and paid a huge sum of money to the Maharaja as *nazrana*. The Maharaja stayed for some days at Jasrota, went deep into jungles for hinting.

Then, he marched towards Chamba, a small hilly State. The Maharaja had hardly reached half way, when the emissaries of the Chamba raja approached him and offered him terms for peace treaty. The Maharaja accepted the *nazrana* and sent back the emissaries with large *Khillats*.

Next came the turn of Basohli, the raja agreed to pay an annual tribute of Rs. 8000. A *nazrana* was also paid. Thus one by one, most of the hill States were annexed to the Lahore *darbar*.

In the plains, Diwan Mukham Chand subdued many chiefs on the left side of the Sutlej. Most of the Sardars offered their allegiance to Lahore *darbar*. They were confirmed In their possessions on the promise of supply of horses and other war material in case of need. They agreed to remain constantly obedient to the *darbar*.

By now the Maharaja had gained much strength. It was difficult to challenge his authority. Diwan Mukham Chand advised the Maharaja to hold the Shahi *darbar*, invite all the chieftains and invest them with the robes of honour. This was a shrewd move as any raja or chieftain who refused to attend the *darbar* would be considered a traitor and punished accordingly.

All the Sardars responded to the invitation except Jiwan Singh of Sialkote and Sahib Singh of Gujarat. In the *darbar* robes of honour were conferred on the Sardars who had accepted the suzerainty of the Lahore ruler. The act of Sialkote and Gujarat Sardars was considered as an act of defiance. Ranjit Singh was infuriated and ordered his army to march on to punish them for their audacity. Sialkote was attacked and the city was stormed. Jiwan Singh with his one thousand armed men and four pieces of artillery offered stout resistance. The fighting continued for 7 days when one of the gates was battered down by the artillery. Ranjit Singh's army entered the fort and occupied it. Jiwan Singh was imprisoned and all arrangements were made for running the administration.

From Sialkote, the Maharaja marched towards Gujarat. While he was still in the way, Sahib Singh's men offered him tribute. A treaty was signed and Sahib Singh accepted the suzerainty of Ranjit Singh. The Maharaja withdrew his forces. After that, Akhnur was attacked the chief Alam Khan paid him the *nazrana* and surrendered without offering any resistance.

In January 1808, the Maharaja deputed Ghouse Khan and Hukma Singh Chimni to subdue Sheikhupura. Its chiefs Arbel Singh and Amir Singh were a constant source of trouble not only to the Maharaja but were disturbing public peace too. They carried depredations throughout the countryside, harassed the innocent villagers and plundered them.

An expedition was sent under Prince Kharak Singh. Arbel Singh and Amir Singh offered stout resistance. The fort was well defended and after its walls were battered with *Bhangian di Tope*, one of the gates of the fort was broken into pieces. The troops entered the fort. Both the Sardars were put in chains. Their army was forced to join the Maharaja's and the place was presented to Prince Kharak Singh as a *Jagir*. Rani Nakai was made the guardian, who lived in the fort till her death.

The campaign continued for two years ceaselessly. It added many new territories to the Lahore *darbar*. Their administration had to be reorganised, finance had to be arranged and other matters put in order. So far, Ranjit Singh's finances were controlled by the banking house of Rama Nand of Amritsar. Now bhwani Dass, an expert in the management of finances, having worked under Shah Zaman, was made incharge of accounts. He opened many treasuries and put the finances of the State on sound footing. He introduced a proper system of accounting.

The Maharaja appointed Khushal Chand of Meerut to manage his household. He was earlier an ordinary soldier. He was now given the rank of Jamedar and was later appointed as *Deoridar*—keeper of the palace. The post gained much importance and Khushal Chand became very powerful. Anybody seeking favour from or interview with the Maharaja had to go through him. He embraced Sikhism and was called Jamedar Khushal Singh. Two of his relations Tej Singh and Ram Singh joined the Maharaja's *darbar*. All of them betrayed the *darbar* after Ranjit Singh's death and played a treacherous role in Anglo-Sikh wars.

REFERENCES

1. Kangra District Gazetteer, p. 35.
2. Asiatic Journal, Vol. XVIII
3. Political Proceedings No. 101, October 23, 1819.
4. Moorcroft: Travels, pp. 75-76.

10

Treaty of Amritsar

In 1807, Ranjit Singh had taken over the territory of Tara Singh Gheba, who had died earlier. His widow was ousted and the estate attached without any resistance. It was a severe blow to the authority of the Sardars who were still dreaming of retaining their petty estates. It caused alarm among the Malwa chiefs, who were convinced that the Maharaja was now bent upon reducing them to the position of tributaries.

Ranjit Singh's General, Dewan Mukham Chand crossed the Sutlej and captured Wadni, near Ferozepur, and proceeded towards Anandpur. This created further stir among the Malwa chiefs and they conspired against the Lahore *darbar* and turned their eyes towards the British who could help them in retaining their territories. They found in the British their saviour.

The Malwa chiefs held a meeting and met Seton, the British Resident at Delhi. They appealed to the resident to give them protection against the designs of Ranjit Singh. They argued that the Cis-Sutlej territory had always been protected by the Government at Delhi and now that the British were in possession of Delhi, they should extend them protection. The resident gave them patient hearings, but could not help them at that stage.

In March 1808, Lord Minto, the Governor-General, wrote, "Although as a principle, we cordially recognise the wisdom and the justice of abstaining from all interferences in the contests, disputes, and concerns of states with which we are unconnected by the obligations of alliance, and are fully convinced of the embarrassment and inconvenience of extending our protection to petty chieftains, who are unable to protect their territories from the aggressions of more powerful neighbours, yet we are disposed to think that cases may occur in which temporary deviation from those general principles may be a measure of defensive policy, the neglect of which might be productive of much more danger and embarrassment than the persecution of it, and that the certain resolution of the Raja of Lahore to subjugate the states situated between the Sutlej and the frontier of our dominion would, under other circumstances than the present constitute a case on which, on grounds of self defence, the interposition of the British power for the purpose of preventing the execution of such a project would be equally just and prudent."[1]

The British, however, did not harm their relations with Ranjit Singh, Though, "the Resident held out no hopes to the deputies of the confederate Sikh chiefs of direct British interference in their relations with the Lahore ruler, but nevertheless they were led to hope that they had the best sympathies of the British authorities, and that, when the time came, a helping hand would not be denied to them. The reply, though encouraging, was not decisive, and by no means sufficient to save the chiefs concerned from eventual ruin."[2]

Thus, the British agent "gave the hint to the Cis-Sutlej chiefs that in emergency they would not be deserted."[3]

However, "the reply to the deputation, though straightforward, was cautious and vague. It practically amounted to this: We can promise nothing definite; but you have our sympathy, and we will do what we can."[4]

This did not satisfy the Cis-Sutlej chiefs. They thought of further means to save themselves from the expansionist designs of Ranjit Singh. However, Ranjit Singh played a diplomatic game. He sent his emissaries to Cis-Sutlej chiefs to calm down their feelings and to assure that he did not want to subdue them. The Cis-Sutlej chiefs too desired to seek Ranjit Singh's protection than to bow down before the British Government. Ranjit Singh proposed a meeting of these chiefs at Amritsar where all the chiefs assembled to settle their own terms with the acknowledged ruler of the land—Ranjit Singh. The Maharaja received them with consideration and did his utmost to allay their fears. The chiefs were convinced and settled their terms with Ranjit Singh, at least, for the time being. The chiefs agreed to come into Ranjit's camp as "between the lion and the wolf they had to come to terms with the deadlier of the beasts."[5]

By this time, in Europe, Napoleon Bonaparte had risen to power. He became a terror for the Europeans and one after another power fell at his feet. However, in July 1807, he signed a treaty with Russia known as the treaty of Tilsit, thus entering into a settlement with the Tzar Alexander. They agreed that if England continued hostilities with France, Russia would join hands with the French in combating the British menace. There is no doubt that the British navy was supreme, the land route to India via Persia, Afghanistan, Sind and the Punjab was open to the combined army of France and Russia. It was also said that Napolean was planning to invade India in league with Turks and the Persians. This created an alarm among the British and Lord Minto was determined to take defensive measures and tried to build up relations not only with the powers beyond by Yamuna and Sutlej but also with those across the Indus river. It was, therefore, decided to send ambassadors to the Court of Shah Shuja, the King of Afghanistan, the Court of the Shah of Persia and to the Lahore *darbar*. Their job was to negotiate with these monarchs and to lay emphasis upon them that they had the common interest with the British and that in the event of an invasion of India by Napolean, the Sikhs were likely to suffer the most. The

Lord urged upon them the necessity of unity which could only stall the enemy. Elphinstone was sent to Afghanistan, John Malcolm to Tehran and Metcalfe, who had already distinguished himself for his political sagacity and firmness was deputed to the Court of Ranjit Singh, and Pottinger was to negotiate with the Sind ruler.

The idea of sending Metcalfe to the Lahore *darbar* was mooted in early 1808. The British government received the intelligence reports that Ranjit Singh was visiting Hardwar, to take bath in the holy Ganges; they desired to take advantage of the situation , "by acts of kindness and attention to render the circumstances of Ranjit Singh's visit to the Company's dominions subservient to the plan of pleasing and conciliating him, thereby rendering it the basis of future intercourse and friendly connection."[6]

Metcalfe was chosen to receive Maharaja and instructions were given to him to proceed to the bank of Yamuna and wait for the arrival of Ranjit Singh and on the return journey, Metcalfe was directed to escort Ranjit Singh upto the British frontier which was the bank of the Yamuna again.

However, at the last moment the Maharaja cancelled his Hardwar visit and Metcalfe had to proceed to Punjab. He set out for Punjab in the last week of July 1808. A month before the visit of Metcalfe, Captain Mathews had visited the Malwa chiefs and held secret discussions with them. He held a secret meeting with Rani Sada Kaur and reported to the British Government that she was hostile to Ranjit Singh. Mathews reported that "This part of the Punjab as well as other parts where the Rajah's authority exists, is under a good police and is safe for travellers; it seldom happens that capital crimes or robberies are committed. The Rajah is not only a most unaffected and pleasing man in his manners but of a very good understanding, brave and liberal, and seem to be quite the soldier and very fond of military exercises. He is both feared and believed by his men and frequently leads them on to the assault of forts, being a fatalist, he says it is in vain for a man to screen himself and that what is to be his end must inevitably be so. He is most capital horseman and rides every morning till 7 O' clock with only with only few attendants on the fine level plain between the walls of the town and the river."

Metcalfe was instructed by the Governor-General that it should be clearly remembered that his Government had no legal rights over the Cis-Sutlej States. He could not promise the protection of the States which were not connected with them. They could not have any alliance with them even for defensive purposes. However, it should be clearly and implicitly understood that the Governor-General desired "to avoid a declared concurrence in Ranjit's hostile designs against the states in question and until it is known in what degree the security of the British Government may require a cordial union of its interests with those of Ranjit Singh it is not easy to determine what sacrifices it may be expedient to make for the attainment of that objects."[7]

However, Ranjit Singh had a doubt about the British intentions. It was just an excuse that the British Government was taking steps to safeguard the selves from the French invasion which was a myth. Napolean had not tried to establish any links with Ranjit Singh, nor with the Amirs of Sind and Shah of Afghanistan. Whereas, on the other hand, the British had established contacts with both of them. The situation was confusing for Ranjit Singh.

Matcalfe reached Patiala on August 22, 1808. He was received with great honour by Raja Sahib Singh. In his first public meeting with Metcalfe, he delivered the keys to him, meaning that he was under the British protection and pleaded that the keys be returned to him only if he agreed to take change of the State as a protector on behalf of the British Government. The British envoy declined to accept the keys but assured the Raja of the British Government's goodwill for him and requested him to keep the keys with him as they had always remained with him and it was hoped that they would remain with him in future too. The Raja was over-whelmed with joy. Later, the Raja strengthened his defences, against the threatened invasion of Ranjit Singh.

While this was happening at Patiala, the Maharaja was holding his *darbar* at Lahore in which were present Raja Bhag Singh of Jind, Raja Jaswant Singh of Nabha, Bhai Lal Singh of Kaithal and Raja Gurdit Singh of Ladwa. Other Cis-Sutlej chiefs had sent their representatives. It seemed that these Rajas were leaning towards Ranjit Singh now as they had received discouragement in their meeting with the British agent, Seton at Delhi. Raja Sahib Singh of Patiala was also ignored by Metcalfe at their recent meeting held at Patiala. Under the circumstances every Cis-Sutlej chief had started looking towards the Lahore *darbar* as his asylum and not to the British Government which could not be relied upon. They had seen the rising power of Ranjit Singh. "The Afghans who were left in possession of the north-weast portion of the Punjab, the Saddozie family of pathans, who held the province of Multan, and the hill raja of Kangra, had already felt the weight of his power and were treated by him as ordinary vassals. His highest ambition now, as Maharaja of Lahore was to unite all the Sikhs under one banner, and extend his sway from the banks of the Sutlej to the Jammu, and to absorb into his own dominions all the independent States encompassed by those rivers. Already his last two Sutlej compaigns had borne good fruit, and his successive inroads and victories had reasonably led him to hope that another season would see the whole country from the Sutlej to the Jamma annexed to his new kingdom of Lahore. He was munificent in his rewards and severe in his exactions. He was dreaded, if not loved, by his subjects, and respected by those around him. His power was absolute and from the chief of a State to the common soldier, everyone implicitly obeyed him."[8]

The Cis-Sutlej chiefs were still playing the double game. They informed Ranjit Singh that the British would soon annex his kingdom. On the other hand, they informed Metcalfe that the Maharaja was massing troops to fight against the British. The atmosphere was full of suspicion and disbelief when Metcalfe was planning of holding a meeting with Ranjit Singh.

The Maharaja directed Fakir Aziz-ud-din and Mit Singh to negotiate with Metcalfe on behalf of the Lahore *darbar*. They were to be assisted by Prabh Dyal; who was considered to be the knowledgeable person as far as the British were concerned.

Metcalfe arrived and the Maharaja had the first two meetings with the British envoy at Khemkaran, near Kasur on September 11, 1808.

Metcalfe was not in a happy mood. He did not like the very idea of holding the meeting at Khemkaran instead of the State capital and that too without any ceremonial formalities. He hated the site of his camp which was arranged in tents in the river bed. There was a thunderstorm which further spoiled the mood of the envoy. The atmosphere was surcharged with suspicion.

However, Ranjit Singh exhibited his diplomacy and received Metcalfe cordially and affectionately. He came out of his tent and embraced Metcalfe warmly. He himself conducted him to the royal enclosure and asked him to sit along with him. There were greetings and presentations of an elephant, a beautiful horse, strings of pearls and costly Kashmiri shawls were made. No talks were held. Rajit Singh only asked Metcalfe as to what brought him here in such a bad weather and what was the purpose of taking so much pains when there was no danger of war from any quarter.

Three days passed in suspense. Now Metcalfe unfolded the real purpose of his visit. In a packed *darbar*, Metcalfe read out a note saying that his Government had information that the French who were itching to establish themselves in Persia also kept an evil eye on Kabul and Punjab and it was in the interest of all the States of this region that there should be complete unity and amity among them, so that their territories were defended and in case of an attack, the enemy's army should be repulsed.

Ranjit Singh expressed his willingness to give Metcalfe full cooperation and declared that since long he had a desire to have an alliance with the British. Metcalfe submitted a draft for the treaty to be signed by the Maharaja and the British. It said that both Ranjit Singh and the English should join hands against any aggression from the French, that Ranjit Singh would check Napolean from passing through the Punjab in case war broke out with the French and Ranjit Singh would extend his protection to the British passing through Punjab.

Ranjit Singh listened to his proposals carefully. However, on the advice of his counsels he informed Metcalfe that he would like to have so me time to consider the proposals and would give his reply only the next day.

Ranjit Singh held discussions with his advisers who apparently were not very happy with the proposals and told Fakir Aziz-ud-din how selfish the British were and how their proposals smacked of nothing but simply to trap him.

The next day, Ranjit Singh's advisers met Metcalfe and told him that while they were agreeable to join defence against the French aggression, they should go further and establish a permanent unity between the British and the Punjab and this way put a curb on the rumours that were afloat throughout the country that the relations between the British Government and the Punjab *darbar* were becoming strained and further disputes might arise anytime.

Metcalfe was stunned. He was not prepared for such an eventuality and replied that his question was only one-sided whereas his ambition was to discuss question of mutual interest. Fakir Aziz-ud-din who was sitting quiet all along said that the settlement of the question of common frontier was as much a question of mutual interest as that of making an alliance. Metcalfe diplomatically replied that as the boundaries of the territories were fixed, there was no intention to exceed it. The *Fakir* asked Metcalfe as to where the Government had fixed the boundaries.

To this Metcalfe had no reply. He was non-plussed for some time, then replied haltingly, "Karnal". He had in mind that the British had already established their army base to defend Delhi. However, he was informed that Karnal belonged to Gurdit Singh, who was friendly to Ranjit Singh. Metcalfe tried to dodge the Sikhs and again harped on the bogey of French invasion. He was given a calm hearing but Dewan Mukham Chand said that the British should first sign an agreement with Ranjit Singh before deputing a mission to Kabul.

Metcalfe could not paciy the *darbar*. He was doubtful whether he would be able to enter into any treaty with the Maharaja. Next day Ranjit Singh met him personally and asked him frankly as to what was the British Government's policy towards the Malwa States. Metcalfe evaded direct replies and only told the Maharaja that the British had no intention of extending their territory up to Sutlej.

But he also stuck a note of warning to Ranjit Singh that it was in his interest that the British policy should remain vague otherwise the Governor-General might declare for the Sutlej. Now Metcalfe tried to entangle Ranjit Singh by out-Manouvering him and told him that the treaty he was proposing was only for defensive purposes and if Ranjit Singh intended to advance towards Afghanistan, the British would not interfere at all.

Ranjit Singh understood the game and was disgusted with the dual policy of the British. He was aware that negotiations were already going on between the British and the Afghans. He was so much disappointed that he ordered breaking of the camp. But before doing so he expressed his desire to sign a defensive treaty with the British on his own terms and conditions and that the English would not interfere in his dispute with the Kabul Amir, the English would not establish friendly relations with that chief and Ranjit Singh would be recognised as the sole sovereign of the Sikhs including the chiefs of Cis-Sutlej and if so desired Metcalfe could also accompany Ranjit Singh in his Cis-Sutlej campaigns.

Metcalfe was caught in his own net. He refused to sign the treaty without the permission of the Governor-General. It is said that Ranjit Singh was so furious that only Fakir-Azız-ud-din dissuaded him from declaring war."[9]

Metcalfe was given a chance to reconsider, However, the Maharaja's entourage moved towards Faridkote whose Raja had revolted against the authority of Patiala chief. Ranjit Singh being an overlord of Patiala was duty bound to force Faridkote to obey the Patiala chief.

The Maharaja reached Faridkote. Metcalfe who arrived on the scene was dazzled. He was now prepared for further negotiations. After about two weeks Ranjit Singh proceeded to Malerkotla where the ruler submitted. This gave a rude shock to Metcalfe and added to his indignation. However, Metcalfe was received at Malerkotla by Ranjit Singh and his courtiers. They advised him to accept Ranjit Singh's sovereignty over the Sikh chiefs without any reservation whatsoever. But Metcalfe showed his reluctance. The discussions continued without any result. The Maharaja decided to proceed to Ambala without caring for remonstrations from Metcalfe who charged the Maharaja with entering the territories of those very chiefs who had solicited the protection of British Government. He at first refused to go to Ambala with the Maharaja.

Ranjit Singh continued his march to Ambala. He was given warm reception wherever he went. From Ambala he went to Shahabad and then to Patiala. The interview between

Raja Sahib Singh of Patiala and Maharaja Ranjit Singh took place at Lakhnaur about 30 km east of Patiala Singh on November 21, 1808 in the presence of Baba Sahib Singh Bedi, the revered Sikh. In Bedi's tent, Ranjit Singh received Raja Sahib Singh with cordiality. Ranjit Singh swore of perpetual friendship with Raja Sahib Singh and exchanged turbans with him as a sign of eternal brotherhood. The next day formal treaties were executed. Ranjit Singh then crossed the Sutlej on December 2, 1808, proceeding to Amritsar. He arrived there on December 4, to be joined by Metcalfe. At Amritsar the Maharaja was given a heroic welcome. There were rejoicings in the city which was bedecked like a bride. Flowers were showered on the Maharaja. For many days the Golden Temple and other houses were illuminated and there were fireworks.

Meanwhile, the decision of the Governor-General was communicated to the Maharaja, that the Cis-Sutlej chiefs had been declared to be under the protection of the British Government and that the State of Lahore must severe all its connections with them. The Maharaja had no claim on the country between the Sutlej and Yamuna. Metcalfe wrote. "Since the British Government has come into this situation, it has relieved the chiefs between the Sutlej and the Jamuna front tribute, and that degree of subserviency which they were used to pay to the Marathas, and has allowed them to carry on their own concerns without interference or control. But this liberality on the part of the British Government was meant for the benefit of those chiefs, not for their injury. It was never intended that the forbearance of the British Government should be take advantage of by another power to oppress and subjugate those whom the British government wished to protect and relieve." On these grounds it was declared that the British Government could not consent to these chiefs being subjugated by the Maharaja or for that matter any other and that those chiefs should remain under the protection of the British Government. The Maharaja was therefore, called upon to restore all the territories lying down between the Sutlej and the Yamuna of which he had taken possession, to their former chiefs and to confine to his army to the right bank of the Sutlej.

The *darbar* was double-minded. Two opinions prevailed. One was for resisting the British threat and the other for restoring peace. Mukham Chand was for fighting and saving the nation's honour. He declared openly that is was more dignified to die fighting on the battlefield than to lick the ground without a shot being fired. He sent orders to all the Sardars to bring their forces to repulse the British on the banks of Sutlej, if any attack was made. The forts of Gobindgarh, Phillaur and Lahore were fortified and provisioned for prolonged battle. On the other hand, *Fakir Aziz-ud-din* wanted to avoid hostilities. However, the Maharaja decided to swallow the bitter pill and accepted Sutlej as the eastern boundary.

The situation was tense. Lord Minto was determined and sent a detachment of British troops to the Sutlej to give support to the British envoy, Metcalfe, to carry on negotiations with the *darbar*. However, the move's main object was to keep the Maharaja's forces to the north of the river. The troops under the command of Sir David Ochterlony, crossed Yamuna on January 16, 1809 and a declaration to the effect was made that all the Sikhs on the south of the river were the protectees of the British Government. The general was enthusiastically received by the Cis-Sutlej chiefs and he advanced further without any hindrance.

The movement of troops irritated Ranjit Singh but he carried on parleys with the British envoy. Metcalfe stayed in Amritsar. He made an offering of a handsome amount at *Darbar Sahib*. He believed that his gesture would please the entire Sikh community.

The negotiations were resumed at Amritsar. Ranjit Singh by now had agreed to all the conditions laid down by the British except giving up his claim on Faridkote. Metcalfe agreed to refer the matter to Governor-General and got an excuse of postponing the signing of a treaty of friendship. However, Raja Bhag Singh of Jind, a relation of Ranjit Singh tried to mediate between the Maharaja and the British. He told Ochterlony that Ranjit Singh was anxious to avoid war though his suspicious nature and wrong advice tendered to him by his counsellors might create complications. Ochterlony plained told him "that the British Government was determined to acquire the restitution of all conquests in the Cis-Sutlej region during his late expedition."[10]

The British force moved upto the Sutlej. The Lahore *darbar* was double minded. Some counsellors were for giving the British the befitting reply, while others were for maintaining peace. Dewan Mukham Chand opined that it was honourable to die fighting than to surrender without resistance. At his instance forces were collected and within a few days about one lakh Punjabis answered the call to arms. On the other hand, Fakir Aziz-ud-din was for negotiations and avoiding hostilities af far as possible. He was supported by Rani Sada Kaur. According to intelligence reports received by Ochterlony, Sada Kaur had "urged Ranjit Singh to avoid hostilities with the British power which was coming from one who had so much cause of complaint and dissatisfaction will probably have greater weight at this moment than he has been accustomed to pay to her representations."[11]

However, Ranjit Singh fully realised that if he was defeated now, all would be lost. If the danger could be avoided now, he could fight again any day after making more was preparations. He made up his mind to accept Sutlej as the boundary between the British and the Sikhs.

On January 2, 1809, Ochterlony left Delhi for Karnal at the head of three infantry battalions, a regiment of cavalry and some artillery. He was to force the Lahore *darbar* to give up its recent conquests. He was also to call upon the Cis-Sutlej chiefs to render all possible assistance to the British. It was declared that all the Sikhs on the south bank of the Sutlej were under the protection of the British Government. Ochterlony advanced via Buria, Patiala and Nabha towards Ludhiana, and was welcomed by the Sirhind chiefs. He restored Ambala to Rani Daya Kaur who waited on Ochterlony and thanked him personally for the generous act done to her. Raja Sahib Singh of Patiala and Raja Jaswant Singh of Nabha received Ochterlony with enthusiasm and relished the sight of British troops marching through their territories. Ochterlony then visited Malerkotla and reinstated the Nawab.

Meanwhile, the decision of the Governor-General was communicated to Maharaja Ranjit Singh, that the Cis-Sutlej chiefs had been declared to be under the protection of the British Government, and that the State of Lahore must severe all its connections with it. The British Government argued "that these chiefs had long been considered under the protection of the power in the north of Hindostan, that by the issue of the War with the Mahrattas, the British Government became possessed of the power and right formerly exercised by that nation in northern India that at that time Maharaja had no claim on the country between the Sutlej and the Jamna and that in an early period of that contest, a communication was received from the Maharaja by the late Lord Lake, which proposed to fix the Sutlej as the boundary between the British Government and his which was clear proof that the Maharaja in those days was well aware that the country in question was dependent on the power paramount in the north of Hindustan."[12]

Metcalfe wrote, "it has relieved the chiefs between the Sutlej and the Jamna from tribute and that degree of subserviency which they were used to pay to the Mahrattas, and has allowed them to carry on their own concerns without interference or control. But his liberality on the part of the British Government was meant for the benefit of those chiefs, not for their injury. It was never intended that the forbearance of the British Government, should be take advantage of by another power to oppress and subjugate those whom the British Government wished to protect and relieve."[13]

"It was on these grounds declared that the British Government could not consent to those chiefs being subjugated by the Maharaja or any other power, and announced that those chiefs, according to established custom were and should remain under the protection of the British Government. The Maharaja was therefore called upon to restore all places situated between the Sutlej and the Jamuna, of which he had taken possession (since the period of the first reference to this question to the British Government), to their former possessors, and to confine his army to the right bank of Sutlej."[14]

Ranjit Singh now seeing the danger of further protracting the negotiations and feeling that the British Government was earnest and in no way to be turned down from the resolution at length awoke to the necessity of a speedy settlement with that power. He also saw that his own authority in the Punjab could hardly be said to be yet firmly established, and was fully sensible that the still independent chiefs of the Punjab might shake off their allegiance to him and go over to the side of the English at any moment.

"A chances of establishing an empire would then be lost, his lofty aspirations effectually humbled, and he himself involved in hostilities with a power which he may very well know he was incapable of effectually opposing in the field. He therefore, prudently made up his mind at once to withdraw his forces to the south of Sutlej, as required by the British authorities."[15]

On February 9, 1809, David Ochterlony made an official proclamation on behalf of the British Government that the chiefs of Malwa were under British protection. The proclamation (*Ittilahnama*), under the Seal of General St. Leger, and under the Seal and signature of Colonel Ochterlony, read: "The British army having encamped near the frontiers of the

Maharaja Ranjit Singh, it has been thought proper to signify the pleasure of the British Government, by means of this precept, in order to make all the chiefs of the Maharaja acquainted with the sentiments of the British Government, which have solely for their object and aim to confirm the friendship with the Maharaja, and to prevent any injury to his country, the preservation of friendship between the two States depending on particular conditions which are hereby detailed."

The Thanas in the fortress of Kharar, Khanpur, and other places on this side of the river Sutlej, which have been placed in the hands of the dependents of the Maharaja, shall be razed and the same places restored to their ancient possessors.

The forces of cavalry and infantry which may have crossed to this side of the Sutlej must be recalled to the other side, to the country of the Maharaja.

The troops stationed at the Ghat of Phillaur must march thence, and depart to the other of side the river as described, and in future the troops of the Maharaja shall never advance into the country of the Chiefs situated on this side of the river, who have called in for their security and protection of Thanas of the British Government; but if in the manner that the British have place Thanas of moderate number of this side of the Sutlej, if in like manner a small force by way of Thana be stationed at the Ghat of Phillaur, it will not be objected to.

If the Maharaja persevere in the fulfilment of the above stipulations which he so repeatedly professed to do in presence of Mr. Metcalfe, such fulfilment will confine the mutual friendship. In case of non-compliance with these stipulations then shall it be plain that the Maharaja has no regard for the friendship of the British, but, on the contrary, resolves on enmity. In such case the victorious British army shall commence every mode of defence.

The communication of this precept is solely with the view to publishing the sentiments of the British, and to know those of the Maharaja. The British are confident that the Maharaja will consider the contents of this precept as abounding to his real advantage, and as affording a conspicuous proof of their friendship; that with their capacity for war, they are also intent on peace.

The British detachment arrived at Ludhiana on February 18, 1809, where Ochterlony established an army post. Raja Bhag Sing of Jind was allowed a paltly compensation of Rs. 500 per mensum for its temporary occupations.

"The proclamation of 9 February, 1809, was the last straw which broke the camel's back. The advance of British detachments under General St. Leger and Col. Ochterlony had considerable effect on the wavering Cis-Sutlej Sikh chiefs who withdrew their loyalty and professions of friendship with the Maharaja one by one. Thus the desertion of Cis-Sutlej chiefs of Patiala Nabha, Jind, Kaithal, Kalsia, Ladwa, Thanaser and Buria who realised the advantages of British protection greatly disheartened the Maharaja. He prudently agreed to withdraw his troops to the right bank of the Sutlej, abandon all claims of sovereignty over the Cis-Sutlej Sikh chiefs and restore all conquests made by him during the third Malwa expedition."[16]

While Matcalfe was staying at Amritsar, an unfortunate incident took place, which added to the tension. On the occasion of Muharram on February 25, 1809, the Shia Muslims in the escort of Metcalfe took out a procession in the bazars of Amritsar. It was also Holi day and the Sikhs, mostly Nihangs, under the command of their leader Akali Phula Singh gathered in the city to celebrate the festival. Mourning and beating their breasts, the Shias came in the front of the Golden Temple where the Sikhs were offering their prayers. The Nihangs asked the Shias not to pass through the streets around Golden Temple. The altercation led to a collision between the Shias and the Nihangs. It is not known as to who had attacked first. However, there was regular exchange of fire. A fierce fighting took place and there were casualties.

As soon as the Maharaja, who was staying in the Gobind-garh fort, came to know of the incident, he rushed to the sport and saw to it personally that the riots were quelled.

Ranjit Singh now did not want to prolong the discussions and felt that the negotiations should be finalised at this stage with the British. Thus, a treaty was signed between the British and Ranjit Singh on April 25, 1809, the terms of which were:

Whereas certain differences which had arisen between the British Government and the Raja of Lahore have been happily and amicably adjusted; and both parties being anxious to maintain relations to perfect amity and concord, the following articles of treaty, which shall be binding on the heirs and successors of the two parties, have been concluded by the Raja Ranjit Singh in person, and by the agency of C. T. Metcalfe, Esquire, on the part of the British Government.

One. Perpetual friendship shall subsist between the British Government and the State of Lahore; the latter shall be considered, with respect to the former, to be on the footing of the most favoured powers and the British Government will have no concern with the territories and subjects of the Raja to the northward of the river Sutlej.

Two. The Raja will never maintain in the territory which he occupies on the left bank of the river Sutlej more troops than are necessary for the internal duties of that territory, nor commit or suffer any encroachments on the possessions or rights of the chiefs in its vicnity.

Three. In the event of a violation of any of the preceding articles, or of a departure from the rules of friendship, this treaty shall be considered null and void.

Four. This treaty consisting of four articles, having been settled and concluded at Amritsar, on the 25th day of April, 1809, Mr. C.T. Metcalfe has delivered to the Raja of Lahore a copy of the same in English and Persian, under his seal and signature; and the Raja has delivered another copy of the same under his seal and signature; and Mr. C. T. Metcalfe engages to procure within the space of two months a copy of the same duly ratified by Right Honourable the Governor-General in Council on the receipt of which by the Raja, the present treaty shall be deemed complete and binding on both parties, and the copy of it now delivered to the Raja shall be returned.

The treaty was rectified by the Governor-General in Council on May 21, 1809.

After the treaty was signed, Metcalfe left Amritsar on May 2, 1809.

The treaty of Amritsar was of great significance in the history of Punjab and it had far-reaching consequences. The cherished objective of Ranjit Singh was to unite all the Sikhs under one single banner but this could not be achieved by him. "Ranjit's intentions over the Cis-Sutlej State were not selfish. He was a man who during his life time never used his crown, nor did he ever sit on his throne, nor strike coins after his own name. The coins were rather struck after the names of Guru Nanak and Guru Gobind Singh. If such a man wanted to unite all the Khalsa, including the Cis-Sutlej states under his banner, he was fighting for a national cause, and the opposition of the Cis-Sutlej States was anti-national, yet more so when they sought the British protection."[17]

"However, the Treaty of Amritsar was a grievous blow to Ranjit Singh's dream of united Punjab. Although for the rest of his life he professed friendship for the English nation, the friendship was strongly tinged with fear of their might."[18]

On the other hand, "the treaty of Amritsar (1809) was the definite beginning of Anglo-Sikh friendship. It confined

Ranjit Singh's activities to the other side of the Sutlej, the British Government taking the Cis-Sutlej States under its protection." Thus, the English alliance began by depriving Ranjit Singh of one of the most cherished objects of his life, the ideal of being the sole ruler of all the Sikhs. But at the same time it seemed to give him a *Carte blanche* so far as the region to the west of the Sutlej was concerned. Sir Charles Metcalfe is said to have told Ranjit Singh on taking leave that in 20 years he would reap the fruits of his alliance with the British.

It is said that the Maharaja told Wade in 1827 that "his words have been verified."[19]

The policy of the Maharaja was skillful, bold and deserved that success which it would probably have achieved had the danger of a French invasion been a real and not an imaginary one. He cared nothing for France, and felt that Napolean was not his enemy but that of the English Government. If the English desired him to join them against France, they must be prepared to pay. Thus the history of the Cis-Sutlej states from this time until the First Sikh War was distinct from that of Lahore. The Maharaja honourably observed his engagements, and recognising that the power of English was invincible, he frankly and for ever abandoned his dream of Cis-Sutlej supremacy and turned his attention to the expulsion of the Afghans from the northern districts of the province."[20]

The treaty of Amritsar was by no means a bad bargain for the Sikh ruler; for though forced to abandon all hope of Cis-Sutlej supremacy, he had the enormous advantage of knowing that from that time forward, he would never be called upon to defend his eastern frontier. For this his sole guarantee was the word of the British Government; but the character of the recent negotiations had taught him that word was to be relied upon. He loyally abided by the terms of the treaty, and from the moment he signed it he became the firm and devoted friend of the paramount power."[21]

In reply to the question whether it was a diplomatic defeat of Ranjit Singh or he might have signed the treaty of Amritsar under coercion and pressure as is stated by Osboren that "the conduct of Ranjit Singh was so unsatisfactory, and he evinced such a strong disposition to continue its encroachments that it was deemed expedient to advance a body of troops under Colonel Ochterlony, to enforce the demands, and to support the negotiations of our agent."[22] Or was it a success of his foreign policy, one can only say that the signing of the treaty of Amritsar was the only alternative left to Ranjit Singh. Ranjit Singh was still building up his empire and the fight with the British could have proved suicidal for Ranjit Singh. Under the circumstances, he adopted the best course.

Moreover, the role of Cis-Sutlej chiefs was anti-national and they could not be relied upon. The future events culminating in the final annexation of Punjab bear ample testimony to the fact that the Cis-Sutlej chiefs in order to protect their self-interests behaved in such a manner. They were only to retain their estates and had no sense of national honour or pride. It were they who had shattered Ranjit Singh's dream of unifying all the Sikhs of Guru Gobind Singh under one banner and unfurl the national flag over the vast territory lying between the Yamuna and the Sutlej.

The relations between Cis-Sutlej chiefs and the paramount power under whose protection they had now come were defined in a separate treaty called *Ittilahanama* executed on May 6, 1809 and duly promulgated to all the chiefs concerned, "who felt very grateful to the British Government for the successful issue of their prayer, and vied with each other in showing their deep sense of obligation to their patrons and protectors. Among themselves, however, the relations of these chiefs were most unsatisfactory. The more powerful chief was inclined to usurp the possession of the weaker chief, and feuds and quarrels, attended with much bloodshed and of loss of life, were the order of the day."[23]

Proclamation of protection to the Cis-Sutlej chiefs against the State of Lahore read:

That the territories of Sirhind and Malwa had been taken under British protection, and Ranjit Singh had bound himself by treaty to exercise in future to interference therein.

That is was not the intention of the British Government to demand any tributes from the chiefs and Sardars benefiting by this arrangements.

That the chiefs and Sardars would be permitted to exercise, and were for the future secured in the rights and authorities they possessed in their respective territories prior to, and at time of, the declaration of protection by the British Government.

That the chiefs and sardars should be bound to offer every facility and accommodation purposes otherwise connected with the general interest of the State, whenever the same might be marched into stationed in their respective territories.

In case of invasion or war the sardars were to join the British standard with their followers, whenever called upon.

Merchants conveying articles, the produce of Europe, for the use of detachments at Ludhiana, or of any other British force or detachment, should not be subjected to transit duty but must be protected on their passage through the Sikh country.

In like manner, horses for the cavalry, when furnished with passports from competent officers, must be exempt from all tax.

A third proclamation, was therefore, issued on August 22, 1811 warning the Cis-Sutlej chiefs that if any of the Sardars had forcibly taken possession of the estates of others, or otherwise injured the lawful owner, it was necessary that, before the institution of any complaint the proprietor should be satisfied.

The proclamation read:

"On the 6th May, 1809, an 'Ittilah Nameh' comprised of seven articles, was issued by the orders of the British Government, purporting that the country of the Sardars of Sirhind and Malwa having come under their protection, Raja Ranjit Singh, agreeable to treaty, had no concern with the possessions of the above Sardars; that British Government had no intention of claiming Peishkashs or Nazarana, and that they should continue in the full control and enjoyment of their respective possessions: The publication of the above 'Ittilah Namah' was intended to effort every confidence to the Sardars, that the protection of the country was the sole object, that they had no intention of control, and that those having possessions should remain in full and complete enjoyment thereof."

Whereas several Zamindars and other Subjects of the Chiefs of this country have preferred complaints to the officers of the British Government who having in view the tenor of the above 'Ittilah Nameh' have not attended, and will not in future pay attention to them; for instance, on the 15th of June 1811 Delawar Ali Khan of Samana complained to the Resident of Delhi against the officers of Raja Sahib Singh for jewels and other property said to have been seized by them, who in reply, observed that the 'Cusba' of Samana being in the Amildari of Raja Sahib Singh his complaint should be made to him. And also, on the 12th of July, 1811, Dussowandha Singh and Gurmukh Singh complained to Colonel Ocheterlony, Agent to the Governor-General against Sardar Charat Singh for their shares of property, and, in reply it was written on the back of their Arzi, "that since, during the period of three years, no claim was preferred against Charat Singh by any of his brothers, nor even the name of any co-partner mentioned; and since it was advertised in the 'Ittilah Namah' delivered to the Sardars, that every Chief should remain in the quite and full enjoyment of his domains, the petition could not be attended to,"—the insertion of these answers to complaints is intended as examples, and also that it may be impressed on the minds of every Zamindar and other subject, that the attainment of justice is to be expected from their respective Chiefs only, that they may not, in the smallest degree, swerve from the observation of subordination. It is, therefore, highly incumbent upon the Rajas and other Sardars of this side of the river Sutlej that they explain this to their respective subjects, and court their confidence, that it may be clear to them, that complaints to the officers of the British Government will be of no avail, and that they consider their respective Sardars as the source of justice, and that, of their free will and accord, they observe uniform obedience.

"And whereas, according to the first proclamation, it is not the intention of the British Government to interfere in the possessions of the Sardars of this country, it is nevertheless for the purpose of ameliorating the condition of the community, particularly necessary to give general information, that several Sardars have, since the last incursion of Raja Ranjit Singh, wrested the estates of others, and deprived them of their lawful possessions, and that in the restoration they have used delays until detachments of the British army have been sent to effect restitution, as in the case of the Rani of Tirah, the Sikhs of Chulian, the Talukas of Karauli and Chehloundy, and the village of Chiba; and the reason of such delays and evasions can only be attributed to the temporary enjoyment of the revenues and subjecting the owners to irremediable losses. It is therefore, by order of the British Government hereby proclaimed that if any one of the Sardars or others has forcibly taken possession of the estates of others, or otherwise injured the lawful owners, it is necessary that before the occurrence of any complaint, the proprietor should be satisfied and by no means to defer the restoration of the property,—in which however, should delays be made, and the interference of the British authority become requisite, the revenues of the estate from the date of ejection of the lawful proprietor, together with whatever other losses the inhabitants of that place may sustain from the march of troops, shall without scruple be demanded from the offending party; and for disobedience of the present orders, a penalty, according to the circumstances of the case and of the offender, shall be levied, agreeable to the decision of the British Government."

The British came to India as conquerers and it was but natural for them to adopt all fair and foul means to annex Punjab too. It was the betrayal of Cis-Sutlej chiefs that resulted in limiting the boundaries of Ranjit Singh empire. Thus, Ranjit Singh had no choice but to enter into treaty with the British and be contented with whatever he had acquired.

After the treaty, the "British officers on the frontier were warned to watch the proceedings of the Lahore ruler, and to see that the terms of treaty were not infringed. It is, however, to the credit of Ranjit Singh that he observed his treaty with the British with fidelity until his dying day. This was due mainly to the shrewd monarch's well-knowing the strength of the British Government and his personal conviction that power was sincere in its professions of friendship and amity, and really desired to see him powerful and prosperous, for the extinction of his sway would unmistakably have been followed by those convulsions, bloodshed and anarchy (on the borders of the British possessions) which had long continued a source of disgrace and misery and a repetition of which would have ruined the Maharaja's Government."[24]

After completing these formalities, a British cantonment was established at Ludhiana under the command of Colonel Ochterlony. Bakshi Nand Singh Bhandari of Batala was then appointed the Maharaja's Ambassador with the British General. Khushwakt Rai was deputed by the British Government as their news writer in the Lahore *darbar*.

REFERENCES

1. Lord Minto in India, p. 81.
2. Latif Mohd., History of the Panjab, p. 373.
3. Murray W. History of the Punjab, p. 64.
4. Payne C. H., A Short History of the Sikhs, p. 81.

5. Thompson E., Lord Metcalfe, p. 75.
6. Seton to Governor General, February 18, 1808.
7. SC 3, June 20, 1808.
8. Latif Mond., History of the Panjab, p. 374.
9. Moorcroft, Travels, Vol. 1, p. 94.
10. Ochterlony to Edmonstone, January 20, 1809 and February 13, 1809.
11. Ochterlony, March 13, 1809.
12. Latif Mohd., History of the Panjab, p. 377.
13. Metcalfe, December 12, 1808.
14. Latif Mohd., History of the Panjab, p. 377.
15. Latif Mohd., History of the Panjab, p. 329.
16. Hasrat, Bikramjit, Life Times of Ranjit Singh, p. 58.
17. Kohli Sita Ram, Ranjit Singh, p. 94.
18. Khushwant Singh, Ranjit Singh, p. 94.
19. Wade, Letters, 1827.
20. Lepel, Griffin, Ranjit Singh, pp. 177, 180-81.
21. Payne, C.H., A Short History of the Sikhs, p. 85.
22. Osborne, W. G., Court and Camp of Ranjit Singh, pp. 27-28.
23. Latif Mohd., History of the Panjab, p. 330.
24. Latif Mohd., History of the Panjab, p. 380.

11

Conquest of Kasur and Multan

After settling the affairs of Lahore, the Maharaja turned his eyes on Kasur. Kasur was a small colony governed by a Pathan, Nawab Nizam-ud-din. It was an eye-sore to the Maharaja. In 1801, an expedition was sent to subdue the Pathan but he offered stubborn resistance. Later, the Nawab joined hands with Sahib Singh Bhangi and raised a banner of revolt against the Maharaja. The Maharaja sent a force under Fateh Singh to Kasur. The Nawab surrendered and agreed to acknowledge the authority of the Lahore *darbar*. He paid *nazrana* and offered a few of his men as a guarantee of future good behaviour.

Hardly a year passed in peace. The Nawab again became hostile and started attacking the Lahore *darbar's* territory. The Maharaja could not tolerate this defiance. A force was sent under Fateh Singh Ahluwalia to subdue Nawab Nizam-ud-din. However, the Maharaja took no chance and himself followed with a strong contingent of troops to chastise the Pathan ruler. Finding it difficult to hold the fort, the Nawab surrendered. He had to pay a huge sum of money as indemnity and was recognised as a tributary of Lahore *darbar*.

However, the situation further changed with the assassination of Nawab Nizam-ud-din and succession of his brother Nawab Qutab-ud-din who, being somewhat arrogant, openly defied the authority of the Maharaja. Immediately a force was sent to subdue him. The Nawab remained inside the fort and fought the battles from within. After a siege lasting several months, the Nawab surrendered with a promise to pay war indemnity.

In 1807, However, trouble erupted again. Qutab-ud-din revolted and challenged the authority of the Maharaja. On February 10, the Maharaja's forces attackead Kasur under the command of Jodh Singh Ramgarhia. Kasur contained many small forts, all of which were full of huge quantity of arms and ammunition and other war material. The march of the Sikhs cut of all the lines of communications. Siege lasted for about a month, by which time the pathans had consumed all their provisions and had begun to live on the flesh of horses and other cattle. The Sikhs laid waste the entire area and, using artillery, levelled the city walls to the ground. The city was plundered and everything the people of the town had was forcibly wrested from them. Qutab-ud-din shut himself within the four walls of the fort. There were internal dissensions in the Nawab's family which resulted in his complete ruin. By the end of March, he was forced to surrender. "Like a moth, Qutab-ud-din fell upon the lamp of the glory of the armies, burnt his wings and having failed to carry on the open battle was besieged."[1] The Nawab's forces laid down their arms and recognised Maharaja Ranjit Singh as the sovereign. The Maharaja however, took pity on the Nawab and bestowed a *Jagir* on him at Mamdoi. In turn, the Nawab promised to give 100 horsemen to the Lahore *darbar*. The *Jagir* had an annual income of Rs. 52,000. This territory had been conquered by Qutab-ud-din and his brother in 1800 from the Rai of Rajkot, Fateh Din Khan, nephew of Qutab-ud-din and son of Nizam-ud-din, was given a *Jagir* at Marup, subject to the same conditions as imposed upon his uncle.

At the time of Metcalfe's mission, the Nawab was present with the army of Ranjit Singh. When the Khan desired latter to transfer his allegiance to the British as a Cis-Sutlej chieftain, the British Government declined protection to him, for he was by now regarded as a follower of the Lahore ruler.

Multan was a rich fertile land in the southern part of Punjab and was a very prosperous agricultural territory. It was a part of the Mughal empire and was known as a *Dar-ul-Amann*. When the Mughal power was disintegrating Multan came in the possession of Pathans. Near Multan there was a territory which was bestowed on a landlord by Nadir Shah in 1739. Later, it came to be known as Bhawalpur. In 1752, Ahmad Shah Abdali conquered Multan but left out Bhawalpur. He appointed a separate Governor for the province. Till 1757, it was governed as a part of Ahmed Shah Abdali's Indian empire. In 1767, Jhanda Singh, the head of Bhangi Misal, launched an attack on multan but was unable to drive out the Durani Shuja Khan from there. Even his ally Mubarak Khan, could not be uprooted. A fierce battle took place on the banks of the river Sutlej but it could not decide the fate of any of them. At last an understanding was reached between Jhanda Singh Bhangi and the Nawab to the effect that Pakpattan would form the boundary between their territories. But the Bhangis did not stick to the terms of the agreement. He again invaded Multan in 1771 but failed to capture it. However, a dispute arose between Shuja Khan and Haji Sharif Beg, the two aspirants for the Governorship of Multan. Haji Beg sought the aid of Bhangis to subdue the former. His request was conceded and Jhanda Singh marched towards Multan alongwith his brother Ganda Singh. Fierce battle ensued in which Nawab Shuja Khan and his ally Mubarak Khan were completely routed. The fort was seized by the Bhangis who refused to hand over he territory to Haji Beg. Multan was proclaimed territory belonging to the Khalsa and Haji Beg was driven out of it. The Bhangis ultimately divided the town amongst themselves. A portion of the city was given to Lehna Singh, the Bhangi commander, and on the remaining portion the authority of Diwan Singh was recognised who was appointed Commander of the fort where Sikh forces were stationed.

The Bhangi rule of Multan did not last more than seven years. They could not administer the territory efficiently which resulted in widespread discontentment. Jhanda Singh was constantly busy in wars and internal wrangles of divergent *Misals*. Although he was able to conquer Jhang, Kala Bagh and Mankera he could not subdue Shujabad. After some time Jhanda Singh was assassinated while at war in Jammu with Kanahiayas and Sukerchakias.

In 1776, Shuja Khan died and his on Muzaffar Khan succeeded him. In 1779, Taimur, the successor of Ahmad Shah Abdali, expelled the Bhangis from Multan and recognised Muzaffar Khan as its Governor. Taimur also overran Sind and Bhawalpur, the rulers of which were again brought under subjugation, making them tributaries of Kabul. Taimur then returned to Afghanistan.

Multan thus again came under the Afghans who ruled it with an iron hand. Taimur died in 1792. Nawab Muzaffar Khan remained loyal to Afghans and paid tribute regularly. However, Wazir Fateh Khan, the Minister of Amir Shah Mohammad of Kabul, conspired to replace Nawab Muzaffar Khan and appointed his own henchman as the Governor of Multan. But the move was strongly resisted by the Nawab Shuja-ul-Malik, who had regained power in the eastern part of Afghanistan from Muzaffar Khan's rescue and confirmed him to the Governorship.

The Nawab governed Multan in a half-hearted way and administered in only to fulfil his own ambition. Multan was surrounded by a wall between forty and fifty feet high. A large portion of the villages was in ruins and there were signs of a well-cultivated country going to decay.

It is estimated that the army of the Nawab consisted of 2,000 fully trained men and 20 guns. He had also 10,000 militia which could be utilized in case of exigencies.

Muzaffar Khan "was a brave and energetic man, and held his own gallantly against both the Sikhs and the neighbouring tribes, Sials and others, who attacked him."[2]

From the very beginning, Ranjit Singh had an eye on Multan and wanted to annex it to his empire. Multan had then a strategic position. It was not only the capital of the State but was also a centre of trade with the countries across the Bolan Pass and had an annual revenue of Rs. 680,975. There was a direct route between Multan and the Bolan Pass, leading to the Kandhar under the Persians. Bolan Pass had to be defended by the forces stationed at Multan. Moreover, it was situated in between the states of Bhawalpur and Southern Sind and could pose a threat to Maharaja Ranjit Singh any time for all these Muslim States could join hands and attack Ranjit Singh's territory. Their power had therefore, to be curbed.

In 1802, Ranjit Singh attacked Multan for the first time. The Nawab came out to meet him 60 km from his capital but could not stand against Ranjit Singh's forces. In the end, he offered *Nazrana* and promised to pay tribute to Ranjit Singh. Some valuable gifts were exchanged and both parted as friends.

In 1806 again, after having captured Jhang, Ranjit Singh marched towards Multan and reached Mahtan, 30 km north of the city. The Nawab did not nave the heart to engage him, so he gave him Rs. 70,000 and requested him to retire to his own territory.

In 1807, the Maharaja again marched to Multan in force. A battle was fought on the outskirts of the town after which it was partially captured but the fort remained impregnable. At last, an agreement was concluded through Fateh Singh Kalianwala, under which the Maharaja retuned to his capital, securing a huge sum of money. "Nawab Muzaffar Khan, weary of war, now made a pilgrimage to Mecca, and on his return vainly tried to induce, the English to take him under their protection. But the British Government declined. Multan was remoted and beyond the sphere they then desired to influence.[3]

At the same time, the Maharaja's desire to capture Multan could not be extinguished. Preparations were on once again to conquer the capital. So in the early days of 1810, Ranjit Singh marched towards Multan with a sizeable force. He had earlier met Shah Shuja of Afghanistan at Khushab. Shah Shuja was an exiled king of Kabul who desired Ranjit Singh to capture Multan and hand over the territory to him. Muzaffar Khan had, in 1803, repulsed an attack of the Shah's troops and in the hope of conciliating him, had more than once offered him an asylum at Multan but the Shah desired to have the capital as his own by conquest. Shah was given due respect by the Maharaja but the Shah did not offer any money to Ranjit Singh who then decided to attack Multan.

A huge force proceeded which reached the outskirts of Multan on February 24.

On February 25, the Maharaja, who was himself commanding the forces sent an ultimatum to Nawab Muzaffar Khan through his General, Fateh Singh Ahluwalia. It was stated that the Nawab had entered into an agreement with the Lahore *darbar* that he would be loyal to the *darbar*; that he would have no connection with the enemies of the *darbar*; that he would pay regularly tribute and *nazrama* to the *darbar* through his own men; and that he would remain faithful and well-wisher of the *darbar* under all circumstances. But he had not implemented the terms of the treaty, was responsible for breaking the various clauses of the treaty by giving shelter to Ahmad Khan Sial of Jhang, who was the confirmed enemy of the *darbar;* was asked to arrest Ahmad Khan according to the terms of the treaty and hand him over to the Maharaja; had helped Nawab Qutab-ud-din of Kasur against the Maharaja and given him arms, ammunition and money for which proof was available and had failed to send tribute and *nazrana* in time.

In the end, the Nawab was called upon to pay the due amount immediately without any further loss of time. If he did not take speedy action in this regard, his territory would be annexed to the Lahore *darbar*. He was further asked to send an immediate reply through Fateh Singh Ahluwalia.

When the ultimatum was read to the Nawab, he became nervous and panicky. He did not give any satisfactory reply and tried to side-track the issue. Ahluwalia no longer stayed with the Nawab and returned to report to the Maharaja the gist of what happened. The Maharaja immediately ordered his forces to attack Multan. The Nawab had also made full preparations for war. However, the Maharaja's forces took possession of the city, and laid siege of the fort. The Nawab had provided the fort with abundance of water, provisions and supplies. The appearance of the Sikh army at Multan and their occupation of the town spread alarm throughout then neighbouring country. Muhammad Khan, the chief of Leia and Bhakkar, bought off the invader by the payment of Rs. 1,20,000 as a ransom for his State and the chief of Bahawalpur. Sadiq Muhammad Khan, through a friend of Muzaffar Khan offered a lakh as tribute but as the Maharaja wanted more substantial aid, the offer was not accepted. The Bahawalpur, chief was at last compelled to furnish a contingent of 500 cavalry of service in the impending Multan campaign.

Now, the Maharaja's attention was diverted towards the capture of the fort. He himself took stock of the situation by going round the fort along its wall and ordered installation of the big guns outside Hathi and Khizri gates. Although, by now, the citadel of Multan was besieged by the Sikh army, the Pathans offered a stout resistance and the most strenuous attempts of the Sikh forces to capture the fort by assault failed miserably. A heavy bombardment was made for several days but without any result.

The Maharaja, finding the situation most critical, thought of an alternative. Under this plan, some of the violent soldiers had to come forward to lay mines under the walls of the fort. But to lay mines was a most difficult task which could have very dangerous consequences. Anyone who tried to lay the mines might himself get grown up in the process.

However, the Maharaja's keen interest encouraged and inspired the soldiers. And with shouts of *Sat Sri Akal*, 75 brave soldiers under the command of Hari Singh Nalwa, Nihal Singh Attari and Attar Singh Dhari proceeded towards the fort. The Nawab's soldiers spat fire on them. But these brave-men unconcernedly went on laying mines under the walls of the fort. "Ranjit Singh made the most solemn and lavish promises to the chiefs who should distinguish themselves in the action, by the earliest effective advance. He personally reconnoitred the enemy's position, examined his posts and fixed his own, marking out the spots of the batteries and assigning lines of approach to the different chiefs, whose sense of duty to their countrymen was appealed to with vehemence. Extensive transport arrangements were made both by land and water from Lahore and Amritsar, and the whole resources of the country were unreservedly placed at the disposal of the military authorities to secure this much coveted possession."[4]

By the time the mines were laid, several Sikh soldiers were injured and many others killed. The fort was besieged but the soldiers inside blew up the battery of Attar Singh Dhari, killing him and his twelve men. Hari Singh Nalwa was seriously injured. On March 21, a general assault was ordered but the Sikhs were repulsed with a heavy loss. The provisions were exhausted and the soldiers were disheartened.

Dewan Mukham Chand, the army general fell dangerously ill and many other notable chiefs were slain. But the Nawab's citadel remained as it was. On March 25, another assault was made but without any remarkable success. At last, no alternative was left with the Maharaja but to accept the terms offered by the Nawab. These terms had been rejected earlier several times. The Maharaja agreed to retire on receiving the payment of two and a half lakh rupees, 20 war horses and a contingent in time of war. On April 14, the Maharaja ordered his forces to be withdrawn after receiving Rs. 30,000 in ransom. Akbar Khan, brother-in-law of Muzaffar

Khan was handed over as a hostage for the payment of the balance. The Maharaja reached Lahore on April 24, highly depressed on his failure to subdue Multan.

"The famous Bhangi top named *Zamzama* was brought from Lahore to batter down the walls of the fort down; but it made little impression on the besieged. It discharged a ball of two-and-a-half maunds (Kacha) or 80 lbs. in weight, but the appliances for working this huge piece of ordnance were wanted in the Sikh camp, while nobody possessed sufficient knowledge and skill to make a proper use of it. Some little impression that was made on the ramparts of the citadel by the Sikh artillery had the effect only of redoubling the zeal of the besieged, who in countermining blew up the battery of Sardar Attar Singh Dhari, close to the fort, killing the Sardar and twelve others and severely wounding many more among whom were Sardar Nihal Singh Attariwala and the youthful Hari Singh Nalwa. Confused and panic-stricken the assailants fled, leaving their dead close to the fort, but the high-minded Pathans sent the bodies to the besiegers, that of Attar Singh being wrapped in a pair of shawls."[5]

When the Maharaja was about to retire he saw the dead body of Attar Singh Dhari and the badly injured Hari Singh Nalwa and Nihal Singh Attariwala. He ordered immediate treatment of these generals and issued special instructions to Fakir Aziz-ud-Din to look after them. Sardar Attar Singh Dhari's body was cremated with full military honours and the wounds of the injured generals were bandaged. The services of the brave soldiers who had laid down mines under the walls of the fort were highly appreciated and grant of *Jagri* was announced for many of them.

After a few days' effective treatment, Hari Singh Nalwa recovered and then he and general Attariwala were taken to Lahore in palanquins. There they admitted in a hospital from where they were discharged after several months in a fit physical state.

It is said that "seeing that his own strength was insufficient for the capture of Multan, Ranjit Singh addressed to Governor-General requesting the cooperation of British troops. His proposition was not well received, the more so as he proposed that the force, instead of marching through the Punjab should pass across the sterile, country south of the Sutlej."[6]

However, the Maharaja could not sit idle. His desire for the capture of Multan increased and he reinforced his forces for another attack as the successive failures had cast a gloom in his *darbar*.

In February 1816, Multan was attacked again. The Sikh forces marched in good numbers, but they were not sufficient to conquer the territory. While some other parts of the fort were captured, the battle on the whole ended without any achievement. Fakir Aziz-ud-din, however, made the Nawab pay the tribute and the Sikh forces proceeded towards Mankera.

At that moment, Nawab Mohammad Khan of Mankera died and his grandson Sher Mohammad Khan succeeded him. He was asked to pay tribute to the extent of rupees one lakh and twenty thousand to the Lahore *darbar*. Akali Phula Singh caused havoc in Khanpur and Mohmudkot forts. On the other hand, Misar Diwan Chand general Ilahi Baksh, Fateh Singh Ahluwalia Nihal Singh Attari and Hari Singh Nalwa bombarded the forts with seven platoons and heavy artillery. The walls of the fort collapsed and heavy casualties occurred in the Nawab's ranks. The Nawab became nervous and offered to pay rupees fifty thousands in cash as *nazrana*.

Hari Singh Nalwa had exhibited exemplary courage in the battle and the Maharaja greatly appreciated his services. As a token of his appreciation the Maharaja offered him a big *jagir* at Gujranwala.

In 1817, the Maharaja issued orders for a large scale campaign to conquer Multan. Troops were collected in large numbers, the entire transport system was re-organised, an effective line of communication was established, military provisions were collected and depots were reinforced. Ranjit Singh's generals were told to subdue Multan once for all. They asked the Nawab to surrender himself completely and hand over the fort to the Lahore *darbar*. No negotiations were to be held with the Nawab unless he surrendered. A 20,000 strong force was collected, to face any eventuality. In January, 1818 the army was sent to Multan under the nominal command of Prince Kharak Singh but in reality commanded by Misal Diwan Chand. It included generals like Hari Sigh Nalwa, Fateh Singh Ahluwalia, Jafar Jang, Dhanna Singh Malwai, Nihal Singh Attari and others.

On the way, the forts of Khangarh and Muzaffargarh were taken. In February 1819, the city of Multan fell before the Sikh forces. Then, the bombardment of the citadel started which continued for many days. The Nawab had an army of only 2000 men, but the fort was very well defended and such arrangements were made that even if the siege lasted several months, the provisions did not fall short.

The Nawab raised a cry of *jehad* to fight the infidels and the entire Muslim population of the surrounding areas joined him. He also made a special appeal to the ruler of Afghanistan for help. The battle continued and he fort remained besieged for about four months. The Nawab's forces resisted the attack with courage and endurance. The Sikh soldiers, with the help of their cannon, made breaches in the thick mud-and-brick wall of the fort, across the wide moat which surrounded it, but the Nawab's forces soon filled them up. Even heavy bombardment of the fort was not showing any result.

In April the Sikh forces were reinforced and an 80 pounder cannon was brought in under the command of Jamedar Khushal Singh. The Sikh forces encouraged by this made renewed assaults but were repulsed. It is said that at one time the Sikh forces lost 1800 men. The gates were blown off, but the garrison raised behind them mounds of earth on which they fought hand to hand with the Sikhs. The defenders of the fort were at last reduced to about two to three hundred fighting men, most of them belonging to the family of tribe of the Nawab. The rest were killed.

The storming of the fort continued till June 2, 1818 when Ilhai Baksh's artillery was able to effect two breaches. Again, many assaults were made by the Sikhs who also crossed the moat, but then they were mowed down by the Nawab's men.

The fighting continued. The Nawab's forces refused to surrender. They were adamant in their resolve to defend the fort. However, on the midnight of June 2, a party of Akalis under the command of Sadhu Singh surprised the defenders by rushing through one of the breaches in Khizri gate, risking their own lives. Sikh forces followed.

"After sieging the fort, the city and fort were now given up to be plundered by the Sikh troops: great were the ravages committed by the Sikhs on this occasion. About 400 to 500 houses in the fort were razed to the ground and their owners deprived of all they had. The precious stones, jewellery, shawls and other valuables belonging to the Nawab were confiscated to the State and kept carefully packed by Diwn Ram Diyal, for the inspection of the Maharaja. The arms were all carried away. In the town many houses were set on fire, and nothing was left with the inhabitants that was worth having. Hundreds were stripped of their clothes. Outrages were committed on the women many of whom committed suicide by drowning themselves in the wells, or otherwise putting an end to their lives, in order to save themselves from dishonour. Hundreds were killed in the sack of the city; and indeed there was hardly a soul who escaped both loss and violence. So great, in short, were the horrors inflicted upon the unfortunate inhabitants that the terrible incidents attendant on the sack of Multan are recollected to this day and still not infrequently form the topics of conversation."[7]

When the news of victory reached the Lahore *darbar*, the Maharaja could not contain his joy. He gave the messenger who brought the news of victory a pair of gold bracelets and rode out on the back of elephant and showered silver and gold on his subjects. Misar Diwan Chand was honoured with the title of *Zafarjang Bahadur*.

As Multan fell, a large booty was collected by the soldiers Maharaja Ranjit Singh himself admitted that at the time of the conquest the wealth of the city was estimated at four crores of rupees. The Sikh officers, he said, did not restrain the soldiers from plunder after the fall of the town, but very little of the booty came to his share even though the soldiery was made to disgorge part of it."[8]

With the capture of Multan, Afghan influence in the south of Punjab was over. Maharaja Ranjit Singh was in occupation of the rich province yielding a revenue of Rs. 7,00,000 annually. It was also a great commercial centre and had its strategic importance.

After the fall the Multan, the walls of the fort were repaired and a garrison of 600 men placed in the fort. The victorious Sikh army then hastened back to Lahore. The Maharaja issued strict orders to his officers and soldiers to deposit their plunder with the State, adding that if any booty was found with them beyond a particular date, the penalty would be death. As a result of this orders, Rs. 5,00,000 were deposited in the State treasury. However. The plunder of Multan was estimated at two million sterling. It was said, in popular belief, that the loot did not bring any luck to its possessors and most of them died in poverty or were killed in battle.

The Maharaja was over-joyous at this victory. It not only consolidated his power but also enhanced his prestige. Cannons were fired in Lahore to celebrate the victory. Celebrations were also held throughout the State. The victorious forces were received with full honour at Lahore and the Maharaja bestowed *Jagirs* on his valiant generals and soldiers.

Hardly Hari Singh Nalwa had been cured to his injuries when he was directed by the Maharaja to subdue the ruler of Mitha Tiwana who had raised a banner of revolt. He was further asked to mend Sayeeds of Uch who were not behaving properly. They had created terror in the area and people were groaning under their cruelty.

Sardar Hari Singh Nalwa, fulfilling the Maharaja's desire and in accordance with the policy of the Khalsa, tried to mend these rulers but without success. The General did not want to pick up quarrel with them, but when they refused to oblige, Sardar Dal Singh and Hari Singh Nalwa came with four platoons of soldiers to subdue them. On February 7, 1812, the Sikh forces and artillery marched towards Mitha Tiwana, the capital of the Tiwana's territory and reached there in the shortest possible time. The Tiwanas under the command of Ahmad Yar Khan, offered stout resistance. Artillery fire was opened and a fierce battle ensued. The Tiwanas fought bravely but suffered heavy casualties. The fighting continued the whole day.

By evening the soldiers felt tired and the battle ceased. A *Gurmatta* was passed by the Sikh leader that it was no use fighting and killing the innocent. Tiwanas were asked to cease hostilities as it would be useless to shed more blood. It was also made clear to them that if they would do so, they would themselves be responsible for the consequences. They could vacate the town by night after which they would not be attacked. Tiwana retreated and their territory was captured. The Khalsa army fulfilled its promise and no blood was shed. Thereafter, the Sikh flag was unfurled.

Now came the turn of the Sayeeds of Uch. The Maharaja made up his mind to punish the Sayeeds for their misdeeds. These *Pirs* had created havoc for the Hindu population. They ill-treated them and looked on them with contempt. Whenever any Hindu used to cross their way, they would either cover their face with a piece of cloth or spit on them. The *Pirs* even went to the extent of looting the houses of these people without caring for any law. The innocent people, however, could not raise their voice against them and were suffering silently.

Uch was attacked by the Khalsa army under the command of Hari Singh Nalwa. The *Pirs* could not offer much resistance and were soon ready to surrender. They were asked to pay *nazrana* of twentyfive thousand rupees which they readily paid. They were then directed to remain in peace.

Hari Singh Nalwa reached Lahore victorious. He was warmly received by the Maharaja who bestowed on him the entire territory as a *Jagir*. Others were also amply rewarded.

REFERENCES

1. Suri, Sohan Lal Umdat-ut-Twarikh Daftar II, p. 53.
2. Griffin Lepel, Ranjit Singh, P. 183.
3. Griffin Lepel, Ranjit Singh, p. 183.
4. Latif Mohd., History of the Punjab, p. 386.
5. Latif Mohd., History of the Panjab, p. 387.
6. Griffin Lepel, Ranjit Singh, pp. 184-85.
7. Latif Mohd., History of the Panjab, p. 142.
8. Moorcroft, William, Travels, p. 61.

12

Acquisition of North-West Regions

Ranjit Singh had brought Peshawer under his sway, but the complete reduction of the province was yet to cost him an arduous warfare of many years. He has become master of the Punjab almost unheeded by the English; but the position and views of that people had changed since they asked his aid against the armies of Napoleon. The Jumna and the sea-cost of Bombay were no longer the proclaimed limits of their empire; the Narbada had been crossed, the states of Rajputana had been rendered tributary, and, with the laudable design of diffusing wealth and of linking remote provinces together in the strong and useful remote provinces together in the strong and useful bonds of commerce, they were about to enter upon schemes of navigation and of trade, which caused them to deprecate the ambition of the king of the Sikhs, and led them, by sure yet unforeseen steps to absorb his dominion in their own, and to grasp, perhaps inscrutably to chasten, with the cold unfeeling hand of worldly rule, the youthful spirit of social change and religious reformation evoked by the genius of Nanak and Gobind.

Appeared to adhere to Dost Muhanmad rather than to others, had nevertheless an ambition of his own, and he was more than suspected of a wish to make his admiration of the amenities of English life the means of acquiring political Power.[1] Thus, doubtful of all about him, Dost Muhammad left Kabul to oppose Shah Shuja, but the Sikhs had, in the meantime, occupied Peshawer, and the perplexed ruler grasped once more at British aid as his only sure resource. [2] He tendered his submission as a dependent of Great Britain, and having thus endeavoured to put his dominions in trust, he gave Shah Shujas battle. But the Shah was defeated, and the rejoicing victor forget his difficulties. He declared war against the Sikhs on account of their capture of Peshawar and he endeavoured to make it a religious contest by rousing the population generally to destroy infidel invaders.[3] He assumed the proud distinction of 'Ghazi', or champion of the faith, and the vague title of 'Amir' which he interpreted 'the noble', for he did not care to wholly offend his brothers, whose submission he desired, and whose assistance was necessary to him.[4]

Dost Muhammad Khan, amid all his exultation, was still willing to use the intervention of unbelievers as well as the arms of the arms of the faithful and he asked English masters of India to help him in recovering Peshawer.[5] The youth who had been sent to Ludhiana to become a student, was invested with the were of a diplomatișt and the Amir sought to Prejudice the British authorities against the Sikhs, by urging that his nephew and their guest had been treated with suspicion and had suffered restraint on his way across the Punjab. But the English had not yet thought of requiring him to an ally for purposes of their own, and Dost Muhammad was simply assured that the son of Nawab Jabbar Khan should be well taken care of on the eastern side of the Sutlej. A direct reply to his solicitation was avoided, by enlarging on the partial truth that the Afghans were a commercial people equally with the English, and on the opening of the Indus to commerce. It was hoped, it was added that the new impulse given to trade would better help the two governments to cultivate a profitable friendship, and the wondering Amir, full of warlike schemes, was naively asked, whether he had any suggestions to offer about a direct route for merchandise between Kabul and the great boundary river of the Afghans.[6] The English rulers had also to reply to Ranjit Singh, who was naturally suspicious of the increasing intimacy between his allies and his enemies, and who desired that the European lords might appear rather as his than as Dost Muhammad's supporters; but the Governor-General observed that any endeavours to mediate would lead to consequences seriously embarrassing, and that Dost Muhammad would seem to have interpreted general professions of amity into promises of assistance.[7]

The two parties were thus left to their own means. Ranjit Singh began by detaching Sultan Muhammad Khan from the Amir, with whom he had sought a refuge on the occupation of Peshawar by the Sikhs; and the ejected tributary listened the more readily to the Maharaja's propositions, as he apprehended that Dost Muhammad would retain Peshawar for himself, should Ranjit Singh be beaten. Dost Muhammad came to the eastern entrance of the Khaibar Pass, and Ranjit Singh amused him with proposals until he had concentrated his forces. On the 11th of May 1835, the Amir was almost surrounded. He was to have been attacked on the 12th, but he thought it prudent to retreat, which he did with the loss of two guns and some baggage. He had designed to carry off the Sikh envoys, and to profit by their presence as hostages or as prisoners; but his brother, Sultan Muhammad Khan, to whom the execution of the project had been entrusted, had determined on joining Ranjit Singh, and the rescue of the agents gave him a favourable introduction to the victor. Sultan Muhammad and his brothers had considerable *Jagirs* conferred on them in the Peshawar district, but the military control and civil management of the province was vested solely in an officer appointed from Lahore.[8]

Dost Muhammad suffered much in general estimation by withdrawing from an encounter with the Sikhs. His hopes in the English had not borne fruit, and he was disposed to court Persia;[9] out the connexion was of less political credit and utility than one with the English, and he tried once more to move the Governor-General in his favour. The Sikhs, he said, were faithless, and he was wholly devoted to the interests of the British Government.[10] The Kandahar brothers, also, being pressed by Shah Kamran of Herat, and unable to obtain aid form Dost Muhammad, made propositions to the English authorities; but Kamram's own apprehensions of Persia soon relieved them of their fears, and they did not press their solicitations for European aid.[11] Ranjit Singh, on his part, disliked an English and Afghan alliance, and sought to draw Dost Muhammad within the vortex of his own influence. He gave the Amir vague hopes of obtaining Peshawar, and he asked him to send him some horses, which he had learnt was a sure way of leading others to believe they had won his favour. Dost Muhammad was not unwilling to obtain a hold on Peshawar, even as a tributary, but he felt that the presentation of horses would be declared by the Sikh to refer to Kabul and not to that province.[12] The disgrace of his retreat rankled in his mind, and he at last said that a battle must be fought at all risks.[13] He was the more inclined to resort to arms, as the Sikhs had sounded his brother, Jabbar Khan, and as Sirdar Hari Singh had occupied the entrance of the Khaibar Pass and entrenched a position at Jamrud, as the basis of his scheme for getting through the formidable defile.[14] The Kabul troops marched and assembled on the eastern side of Khaibar, under the command of Muhammad Akbar Khan,[15] the most warlike of the Amir's sons. An attack was made on the post of Jamrud, on the 30th of April 1837; but the Afghans could not carry it, although they threw the Sikhs into disorder. Hari Singh, by feigning a retreat, drew the enemy more fully into the plains; the brave leader was present everywhere amid his retiring and rallying masses, but he fell mortally wounded, and rallying masses, but he fell mortally wounded, and the opportune arrival of another portion of the Kabul forces converted the confusion of the Sikhs into a total defeat. But two guns only were lost; the Afghans could not master Jamrud or Peshawar itself, and after plundering the valley for a few days, they retreated rather than risk a second battle with the reinforced army of Lahore.[16]

The death of Hari Singh and the defeat of his army caused some anxiety in Lahore; but the Maharaja promptly roused his people to exertion, and all readily responded to his call. It is stated that field guns were dragged from Ramnagar, on the Chenab, to Peshawar in six days, a distance by road of more than two hundred miles.[17] Ranjit Singh advanced in person to Rohtas, and the active Dhian Singh hastened to the frontier, and set an example of devotion and labour by working with his own hands on the foundations of a regular fort at Jamurud.[18] Dost Muhammad was buoyed up by his fruitless victory, and he became more than ever desirous of recovering a province so wholly Afghan; but Ranjit Singh contrived to amuse him, and the Maharaja was found to be again in treaty with the Amir, and again in treaty with Shah Shuja, and with both at the same time.[19] But the commercial envoy of the English had gradually sailed high up the Indus of their imaginary commerce, and to his Government the time seemed to have come when political interference would no longer be embarrassing, but, on the contrary, highly advantageous to schemes of peaceful trade and beneficial intercourse. It was made known that the British rulers would be glad to be the means of negotiating a peace honourable to both parties, yet the scale was turned an favour of the Afghan, by the simultaneous admission that Peshawar was a place to which Dost Muhammed could scarcely be expected to resign all claim.[20] Nevertheless, it was said, the wishes of Ranjit Singh could be ascertained by Capt. Wade, and Capt. Burnes could similarly inquire about the views of the Amir. The latter officer was formally invested with diplomatic powers,[21] and the idle designs or restless intrigues, of Persians and Russians, soon caused the disputed of Sikhs and Afghans to merge in the British scheme of reseating Shah Shuja on the throne of Kabul. At the end of a generation the repose of the English masters of India was again disturbed by the rumoured march of European armies,[22] and their suspicions were further roused buy the conduct of the French General, Allard. That officer, after a residence of several years in the Punjab, had been enabled to visit his native country, and he returned by way of Calcutta in the year 1836. While in France he had induced his Government to give him a document, accrediting him to Ranjit Singh, in case his life should mission to quit the Lahore dominions. It was understood by the English that the paper was only to be produced to the *Maharaja* in an extremity of the kind mentioned; but General Allard himself considered that it was only to be so laid in form before the *English authorities*, in support of a demand for aid when he might chance to be straitened. He at once delivered his credentials to the Sikh ruler; it was rumoured that General Allard had become the British authorities forgave the fancied deceit, or the vain effrontery of their guest.[23]

Ranjit Singh had invited the Governor-General of India, the Governor of Agra (Sir Charles Mecalfe), and the Commander-in-Chief of the British forces to be present the nuptials of his grandson, which he designed to celebrate with much splendour. The prince was wedded to a daughter of the Sikh chief, Sham Singh Atariwala, in the beginning of March 1837, but of the English authorities Sir Henry Fane alone was able to attend. That able commander was ever a careful observer of military means and of soldierly qualities; he formed an estimate of the force which would be required for the complete subjugation of the Punjab, but at the same time he laid it down as a principle, that the Sutlej and the wastes of Rajputana and Sind were the best boundaries which the English could have in the east.[24] The prospect of a war with the Sikhs was then remote, and hostile designs could not with honour be entertained by a guest. Sir Henry Fane, therefore, entered a artily into the marriage festivities of Lahore, End his active mind was amused with giving shape to a scheme, which the intuitive sagacity of Ranjit Singh had acquiesced in as pleasing it the just pride or useful vanity of English soldiers. The project of establishing an Order of merit similar to those dying exponents of warlike skill and chivalrous fraternity among European nations had been for some time entertained, and although such a system of distinction can be adapted to the genius of any people, the object of the Maharaja was simply to gratify his English neighbours, and advantage was accordingly taken of Sir Henry Fane's presence to establish the 'Order of the auspicious Star of the Punjab' on a purely British model.[25] This method of pleasing, or occupying the attention of the English authorities, was not unusual with Ranjit Singh, and he was always ready to inquire concerning matters which interested them, or which might be turned to account by himself. He would ask for specimens of and for information about, the manufacture of Sambhar salt and Malwa opium.[26] So early as 1812 he had made trial of the sincerity of his new allies, for five hundred muskets. These were at once furnished to him, but a subsequent request for a supply of fifty thousand such weapons excited a passing suspicion.[27] He readily entered into a scheme of freighting a number of boats with merchandise for Bombay, and he was praised for the interest he took in commerce, until it was known that he wished the return cargo to consist of arms for his infantry.[28] He would have his artillerymen learn gunnery at Ludhiana,[29] and he would send shells of zinc to be inspected in the hope that he might receive some hints about the manufacture of iron shrapnels.[30] He would inquire about the details of European warfare, and he sought for copies of the pay regulations of the Indian army and of the English practice of courts martial, and bestowed dresses of honour on the translator of these complicated and inapplicable systems;[31] while, to further satisfy himself, he would ask what punishment had been found an efficient substitute for Logging.[32] He sent a lad, the relation of one of his chiefs, to learn English at the Ludhinana school, in order, he said that the youth might aid him in his correspondence with the British Government, which Lord William Bentinck had wished to carry on in the English tongue instead of in Persian;[33] and he sent a number of young men to learn something of medicine at the Ludhiana dispensary, which had been set on foot by the political agent—but in order, the

Maharaja said that they might be useful in his battalions.[34] In such ways, half-serious, half-idle, did Ranjit Singh endeavour to ingratiate himself with the representatives of a power he could not withstand and never wholly trusted.

Ranjit Singh's rejoicings over the marriage and youthful promise of his grandson were rudely interrupted by the success of the Afghans at Jamrud, and the death of his able leader Hari Singh, as has been already related. The old man was moved to tears when he heard of the fate of the only genuine Sikh chief of his creation;[35] and he had scarcely vindicated his supremacy on the frontier, by filling the valley of Peshawar with troops, when the English interfered to embitter the short remainder of his life, and to set bounds to his ambition on the west, as they had already done on the east and south. The commercial policy of the English people required that peace and industry should at once be introduced among the half-barbarous tribes of Sind, Khorasan, and the Punjab; and it was vainly sought to give fixed limits to newly-founded feudal governments, and to impress moderation of desire upon grasping military sovereigns. It was wished that Ranjit Singh should be content with his past achievements; that the Amirs of Sindh, and the chiefs of Herat, Kandahar, and Kabul should feel themselves secure in what they held, but incapable of obtaining more; and that the restless Shah Shuja should quietly abandon all hope of regaining the crown of his daily dreams.[36] There were the views which the English viceroy required his agents to impress on Talpurs, Barakzais, and Sikhs; and their impracticability might have quietly and harmlessly become apparent, had not Russia found reason and opportunity to push her intrigues, through Persia and Turkestan, to the banks of the Indus.[37] The desire of effecting a reconciliation between Ranjit Singh and Dost Muhammad induced the British Government to offer its mediation;[38] the predilections of its frank and enterprising envoy led him to seize upon the admission that the Amir could scarcely be expected to resign all pretensions to Peshawar.[39] The crafty chief made use of this partiality, and of the fact that his friendship was courted, to try and secure himself against the only power he really feared, viz. that of the Sikhs; and he renewed his overtures to Persia and welcomed a Russian emissary, with the view of intimidating the English into the surrender of Peshawar, and into a guarantee against Ranjit Singh. Friendly assurances to the Kandahar brothers, and a hint that the Sikhs were at liberty to march on Kabul, would have given Dost Muhammad a proper sense of his insignificance;[40] but the truth and the importance of his hostile designs were both believed or assumed by the British Government, while the rumours of a northern invasion were eagerly received and industriously spread by the vanquished princes of India, and the whole country vibrated with the hope that the uncongenial domination of the English was about to yield to the ascendancy of another and less dissimilar race.[41] The recall of Capt. Burnes from Kabul gave speciousness to the wildest statements; the advantage of striking some great blow became more and more obvious; for the sake of consistency it was necessary to maintain peace on the Indus, and it was wisely resolved to make a triumphant progress through Central Asia, and to leave Shah Shuja as a dependent prince on his ancestral throne. The conception was bold and perfect; and had it been steadily adhered to, the whole project would have eminently answered the ends intended, and would have been in every way, worthy of the English name.[42]

In the beginning of 1838 the Governor-General did not contemplate the restoration of Shah Shuja;[43] but in four months the scheme was adopted, and in May of that year Sir William Macnaghten was sent to Ranjit Singh to unfold the views of the British Government.[44] The Maharaja grasped at the first idea which presented itself, of making use of the Shah at the head of *his* armies, with the proclaimed support of the paramount power in India; but he disliked the complete view of the scheme, and the active co-operation of his old allies. It chafed him that he was to resign all hope of Shikarpur, and that he was to be enclosed within the iron arms of the English rule. He suddenly broke up his camp at Dinanagar, leaving the British envoys to follow at their leisure, or to return, if they pleased, to Simla; and it was not until he was told the expedition would be undertaken whether he chose to share in it or not, that he assented to a modification of his own treaty with Shah Shuja, and that the triple alliance was formed for the subversion of the power of the Barakzais.[45] The English, on their part, insisted on a double invasion of Afghanistan: first, because the Amirs of Sind disliked a proffered treaty of alliance or dependence, and they could conveniently be coerced as tributaries by Shah Shuja on his way to Kandahar; and, secondly because it was not deemed prudent to place the ex-king in the hands of Ranjit Singh; who might be tempted to use him for Sikh rather than for British objects.[46] It was therefore arranged that the Shah himself should march by way of Shikarpur and Quetta, while his son moved on Kabul by the road of Peshawar, and at the head of a force provided by the Maharaja of the Punjab. The British force assembled at Ferozepore towards the close of 1838, and further eclat was given to the opening of a memorable campaign, by an interchange of hospitalities between the English viceroy and the Sikh ruler.[47] Ostensibly Ranjit Singh had reached the summit of his ambition; he was acknowledged to be an arbiter in the fate of that empire which had tyrannized over his peasant forefathers, and he was treated with the greatest distinction by the foreign paramounts of India; but his health had become seriously impaired; he felt that he was in truth fairly in collision with the English, and he became indifferent about the careful fulfilment of the engagements into which he had entered. Shahzada Taimur marched from Lahore in January 1839 accompanied by Col. Wade as the British representative; but it was with difficulty the stipulated auxiliary force was got together at Peshawar, and although a considerable army at last encamped in the valley, the commander, the Maharaja's grandson, thwarted the negotiations of Prince Taimur and the English agent, by endeavouring to gain friends for Lahore rather than for the proclaimed sovereign of the Afghans.[48] Ranjit Singh's health continued to decline. He heard of the fall of Kandahar in April, and the delay at that place may have served to cheer his vexed spirit with the hope that the English would yet be baffled; but he died on the 27th of June, at the age of fifty-nine, before the capture of Ghazni and the occupation of Kabul, and the forcing of the Khaibar Pass with the aid of his own troops, placed the seal of success on a campaign in which he was an unwilling sharer.

Ranjit Singh found the Punjab a waning confederacy, a prey to the factions of its chiefs, pressed by the Afghans and the Marathas, and ready to submit to English supremacy. He consolidated the numerous petty states into a kingdom, he wrested from Kabul the fairest of its provinces, and he gave the potent English no cause for interference. He found the military array of his country a mass of horsemen, brave indeed, but ignorant of war as an art, and he left it mustering fifty thousand disciplined soldiers, fifty thousand well-armed yeomanry and militia, and more than three hundred pieces of cannon for the field. His rule was founded on the feelings of a people, but it involved the joint action of the necessary principles of military order and territorial extension; and when a limit had been set to Sikh dominion and his own commanding genius was no more, the vital spirit of his race began to consume itself in domestic contentions.[49]

When Ranjit Singh was Lord Auckland's host at Lahore and Amritsar, his utterance was difficult and the powers of his body feeble; he gradually—the use of his speech, and of the faculties of his mind; and, before his death, the Rajas of Jammu had usurped to themselves the whole of the functions of government, which the absence of Nau Nihal Singh enabled them to do with little difficulty. The army was assembled, and a litter, said to contain the dying Maharaja was carried along the extended line. Dhian Singh was assiduous in his mournful attentions; he seemed to take orders as if from his departing sovereign, and from time to time during the solemn procession, he made known that

Ranjit Singh declared the Prince Kharak Singh his successor, and himself, Dhian Singh, the wazir or minister of the kingdom.[50] The soldiery acquiesced in silence, and the British Government was perhaps more sincere than the Sikh people in the congratulations offered, agreeably to custom to the new and unworthy master of the Punjab.

In the year 1824, the turbulent Muhammadan tribes on either side of the Indus above Attock arose in rebellion, and the Sikh General Hari Singh received a severe check. The Maharaja hastened by forced marches to that quarter and again forded the rapid, stony-bedded Indus; but the mountaineers dispersed at his approach and his display of power was hardly rewarded by Yar Muhammad Khan's renewed protestations of allegiance.[51] In 1825 Ranjit Singh's attention was amused with overtures from the Gurkhas, who forgot his former rivalry in the overwhelming greatness of the English; but the precise object of the Nepalese did not transpire and the restless spirit of the Sikh chief soon led him to the Chenab, with the design of seizing Shikarpur.[52] The occurrence of a scarcity in Sind, and perhaps the ramours of the hostile preparations of the English against Bharatpur,[53] induced him to return to his capital before the end of the year. The *Jat* usurper of the Jumna asked his brother *Jat* of the Ravi to aid him; but the Maharaja acted to discredit the mission, and so satisfied the British authorities without compromising himself with the master of fortress which had successfully resisted the disciplined troops and the dreaded artillery of his neighbours.[54] But about the same time Ranjit Singh likewise found reason to distrust the possessors of strongholds; and Fateh Singh Ahluwalia was constrained by his old brother in arms to leave a masonry citadel unfinished and was further induced by his own fears to fly to the south of the Sutlej. He was assured of English protection in his ancestral estates in the Sirhind province, but Ranjit Singh remembering perhaps the joint treaty with Lord Lake earnestly endeavoured to ally the fears of the fugitive, and to recall a chief so dangerous in the hands of his allies. Fateh

Singh returned to Lahore in 1821; he was received with marked honour, and he was confirmed in nearly all his possessions.[55]

Towards the end of 1826, Ranjit Singh was attacked with sickness and he sought the aid of European skill. Dr. Murray, a surgeon in the British-Indian army, was sent to attent him, and he remained at Lahore for some time, although the Maharaja was more disposed to trust to time and abstinence, or to the empirical remedies of his own physicians than to the prescribers of unknown drugs and the practisers of new ways. Ranjit Singh, nevertheless, liked to have his foreign medical adviser near him as one from whom information could be gained, and whom it might be advantageous to please. He seemed anxious about the proposed visit of Lord Amherst, the Governor-General, to the northern provinces; he asked about the qualities of the Burmese troops,[56] and the amount of money demanded by the English victors at the end of the war with that people; he was inquisitive about the mutiny of a regiment of Sepoys at Barrackpore, and he wished to know whether native troops had been employed in quelling it.[57] On the arrival of Lord Amherst at Simla, in 1827, a further degree of intimacy became inevitable a mission of welcome and inquiry was sent to wait upon his lordship, and the compliment was returned by the deputation of Capt. Wade, the British frontier authority, to the Maharaja's court.[58] During the following year the English Commander-in-Chief arrived at Ludhiana, and Ranjit Singh sent an agent to convey to him his good wishes; but an expected invitation to visit the strongholds of the Punjab was not given to the captor of Bharatpur.[59]

The little business to be transacted between the British and Sikh governments was entrusted to the management of the Resident a Delhi, who gave his orders to Capt. Murray the political agent at Ambala, who again had under him an assistant, Capt. Wade, at Ludhiana, mainly in connexion with the affairs of the garrison of that place. When Capt. Wade was at Lahore, the Maharaja expressed a wish that, for the sake of dispatch in business, the agency for his Cis-Sutlej possessions should be vested in the officer at Ludhiana subordinate to the resident at Delhi, but independent of the officer at Ambala.[60] This wish was complied with;[61] but in attempting to define the extent of the territories in question, it was found that there were several doubtful points to be settled. Ranjit Singh claimed supremacy over Chamkaur, and Anandpur Makhowal, and other places belonging to the Sodhis, or collateral representatives of Guru Gobind. He also claimed Whadni, which a few years before, had been wrested from him on the plea that it was his mother-in-law's; and he claimed Ferozepore, then held by a childless widow, and also all the Ahluwalia districts, besides others which need not be particularized.[62] The claims of the Maharaja over Ferozepore and the ancestral possessions of Fateh Singh Ahluwalia were rejected; but the British title to supremacy over Whadni could not longer, it was found, be maintained. The claims of Lahore to Chamkaur and Anandpur Makhowal were expediently admitted. For the British right did not seem worth maintaining, and the affairs of the priestly class of Sikhs could be best managed by a ruler of their own faith.[63] Ranjit Singh disliked the loss of Ferozepore, which the English long continued to admire as a commanding position;[64] but the settlement generally was such as seemed to lessen the chances of future collision between the two governments.

Ranjit Singh's connexion with the English thus became more and more close, and about the same time he began to resign himself in many instances to the views of his new favourites of Jammu. The Maharaja had begun to notice the boyish promise of Hira Singh the son of Dhian Singh, and he may have been equally pleaded with the native simplicity, and with the turored deference, of the child. He gave him the title of Raja, and his father true to the Indian feeling, was desirous of establishing the purity of local power and of spotless genealogy. The betrothal of a daughter of the deceased Sansar Chand of Kangra was demanded in the year 1828, and the reluctant consent of the new chief, Anrudh

Chand, was obtained when he unwittingly had put himself wholly in the power of Dhain Singh by visiting Lahore with his sister for the purpose of joining in the nuptial ceremonies of the son of Fateh Singh Ahluwalia. The proposed degradation rendered the mother of the girls more indignant perhaps than the head of the family, and she contrived to escape with them to the south of the Sutlej. Anrudh Chand was required to bring them back, but he himself also fled, and his possessions were seized. The mother died of grief and vexation, and the son followed her to the grave, after idly attempting to induce the English to restore him by force of arms to his little principality. Sansar Chand had left several illegitimate children, and in 1829 the disappointed Maharaja endeavoured to obtain some revenge by marrying two of the daughters himself, and by elevating a son to the rank of Raja, and investing him with an estate out of his father's chiefship. The marriage of Hira Singh to a maiden of his own degree was celebrated during the same year with much splendour, and the greatness of Ranjit Singh's name induced even the chiefs living under British protection to offer their congratulations and their presents on the occasion.[65]

In the meanwhile a formidable insurrection had been organized in the neighbourhood of Peshawar, by an unheeded person and in an unlooked-for manner. One Ahmad Shah a Muhammadan of a family of Saiyids of Bareilly in Upper India had been a follower of the great mercenary leader Amir Khan but he lost his employment when the military force of his chief was broken up on the successful termination of the campaign against the joint Maratha and Pindari powers, and after Amir Khan's own recognition by the English as a dependent prince. The Saiyid went to Delhi, and a preacher of that city, named Abdul Aziz, declared himself greatly edified by the superior sanctity of Ahmad who denounced the corrupt forms of worship then prevalent, and endeavoured to enforce attention to the precepts of the Koran alone, without reference to the expositions of the early Fathers. His reputation increased, and two Maulais, Ismail and Abdul Hai, of some learning, but doubtful views, attached themselves to the Saiyid as his humble disciples and devoted followers.[66] A pilgrimage was preached as a suitable beginning for all undertakings, and Ahmad's journey to Calcutta in 1822, for the purpose of embarkation, was one of triumph, although his proceedings were little noticed until his presence in a large city gave him numerous congregations. He set sail for Mecca and Medina, and he is commonly believed, but without reason to have visited Constantinople. After an absence of four years he returned to Delhi, and called upon the faithful to follow him in a war against infidels. He acted as if he meant by unbelievers the Sikhs alone, but his precise objects are imperfectly understood. He was careful not to offend the English; but the mere *supremacy* of a remote nation over a wide and populous country gave him ample opportunities for unheeded agitation. In 1826 he left Delhi with perhaps five hundred attendants, and it was arranged that other bands should follow in succession under appointed leaders. He made some stay at Tonk, the residence of his old master, Amir Khan, and the son of the chief, the present Nawab, was enrolled among the disciples of the new saint. He obtained considerable assistance, at least in money, from the youthful convert, and he proceeded through the desert to Khairpur in Sind, where he was well received by Mir Rustam Khan and where he awaited the junction of the 'Ghazis', or fighters for the faith, who were following him. Ahmad marched to Kandahar, but his projects were mistrusted or misunderstood; he received no encouragement from the Barakzai brothers in possession, and he proceeded northward through the Ghilzai country, and in the beginning of 1827 he crossed the Kabul river to Panjtar in the Usufzai hills, between Peshawar and the Indus.[67]

The Panjtar family is of some consequence among the warlike Usufzais, and as the tribe had become apprehensive of the designs of Yar Muhammad Khan, whose dependence on Ranjit Singh secured him from danger on the side of Kabul, the Saiyid and his 'Ghazis' were hailed as deliverers, and the authority or supremacy of Ahmad was generally admitted. He led his ill-equipped host to attack a detachment of Sikhs, which had been moved forward to Akora, a few miles above Attock, under the command of Budh Singh Sindhanwala, of the same family as the Maharaja. The Sikh commander entrenched his position, and repulsed the tumultuous assault of the mountaineers with considerable loss, but as he could not follow up his success, the fame and the strength of the Saiyid continued to increase, and Yar Muhammad deemed it prudent to enter into an agreement obliging him to respect the territories of the Usufzais. The curbed governor of Peshawar is accused of a base attempt to remove Ahmad by poison, and in the year 1829, the fact or the report was made use of by the Saiyid as a reason for appealing to arms. Yar Muhammad was defeated and mortally wounded, and Peshawar was perhaps saved to his brother Sultan Muhammad, by the presence of a Sikh force under the Prince Sher Singh and General Ventura, which had been moved to that quarter under pretence of securing for the Maharaja a long-promised horse of famous breed named Laila, the match of one of equal renown named Kahar, which Ranjit Singh had already prided himself on obtaining from the Barakzai brothers.[68]

The Sikh troops withdrew to the Indus, leaving Sultan Muhammad Khan and his brothers to guard their fief or dependency as they could, and it would even seem that Ranjit Singh hoped the difficulties of their position, and the insecurity of the province, would justify its complete reduction.[69] But the influence of Saiyid Ahmad reached to Kashmir, and the mountaineers between that valley and the Indus were unwilling subjects of Lahore. Ahmad crossed the river in June 1830, and planned an attack upon the Sikh force commanded by Hari Singh Nalwa and General Allard; but he was beaten off, and forced to retire to the west of the river. In a few months he was strong enough to attack Sultan Muhammad Khan; the Barakzai was defeated and Peshawar was occupied by the Saiyid and his 'Ghazis'. His elation kept pace with his success, and according to tradition, already busy with his career, he proclaimed himself Khalif, and struck a coin in the name of 'Ahmad the Just, the defender of the faith, the flitter of whose sword scattereth destruction among infidels'. The fall of Peshawar caused some alarm in Lahore, and the force on the Indus was strengthened, and placed under the command of Prince Sher Singh. The petty Muhammadan chiefs generally, with whom self-interest overcame faith, were averse to the domination of the Indian adventurer, and the imprudence of Saiyid Ahmad gave umbrage to his Usufzai adherents. He had levied from the peasants a tithe of their goods, and this measure caused little or no dissatisfaction, for it agreed with their notion of the rights of a religious teacher; but his decree that all the young women of marriageable age should be at once wedded, interfered with the profits of Afghan parents proverbially avaricious, and who usually disposed of their daughters to the wealthiest bridegrooms. But when Saiyid Ahmad was accused perhaps unjustly, of assigning the maidens one by one to his needy India followers, his motives were impugned and the discontent was loud. Early in November 1830 he was constrained to relinquish Peshawar to Sultan Muhammad at a fixed tribute, and he proceeded to the left bank of the Indus to give battle to the Sikhs. The Saiyid depended chiefly on the few 'Ghazis' who had followed his fortunes throughout, and on the insurrectionary spirit of the Muzaffarabad and other chiefs, for his Usufzai adherents had greatly decreased. The hill 'khans' were soon brought under subjection by the efforts of Sher Singh and the Governor of Kashmir; yet Ahmad continued active, and, in a desultory warfare amid rugged mountains, success for a time attended him; but during a cessation of the frequent conflicts, he was surprised, early in May 1831, at a place called Balakot, and fallen upon and slain. The Usufzais at once expelled his deputies, the

'Ghazis' dispersed in disguise, and the family of the Saiyid hastened to Hindustan to find an honourable asylum with their friend the Nawab of Tonk.[70]

The fame of Ranjit Singh was now at its height, and his friendship was sought by distant sovereigns. In 1829, agents from Baluchistan brought horses to the Sikh ruler, and hoped that the frontier posts of Harrand and Dajal, westward of the Indus, which his feudatory of Bahawalpur had usurped would be restored to the Khan.[71] The Maharaja was likewise in communication with Shah Mahmud of Herat,[72] and in 1830 he was invited, by the Baiza Bai of Gwalior, to honour the nuptials of the young Sindhia with his presence.[73] The English were at the same time not without a suspicion that he had opened a correspondence with Russia,[74] and they were themselves about to flatter him as one necessary to the fulfilment of their expanding views of just influence and profitable commerce.

In the beginning of 1331, Lord William Bentinck, the Governor-General of India, arrived at Simla, and a Sikh deputation waited upon his Lordship to convey to him Ranjit Singh's complimentary wished for his own welfare and the prosperity of his Government. The increasing warmth of the season prevented the dispatch of a formal return mission, but Capt. Wade, the political agent at Ludhiana, was made the bearer of a letter to the Maharaja thanking him for his attention. The principal duty of the agent was, however to ascertain whether Ranjit Singh wished and would propose, to have an interview with Lord William Bentinck, for it was a matter in which it was thought the English Viceroy could not take the initiative.[75] The object of the Governor-General was mainly to give the world an impression of complete unanimity between the two states; but the Maharaja wished to strengthen his own authority, and to lead the Sikh public to believe his dynasty was acknowledged as the proper head of the 'Khalsa', by the predominant English rulers. The able chief, Hari Singh, was one of those most averse to the recognition of the right of the Prince Kharak Singh, and the heir apparent himself would seem to have been aware of the feelings of the Sikh people for he had the year before opened a correspondence with the Governor of Bombay, as if to derive hope from the vague terms of a complimentary reply.[76] Ranjit Singh thus readily proposed a meeting and one took place at Rupar on the banks of the Sutlej in the month of October (1831). A present of horses from the King of England had, in the meantime, reached Lahore, by the Indus and Ravi rivers, under the escort of Lieut. Burnes, and during one of the several interviews with the Governor-General Ranjit Singh had sought for and obtained a written assurance of perpetual friendship.[77] The impression went abroad that his family would be supported by the English Government, and ostensibly Ranjit Singh's objects seemed wholly as they had been partly gained. But his mind was not set at ease about Sind: vague accounts had reached him of some design with regard to that country; he plainly hinted his own schemes, and observed the Amirs had no efficient troops, and that they could not be well-disposed towards the English as they had thrown difficulties in the way of Lieut. Burnes's progress.[78] But the Governor-General would not divulge to his inquiring quest and ally the tenor of propositions already on their way to the chiefs of Sind confessedly lest the Maharaja should at once endeavour to counteract his peaceful and beneficial intentions.[79] Ranjit Singh may or may not have felt that he was distrusted, but as he was to be a party to the opening of the navigation of the Indus, and as the project had been matured, it would have better suited the character and the position of the British Government had no concealment been attempted.

The traveller Moorcroft had been impressed with the use which might be made of the Indus as a channel of British commerce,[80] and the scheme of navigating that river and its tributaries was eagerly adopted by the Indian Government, and by the advocates of material utilitarianism. One object of sending King William's utilitarianism. One object of sending King William's presents for Ranjit Singh by water was to ascertain, as if undesignedly, the trading value of the classical stream,[81] and the result of Lieut. Burnes's observations convinced Lord William Bentinck of its superiority over the Ganges. There seemed also, in his Lordship's opinion, good reason to believe that the great western valley had a one time been as populous as that of the east, and it was thought that the judicious exercise of the paramount influence of the British Government might remove those political obstacles which had banished commerce from the rivers of Alexander.[82] It was therefore resolved, in the current language of the day, to open the Indus to the navigation of the world.

Before the Governor-General met Ranjit Singh, he had directed Col. Pottinger[83] to proceed to Hyderabad, to negotiate with the Amirs of Sind the opening of the lower portion of the river to all boats on the payment of a fixed toll;[84] and, two months afterwards or towards the end of 1831, he wrote to the Maharaja that the desire he had formerly expressed to see a steamboat, was a proof of his enlightened understanding, and was likely to be gratified before long, as it was wished to draw closer the commercial relations of the two states. Capt. Wade was at the same time sent to explain in person the object of Col. Pottinger's mission to Sind, to propose the free navigation of the Sutlej in continuation of that of the Lower Indus, and to assure the Maharaja that, by the extension of British commerce, was not meant the extension of the British power.[85] But Ranjit Singh also had his views and his suspicions.[86] In the south of the Punjab he had wrought by indirect means as long as it was necessary to do so among a newly conquered people. The Nawab of Bahawalpur, his manager of the country across to Dera Ghazi Khan, was less regular in his payments than he should have been, and his expulsion from the Punjab Proper would be profitable and unaccompanied with danger, if the English remained neutral. Again, Bahawal Khan was virtually a chief protected by the British Government on the left bank of the Sutlej and Lieut. Burnes was on his way up the Indus. The Maharaja, ever mistrustful, conceived that the political status of that officer's observation would be referred to and upheld by his Government as the true and permanent one,[87] and hence the envoy found affairs in process of change when he left the main stream of the Indus, and previous to the interview at Rupar, General Ventura had dispossessed Bahawal Khan both of his Lahore farms and of his ancestral territories on the right bank of the Sutlej.[88] Further, Shikarpur formed not part of the Sind of the Kalhoras or Talpurs; it had only fallen to the latter usurpers after the death of Muhammad Azim Khan, the wazir of the titular king, Shah Ayub, and it continued to be held jointly by the three families of Khairpur, Mirpur, and Hyderabad, as a fortuitous possession. Ranjit Singh considered that he, as the paramount of the Barakzais of the Indus, had a better right to the district than the Amirs of south-eastern Sind, and he was bent upon annexing it to his dominions.[89]

Such was Ranjit Singh's temper of mind when visited by Capt. Wade to negotiate the opening of the Sutlej to British traders. The Maharaja avowed himself well pleased, but he had hoped that the English were about to force their way through Sind; he asked how many regiments Col. Pottinger had with him, and he urged his readiness to march and coerce the Amirs.[90] It was further ascertained that he had made propositions to Mir Ali Murad of Mirpur, to farm Dera Ghazi Khan, as if to sow dissensions among the Talpurs, and to gain friends for Lahore, while Col. Pottinger was winning allies for the English.[91] But he perceived that the Governor-General had resolved upon his course, and he gave his assent to the common use of the Sutlej and Indus, and to the residence of a British officer at Mithankot to superintend the navigation.[92] He did not desire to appear as if in opposition to his allies of many years, but he did not seek to conceal from Capt. Wade his opinion that the commercial measures of the English had really abridged his political power, when he gave up for the time the intention of seizing Shikarpur.[93]

The connexion of the English with the nations of the Indus was about to be rendered more complicated by the revived hopes of Shah Shuja. That ill-fated king had taken up his abode, as before related, at Ludhiana, in the year 1821 and he brooded at his leisure over shemes for the reconquest of Khorasan. In 1826 he was in correspondence with Ranjit Singh who ever regretted that the Shah was not his guest or his prisoner.[94] In 1827 he made propositions to the British Government, and he was told that he was welcome to recover his kingdom with the aid of Ranjit Singh or of the Sindians, but that, if he failed his present hosts might not again receive him.[95] In 1820 the Shah was induced by the strange state of affairs in Peshawar consequent on Saiyid Ahmad's ascendancy, to suggest to Ranjit Singh, that Sikh aid, he could readily master it, and reign once more an independent sovereign. The Maharaja amused him with vain hopes, but the English repeated their warning, and the ex-king's hopes soon fell.[96] In 1831 they again rose, for the Talpur Amris disliked the approach of English envoys, and they gave encouragement to the tenders of their titular monarch.[97] Negotiations were reopened with Ranjit Singh who was likewise out of humour with the English about Sind, and he was not unwilling to aid the Shah in the recovery of his rightful throne; but the views of the Sikh reached to the Persian frontier as well as to the shores of the ocean, and he suggested that it would be well if the slaughter of kine were prohibited throughout Afghanistan, and if the gates of Somnath were restored to their original temple. The Shah was not prepared for these concessions, and he evaded them by reminding the Maharaja that his chosen allies, the English, freely took the lives of cows and that a prophecy foreboded the downfall of the Sikh empire on the removal of the gates from Ghazni.[98]

In 1832 a rumoured advance of the Persians against Herat gave further encouragement to Shah Shuja in his designs.[99] The perplexed Amirs of Sind orrered him assistance if he would relinguish his supremacy and the Shah promised acquiescence if he succeeded.[100] To Ranjit Singh the Shah offered to waive his right to Peshawar and other districts beyond the Indus, and also to give an acquittance for the Koh-i-nur diamond, in return for assistance in men and money. The Maharaja was doubtful what to do; he was willing to secure an additional little Peshawar, but he was apprehensive of the Shah's designs should the expedition be successful.[101] He wished, moreover to know the precise views of the English, and he therefore proposed that they should be parties to any engagement entered into, for he had no confidence, he said in Afghans.[102] Each of the three parties had distinct and incompatible objects. Ranjit Singh wished to get rid of the English *commercial* objections to disturbing the Amirs of Sind, by offering to aid the rightful *political* paramount in its recovery. The ex-king thought the Maharaja really wished to get him into his power and the project of dividing Sind fell to the ground.[103] The Talpur Amirs, on their part, thought that they would save Shikarpur by playing into the Shah's hands, and they therefore endeavoured to prevent a coalition between him and the Sikh ruler.[104]

The Shah could not come to and satisfactory terms with Ranjit Singh but as his neutrality was essential, especially with regard to Shikarpur, a treaty of alliance was entered into by which the districts beyond the Indus and in the possession of the Sikhs, were formally ceded to the Maharaja.[105] The English had also become less averse to his attempt, and he was assured that his annual stipend would be continued to his family, and no warning was held out to him against returning as had before been done.[106] A third of his yearly allowance was even advanced to him: but the political agent was at the same time desired to impress upon all people, that the British Government had no interest in the Shah's proceedings that its policy was one of complete neutrality and it was added that Dost Muhammad could be so assured in reply to a letter received from him.[107] Dost Muhammad had mastered Kabul shortly after Muhammad Azim Khan's death and he soon learnt to become apprehensive of the English. In 1832 he cautioned the Amirs of Sind against allowing them to establish a commercial factory in Shikarpur, as Shah Shuja would certainly soon follow to guard it with an army[108] and he next sought, in the usual way to ascertain the views of the paramounts of India by entering into a correspondence with them.

Shah Shuja left Ludhiana in the middle of February 1833. He had with him about 200,000 rupees in treasure, and nearly 3,000 armed followers.[109] He *got* a gun and some camels from Bahawal Khan, he crossed the Indus towards the middle of May, and he entered Shikarpur without opposition. The Sindians did not oppose him but they rendered him no assistance, and they at last thought it better to break with him at once than to put *their* means into his hands for their own more assured destruction.[110] But they were signally defeated near Shikarpur on the 9th January 1834 and they willingly paid 500,000 rupees in cash and gave a promise of tribute for Shikarpur to get rid of the victor's presence.[111] The Shah proceeded towards Kandahar, and he maintained himself in the neighbourhood of that city for a few months; but on the 1st July, he was brought to action by Dost Muhammad Khan and his brothers, and fairly routed.[112] After many wanderings, and an appeal to Persia and to Shah Kamran of Herat, and also an attempt upon Shikarpur,[113] he returned to his old asylum at Ludhiana in March 1835, bringing with him about 250,000 rupees in money and valuables.[114]

Ranjit Singh on his part, was apprehensive that Shah Shuja might set aside their treaty of alliance so he resolved to guard against the possible consequences of the ex-king's probable success, and to seize Peshawar before his tributaries could tender their allegiance to Kabul.[115] A large force, under the nominal command of the Maharaja's gandson, Nau Nihal Singh, but really led by Sirdar Hari Singh, crossed the Indus, but really led by Sirdar Hari Singh crossed the Indus, and an increased tribute of horses was demanded on the plea of the prince's presence for the first time, at the head of an army. The demand would seem to have been complied with but the citadel of Peshawar was nevertheless assaulted and taken on the 6th May 1834.[116] The hollow negotiations with Sultan

Muhammad Khan are understood to have been precipitated by the impetuous Hari Singh, who openly expressed his contempt for all Afghans, and did not conceal his design to carry the Sikh arms beyond Peshawar.[117]

The Sikhs were, in the meantime, busy elsewhere as well as in Peshawar itself. In 1832 Hari Singh had finally routed the Muhammadan tribes above Attock, and to better ensure their obedience, he built a fort on the right side of the Indus.[118] In 1834 a force was employed against the Afghans of Tak and Bannu beyond Dera Ismal Khan; but considerable detachment signally failed in an attack upon a mountain stronghold, and a chief of rank and upwards of 300 men were slain. The ill success vexed the Mahraja, and he desired his agent to explain to the British authorities the several particulars; but lest they should still be disposed to reflect upon the quality of his troops, he reminded Capt. Wade that such things had happened before, that his rash officers did not wait until a breach had been effected, and that, indeed the instance of General Gillespie and the Gurkhas at Kalanga afforded an exact illustration of what had taken place![119] In 1833 the grandson of Sansar Chand, of Katotch, was induced to return to his country, and on his way through Ludhiana he was received with considerable ceremony by the British authorities, for the fame of Sansar Chand gave to his posterity some semblance of power and regal dignity. A jagir or fief of 50,000 rupees was conferred upon the young chief, for the Maharaja was not disposed from nature to be wantonly harsh, nor from policy to drive any one to desperation.[120] During the same year Ranjit Singh proposed to send a chief to Calcutta with presents for the King of England and not improbably with the view of ascertaining the general opinion about his designs on Sind. The mission under Gujar Singh Majithia finally took its departure in September 1834 and was absent a year and a half.[121]

When Mr. Moorcroft was in Ladakh (in 1821, &c.), the fear of Ranjit Singh was general in the country, and the Sikh governor of Kashmir had already demanded the payment of tribute;[122] but the weak and distant state was little molested until the new Rajas of Jammu had obtained the government of the hill principalities between the Ravi and Jhelum, and felt that their influence with Ranjit Singh was secure and commanding. In 1834 Zorawar Singh, Raja Gulab Singh's commander in Kishtwar, took advantage of internal disorders in Leh, and declared that an estate, internal disorders in Leh, and declared that an estate, anciently held by the Kishtwar chief, must be restored. He crossed into the southern districts, but did not reach the capital until early in 1835. He sided with one of the contending parties, deposed the reigning Raja, and set up his rebellious minister in his stead. He fixed a tribute of 30,000 rupees, he placed a garrison in the fort, he retained some districts along the northern slopes of the Himalayas, and reached Jammu with his spoils towards the close of 1835. The dispossessed Raja complained to the Chinese authorities in Lassa; but as the tribute continued to be regularly paid by his successor, no notice was taken of the usurpation. The Governor of Kashmir complained that Gulab Singh's commercial regulations interfered with the regular supply of shawl wool, and that matter was at once adjusted; yet the grasping ambition of the favourites nevertheless caused Ranjit Singh some misgivings amid all their protestations of devotion and loyalty.[123]

But Ranjit Singh's main apprehensions were on the side of Peshawar, and his fondest hopes in the direction of Sind. The defeat which the Amirs had sustained diminished their confidence in themselves, and when Shah Shuja returned beaten from Kandahar; Nur Muhammad of Hyderabad was understood to be willing to surrender Shikarpur to the Maharaja, on condition of his guarantee against the attempts of the ex-king.[124] But this pretext would not get rid of the English objections; and Ranjit Singh, moreover, had little confidence in the Sindians. He kept, as a check over them, a representative of the expelled Kalhoras, as a pensioner on his bounty, in Rajanpur beyond the Indus;[125] and, at once to overawe both them and the Barakzais, he again opened a negotiation with Shah Shuja as soon as he returned to Ludhiana.[126] But his main difficulty was with his British allies; and, to prove to them the reasonableness of his discontent he would instance the secret aid which the Mazari freebooters received from the Amirs;[127] he would again insist that Shikarpur was a dependency of the chiefs of Khorassan,[128] and he would hint that the river below Mithankot was not the Indus but the Sutlej, the river of the treaty,—the stream which had so long given freshness and beauty to the emblematic garden of their friendship, and which continued its fertilizing way to the ocean, separating, yet uniting, the realms of the two brotherly powers of the East![129]

But the English had formed a treaty of navigation with Sind, and the designs of Ranjit Singh were displeasing pleasing to them. They said they could not view without regret and disapprobation the prosecution of plans of unprovoked hostility against states to which *they* were bound by ties of interest and goodwill.[130] They therefore wished to dissuade Ranjit Singh against any attempt on Shikarpur; but they felt that this must be done discreetly, for their object was to remain on terms of friendship with every one, and to make their influence available for the preservation of the general peace.[131] Such were the sentiments of the English; but, in the meantime, the border disputes between the Sikhs and Sindians were fast tending to produce a rapture. In 1833 the predatory tribe of Mazaris, lying along the right bank of the Indus, below Mithankot, had been chastised by the Governor of Multan, who proposed to put a garrison in their stronghold of Rojhan, but was restrained by the Maharaja from so doing.[132] In 1835 the Amirs of Khairpur were believed to be instigating the Mazaris in their attacks on the Sikh posts; and as the tribe was regarded by the English as dependent on Sind, although possessed of such a degree of commercial arrangements as being entitled to a fixed portion of the whole toll, the Amirs were informed that the English looked to them to restrain the Mazaris, so as to deprive Ranjit Singh of all precext for interference.[133] The aggressions the nevertheless continued, or were alleged to be continued; and in August 1836, the Multan governor took formal possession of Rojhan.[134] In the October following the Mazaris were brought to action and defeated, and the Sikhs occupied a fort called Ken, to the south of Rojhan, and beyond the proper limit of that tribe.[135]

Thus was Ranjit Singh gradually feeling his way by force; but the English had, in the meantime, resolved to go far beyond him in diplomacy. It had been determined that Capt. Burnes should proceed on a commercial mission to the countries bordering on the Indus, with the view of completing the reopening of that river to the traffic of the world.[136] But the Maharaja, it was said, should understand that their objects were purely mercantile, and that, indeed, his aid was looked for in establishing somewhere a great entrepot of trade, such as, it had once been hoped, might have been commenced at Mithankot.[137] Yet the views of the British authorities with regard to Sind were inevitably becoming political as well as commercial. The condition that country, said the Governor-General, had been much thought about, and the result was a conviction that the connexion with it should be drawn closer.[138] The Amirs he continued, might desire the protection of the English against Ranjit Singh, and previous negotiations, which their fears or their hostility had broken off, might be renewed with a view to giving them assistance; and, finally, it was determined that the English Government should mediate between Ranjit Singh and the Sindians, and afterwards adjust the other external relations of the Amirs when a Resident should be stationed at Hyderabad.

With regard to Ranjit Singh, the English rulers observed that they were bound by the strongest considerations of political interest to prevent the extension of the Sikh power along the course of the Indus, and that, although they would respect the acknowledged territories of the Maharaja, they desired that his existing relations of peace should not be disturbed; for, if war took place, the Indus would never be opened to commerce. The political agent was directed to use every means short of menace to induce Ranjit Singh to abandon his designs against Shikarpur; and Shah Shuja, whose hopes were still great, and whose negotiations were still talked of, was to be told that if he left Ludhiana he must not return, and that the maintenance for his family would be at once discontinued. With regard to the Mazaries, whose lands had been actually occupied by the Sikhs, it was said that their reduction had effected an object of general benefit; and that the question of their permanent control could be determined at a future period.[139]

The Sindians, on their part, complained that the fort of Ken had been occupied, and in reply to Ranjit Singh's demand that their annual complimentary or prudential offerings should be increased, or that a large sum should be paid for the restoration of their captured fort, they avowed their determination to resort to arms.[140] Nor can there be any doubt that Sind would have been invaded by the Sikhs, had not Col. Pottinger's negotiations for their protection deterred the Maharaja from an act which he apprehended the English might seize upon to declare *their* alliance at an end. The princes Kharak Singh and Nau Nihal Singh were each on the Indus, at the head of considerable armies, and the remonstrances of the British political agent alone detained the Maharaja himself at Lahore. Nevertheless, so evenly were peace and war balanced in Ranjit Singh's mind, that Capt. Wade thought it advisable to proceed to his capital to explain to him in person the risks he would incur buy acting in open opposition to the British Government. He listened, and at last yielded. His deference, he said, to the wishes of his allies took place of every other consideration; he would let his relations with the Amirs of Sind remain on their old footing, he would destroy the fort of Ken, but he would continue to occupy Rojhan and the Mazari territory.[141] Ranjit Singh was urged by his chiefs not to their understanding it was not clear where such demands would stop; but he shook his head, and asked them what had become of the two hundred thousand speares of the Marathas![142] and, as if to show how completely he professed to forget or forgive the check imposed on him, he invited the Governor-General to be present at Lahore on the occasion of the marriage of the grandson whom he had hoped to hail as the conqueror of Sind.[143] Nevertheless he continued to entertain a hope that his objects might one day be attained; he avoided a distinct settlement of the boundary with the Amirs, and of the question of supremacy over the Mazaris.[144] Neither was he disposed to relinquish Rojhan; the place remained a Sikh possession, and it may be regarded to have become formally such by the submission of the chief of the tribe in the year 1838.[145]

It is now necessary to go back for some years to trace the connexion of the English Government with the Barakzai rulers of Afghanistan. Muhammad Azim died in 1823, as has been mentioned, immediately after Peshawar became tributary to the Sikhs. His son Habib-ullah nominally succeeded to the supremacy which Fateh Khan and Muhammad Azim had both exercised; but it soon became evident that the mind of the youth was unsettled, and his violent proceedings enabled his crafty and unscrupulous uncle, Dost Muhammad Khan, to seize Kabul Ghazni, and Jalalabad as his own, while a second set of his brothers held Kandahar in virtual independence, and a third governed Peshawar as the tributaries of Ranjit Singh.[146] In the year 1824 Mr. Moorcroft, the traveller, was upon the whole well satisfied with the treatment he received from the Barakzais although their patronage cost him money.[147] A few years afterwards Sultan Mohammed Khan of Peshawar, who had most to fear from strangers, opened a communication with the political agent at Ludhiana,[148] and in 1829 he wished to negotiate as an independent chief with the British.

Government.[149] But the several brothers were jealous of one another, many desired separate principalities, Dost Muhammad aimed at supremacy, rumours of Persian designs alarmed them on the west, the aggressive policy of Ranjit Singh gave them on the west, the aggressive policy of Ranjit Singh gave them greater cause of fear on the east, and the chance presence of English travellers in Afghanistan again led them of hope that the foreign masters of India might be induced to give them stability between contending powers.[150] In 1832 Sultan Muhammad Khan again attempted to open a negotiation, if only for the release of his son, who was a hostage with Ranjit Singh.[151] The Nawab, Jabbar Khan of Kabul, likewise addressed letters to the British frontier authority, and in 1832 Dost Muhammad himself directly asked for the friendship of the English.[152] All these communications were politely acknowledged, but at the time it was held desirable to avoid all intimacy of connexion with rulers so remote.[153]

REFERENCES

1. Capt. Wade to Government, 17th May 1834. Cf. Masson, *Journeys,* iii. 218, 220.
2. Capt. Wade to Government, 17th June 1834.
3. Capt. Wade to Government, 25th Sept. 1834.
4. Capt. Wade to Government, 27th Jan. 1835.
5. Capt. Wade to Government, 4th Jan. and 13th Feb. 1835.
6. Government to Capt. Wade, 19th April 1834, and 11th Feb. 1835. Abdul Ghias Khan, the son of Jabbar Khan, reached Ludhiana in June 1834, and the original intention of sending him to study at Delhi was abandoned.
7. Government to Capt. Wade, 20th April 1835.
8. Capt. Wade to Government, 25th April, and 1st, 15th, and 19th May 1835. Cf. Masson, *Journeys,* iii. 342, &c.; Mohan Lal, *Life of Dost Muhammad,* i. 172, &c.; and also Dr. Harlan's *India and Afghanistan,* pp. 124, 158. Dr. Harlan himself was one of the envoys sent to Dost Muhammad on the occasion.

   The Sikhs are commonly said to have had 80,000 men in the Peshawar valley at this time.

9. Capt. Wade to Government, 23rd Feb. 1836. Dost Muhammad's overtures to Persia seem to have commenced in Sept. 1835.
10. Capt. Wade to Government, 19th July 1836.
11. Capt. Wade to Government, 9th March 1836.
12. Capt. Wade to Government, 12th April 1837.
13. Capt. Wade to Government, Ist May 1837.
14. Capt. Wade to Government, 13th Jan. 1837.
15. [Afterwards the murderer of Sir W. Macnaghten and the chief actor in the tragedy of the retreat from Kabul (1842).—Ed.]
16. Capt Wade to Government, 13th and 23rd May and 5th July 1837. Cf. Masson. *Jaurneys,* iii. 382, 387, and Mohan Lal, *Life of Dost Muhammad,* i. 226, &c.

    It seems that the Afghans were at first routed or repulsed with the loss of some guns, but that the opportune arrival of Shams-ud-din Khan, a relation of the Amir, with a considerable detachment, turned the battle in their favour. It is nevertheless believed that had not Hari Singh been killed, the Sikhs would have retrieved the day. The troops in the Peshawar valley had been considerably reduced by the withdrawal of large parties to Lahore, to make a display on the occasion of Nau Nihal Singh's marriage, and of the expected visit of the English Governor-General and Commander-in-Chief.
17. Lieut.-Col. Steinbach (*Punjab,* pp. 64, 68) mentions that he had himself marched with his Sikh regiment 300 miles in twelve days, and that the distance had been performed by others in eleven.
18. Mr. Clerk's Memorandum of 1842, regarding the Sikh chiefs, drawn up for Lord Ellenborough.
19. Cf. Capt. Wade to Government, 3rd June 1837, and Government to Capt. Wade, 7th Aug. 1837.
20. Government to Capt. Wade, 31th July 1837,
21. Government to Capt. Wade, 11th Sept. 1837.
22. The idea of Russian designs on India engaged the attention of the British viceroy in 1831 (see Murray, *Ranjit Singh,* by Prinsep, p. 168), and it at the same time possessed the inquiring but sanguine mind of Capt. Burnes, who afterwards gave the notion so much notoriety. (See Capt. Wade to Government, 3rd Aug. 1831.)
23. The author gives what the French officers held to be the intended use of the credentials, on the competent authority of General

Ventura, with whom he formerly had conversations on the subject. The English view, however, is that which was taken by the British ambassador in Paris, as well as by the authorities in Calcutta, with whom General Allard was in personal communication. (Government to Capt. Wade 16th Jan. and 3rd April 1837.)

Of the two views, that of the English is the less honourable, with reference to their duty towards Ranjit Singh, who might have justly resented any attempt on the part of a servant to put himself beyond the power of his master, and any interference in that servant's behalf on the part of the British Government.

In the letter to Ranjit singh, Louis Philippe is styled, in French, 'Empereur' (Capt. Wade to Government, 15th Sept, 1837); a title which, at the time, may have pleaded the vanity of the French, although it could not have informed the understandings of the Sikhs, as, agreeably to Persian and Indian practice, king or queen is always translated 'Padshah' equally with emperor. Sir Claude Wade seems to think that the real design of the French was to open a regular intercourse with Ranjit Singh, and to obtain a political influence in the Punjab. The Maharaja, however, after consulting the British Agent, decided on not taking any notice of the overtures. (Sir Claude Wade, *Narrative,* p. 38, note.) [A piece of diplomacy on the part of the French Government, typical of the chicanery of Louis Philippe and his advisers. The monarch who could perpetrate the sordid of an underhand intrigue with Ranjit Singh. —Ed.]

24. These views of Sir Henry Fane's may be on record, but they were well-known to those about his Excellency. His estimate was, as I remember to have heard from Capt. Wade, 67,000 men, and he thought there might be a two years' active warfare.

    This visit to Lahore was perhaps mainly useful in enabling Lieut.-Col. Garden, the indefatigable quarter-master-general of the Bengal Army, to compile a detailed map of that part of the country, and which formed the groundwork of all the maps used when hostilities did at last break out with the Sikhs.

25. Cat. Wade to Government, 7th April 1837. [On the occasion of this visit the Maharaja displayed considerable interest in the great wars of Europe. He was particularly interested in the career of Napoleon. Col. Wallis, one of Sir Henry's staff, had fortunately been at Waterloo, the battle.-Ed.]

26. Capt. Wade to the Resident at Delhi, 2nd Jan. 1831, and to Government, 25th Dec. 1835.

27. Capt. Wade to Government, 22nd July 1836.
28. Cf. Government to capt. Wade, 11th Sept. 1837.
29. Capt. Wade to Government, 7th Dec. 1831.
30. When the restoration of Shah Shuja was resolved on, Ranjit Singh sent shells to Ludhiana to be looked at and commented on, as if, being engaged in one political cause, there should not be any reserve about military secrets!
31. Major Hough, who has added to the reputation of the Indian army by his useful publications, put the practice of courts martial into a Sikh dress for Ranjit Singh. (Government to Capt. Wade, 21st November 1834).
32. Government to Capt. Wade, 18th May 1835, intimating that solitary confinement had been found a good substitute.
33. Capt. Wade to Government, 11th April. 1835. Some of the princes of India, all whom are ever pron suspicion, were not without a belief that, by writing in English, it was designed to keep them in ignorance of the real views and declarations of their paramount.
34. Some of these young men were employed with the force raised at Peshawar, in 1839, to enable Prince Taimur to march through Khaibar.
35. Capt. Wade to Government, 13th May 1837, quoting Dr. Wood, a surgeon in the British army, temporarily deputed to attend on Ranjit Singh, and who was his camp at Rohtas on this occasion.
36. Cf. Government to Capt. Wade, 13th Nov. 1837, and to Capt. Burnes and Capt. Wade, both of the 20th January 1838. With regard to Sind, also, the views of Ranjit Singh were not held to be pleasing, and the terms of his communication with the Amirs were thought equivocal, or denotative of a reservation, or of the expression of a right he did not possess. (Government to Capt. Wade, 25th Sept. and 13th Nov. 1837.)
37. Without reference to the settled policy of Russia, or to what she may always have thought of the virtual support which England gives to Persia and Turkey against her power, the presence of inquiring agents in Khorasan and Turkestan, and the progressive extension of the British Indian dominion, must have put her on the alert, if they did not fill her with reasonable suspicions.
38. Government to Capt. Wade, 31st July 1837.
39. These predilections of Sir Alex. Burnes, and the hopes founded on them by Dost Muhammad, **were** sufficiently notorious to

those in personal communication with that valuable pioneer of the English; and his strong wish to recover Peshawar, at least for Sultan Muhammad Khan, is distinctly stated in his own words, in Masson, *Journeys*, iii. 423. The idea of taking the district from the Sikhs, either for Dost Muhammad or his brothers, is moreover apparent from Sir Alex. Burnes's published letters of 5th Oct. 1837, and 26th Jan. and 13th March 1838 (Parliamentary Papers, 1839), from the Government replies of remark and caution, dated 20th Jan., and especially of 27th April 1838, and from Mr. Masson's statement (*Journeys*, iii 423, 448). Mr. Masson himself thought it would be but justice to restore the district to Sultan Muhammad Khan, while Munshi Mohal Lal (*Life of Dost Muhammad*, i. 257, &c.) represents the Amir to have thought that the surrender of Peshawar to his brother would have been more prejudicial to his interests than its retention by the Sikhs.

40. Such were Capt. Wade's views, and they are sketched in his letters of the 15th May and 28th Oct.. 1837, with reference to commercial objects, although the line of policy may not have been steadily adhered to, or fully developed.

41. The extent to which this feeling was prevalent is known to those who were observers of Indian affairs at the Governor-General's minute of the 20th Aug. 1839.

42. The Governor-General's minute of 12th May 1838, and his declaration of the 1st October of the same year, may be referred to as summing up the views which moved the British Government on the occasion. Both were published by order of Parliament in March 1839.

43. Government to Capt. Wade, 20th Jan. 1838.

44. The proximate cause of the resolution to restore Shah Shuja was, of course, the preference given by Dost Muhammad to a Persian and Russian over a British alliance, and the immediate object of deputing Sir W. Macnaghten to Lahore was to make Ranjit Singh as much as possible a party to the policy adopted. (See, among other letters, Government to Capt. Wade, 15th May 1838.) The deputation crossed into the Punjab at Rupar on the 20th May. It remained some time at Dinanagar, and afterwards went to Lahore. The first interview with Ranjit Singh was on the 31st May, the last on the 13th July. Sir William Macnaghten recrossed the sutlej at Ludhiana on the 15th July, and on that and the following day the arranged with Shah Shuja in person the terms of his restoration.

Two months before the deputation waited upon Ranjit Singh, he had visited Jammu for apparently the first time in his life, and the same may be regarded as the last in which the worn-out prince tasted of unalloyed happiness. Gulab Singh received his sovereign with every demonstration of loyalty, and, bowing to the Maharaja's feet, he laid before him presents worth nearly forty thousand pounds, saying he was the humblest of his slaves, and the most grateful of those on whom he had heaped favours. Ranjit Singh shed tears, but afterwards pertinently observed that, in Jammu, gold might be seen where formerly there was naught but stones. (Major Mackeson's letter to Capt. Wade of 31st March 1838.)

45. That Ranjit Singh was told he would be left out if he did not choose to come in, does not appear on public record. It was, however, the only convincing argument used during the long discussions, and I think Major Mackeson was made the bearer of the message to that effect.

46. Cf. the Governor-General's minute of 12th of May 1838, and his instructions to Sir William Macnaghten of the 15th of the same months. Ranjit Singh was anxious to get something lasting and tangible as his share of the profit of the expedition, and he wanted Jalalabad, as there seemed to be a difficulty about Shikarpur. The Maharaja got, indeed, a subsidy of two hundred thousand rupees a year from the Shah for the use of his troops; a concession which did not altogether satisfy the Governor-General (see letter to Sir William Macnaghten, and July, 1838), and the article became, in fact, a dead letter.

The idea of creating a friendly power in Afghanistan, by guiding Ranjit Singh upon Kabul, seems to have been seriously entertained, and it was a scheme which promised many solid advantages. Cf. the Governor-General's minute, 12th May 1838, the author's abstract of which differs somewhat from the copy printed by order of Parliament in 1839, and Mr. Masson (*Journeys*, iii. 487, 488) who refers to a communication from Sir William Macnaghten on Shah Shuja, see Appendix XXX

47. At one of the several meetings which took place on this occasion, there was an interchange of compliments, which may be noticed. Ranjit Singh likened the friendship of the two states to an apple, the red and yellow colours of which were, he said so blended, that although the semblance was twofold the reality was one. Lord Auckland replied that the Maharaja's simile was very happy, inasmuch as red and yellow were the national colours of

the English and Sikhs respectively; to which Ranjit Singh rejoined in the same strain that the comparison was indeed in every way appropriate, for the friendship of the two powers was, like the apple, fair and delicious. The translations were given in English and Urdu with elegance and emphasis by Sir William Macnaghten and Fakir Aziz-ud-din, of language, whether written or spoken.

48. See, among other letters, Capt, Wade to Government, 18th Aug. 1839. For some interesting details regarding Capt. Wade's military proceedings see Lieut. Barr's published *Journal;* and for the diplomatic history, so to speak, of his mission, see Munshi Shahamat Ali, *Sikhs* and *Afghans.*

49. In 1831, Capt.. Murray estimated the Sikh revenue at little more than 2½ millions sterling, and the army at 82,000 men, including 15,000 regular infantry and 376 guns. (Murray, Ranjit Singh, by Prinsep, pp. 185-186.) In the same year Capt. Burnes (*Travels,* i. 289-291) gives the revenue at 2½ millions, and the army at 75,000, including 25,000 regular infantry. Mr. Masson (*Journeys.* i. 430) gives the same revenue; but fixes the army at 70,000 men, of whom 20,000 were disciplined. This may be assumed as an estimate of 1838, when Mr. Masson returned from Kabul. In 1845, Lieut.-Col, Steinbach (*Punjab,* p. 58) states the army to have amounted to 110,000 men, of whom 70,000 were regulars. The returns procured for Government in 1844, and which cannot be far wrong, show that there were upwards of 40,000 regularly drilled infantry, and a force of about 125,000 men in all, maintained with about 375 guns or field carriages. Cf. the *Calcutta Review,* iii. 176; Dr. Macgregor, Sikhs, ii. 86, and Major Smith, *Reigning Family of Lahore,* appendices. p. xxxvii, for estimates, correct in some particulars, and moderate in others.

For a statement of the Lahore revenues, see Appendix XXXVIII; for a list of the Lahore army, see Appendix XXXIX.

Many descriptions of Ranjit Singh's person and manners have been written, of which the fullest is perhaps that in Prinsep's edition of Murray, *Life,* p. 187, &c; while Capt. Osborne's *Court and Camp,* and Col. Lawrence's *Adventurer in the Punjab,* contain many illustrative touches and anecdotes. The only good likeness of the Maharaja which has been published is that taken by the Hon. Miss Eden; and it, especially in the original drawing, is true and expressive. Ranjit Singh was of small stature. When young he was dexterous in all manly exercises, but in his old age he became weak and inclined to corpulency. He lost an eye when a child by the small-pox, and the most marked characteristic of his mental powers was a broad and massive forehead, which the ordinary portraits do not show.

50. Mr. Clerk's memorandum of 1842 for Lord Ellenborough.

51. Capt. Murray, *Ranjit Singh*, pp. 141-142.

52. Agent at Delhi to Capt. Murray, 18th March 1825, and Capt. Murray in reply, 28th March. Cf. also Murray, *Ranjit Singh*, p. 144.

53. [This famous fortress was besieged by the English orces (20,000 men and 100 guns) on 10th Dec. 1825, and fellon 18th Jan. 1826. Its capture made a great impression, as it had been deemed impregnable. The operations were under the direction of Lord Combermere, the Commander-in-Chief who, as Sir Stapleton Cotton, had fought under Wellington in the Peninsula.—Ed.]

54. Capt. Murray to the Resident at Delhi, 1st and 3rd Oct. 1825, and Capt. Wade to Capt. Murray, 5th Oct. 1825. Capt. Wade, however, in the printed *Narrative of his Services*, p. 7, represents Ranjit Singh as pausing to take advantage of any disasters which might befall the English.

55. Resident at Delhi to Capt. Murray, 13th Jan. 1826, and Capt. Murray, *Ranjit Singh*, p. 144. The old chief had, as early as 1811, desired to be regarded as separately connected with the English, sofearful had he become of his 'turban-brother' (Government to Sir D. Ochterlony, 4th Oct. 1811.)

    The Cis-Sutlej Muhammadan Chief of Mamdot, formerly of Kasur, fled and returned abut the same time as Fateh Singh, for similar reasons and after aming similar endeavours to be recognized as an English dependant (Government to Resident at Delhi, 28th April 1827, with correspondence to which it relates, and cf. Murray, *Ranjit Singh*, p. 145.)

56. [The Burmese War broke out on 24th Feb. 1824 as the result of disturbed relations going back as far as 1818. It lasted till 24th Feb. 1826, when by the Treaty of Yandabu, the Burmese Government ceded the provinces of Tenasserim, Aracan, and Assan, and paid an indemnity of one million sterling—Ed.]

57. Capt. Wade to the Resident at Delhi, 24th Sept, and 30th Nov. 1826, and 1st Jan. 1827. Cf. Murray, *Ranjit Singh*, p. 145. {The mutiny at Barrackpore was the result of the disinclination of the troops to go on service in Burma. There were three native regiments at this station—26th, 47th, and 62nd—and all of them became disaffected. On 1st Nov. 1824, the 47th—broke into open mutimy. English troops were sent to the station, and the 47th

were dispersed by artillery and the regiment was struck off the army list. The other two regiments escaped without punishment.—Ed.]

58. Government to Capt. Wade, 2nd May, 1827.

59. Murray, *Ranjit Ranjit Singh*, p. 147. About this time the journeyings and studies of the enthusiastic scholar Csoma de Koros; and the establishment of Simla as a British post, had made the Chinese of Tibet as Simla as a British post, had made the Chinese of Tibet as curious about the English in one way as Ranjit Singh was in another. Thus the authorities at Garo appear to have addressed the authorities of Bissehir, an English dependency, saying "that in ancient times there was no mention of the 'Filingha' (*i.e.* Faranghis or Franks), a bad and small people, whereas now many visited the upper countries every year, and had caused the chief of Bissehir to maks preparations for their movements. The Great Lama was displeased, and armies had been ordered to be watched. The English should be urged to keep within their own limits, or, if they wanted an alliance, they could go by sea to Pekin. The people of Bissehir should not rely on the wealth and the expertness in warfaring of the English: the emperor was 30 *paktsat* (120 miles) higher than they; he ruled over the four elements; a war would involve the six nations of Asia in calamities; the English should remain within their boundaries;" —and so on, in a strain of deprecation and hyperbole. (Political Agent, Sabathu, to Resident at Delhi, 26th March 1827.)

60. Capt. Wade to Resident at Delhi, 20th June 1827).

61. Government to Resident at Delhi, 4th Oct. 1827.

62. Capt. Wade to the Resident at Delhi, 20th Jan. 1828, and Capt. Murray to the same, 19th Feb. 1828.

    In the case of Ferozepore, Government subsequently decided (Government to Agent at Delhi, 24th Nov. 1838) that certain collateral heirs (Who had put in a claim) could not succeed, as according to Hindu law and Sikh usage, no right of descent existed after a division had taken place. So uncertain however is the practice of the English, that one or more precedents in favour of the Ferozepore claimants might readily be found within the range of cases connected with the Sikh states.

63. Government to the Resident at Delhi, 14th Nov. 1828.

64. In 1823 Capt. Murray talked of the 'strong and important fortress' of Ferozepore having been recovered by Ranjit Singh,

for the widow proprietress from whom it had been seized by a claimant (Capt. Murray to the Agent at Delhi, 20th July 1823), and the supreme authorities similarly talked (Government to Agent at Delhi, 30th Jan. 1824) of the political and military advantages of Ferozepure over Ludhiana.

65. Murray, *Ranjit Singh*, pp. 147-148, and Resident at Delhi to Government 28th Oct. 1828.

66. A book was composed by Mauli Ismail, on the part of Saiyid Ahmad, in the Urdu or vernacular language of Upper India, at once exhortative and justificatory of his views. It is called the *Takvia-ul-Iman*, or 'Basis of the Faith', and it was printed in Calcutta. It is divided into two portions, of which the first only is understood to be the work of Ismail, the second part being inferior, and the production of another person.

In the preface the writer deprecates the opinion that the wise and learned alone can comprehend God's word. God himself had said a prophet had been raised up among the rude and ignorant for their instruction, and that He, the Lord, had rendered obedience easy. There were two things essential: a belief in the unity of God, which was to know to other, and a knowledge of the Prophet, which was obedience to the law. Many held the sayings of the saints to be their guide; but the word of God was alone to be attended to although the writings of the pious, which agreed with the Scriptures, might be read for edification.

The first chapter treats of the unity of God, and in it the writer deprecates the supplication of saints, angels, &c., as impious. He declares the reasons given for such worship to be futile, and to show an utter ignorance of God's word. The ancient idolaters had likewise said that they merely venerated powers and divinities, and did not regard them as the equal of the Almighty; but God himself had answered these healthens. Likewise the Christians had been admonished for giving to dead monks and friars the honour due to the Lord. God is alone, and companion he has none; prostration and adoration are due to him, and to no other." The writer proceeds in a similar strain, but assumes some doubtful positions, as that Muhammad says God is one, and man learns from his parents that he was born; he believes his mother, and yet he distrusts the apostle: or that an evil-doer who has faith is a better man than the most pious idolater.

The printed Urdu korans are eagerly bought by all who can afford the money, and who know of their existence.

67. Ct. Murray, *Ranjit Singh*, pp. 145-146. About Saiyid Ahmad, the author has learnt much from the 'Ghazi's' brother-in-law, and from a respectable Mauli, who likewise followed his fortunes, and both of whom are now in honourable employ in the chiefship of Tonk. He has likewise learnt many particulars from Munshi Shahamat Ali, and especially from Pir Ibrahim Khan, a straightforward and intelligent pathan of Kasur, in the British service, who thinks Ahmad right, notwithstanding the holy neighbourhood of Pakpattan, Multan, and Utch! Indeed most educated Muhammadans admit the reasonableness of his doctrines, and the able Regent-Begum of Bhopal is not indisposed to emulate the strictness of the Chief to Tonk, as an abhorrer of vain ceremonies. Among humbler people the Saiyid likewise obtained many admirers, and it is said that his exhortations generally were so efficacious that even the tailors of Delhi were moved to scrupulously return remnants to cloth to their employers!

68. Cf. Murray, *Ranjit Singh*, pp. 146, 149. The followers of Saiyid Ahmad believe that poison was administered, and describe the 'Ghazi' as suffering much from its effects.

    General Ventura at last succeeded in obtaining a Laila, but that the real horse, so named, was transferred, is doubtful, and at one time it was declared to be dead. (Capt. Wade to the Resident, Delhi, 7th May 1829).

69. Capt. Wade to the Resident, Delhi, 13th Sept. 1830. The Maharaja also reserved a cause of quarrel with the Barakzais, on account of their reduction of the Khattaks, a tribe which Ranjit Singh said Fateh Khan, the Wazir had agreed to leave independent. (Capt. Wade to Government, 9th Dec. 1831.)

70. Apt. Wade to Resident at Delhi, 21st March 1831, and other dates in that and the previous year. Cf. Murray, *Ranjit Singh*, p. 150. The followers of the Saiyid strenuously deny his assumption of the title of Khalif, his new coinage, and his bestowal of Usufzai maidens on his new coinage, and his bestowal of Usufzai maidens on his Indian followers.

71. Capt. Wade to the Resident at Delhi, 3rd May 1829, and 29th April 1830. Harrand was once a place of considerable repute. (See Munshi Mohan Lal, *Journal*, under date 3rd March 1836) The Bahawalpur Memoirs show that the Nawab was aided by the treachery of others in acquiring it. The place had to be retaken by General Ventura (as the author learnt from that officer), when Bahawal Khan was deprived of his territories west of the Sutlej.

72. Capt. Wade to Resident at Delhi, 21st Jan. 1829, and 3rd Dec., 1830.

73. Capt. Wade to Resident at Delhi, 7th April 1830. The Maharaja declined the invitation, saying Sindhia was not at Lahore when *his* son was married.

74. Capt. Wade to Resident at Delhi, 24th August 1830.

75. Government to Capt. Wade, 28th April 1831, and Murray, *Ranjit Singh*, p. 162.

76. With regard to this interchange of letters, see the Persian Secretary to the Political Secretary at Bombay, 6th July 1830.

    That Ranjit Singh was jealous, personally, of Hari Singh, or that the servant would have proved a traitor to the living master, is not probable: but Hari Singh was a zealous Sikh and an ambitious man, and Kharak Singh was always full of doubts and apprehensions with respect to his succession and even his satefy. Ranjit Singh's anxiety with regard to the meeting at Rupar, exaggerated, perhaps by Mr. Allard, may be learnt from Mr. Prinsep's account in Murray, *Ranjit Singh*, p. 162. Col. Wade has informed the author that the whole of Sikh chiefs were said by Ranjit Singh himself to be averse to the meeting with the British Governor-General.

77. Murray, *Ranjit Singh* p. 166.

78. Murray, *Ranjit Singh*, p. 167. This opinion of Ranjit Singh about Sindian troops may not be pleasing to the victors of Dabo and Miani, although the Maharaja impugned not their courage, but their discipline and equipment. Shah Shuja's expedition of 1834, nevertheless, served to show the fairness of Ranjit Singh's conclusions.

79. Murray, *Ranjit Singh*, pp. 167, 168. The whole of the tenth chapter of Capt. Murray's book, which includes the meeting at Rupar, may be regarded as the composition of Mr. prinsep. The Secretary to Government, with the Governor-General.

80. Moorcroft. *Travels*, ii. 338.

81. Government to Col. Pottinger, 22nd Oct. 1831, and Murray, *Ranjit Singh*, p. 153.

82 Government to Col. Pottinger, 22nd Oct. 1831.

83. [Afterwards Sir H. E. Pottinger, Bart., first Governor of Hong Kong.—Ed.]

84. Murray, *Ranjit Singh*, p. 168.

85. Government to Capt. Wade, 19th Dec. 1831. It is admitted that the mission, or the schemes, had a political preference to Russia and her designs, but the Governor-General would not avow his motives. (Murray, *Ranjit Singh*, p. 168.)

86. Ranjit Singh's attention was mainly directed to Sind, and a rumoured matrimonial alliance between one of the Amirs, or the son of one of them, and a Persian princess, caused him some anxiety. (Capt. Wade to Government, 5th Aug. 1831.)

87. This view appears to have subsequently occurred to Capt. Wade as having influenced the Maharaja. See his letter to Government, 18th Oct. 1836.

88. Capt. Wade to Government, 5th Nov. 1831.

89. This argument was continually used by Ranjit Singh. See, for instance. Capt. Wade to Government, 15th Jan. 1837.

90. Capt. Wade to Government, 1st and 13th Feb. 1832.

91. Capt. Wade to Government 21st Dec. 1831; and Col. Pottinger to Government, 23rd Sept. 1837.

92. See Appendices XXVII and XXIX. A tariff on goods was at first talked of but subsequently a toll on boats was preferred. From the Himalayas to the sea the whole toll was fixed at 570 rupees, of which the Lahore Government got Rs. 155, 4, 0 for territories on the right bank, and Rs. 39, 5, 1 for territories on the left bank of the Sutlej. (Government to Capt. Wade, 9th June 1834, and Capt. Wade to Government, 13th Dec. 1835.)

93. Capt. Wade to Government 13th Feb. 1832.

94. Capt. Wade to the Resident at Delhi, 25th July 1826.

95. Resident at Delhi to Capt. Wade, 25th July 1827.

96. Government to Resident at Delhi, 12th June 1829.

97. Capt. Wade to Government, 9th Sept. 1831.

98. Capt. Wade to Government, 21st Now. 1831.—Considering the ridicule occasioned by the subsequent removal by the English of these traditional gates, it may gratify the approvers and originators of the measure to know that they *were* of some local importance. When the author was at Bahawalpur in 1845, a number of Afghan merchants came to ask him whether their restoration could be brought about—for the repute of the fane (a tomb made a temple by superstition), and the income of its *pir* or saint, had much declined. They would carefully convey them back, they said, and they added that they understood the

Hindus did not want them, and that of course they could be of no value to the Christians!

99. Government to Capt. Wade, 19th Oct. 1832.
100. Capt. Wade to Government, 15th Sept. 1832.
101. Capt. Wade to Government, 13th Dec. 1832.
102. Capt. Wade to Government, 31st Dec. 1832.
103. Capt. Wade to Government, 9th April 1833.
104. Capt. Wade to Government, 27th March 1833.
105. This treaty, which became the foundation of the Tripartite Treaty of 1838 was drawn up in March 1833, and finally agreed to in August of that year. (Capt. Wade to Government, 17th June 1834.)
106. Government to Capt. Wade, 19th Dec. 1832.
107. Government to Capt. Faithful, Acting Political Agent, 13th Dec. 1832, and to Capt. Wade, 5th and 9th of March 1833.
108. The Bahawalpur Memories state that such a recommendation was pressed by Dost Muhammad on the Amris; the belief in the gradual conversion of 'Kothis' or residencies or commercial houses, into 'Chaonis', or military cantonments, having it may be inferred become notorious as far as Kabul. Dost Muhammad's main object, however, was to keep Shah Shuja at a distance; and he always seems to have held that he was safe from the English themselves so long as Lahore remained unshaker. For another instance of the extent to which the English were thought to be identified with Shah Shuja, see the *Asiatic Journal*, xix. 38, as quoted by Professor Wilson in Moorcroft's *Travels*, p. 340 *n*., vol ii.
109. Capt. Wade to Government, 9th April 1833.
110. Capt. Wade to Government, 25th Aug. 1833, and the Memoirs of the Bahawalpur Family.
111. Capt. Wade to Government, 30th Jan. 1834.
112. Capt. Wade to Government, 25th July 1834.
113. Capt. Wade to Government, 21st Oct, and 29th Dec. 1834 and 6th Feb. 1845.
114. Capt. Wade to Government, 19th March 1835.
115. Capt. Wade to Government, 17th June 1834.
116. Capt. Wade to Government, 19th May 1834.
117. These views of Hari Singh's were sufficiently notorious in the Punjab some years ago, when that chief was a person before the public.

118. Capt. Wade to Government, 7th Aug. 1832.

119. Capt. Wade to Government, 10th May 1834. Dera Ismail Khan and the country about it was not fairly brought into order until two years afterwards. (Capt. Wade to Government 7th and 13th July 1836).

120. Capt. Wade to Government, 9th Oct. 1833 and 3rd Jan. 1835.

121. Capt. Wade to Government, 11th Sept. 1834 and 4th April 1836.

122. Moorcroft, *Travels, i.* 420.

123. Capt. Wade to Government, 27th Jan. 1835, and Mr. Vigne, *Travels in Kashmir and Tibet,* ii. 352; their statements being corrected or amplified from the author's manuscript notes. The Prince Kharak Singh became especially apprehensive of the designs of the Jammu family. (Capt. Wade to Government, 10th Aug. 1836).

124. Capt. Wade to Government, 6th Feb. 1835.

125. Capt. Wade to Government, 17th June 1834. Sarafraz Khan, otherwise called Ghulam Shah, was the Kalhora expelled by the Talpurs. He received Rajanpur in Jagir from Kabul, and was maintained in it by Ranjit Singh. The place was held to yield 100,000 rupees, including certain rents reserved by the state, but the district was not really worth 30,000 rupees.

126 Capt. Wade to Government, 17th April 1835, and other letters of the same year. The Maharaja still urged that the English should guarantee, as it were, Shah Shuja's moderation in success; perhaps, because the greatness of the dynasty of Ahmad Shah still dwelt in the mind of the first paramount of the Sikhs, but partly also with the view of sounding his European allies as to *their* real intentions.

127. Capt. Wade to Government, 5th Oct. 1836

128. Capt. Wade to Government, 15th Jan. 1837

129. Capt. Wade to Government, 5th Oct. 1836

130. Government to Capt. Wade, 22nd Aug. 1836—This plea will recall to mind the usual argument of the Romans for interference, viz. that their friends were not to be molested by strangers.

131 Government to Capt. Wade, 22nd Aug. 1836.

132 Capt. Wade to Government, 27th May 1835.

133. Government to Capt. Wade, 27th May 1835 and 5th Sept. 1836; and Government to Col. Pottinger, 19th Sept. 1836.

134. Capt. Wade to Government, 29th Aug. 1836.

135. Capt. Wade to Government, 2nd Nov. 1836.

136. Government to Capt. Wade, 5th Sep. 1836.

137. Government to Capt. Wade, 5th Sep. 1836.

138. Government to Col. Pottinger, 26th Sept. 1836.

139. Government to Capt. Wade, 26th Sept. 1836.

140. Capt. Wade to Government, 2nd Nov. and 13th Dec. 1836.

141. Capt. Wade to Government, 3rd Jan. 1837.

142. Cf. Capt. Wade to Government, 11th Jan. 1837. Ranjit Singh not unfrequently referred to the overthrow of the Maratha power as a reason for remaining, under all and any circumstances, on good terms with his European allies . See also Col. Wade's *Narrative of Personal Services*, p. 44, note. [Though the Maharaja kept loyally to his treaty of friendship with the English, he occasionally manifested some suspicion of their victorious advance in India. On one occasion he was shown a map of the country in which the English possessions were marked in red. The Maharaja asked what the red portions indicated, and on being told tossed the map aside with the impatient remark, *Sab lal hojaega* (All will become red).—Ed.]

143. Capt. Wade to Government, 5th Jan. 1837.

144. Capt. Wade to Government, 13th and 15th Feb., 8th July, and 10th Aug. 1837.

145. Capt. Wade to Government, 9th Jan. 1838.

146. Cf. Moorcroft, Travels, ii. 345, &c, and Munshi Mohan Lal, *Life of Dost Muhammad Khan*, i. 130, 153, &c.

147. Moorcroft, Travels, ii. 346-347.

148. Capt. Wade to the Resident at Delhi, 21st April 1828.

149. Capt. Wade to Government, 19th May 1832. The brothers had already (1823, 1824) made similar proposal through Mr. Moorcroft. (See *Travels*, ii. 340.)

150. Mr. Fraser and Mr. Stirling, of the Bengal Service, were in Afghanistan the former in 1826, apparently; and the latter in 1828. Mr. Masson also entered the country by way of the Lower Punjab in 1827, and the American, Dr. Harlan, followed him in a year by the same route. Dr. Harlan came to Lahore in 1929, after leading the English authorities to be live that he desired to constitute himself an agent between their Government and Shah

Shuja, with reference doubtless to the ex-king's designs on Kabul. (Resident at Delhi to Capt. Wade, 3rd Feb. 1829.) The Rev. Mr. Wolff should be included among the travellers in Central Asia at the time in question.

151. Capt. Wade to Government, 19th May and 3rd July 1832.

152. Capt. Wade to Government, 9th July 1832 and 17th Jan. 1833. Col. Wade in the *Narrative of Personal Services*, p. 23, note, regards these overtures of Dost Muhammad, and also the increased interest of Russia and Persia in Afghan affairs, to Lieut. Burnes's Journey (to Bokhara, in 1832) and to Shah Shuja's designs.

153. Government to Capt. Wade, 28th Feb. 1833.

13

Conquest of Attock and Kashmir

The Attock fort had its historical importance as it was built at a strategic point. It lay on the main route through which all the Central Asian invaders came to India and plundered it to their heart's fill. The fort could act as a strong guard for the defence of India. Ranjit Singh had realised this and was convinced that once the fort was occupied he could not only close this highway to India to future invaders but, with the fort beyond the Indus under his control, also expand his territory right up to the Kheyber Pass where Afghans had built up strong defences.

The Attock fort was built by Akbar with good quality stone in 1583 at a high altitude. Its construction was supervised by Khwaja Shams-ud-din who had earlier designed it too. Its front wall was 400 yards long while the other three walls were 500 yards long. On the eastern side of the fort, it was engraved in Persian that it had been built by King Akbar in Hizri 991.

The Kabul *wazir* was awfully annoyed with Ata Mohammad for the assistance he had given to Shah Mohammad and made up his mind to invade and capture Kashmir. In 1812, he put his designs into action. This was the time when Maharaja Ranjit Singh had also sent his forces, to attack Kashmir. When they came to know each other's aim they decided to cooperate and attack the Kashmir valley jointly. Fateh Khan sought Ranjit Singh's help as he was afraid that Ranjit Singh might help Ata Mohammad against him. On the other hand, Ranjit Singh had a definite motive in extending his hand of friendship to Fateh Khan. As he had not captured all the hill States, he felt unsure of himself to capture Kashmir alone. In the venture, he needed somebody's help which was now readily available.

Ranjit Singh promised assistance to Fateh Khan with 12,000 men under the command of Mukham Chand besides facility to the Afghans to pass through Rajouri and Pir Panjal in return for Rs. 9 lakhs from the Kashmir plunder and Afghan help in subduing Multan. It is said that "neither was inclined to advance into the hills with the possibility of having its retreat cut off by the other." There was but one alternative. The leaders met and agreed to finish the hunt together, and divide the spoils. On this understanding the parties advanced, each having made a mental reservation to outwit the other if the opportunity offered.

Kashmir was occupied by Fateh Khan with the help of Ranjit Singh's forces. But he now refused to allow Ranjit Singh his share of the plunder as agreed upon. When the Maharaja came to know that Mukham Chand had returned empty handed, his wrath knew no bounds, he became so furious that he decided to take revenge immediately.

Finding that this brother Ata Mohammad Khan, Governor of Kashmir had been driven out from his position. Jahandad Khan, the Governor of Attock also became panicky. Ranjit Singh started negotiations with him and offered him a big *Jagir* in return for the surrender of the fort of Attock. Jahandad Khan agreed to the Maharaja's proposals and allowed Dia Singh, who was already present in the vicinity of Attock with a contingent of Sikh soldiers as a precautionary measure, to occupy the fort. The fort was occupied by Ranjit Singh at a very low cost of Rs. 1 lakh. This amount had to be paid to Jahandad Khan's soldiers who would leave the fort only after the long outstanding arrears of pay were paid to them. It is also said that the Sikhs got in the fort 3510 maunds of grains, 439 rounds of ammunition, 70 pieces of guns and mortars, and 255 maunds of rock salt.

However, the Maharaja could not remain complacent and despatched a strong detachment of his troops under the command of *Fakir* Aziz-ud-din, Dewan Devi Das and Sardar Hari Singh Nalwa. Fateh Khan also became furious, remonstrated with the Maharaja and accused him of treachery. He demanded immediate surrender of the fort of Attock which the Maharaja bluntly refused as he was confident of his strength. Instead, Ranjit Singh asked for his share of the Kashmir plunder. No compromise was visible and Fateh Khan marched towards the fort of Attock at the head of a 15,000 strong army, leaving the affairs of Kashmir to the care of his brother Azim Khan. Thus the situation became tense. More troops were then sent from Lahore under the command of Karam Chand Chahal and Dewan Mukham Chand was directed to proceed towards the fort from Burhan. The Afghan and Sikh armies were not poised against each other.

Frequent skirmishes took place in which both sides lost heavily. But the Sikhs waited for their chance. On July 12, 1813 the Sikh forces took action when the Afghan supplies were exhausted. The Dewan marched towards Haidru, situated on the bank of river Indus, 8 km from the fort of Attock. The Afghan troops took up positions to oppose the advance of the Sikhs, a portion of their cavalry being led by Dost Mohammad Khan, brother of Fateh Khan.

Dewan Mukham Chand formed the cavalry into four divisions, one of them under the command of Hari Singh Nalwa. The only infantry battalion, forming a square and the artillery under Ghouse Khan supported the entire body of troops. Dost Mohammad first made a resolute cavalry charge which was repulsed by heavy fire from the Sikh side. The Afghans mustered strength and rallied under Dost Mohammad who launched an attack riding his horse. The Sikh troops were thrown into confusion and some of their guns were captured. It seemed the Sikhs were giving way but Mukham Chand, riding a mighty elephant with two guns, fired on Afghans, checking their further movement. The scorching heat also compelled the Afghans to retire. The lost guns were recovered by the Sikhs and Fateh Khan, fearing Dost Mohammad's death, fled. There from the victorious Sikh army pursued the Afghans and drove them out of Khyrabad.

"The battle of Haidru was fought on the 13th of July, 1813, and was the first on record in which the Sikh troops, under the Lahore *darbar*, had beaten the Afghans, who from this time began to entertain a dread of their powers. There were great rejoicing at Lahore in honour of this great and decisive victory, royal salutes being fired at all the principal stations in the Raj, while the cities of Lahore, Amritsar and Batala were brilliantly illuminated. Two months were spent in Lahore in these rejoicings, at the end of which in Asu (September), the Maharaja himself paid a visit to his newly conquered province of Attok, with the view of further intimidating the Pathans, as well as of consolidating his authority in those distant regions."[1]

After a couple of days when the Maharaja personally visited the fort of Attock, he conferred *jagirs* on the generals and the Maharaja joyously inspected the tents, horses, food articles and ammunition captured from the fort.

After the astonishing victory of Attock, Maharaja Ranjit Singh gained more confidence and thought of annexing other strategic areas to his empire. Kashmire came to his mind first. Kashmir had great importance because of its trade routes. It was a wealthy area, rich in forests and other products. The valley grew fruit in abundance. Walnuts, apples peaches and cherries were among the superior varieties of fruits grown in Kashmir. It had several health resorts and beauty spots.

Trade and commerce flourished between Kashmir and Tibet. Kashmir imported from Tibet annually 60,000 seers of raw wool and woollen cloth, tea, gold and silver ingots and dry fruit. The Kashmir exports included cotton cloth, iron and spices.

Kashmir's capital, Srinagar, was a flourishing town. Its shawls were known the world over. Finer quality shawls fetched 300 to 7000 rupees in those days. Leather goods, wooden products and woollen cloth were the other itmes produced in the Valley.

In 1814, Maharaja Ranjit Singh made full preparations for a massive invasion of Kashmir. On June 6, 1814, the Maharja himself reached Bhimber. The Raja of Poonch, Bahullah Khan, was asked to cooperate in the operations. But he refused to oblige the Maharaja. Upon this the Maharaja sent a detachment of troops under Sardar Fateh Singh Ahluwalia and Dewan Ram Dayal. They were able to subdue the Raja and the Bakram Kalla Pass was seized. Then two divisions of the Khalsa army marched towards Kashmi; the main body commanded by the Maharaja himself advanced through the Poonch route, towards the Toshu Maidan Pass while another under Ram Dayal and Sardar Dal Singh passed through Baramula towards Supin in the heart of the Valley.

However, the expedition could not succeed as the rains set in. Pir Panjal was still snow-clad. The inclement weather had an adverse effect on the Sikhs, as they were not used to fighting in the hills. The supply line also could not be maintained and the operations had to be abandoned temporarily. When the rains ceased, the Maharaja's division reached Poonch, the supplies were replenished and the forces marched towards Mandi. On July 18, 1814, they reached Toshu Maidan. Here Ata Mohammad Khan, the Governor of Kashmir, was ready to face the Sikh army. At the same time, the news was received that the Sikh forces had ascended Pir Panjal Pass, occupied Haripur and were advancing towards Supin. The Sikhs attacked the well-defended town but did not succeed in dislodging the enemy forces. Meanwhile Azim Khan's cavalry reached there. A fierce battle was fought but due to heavy rains, the Sikhs were badly mauled. The defeated Khalsa army returned to Pir Panjal. They suffered heavy losses in men and material and the situation became grave for the Sikhs. Azim Khan attacked the Sikhs at Toshu

Maidan. No defence could be offered and the Sikh soldiers retreated to Mandi. The town was set on fire. The Afghans pursued the Sikhs and Ranjit Singh ordered reorganisation of the demoralised Sikh army. The roads were under deep water. The Sikhs could not fight and desertions began to take place. Many were slain. Much of the war material was lost.

"The remnants of the Sikh army fell back on Puch but the retreat was conducted so irregularly and in such disorder, that it became a disgraceful flight."[2] The Maharaja was forced to be back to Bhimber and from there he returned to Lahore were he reached on August 12, 1814.

"Thus the whole expedition returned to Lahore, having lost its best officers and men, and being short of everything that constituted its strength and utility as a military body. The Maharaja lamented that in the campaign he could not avail himself of his aged Dewan's determination and judgement, as well as of his skill and valour. Everything had come to pass exactly as the old Dewan had predicted and the ruler of Lahore sighed at the political blunder he had committed."[3]

The Maharaja could not sit idle. He still nourished the ambition of conquering Kashmir at the earliest possible opportunity. So he strengthened his forces, re-equipped them and gave them proper training to fight in the hills. However, it took him five years to give shape to his plans.

Early in the year Bir Dhar a minister under Jabber Khan, the Afghan Governor of Kashmir betrayed Jabber Khan and sought asylum with the Maharaja. Bir Dhar informed Ranjit Singh that Mohammad Azim Khan had gone to Kabul with his forces and the Kashmir valley was without any defence. The remnants of Jabber Khan's forces were incapable of protecting Kashmir and the Maharaja had a good opportunity to annex the valley to his territory.

Ranjit Singh the shrewed diplomat as he was, ordered his commanders to make preparations to attack Kashmir on massive scale. Arms and ammunition were collected at

Gurarat and Wazirabad and nothing was left to chance. On April 20, 1819, the Maharaja marched from Lahore at the head of 30,000 strong force. The forces marched with shouts of *Sat-Sri-Akal* resounding in the sky. These were followed by more troops under the command of Diwan Chand, Jaffer Jang, Hukma Singh Chimni, Sardar Jawala Singh and Sardar Sham Singh Attari. Besides, the Maharaja kept in reserve a force of 10,000 strong army so that in case of any exigency, it could be sent at a moment's notice.

The Khalsa forces reached Bhimber from where the hill tract started. Drinking water was not available in the hills, so the soldiers were asked to fill up their buckets. Then they reached Saidabad, where on old fort could be used for halt. The *Hakim* of the fort fled without offering any resistance. The Khalsa army captured the fort without any loss of men or material. This was their first victory. The forces marched further and reached Rajouri on May 1, 1819. The garden, situated on the bank of river Tawi, with a spacious *baradari,* was occupied. The local *Hakim* tried to offer some resistance, but his forces were overpowered by the division under the command of Hari Singh Nalwa who gave him a crushing defeat. Agar Khan fled and his force was so much demoralised that it surrendered unconditionally. Many of Agar Khan's soldiers were slain and much of his war equipment was lost. The Sikhs too lost ten of their brave men of whom Sardar Jodh Singh Russa deserves a mention. He was a man of indomitable spirit and his dynamism impressed one and all. However, while fleeing Agar Khan was captured and was sent to Bhimber where Maharaja Ranjit Singh help his *darbar*.

Agar Khan sought mercy from the Maharaja and promised to remain loyal to him in future. He offered to assist the Maharaja in the annexation of Kashmir. The Maharja pardoned him and made him Raja of Rajouri.

The Sikh forces marched further and halted at Behram Pass. The route was hilly and rugged and the entire journey was strenuous. Here an Afghan *faujdar* was a petty chief and when he came to know of the massive Sikh forces he fled in panic towards Srinagar, leaving his fortress unprotected. Behram Pass was thus captured. Mir Mohammad Khan, the *kotwal* of Poonch, submitted to the Sikh general and the kotwal of Supin, Mohammad Ali followed in his footstep. Jabbar Dost Khan, the Raja of Poonch, who had closed the fort, did not surrender and offered some resistance. Raja Sultan Chand, who was acquainted with the topography of the area, was ordered to attack the fort. The Raja sealed the walls of the fort. Many soldiers defending the fort were slain in the battle that ensued. At last, Jabbar Dost Khan was left with no alternative but to surrender to the Sikhs. The Governor of *Basara* who also made to swear allegiance to Maharaja Ranjit Singh. Thus the route to Pir Panjal Pass was fully secured. Missar Diwan Chand divided the army into three divisions and directed them to march towards the valley of Kashmir through different routes. The Missar himself headed the forces which were to cross Pir Panjal. They marched at a lighting speed and entered the Valley. Some resistance was offered by the Pathans and after many dead and wounded, they were made to flee in dismay, leaving behind huge war equipment which was taken possession of by the Sikhs. The Sikh morale was very high and on June 16, 1819 the entire Sikh force took up their positions at Serai Ali, leading to Supin. Meanwhile, Maharaja Ranjit Singh himself arrived at Shahabad to supervise the arrangements and to see that the supply position was in perfect order.

Sardar Jabbar Khan faced the Sikh forces in the plains of Supin with a 5000 strong force. The bugles sounded and the sky resounded with the cries of *Sat-Sri-Akal*. On July 5, 1819, a fierce battle was fought between the opposing armies. For some time the Afghans held the Sikh forces and were also able to capture two of their guns. But then the Sikhs rallied and regrouped their forces and made a severe attack on the Afghans who fled towards Shergarh. Sardar Jabbar Khan was wounded and had a narrow escape. Kashmir was now captured and the Sikh territory was enlarged. The Maharaja's forces then made a triumphant entry into

Srinagar. Next day the city was fully occupied. Jabbar Khan fled with a few of his men, crossed the mountains and eventually reached Peshawar.

In Srinagar, Prince Kharak singh announced that nobody should feel panicky, adding that full protection would be afforded to the peaceful citizens. No distinction would be made on the basis of caste, creed or colour. The soldiers were strictly warned not to plunder the city. A huge procession was taken out in the city. It was a unique thing in the history of Kashmir. Earlier, the town had been ransacked several times. For the first time the victorious forces had remained peaceful and not a single case of loot or arson had taken place. The Sikh forces were therefore welcomed with open arms. Prince Kharak Singh encamped in Shergarh fort.

"The Maharaja on receiving the news of the conquest of the important and fertile province of Kashmir made great rejoicings, and sending *Fakir* Aziz-ud-din to make enquiries about the climate and Dewan Devi Dass to take charge of the assessment and revenues returned to Lahore. As usual with him on such occasions, the Maharaja spent several days in rejoicings at Lahore in commemoration of the victory won by his troops. The cities of Lahore and Amritsar were illuminated for three nights. The Maharaja visited Amritsar where he paid his benediction at the Darbar Sahib, and made a large offering of money. On his return to Lahore, he recalled Missar Dewan Chand and sent Dewan Moti Ram son of late Dewan Mukhan Chand as the first governor of Kashmir."[4]

On Maharaja's orders Hari Singh Nalwa and Sham Singh Attari marched towards Muzzafrabad and Darband. They succeeded in the complete subjugation of those parts.

"The conquest of Kashmir added an annual revenue of 4,000,000 rupees to the Kingdom of Lahore and brought under Sikh rule an extensive area inhabited by varied races, Aryans and Turanians in the valley and its loftier mountains. It raised the prestige of the Maharaja and the majesty of his power at Leh, Lhasa and beyond the Karakuram mountains.

It struck a heavy blow at the warring Afghan satrapies in northern India, the only one left now was Peshawar."[5]

After its conquest, Kashmir was put under military rule for some time. Dewan Ram Dayal was made incharge of Bhimber. Bhai Ram was appointed as *Parganadar* of the river. Likewise, Sardar Sham Singh Attari and Sardar Jawala Singh and Missar Dewan Chand were made heads of Baramula and Srinagar respectively. Sardar Hari Singh Nalwa was made overall incharge of the forces.

Army ruled the province of Kashmir well and won the hearts of the people who by and large cooperated with them. When everything was settled, Dewan Moti Ram was appointed its first Governor. The forces were ordered to be withdrawn, leaving behind a few soldiers in the valley to meet any exigency. When the army reached Lahore, the soldiers were received by the Mahraja himself, giving them a right royal reception near Shadhara. A huge procession was taken out in which royal bands played martial tunes, the Mahraja and the Princes leading it. When it entered Lahore, the people received the victorious army with enthusiasm. The bazars were decorated and huge arches were put up. When the procession entered the fort, cannons were fired and a gun salute was given. At night the entire town was illuminated and crackers were fired. Next day an open *darbar* was help by Maharaja in which *Khillats* were offered to those who had conquered Kashmir.

Dewan Moti Ram continued as Governor of Kashmir for about a year. Though he governed the province with a firm hand, he had to levy heavy taxes as ahuge sum of money was required for administering the territory. But it broke the backbone of the peasantry and the working class. "Everywhere however, the people are in the most abject condition. Exhorbitantly taxed by the Sikh Government, and subjected to every kind of extortion and oppression by its officers. The consequences of the system are the general depopulation of the country. Not more than one-sixteenth of the cultivable surface is in cultivation, and the inhabitants, starving at home, are driven in great numbers to the plains of Hindustan. In the like manner the people of the city are thinning, though less from emigration than poverty and disease; the prevalance of the latter in its most aggravated from was fearfully extensive."[6]

This statement of Moorcroft exaggerated yet is clear that the great resentment prevailed among the people or Kashmir who lived in depressing conditions. Signs of rebellion were visible and efforts were on to sabotage the Government from inside. Many people refused to pay land revenue. The Government's orders were not implemented. Besides, cases of loot and arson were also reported. Ultimately complaints were lodged with the Maharaja about the mismanagement of Kashmir affairs. He ordered Dewan Moti Ram to bring about improvement in the administration but not much could be achieved. Then he sent Dewan Devi Das to Kashmir to enquire into its problems. When he reached Kashmir, he found the administration totally at a breaking point. There was no respect for law and order, and general condition of the people had very much deteriorated. He reported to the Maharaja that if such a state of affairs continued for some time more, there would be an open rebellion which would be difficult to control.

As the Maharaja read Dewan Devi Das's report on Kashmir he became grim. Soon he took a firm decision to set matter right. Hari Singh Nalwa was appointed Governor of Kashmir.

Hari Singh Nalwa reached Kashmir on August 20, 1920. He took charge as Governor of Kashmir from Dewan Moti Ram the next day. As Hari Singh Nalwa took charge, he found that no land revenue had been collected nor soldiers had been paid their salaries for the last four months. On account of Dewan Moti Ram's lenient attitude, people were openly disobeying Government orders. There were many cases of loot and arson and powerful were sucking the blood of the poor and the down-trodden. The honour of women was not safe. In fact, there was no rule of law and complete chaos prevailed.

These conditions were unbearable. Nalwa made a proclamation to the effect that he would rule the people of Kashmir with love. No harsh treatment would be meted out to anyone and steps would be taken to improve the lot of the poor. To achieve this, he solicited the cooperation of the people of Kashmir. People were directed to pay forthwith the land revenue and other taxes due. They were further warned that if after the issue of the proclamation, any untoward incident took place and people failed in their duty, they would be taken to task and would be dealt with severely. It was upto the people to choose the path they wanted to.

The proclamation had the desired effect. People started paying their dues to the Government and respect for the law restored. Peace prevailed in the valley yet some signs of discontentment were still there.

When things settled down a little, Nalwa sought the Maharaja's permission to strike coins in his name, as it was necessary to do so to uphold the state's authority. The Maharaja readily agreed to the proposal and a coin was struck which contained ten *massas* of silver and six *massas* of bronze. The coin was known as Hari Singh's rupee. It was equal to fifty paisa. Besides, a rupee coin was also minted. The undermentioned words were engraved on the coin:

Sri Akal Sahai, Samat 1878. On other side was Hari Singh's likeness and the words *Zak rupehia* (one rupee).

The next step was to take drastic action against the inhabitants of Baramula and the people settled on the banks of the river. These people were originally Hindu *Brahmins* and *Khatris* who had been converted to Islam during the Mughal period. They still put B and K after their names denoting *Brahmins* and *Khatris*. There present leaders were Raja Ghulam Ali Khan and Zulfikar Ali Khan who had revolted openly during the Governorship of Dewan Moti Ram and had refused to pay land revenue. Dewan Moti Ram had summoned them to his *darbar* many a time but they had refused to obey his orders. The situation was grim and demanded firm but diplomatic action.

Baramula was attacked and the people were not only forced to pay the balance of land revenue but were also made to pay Rs. 5 per family as war indemnity. Then Sardar Nalwa turned his attention towards B's and K's. One night Nalwa, along with Sardar Tek Singh, marched towards these villages with an infantry platoon. People were surrounded and their leaders arrested. No resistance was offered. Some of them tried to make michief but they were taken to task. Both the top leaders Raja Ghulam Ali Khan and Zulfikar Ali Khan were put in chains and were sent to Lahore under heavy escort. Their arms were confiscated and they were made to pay land revenue. They were further ordered to pay regular visits to Srinagar. Complete peace was now restored in the villey. The Maharaja issued a *firman* praising the services rendered by Sardar Nalwa.

After restoring order Nalwa attended to land reforms. Land revenue records were studied and new rates of revenue fixed. This was the most difficult task. Nalwa solved the problem efficiently without making much changes in the system and without hurting the feelings of the people. A man of shrewd disposition, Nalwa tried to pacify all sections of the people.

According to *Ain-e-Akbari*, Kashmir's land revenue amounted to Rs. 3,01110,619 Kharwar equivalent to Rs. 1,552,025. During the Afghan regime, it was 6,000,000 *chilak* rupees and under Dewan Moti Ram it amounted to 2,100,000 Nanak Shahi rupees. Hari Singh reduced this figure to 1,300,000 Hari Singh rupees. This proved beneficial both to Government and the people. Nalwa fixed this figure after careful consideration and giving due weightage to the aspirations of the people. The result was that the people started paying land revenue willingly without any hesitation. The step was highly applauded by the Maharaja.

Another evil that prevailed in Kashmir at that time was that of bonded labour. The system had been prevalent since the days of Shanker Verma who had ruled Kashmir in 907 A.D. Whenever any State official proceeded on tour or attended to some other official duty, thousands of labourers were forcibly caught and put to all sorts of odd jobs. It is said that the Raja got the town of Pattan constructed by these labourers without paying them a single paisa. In 1664 A.D., when Aurangzeb visited Kashmir, 30,000 Kashmiri labourers were used to carry the luggage.

When for the first time Sardar Nalwa toured the province his subordinates engaged hundreds of labourers to carry his luggage and provide him all sorts of facilities. Those were the days of harvesting and the labourers were extremely busy in their operations. They requested the *chaudries* with folded hands, to let them free so that their work did not suffer. But no heed was paid to their request; rather they were beaten with *lathis,* as was the prevailing custom. When this came to Nalwa's notice, he wanted to know what all the hue and cry was about. He was informed that the labourers had been collected to provide him the necessary facilities and to carry his luggage and other effects.

Nalwa refused to proceed further with the labourers and ordered that horses and donkeys be arranged for the transportation of his luggage. Immediately a *firman* was issued banning the system of bonded labour. Orders were also issued to the effect that when labour was required, paid workers should be engaged for the purpose.

Many other improvements were made in the administration. Relief was provided to flood victims—2000 *Kharwar* of rice was procured and distributed among the sufferers.

Another tax *Tera* was in force which all the subjects were required to pay. This was levied at the time of birth, betrothal and marriage. It was abolished.

In the system of administration, several other changed were made. A number of new Police Stations were opened in the villages. Hardened criminals were produced before the Governor and judgements were delivered there and then after hearing the arguments of both the parties. Officials were forbidden to implicate persons in false cases. The system of weights and measures was regularised. Iron measures were introduced and a uniform yard was put into use. This gave relief to people who were being cheated by unscrupulous traders. The result was that trade and industry flourished in Kashmir and many people who had fled the valley during the Afghan regime returned to their hearths and homes.

Another custom prevalent in Kashmir was that no non-Muslim was allowed to tie turban on his head or wear shoes. Orders were issued that no restriction would be imposed on anybody's dress. Everyone was free to put on the dress of his choice. All those who desired or could effort could ride horses. Everybody was equal in the eyes of law.

In 1821, Kashmir was faced with the worst flood in its history. It rained continuously for several days and the overflowing rivers created havoc. Some dams were damaged and hundreds of people were encircled in the gushing waters of the rivers. Houses were damaged and crops destroyed. Bridges were washed away. Sardar Nalwa provided all possible help and assistance to the people. Cash relief was give bridges were reconstructed, foodgrains were imported from Punjab and distributed freely among the people. More foodgrains were purchased from non-affected areas at a higher price per *Kharwar* and sold in the affected areas at lower price.

Another notable feature to Kashmir was that crops were grown on water in the lakes. Special attention was paid to this form of agriculture and liberal *taccavi* loans were given to the people besides reducing their land revenue. The production, specially of vegetables, increased and economy of the province was put on a firm footing.

New fields were laid on the water and cultivation of saffrom was encourages. The farmers of Palmpur, where saffron was cultivated on a very large scale, were given all facilities.

Rural industries were encourages. Special attention was given to papier machie industry and fillip was given to shwal manufacture. With the development of these industries the condition of the people improved considerably.

The administration was now on a sound footing. The rule of law prevailed and people's respect for law also increased. In 1921, Nalwa attacked Poonch and Rajouri and annexed these areas to Kashmir. He prepared a balance sheet of all the accounts of Kashmir and submitted it to the Maharaja who was extremely pleased to see the progress of the province. He appreciated Nalwa's services and offered him a *Khillat*. According to Maulana Mohammad Din, the Maharaja was so overwhelmed with joy that he presented to Nalwa a chain, an elephant and a pair of golden bangles.

In short, Kashmir prospered considerably under the Sikh rule. Trade and industry flourished. Cottage industry was revived. Hindus, Muslims and Siksh atarted living like brothers and in the eyes of law no distinction was made on the basis of caste, creed or colour. It was a unique thing to see that after so many years of communal rule, secular rule had been established in the valley. Even Shias and Sunnis among the Muslims joined hands and lived like one community. Land revenue was collected without use of any force and the soldiers were paid regularly. There was no resentment among them. When the Maharaja found the conditions in Kashmir well-settled, the decided to call back Nalwa to utilise his services elsewhere. Dewan Moti Ram was again appointed Governor of Kashmir.

Hari Singh Nalwa returned to Punjab with fully armed 7000 strong troops to meet any exigency enroute. When Sardar Nalwa reached Pakhli through Muzzafarabd, an intelligence report was received, according to which 30,000 tribesmen were making preparations to oppose the Sikh forces at Mangli. As was the practice with him, Hari Singh first negotiated with the *Ghazis* and made every effort to avoid war. He sent his *Kardars*, Mohammad Ismil and Sardar Dhanna Singh Malwai to meet the *Ghazis* and reach an amicable settlement. They told the *Ghazis* that Sardar Nalwa was interested in only passing through Mangli and had no intention of annexing any territory or fighting a war. But the *Ghazis* rejected a peaceful settlement and refused to allow the Sikhs to pass through Mangli. The emissaries returned and reported the result of their deliberations to the Nalwa Sardar.

As the war was inevitable, Nalwa visited forward areas in disguise and watched the defence arrangements. It rained for some time and then cleared. The inhabitants of Mangli were seen levelling the earth on their roofs with wooden pieces in their hands, Nalwa was surprised to see this and enquired from the inhabitants whether all the roofs were leaking. They replied that the earth of that area could be levelled with only wooden pieces. Then Nalwa returned to his campt and called an emergency meeting of his Sardars who were told that it was extremely easy to defeat the people of Mangli. The attack, he said, should be sudden and massive. The offensive was made from three sides. The *Ghazis* unsheathed their swords and put up stiff resistance.

Sardar Megh Singh Russa entered the enemy ranks with his platoon and broke their defences. A fierce battle ensured as Khalsa army advanced from all sides. Soon Russa was dead. Hundreds were killed and wounded on both sides. At the same time some 2,000 *Ghazis* were dead. About 180 Sikh soldiers laid down their lives and another 350 were injured. The enemy was completely demoralised and fled away from the battlefield. Mangli was captured. The Sikhs seized a good deal of arms and ammunition which the Pathans had left behind. Besides, there was substantial quantity of foodgrains and a large number of cows and buffaloes. It was a unique victory for Nalwa which he had won by his sheer dash and dynamism.

Early next day with white flags in their hands, the *Ghazis* presented themselves before the Nalwa Sardar and sought his pardon. Their backbone was already broken, so they were prepared for any peace settlement, on Nalwa's terms. Nalwa pardoned them but imposed a fine of rupees five per family, which was collected without delay. This happened on November 10, 1821. Nalwa then allowed his army to take rest for three days.

Mangli was the capital of Hazara for a very long time. Huen-Tsang, a well-known Chinese traveller, has referred Mangli in his writing. He said: "I visited Mangli in 200 A.D. The city was flourishing and it is the capital of Raja Vulashi's kingdom. It is situated in the north-west division of Kashmir. Nearby flows the Mangli stream."[7]

Nalwa left Mangli on November 14, 1821 and on November 28 reached Khushab were the Maharaja was camping. Hari Singh was honoured with the firing of guns. Nalwa gave a detailed account of his victory in Mangli. The Maharaja was so happy that he embraced him in the open *darbar*.

Sardar Nalwa presented to the Maharaja two lakh rupees collected as land revenue in Kashmir but the latter returned him the money as a prize for the notable work done by him. Moreover, Pakhli and Dhantor in Kashmir were bestowed as a *Jagir* on the gallant Hari Singh Nalwa, in recognition of his services in that country. However, during the same year, the tribes of Pakhli and Dhantor rebelled and Sardar Hari Singh Nalwa to whom these places had been given in *jagir*, was sent at the head of the troops to punish the offenders. Hari Singh spread havoc in the invaded country, and put the population of the affected villages to the sword. Pakhil and Dhantor were set on fire.

Paragana Mungher was situated on the right bank of river Attock. It was ruled by the Afghans and was one of their best governed territories. Its annual revenue was 10 lakh rupees. Its present *Hakim* was Hafiz Ahmad Khan, who was a gallant soldier, ell versed in horsemanship and archery.

Hafiz Ahmad Khan was not cooperating with the Khalsa *darbar*. He was strengthening his army and was preparing to defy Maharaja Ranjit Singh any time. Earlier, the Maharaja had subdued the Tiwanas, who had surrendered to the Sikh forces and promised to pay tribute to them. Missar Dewan Chand sent an intelligence report to the Maharaja to the effect that Hafiz Ahmad Khan was openly supporting the Tiwanas and was instigating them against the Maharaja. He had also given refuge to Ahmad Yar Khan, the leader of the Tiwanas. Besides the Nawab had entered into a treaty with the Afghans and was spying against the Lahore *darbar*. The situation was grim and unbearable for the Maharaja. He became furious. So he had by now captured Kashmir and Multan and was well entrenched in these areas, he decided to attack Mungher and annex it to the Sikh empire although the task was difficult. It was approached by a sandy track without any road or other means of communications. For miles together no drinking water was available which was of prime necessity for the invading army. Besides, the Nawab had constructed 12 forts around Mungher which were strong enough to repulse any invader. Thus, capturing the territory was an uphill task. The difficult terrain, lack of drinking water facility absence of means of communications and Afghans' support to the Nawab had detained Ranjit Singh from attacking the territory earlier.

Besides other defensive measures, the Nawab had an army of 25,000 strong, ever-ready to fight the invaders. Maharaja Ranjit Singh marched on the enemy territory at the head of his 3,000 troops. When he reached Khushab, Hari Singh Nalwa joined him along with his troops. They discussed war strategy and on December 3, 1821 the Khalsa forces proceeded further after performing Bhog of Sri Akhand path and offering prayers to the Almighty for strength and courage.

The army was divided in such a way as to gain maximum ground. Sardar Dal Singh and Khushal Singh were sent with 8,000 soldiers to attack the forts in Dera Ismail Khan area, Dewan Chand and Kirpa Ram were directed to attack Khangarh and Manjgarh with a 10,000 force and Sardar Hari Singh Nalwa was required to proceed towards Mungher with a 6,500 strong force. The remaining army was kept in reserve under the Maharaja himself so that in case of any exigency, additional forces could be despatched forthwith.

The Khalsa army was able to capture all the seven forts en route without any resistance from the enemy. This took just three days and on the fourth day a massive attack was launched on Mungher. Hafiz Ahmad Khand offered stout resistance and his soldiers fought bravely. A fierce battle took place in which cannon fire dominated. The battle continued for several days. On the fifth day, after heavy artillery fire, the town of Mungher was captured by the Khalsa forces. The fort was besieged and the Nawab's forces were completely demoralised. Many of his soldiers deserted him and fled in whatever direction they could. Some of his principal Sardars, having secretly come out of the fort, joined Ranjit Singh and pointed out the spots at which an attack could be successfully made. The dispositions for the attack were accordingly changed and the Nawab, seeing treachery on all sides and conceiving that he had done enough to preserve the honour of his ancestors, sent his agents, Qazi Gul Mohammad and Ali Jah Sikander Khan, to propose terms of capitulation. These were: the Nawab should be allowed safe conduct from the citadel of his camp taking with him all the members of his family, men, arms and property; should be permitted to retain possession of Dera Ismail Khan; and receive a suitable *jagir*. The Maharaja agreed to these terms. The Nawab had studied the Sikh character well and knew of the Sikh ruler's belief in good faith. He, therefore, asked him to put the impression of his hand, with the fingers extended, on a blank piece, of paper with saffron, as a solemn pledge for the execution of the agreement; Ranjit Singh anxious to set an example of the Khalsa faith no less than to close a costly campaign in a country so ill-provided with the means of prosecuting it went through the formality. Rich dresses were sent to the Nawab who, his suspicions having been thus allayed, surrendered the fort and came out with 300 followers, bringing with him all his arms and property. His camp pitched within the lines of the Sikhs, he had an interview with the Maharaja on the 20th. The Maharaja half-stood up to receive him, and was seated close to him on the same *Masnad*. The Nawab implored his conquerer to save that city from plunder and to provide his loyal troops with suitable employment. Both these requests were granted by the Maharaja who as a further proof of his friendship for the Nawab, discarded those who had joined him as deserters from their now-vanquished sovereign. The Nawab made over 22 guns, with a large quantity of ammunition, to the Maharaja and was sent to Dera Ismail Khan under proper escort with the whole of his harem, family and attendants. "The country of Nawab Hafiz Ahmad Khan, annexed by the Maharaja was worth annually ten lakhs of rupees, and its acquisition was the source of intense pleasure to Ranjit Singh, who ordered the towns of Lahore and Amritsar to be illuminated in honour of the occasion."[8]

Sardar Amar Singh Sindhawalia was appointed the first Governor. Before departure from Mungher the Maharaja held a *Shahi darbar*. The Maharaja returned to Lahore on January 27, 1821. Victory parades were held, processions were taken out in the bazars and the town was illuminated.

After the capture of Mungher, Maharaja turned his attention of Hazara which wus considered to be the abode of the Aryans. The entire area lies on the foothills of Kashmir and is well-known for its scenic beauty. Its boundaries were never static but in 19th century its area was about 100 km long and 40 km wide. On its east lay Kashmir and river Jhelum, on the west Peshawar, on the south Rawalpindi and on the north the Himalayas.

When Maharaja Ranjit Singh was engaged in the Kashmir campaign the Pathans of Hazara, who had never admitted the authority of any other power, created some trouble. They attacked both the Sikh forces and the Afghans. In fact, they could never live in peace. Earlier, the Maharaja had captured the fort of Attock and had closed all the routes of Afghanistan, so the local Pathans started plundering the Hazara territory.

In those days, Hukma Singh Chimni a brave general was the *Qiledar* of Attock and under him was posted Bhai Makhan Singh. Everything was going on peacefully when suddenly there was a change in the situation. Hashim Khan of Hazara who had murdered his neighbour Kamal Khan and was attacked by the latter's brother Sardar Mohammad Khan, sought the Maharaja's protection. The Maharaja issued orders to Sardar Makhan Singh through Sardar Hukma Singh Chimni to redress the grievances of Hashim Khan.

Makhan Singh carried out the Maharaja's orders and invaded the Hazara territory along with 500 horsemen. Mohammad Khan surrendered. Makhan Singh realised tribute from Mohammad Khan and imposed strict restrictions on him. He was forced to implement all the terms of the treaty vigorously. But hardly a year had passed when in 1819 he collected a number of *Ghazis* and launched massive attack on the Sikh forces which were taken by surprise. Not only several Sikh soldiers were put to death but Bhai Makhan Singh was also slain.

This was unberable for the Sikh General Sardar Hukma Singh Chimni who became red with rage and marched on Hazara from Attock. Sardar Mohammad Khan offered stout resistance and a bloody battle ensued but in the end he had to flee leaving a large number of *Ghazis* dead. But as the entire population of Hazari had risen in revolt, complete peace could not be restored in the territory and Sardar Chimni had to hasten back to Attock.

When the news of the failure of Hazara campaign was broken to the Maharaja he lost his temper. Meanwhile more complaints were received against Sardar Hukma Singh Chimni. Mian Dhian Singh had complained that the Chimni

Sardar had hanged Sayeed Khan Kot Hussan Ali, who was loyal to the Maharaja. The Maharaja , in his fury, called the Chmni Sardar back to Lahore fined him Rs. 25,000 and appointed Dewan Ram Dayal as the Governor of Attock. At the same time the Maharaja could not tolerate the rebellion in Hazara and directed Kanwar Sher Singh and Rani Sada Kaur, his mother-in-law who was bold and courageous lady, to proceed to Hazara with a huge force. They Sham Singh Attari and new Governor Dewan Ram Dayal. This way in January, 1820.

The Hazara rebellion was widespread and was not confined to any one part. Sardar Mohammad Khan had instigated the *Ghazis* to such an extent that they were filled with a revengeful spirit and the atmosphere was surcharged with deep enmity. The Sikh forces had, therefore an uphill task to accomplish. The entire force was divided and put under different commanders Pakhli, Dhamtor, Dharband, Terbela and Ghandgarh, in short, all the areas were surrounded. Skirmishes took place at many places, but in the end the *Ghaziz* fled and were chased into the deep corners of the hills. However, the newly appointed Governor, Dewan Ram Dayal, was surrounded in one of the hill streams and fired upon. Firing back he offered resistance, but was finally killed in the encounter. It was a great loss to the Khalsa and gloom was cast in the army's rank and file. Lahore *darbar* expressed sympathy to the bereaved family and the Maharaja himself sent a message of condolence.

The Khalsa forces were not enraged and revengeful spirit engulfed them. They were looking for an opportunity to attack the *Ghazis* to fulfil this task, they made fresh preparations. A massive attack was made with full strength. After some resistance the *Ghazis* fled in whichever direction they could. Hazara was captured and the hills resounded with the cries of *Sat Sri Akal*. The rebellion was crushed once for all. After the victory, Rani Sada Kaur held a *darbar* and announced that whosoever would raise the banner of revolt would be severely dealt with. Complete peace should prevail and nobody should create any trouble. Land revenue should be paid regularly in future and previous dues cleared. War indemnity was imposed on the *Ghazis* which they promised to pay, putting their hand on the *Quran*.

The Sikhs did not want to take any risk and so strengthened their forts. A lot of arms and ammunition were kept there and new forts like Ghandgarh, Terbela, Dharband and Ghazigarh were constructed and fortified. A *samadhi* of Dewan Ram Dayal was constructed to commemorate his memory.

After peace was restored. Sardar Amar Singh was appointed the new Governor. He ruled the territory with the best of his ability and the situation remained under control. However, after two years in 1822 an intelligence report was received to the effect that Hassan Ali, leader of *Karalas,* had raised the banner of revolt. Sardar Amar Singh marched at the head of his forces to crush the rebellion. He succeeded in putting down the revolt but on the way back to his head-quarters, he was attacked by *Ghazis* hiding in bushes while he was drinking water in the stream. Amar Singh tried to defend himself but was fatally wounded with a dagger. When the news was conveyed to the Maharaja, he was deeply shocked.

The Maharaja now appointed Sardar Hari Singh Nalwa as the Governor of Hazara. As desired by the Maharaja, Nalwa reached Hazara on February 26, 1822 along with his contingent. After taking stock of the situation for a couple of days, Nalwa's first action in Hazara was to attack the territory of Hashim Khan Karal, who had treacherously slain Sardar Amar Singh. The area was surrounded and Hashim Khan was arrested, his area was set on fire and he was presented before the Nalwa Sardar. He was trembling with fear. Nalwa gave him an option of either producing before him the murder of Sardar Amar Singh or he himself facing the consequences by standing before the cannon and getting killed. Putting his hands on the *Quran,* he promised to produce the real culprits. Nalwa readily agreed. Hashim Khan was allowed to go with Sikhs and soon the real culprits were produced before Nalwa. Further investigations established their guilt. The Nalwa Sardar held a big *darbar* in which all the inhabitants of the area were ordered to participate. The *darbar* was attended by a large number of people. The culprits were fired upon by guns to teach a lesson to all. The people were so much terrified that for years they aid not rise against the Khalsa. Hashim Khan promised to remain loyal to the *darbar*. His territory was annexed to the Sikh empire and he was let off. A big fort was got constructed at narra and army was stationed in it.

To provide permanent defence in the plains of Hazara, a fort was constructed and named Harikrishangarh after the eighth Guru. A town was also constructed near the fort which was named Haripur. When Baron Hugel visited the Hazara territory on December 23, 1835 he found the town of Haripur flourishing. He said no other town was as humming with activity as Haripur. Around the town a wall four yards thick and 16 years high was built. Four gates were constructed for entry into the town. Drinking water was provided by digging a tank. Many small drains were dug to carry water into the streets of the town. A shrine named Shahidganj was constructed in the memory of all those who had laid down their lives for the liberation of Hazara. A permanent *Granthi* was employed to ensure uninterrupted *kirtan* and *path*. A *mandir* called Ganesh Giri was also built. A mosque was constructed too. This was a step in the direction of real integration of the people of all castes and creeds.

Many gardens and parks were laid to beautiful the town. Some more forts were constructed at Nawan Shair, Dhamtor, Dharband and Sheenkiari. The whole of the year 1822 was spent in restoring peace in the area.

However, peace was broken shortly afterwards. Sardar Mohammad Khan, who had earlier revolted against the

Khalsa, became nervous and fearful when the people responsible for the murder of Sardar Amar Singh were given severe punishment. He lodged a complaint with the Maharaja against the Nalwa Sardar and was given a patient hearing by the Maharaja who sent instructions to Nalwa to grant Sardar Mohammad Khan a *Jagir* worth Rs. 2,000 annually. Nalwa reluctantly offered a *Jagir* worth Rs. 1,700 which he refused to accept and once again complained to the Maharaja. The Maharaja granted to Sardar Mohammad Khan a Jagir worth Rs. 2,700 in some other area. Thus both Nalwa and Mohammad Khan were apparently satisfied for a while. But soon afterwards the Khan instigated the people of Sirikot and raised the banner of revolt in Ghandgarh. But Nalwa crushed the rebellion with an iron hand and thus nipped the evil in the bud. Many *Ghazis* were killed and the Khan fled to some unknown place.

REFERENCES

1. Latif Mohd., History of the Panjab, p. 397.
2. Ochterlony to Adams, August 13, 1814.
3. Latif Mohd., History of the Panjab, p. 405.
4. Latif Mohd., History of the Panjab.
5. Hasrat, Bikramjit, Life and Times of Ranjit Singh, p. 105.
6. Moorcroft, Travels, p. 344.
7. Latif Mohd., History of the Panjab, p. 427.
8. Latif Mohd., History of the Panjab, p. 426.

Index

L

M

N

O

P

□□□